JEAN 'DJANGO' REINHARDT

Dedication

It is probably true to say that Django found me, rather than the other way around, because his music was waiting for me when I came home from the maternity ward. I cannot, therefore, remember the time when I first heard Django, because I cannot remember a time when he wasn't there.

My father, an amateur guitarist and general music fan, had seen the Quintette in London in 1938. Utterly smitten by the experience, he bought as many records as he could afford and also invested in a cheap guitar. It was an enthusiasm that stayed with him until the day he died, and in growing up around him I shared in it.

It is for these reasons that I humbly dedicate this volume to the man who, more than any other, shaped my tastes, views and philosophies: my father, Edward Vernon (1920–80).

It is also, of course, for Babik (1944–2001).

Jean 'Django' Reinhardt

A contextual bio-discography 1910–1953

PAUL VERNON

ASHGATE

Published by

Ashgate Publishing Limited
Gower House
Croft Road
Aldershot
Hampshire GU11 3HR
England

Ashgate Publishing Company
Suite 420
101 Cherry Street
Burlington, VT 05401-4405
USA

Ashgate website: http://www.ashgate.com

British Library Cataloguing in Publication Data
Jean 'Django' Reinhardt : a contextual
bio-discography 1910-1953
1. Reinhardt, Django, 1910-1953 2. Reinhardt, Django,
1910-1953 - Discography 3. Jazz musicians - Belgium -
Biography 4. Guitarists - Belgium - Biography
I. Vernon, Paul, 1949-
787.8'7165'092

Library of Congress Cataloging-in-Publication Data
Vernon, Paul, 1949-
Jean 'Django' Reinhardt : a contextual bio-discography 1910-1953 / Paul Vernon.
p. cm.
Includes bibliographical references, filmography, and indexes.
ISBN 0-7546-0694-5 (alk. paper)
1. Reinhardt, Django, 1910-1953 -- Discography. I. Title.

ML156.7.R46 V47 2003
787.87'165'092--dc21
[B]

2002027788

ISBN 0 7546 0694 5

Typeset in Baskerville by Bookcraft Ltd, Stroud, Gloucestershire
Printed and bound in Great Britain by MPG Books Ltd, Bodmin, Cornwall.

Contents

Illustrations

Introduction

This work gathers together and organizes all known information relevant to the life and works of Django Reinhardt. It assumes a working knowledge of the artist by the reader, as well as the reader's access to readily available source material. However, the appendix 'Advice for the beginner' makes allowances for those who are new to the field and points the way to relevant material.

Essentially discographical in format, the work therefore adheres to well-established discographical practices:

- All information is presented in as strict a chronological order as possible. Within recording sessions, the company matrix number sequence has been followed, as it will be, with a few noted exceptions, the order in which recordings were actually made.
- The order in which instrumentation is presented within the personnel section follows strict discographical principals first established in the early 1930s.
- Where contextual material has been inserted, it appears as closely as possible to known facts regarding Django Reinhardt's movements.
- All secondary information is presented in alphabetical and/or numerical order.

Many writings about Django Reinhardt have been extremely romantic in tone, which is in perfect keeping with the spirit of both man and music; however, the purpose of this book to present only established facts or likely scenarios.

The discography is, of course, based upon the originals published by Gates and Neill in 1944 and Charles Delaunay in 1960, taking his 1981 revisions into account. It has, however, been thoroughly revised by making comparisons with a number of other discographical works, including Abrams, Gould, Nevers, Royal, Rousseau and Rust; by integrating material from Abrams, Cherrett, Cruickshank, Delaunay and Nevers; by searching every other available resource and database; and by re-listening to every available recording.

A very real attempt has been made to include the details of every known shellac and vinyl release, although some gaps, especially in vinyl, still exist. Compact discs are represented by a carefully balanced selection of currently available issues that both offer the reader as much choice as possible, and are likely to remain in catalogue for some considerable time. Due to the vast ongoing proliferation of both legitimate and illegal pressings available worldwide, a comprehensive presentation of CD issues would be both confusing to the reader and, ultimately, of little real value. The diligent reader is therefore likely to encounter much CD product not mentioned in this present work. See the 'Advice for the beginner' section for further discussion of CD issues.

In keeping with the original works by Delaunay and Abrams, each individual recording has been allocated a three-figure reference number. However, significant re-numbering occurs very early in order to reflect both recently discovered material and the fact that every known Django recording, whether issued or not, has been logged. This system, like the Abrams system, is employed as a cross-reference to the files for shellac, vinyl, magnetic tape, compact disc, accompanying musicians and song titles. The 'Comparative table of allocated recording numbers' correlates the three systems.

Contextual information is provided so that the reader may better understand the world in which Django Reinhardt operated. Contemporary material found in Cherret, Cruickshank and Delaunay is logged in sequence and referenced to the original works by page number. It is therefore useful to have access to these three books (the 1981 edition of Delaunay for preference) to hand while consulting this work. Material presented by Abrams is mentioned in some depth where relevant, since his work is currently unavailable. Previously unpublished or long-unavailable material is presented in full where possible. These contemporary reports and reviews sometimes tell us more about the horizons of the reviewer than the art under their review, but they are, if nothing else, historically interesting.

Recording sessions by Django's associates, but without his participation, are noted, as are selected Parisian recording sessions by other Paris-based or visiting artists. The note 'See Rust for details' refers the reader to Brian Rust's standard works of jazz discography, *Jazz Records, 1897–1942.* All known film, radio and television appearances, whether they survive or not, are also logged (although provably unrecovered broadcasts are not logged into the numerical system), as are appearances within France at clubs and theatres, and overseas tours.

The careers of artists who played a significant role in Django's recording career are traced throughout the main body of this work to provide greater context. Furthermore, significant Parisian, French and global history has been inserted where relevant to provide some historical context.

It is my hope that by adhering strictly to discographical and chronological principles, a clearer picture of the life and work of Django Reinhardt will emerge, allowing readers to draw their own conclusions. Knowing full well that dedicated Django collectors will use the book, I have attempted to compile this information with the true aficionado, as well as the researcher and the eager newcomer, in mind.

Paul Vernon

How to use this work

DISCOGRAPHICAL INFORMATION

This is included in the following format:

- **Location of recording** Specific addresses in Paris will be found in the 'Parisian music business addresses' section.
- **Date of recording** If a specific date is not given, the closest known time is given, e.g. 'December'. The presence of a day and calendar date indicates that the information has been verified as correct.
- **Artist credits** These are given as they appear on the labels of the original issues, in alphabetical order of the record company name.
- **Personnel and instruments** See 'Abbreviations' for a key to instruments. The way in which the instrumentation is arranged adheres strictly to discographical rules devised by Charles Delaunay and others in the 1930s, and are generally accepted as standard practice in popular music discographies (Dixon, Godrich and Rye; Rust). If the engineer's name for the session is known, it follows the personnel listing in *italics.*
- **Tune number, matrix number and title** Tune numbers have been allocated by the author and are used throughout the book for identification and cross-reference purposes. The title is given as it appears on the original label.
- **Exact timing** This is given in minutes and seconds {0:00} and has been checked electronically.
- **Recording history** ***78*** indicates 78rpm issues: the company name is given first, followed by the catalogue number, which sometimes (but not always) includes an alpha prefix. These are alphabetized for easy reference; the issue considered to be the first or original pressing is listed in **bold**.
  LP indicates vinyl long-playing issues, again alphabetized by company name followed by catalogue number. Where a recording is appearing for the first time the label and catalogue number are shown in **bold**. ***25cm LP*** indicates that the record in question is 25 centimetres (10") in diameter; all other issues are 30 centimetres (12"). In the relatively rare cases where tracks appear in 7" EP/45 format, this is noted.
  CD indicates compact disc issues, as usual aphabetized by company name followed by catalogue number, with **bold** to show where a recording is appearing for the first time.
  The use of commas after numbers indicates that the record company is the same, but the recording has been issued more than once by that company. Semi-colons are employed to differentiate between record companies.

A typical entry is shown below:

Ultraphone Studios, Paris — between Thursday 27 and Monday 31 December 1934

Django Reinhardt et le Quintette du Hot-Club de France (Oriole)/**Hot-Club of France** (Royale)/**Djungo Reinhardt and the Quintette of the Hot Club de France** (Supraphon)/**Djungo Reinhardt et le Quintette du Hot-Club de France avec Stéphane Grappelli** (Ultraphone)

Stéphane Grappelli (vln); Django Reinhardt (gtr solo); Joseph Reinhardt, Roger Chaput (gtrs); Louis Vola (sb).
Engineer: Willy Kuhn

080 P 77161 **Dinah** (fox-trot) {2:33}
[***78*** DA17-1; JD 8004; Od D286044; Or LV100, LB1000; Roy 1753; Supra B-22642; Tel A-1959; **Ultr AP 1422**, B-14286; Var 8377]
[***25cm LP*** Or MG10019] [***EP*** Or 7045; Sup SUK35615]
[***LP*** Pac LDP D6272; Vog DPO5, COF03, 500740] [***CD*** AA24; ABM 1194; Cas MACD132; Cly DIG12, Cls 703; Dig CO3506; Ea EABCD71; Fmx FA302; Hab 111200; JSP 341; Kaz EUKCD913; LE JA5138, 5267; Mil 74321308652; Music CD6048; QED71; Recall SMCD307]
etc.

Contemporary reviews of 78rpm records are cross-referenced, by date, between the main body of the work and the 78rpm record release file. For example, an entry marked '5–6/36 *JH*' in the record release file indicates that a full review of the record may be found in *Jazz Hot* for May/June of 1936. These reviews often, but unfortunately not always, appear in the main body of this work.

CONTEXTUAL INFORMATION

Further useful information includes:

- A specific time period during which Django Reinhardt's activities can be proven, together with as much information as possible about those activities.
- A note of a contemporary article or review concerning Django Reinhardt or a significant associate. This is referenced to the known source, and the reader is referred to the relevant source in the bibliography. In cases where the material is previously unpublished or currently difficult to locate, it is reproduced in full. Note that the use of upper and lower case, italics and bold type in the reproduced material reflects, as accurately as possible, original usage, and it is for this reason that the styles vary. Note too that original grammar, punctuation and syntax have been preserved.

- A note of a recording session involving a close associate of Django Reinhardt's, but which does *not* involve Django.
- A contextual historical event, usually in Paris but sometimes elsewhere.

Please note that I have made the decision to spell Stéphane Grappelli's name with an 'i' throughout the entire discography, except for those instances where the label credits or a mention in contemporary journals specifically states otherwise. This usage most accurately reflects the origins of his family name.

Abbreviations

Countries

A	United States of America
Ar	Argentina
Au	Australia
B	Belgium
Br	Brazil
Can	Canada
Cz	Czechoslovakia (first republic)
F	France
G	Germany
H	Holland
I	Italy
In	India
J	Japan
N	Norway
Sd	Sweden
Sp	Spain
Sw	Switzerland
UK	United Kingdom

Instruments

acc	accordion
arr	arranger
as	alto saxophone
bjo	banjo
bs	baritone saxophone
celeste	celeste
cl	clarinet
ct	cornet
dir	director
dms	drums
elgtr	electric guitar
fl	flute
gtr	acoustic guitar
orch	orchestra
pno	piano
sax	saxophone, where the pitch of the instrument is unknown

sb	string bass, *aka* double bass, contra-bass
ss	soprano saxophone
tb	trombone
tp	trumpet
ts	tenor saxophone
tu	tuba
vb	vibraphone
vcl	vocal
vln	violin
xyl	xylophone

Record labels

AA	Audio Archives	United Kingdom
ABC	ABC	France
ABM	Audio, Book & Music Co	United Kingdom
Aff	Affinity	EU
An	Angel	USA
AoC	Ace Of Clubs	United Kingdom
ARC	ARC	EU
Ast	Astan	United Kingdom
Atl	Atlantic	USA
Aus	Ausland	Germany
Avid	Avid	United Kingdom
Bar	Barclay	France
BBC	BBC Records	United Kingdom
BGO	Beat Goes On	United Kingdom
Br	**Brunswick**	
	500, 505-series	France
	A9000, A81000, LPB series	Germany
	1600 series	South Africa
BS	Blue Star	France
BT	Black Tulip	United Kingdom
Cam	Camden	USA
Cap	Capitol	USA
Cas	Castle	United Kingdom
CC	Crown Collection	United Kingdom
Cel	Celson	Italy
Clef	Clef	USA
Cls	Classics	France
Cly	Charly	United Kingdom/EU
Col	**Columbia**	
		Belgium
	100000 series	Brazil
	BF, DCF, DF, KC series	France

	MC series	International (pressed in UK)
		Italy
	GN series	Norway
	R14000	Spain
	F49000, MZ series	Switzerland
	DF series	United Kingdom
	4000M series	USA
Coll	Collector	United Kingdom
Com	Comet	United Kingdom
De	**Decca**	
	Y series	Australia
	F, MB, SB, 20200, 21700 series	Belgium
	23000 series	Canada
	59000, 89000, F, FM, MF, F41000, 5000, 13300 series	France
	F series	Holland
	500, 600 series	Italy
	RD	Spain
	F series	Switzerland
	C, DFE, F, F10000 series	United Kingdom
	23000 series	USA
Des	Design	USA
Dial	Dial	USA
DJM	DJM	United Kingdom
DRG	DRG	Germany
Ea	Eagle	United Kingdom
Ecl	Eclipse (Decca)	United Kingdom
El	Electrola	Germany
Eli	Elite	USA
Emb	Ember	United Kingdom
Emp	Empress	United Kingdom
Esq	Esquire	United Kingdom
Ev	Everest	USA
Fel	Felsted	United Kingdom
Fla	Flapper	United Kingdom
Fmx	Fremeaux	France
Fo	Fonit	Italy
Fr	Frog	UK
Ga	Galaxy	EU
Gal	Gallerie	EU
Gr	**The Gramophone Company *aka* His Master's Voice**	
	B series	Australia
		Britain

	K, SG100 series	France (La Voix de son maître)
	Holland	(De Stem van zyn Meester)
	B, N4000 series	India
	JO series	(international export)
	GW, HN series	Italy (La voce del padrone)
		Norway
	AL series	(Sin Herres Stemme)
	G, GY series	Spain (La voz de su amo)
		Sweden
	X series	(Husbondens Rost)
	JK, SG20000 series	Switzerland
	(All shellac Gramophone Company products, regardless of their origin, are noted in the main section of this work as 'Gr'. The brand names given in parentheses here are those that appear on the disc in the countries noted.)	
Ha	Habana	
Har	Harmonic	France
HD	Happy Days	United Kingdom
Henry	Henry	France
HMV	**His Master's Voice *aka* The Gramophone Company**	
	(vinyl issues)	
	OC	Australia
	FELP	France (La Voix de son maître)
	HCLP	Holland (De Stem van zyn Meester)
	CLP, DLP	United Kingdom
	(All vinyl Gramophone Company products, regardless of their origin, are noted in the main section of this work as 'HMV'. The brand names in parentheses here are those that appear on the discs in the countries noted.)	
HRS	Hot Record Society	USA
Ideal	Ideal	France
JA	Jazz Archives	EU
Jass	Jass	USA
Jay	Jay	USA
JCF	Jazz Club Français	France
JD	Joe Davis	
	8000, DA series	USA
JSP	JSP	United Kingdom
JH	Jazz Hour	United Kingdom
JT	Jazz Time	EU
JTD	Jazzterdays	United Kingdom
Kaz	Kaz	United Kingdom
KC	KC	United Kingdom
La Roulotte	La Roulotte	France
LE	Living Era	United Kingdom

Lon	London	United Kingdom
		USA
Met	Meteor	United Kingdom
MD	Musidisc	France
MFP	Music For Pleasure (EMI)	United Kingdom
Mil	Milan	EU
Mo	Mode (Vogue)	France
Mos	Mosiac	USA
OB	Old Bean	United Kingdom
Od	**Odéon**	
	284000	Argentina
	286000	Argentina
	283000	Brazil
		Germany
Oly	Oly	Belgium
Om	Omega	France
Or	**Oriole**	
	LV, LB, MG series	United Kingdom
		USA
OWI	Office of War Information	USA
Pac	Pacific	France
Pampa	Pampa	Argentina
Pat	**Pathé**	
	PN series	Argentina
	400, 600, 1000,	
	AT, PA, PG series	France
	PI series	Germany
Pe	Period	USA
PG	Polygram	International
Pol	**Polydor**	
	F512, F524000, 2344	
	58000 series	France
	A-100, A-200, A-300 series	Japan
	624000 series	Netherlands
Pop	Pop (a Vogue subsidiary)	France
Pre	Prestige	USA/EU
Pu	Pulse	United Kingdom
QED	QED	United Kingdom
RAR	Rarities	United Kingdom
RCA	**RCA and RCA-Victor**	
	430.000, 731.000 series	France
	EPC	Germany
	LPM	USA
	see also Victor, *qv*	
Recall	Recall	United Kingdom

Ri	Riviera	France
Roy	Royale	USA
Rythme	Rythme	Belgium
RZ	Regal-Zonophone	Australia
Sof	Sofradi	France
Su	Sutton	USA
Sup	Supraphon	Czechoslovakia
Swa	Swaggie	Australia
Swi	Swing	France
Tel	**Telefunken**	
	SH series	Argentina
	A series	France
	A series	Germany
Ultr	**Ultraphone**	
	B14000 series	Czechoslovakia (first republic)
	AP series	France
	Var	Varsity
		USA
Verve	Verve	USA
Vi	**Victor**	
	LVT, 68–0000 series	Argentina
	27000 series	Canada
	1000, 26000, A, DC, JA series	Japan
	255000, 26000, 20-000, BP, LPM, ND, RD, 40-0000 series	USA
Victory	Victory	Belgium
Vo	**Vogue** (all series except those listed as United Kingdom)	France
	000, EPL, EPV, LDE	United Kingdom
Vox	Vox	USA
Wax	Wax	USA
WRC	World Record Club	United Kingdom

Acknowledgements

First and foremost, credit must go to the late Charles Delaunay, without whose enthusiasms, beliefs and drive we would know Django far less well than we do.

Other early enthusiasts who should also be mentioned are Diz Dizley, Alexis Korner, Billy Neill, A P Sharpe (*aka* 'E Gates') and Ken Sykora.

Especially deserving of credit is Dr Roger Baxter. Involved almost from the start of the project, he has freely and willingly devoted expertise, time and energy to the growth of this book. He has challenged my assumptions, pointed out errors, proofread the whole manuscript, offered suggestions that had not occurred to me and, finally, supplied the best available print of the front cover photograph. Without Dr Baxter's input this work would be less complete.

For direct involvement in this present work, I especially wish to thank the following people and organizations, who have willingly donated both time and expertise to enriching this project:

Tony Baldwin	France
Bruce Bastin	Interstate Music, UK
Alasdair Blaazer	National Discography, London
British Library	London
Gene Deitch	Prague
Michael Dregni	USA
EMI Archives	UK
Dave Gould	UK
Ted Kendall	UK
Gary LeGallant	Australia
Marc Masselin	France
Music on Earth Productions (Paul Balmer and Judy Caine)	London
Daniel Nevers	Director, Django Reinhardt reissue project for Fremeaux, France
Lana Noitneter	Czech Republic
Ray's Jazz Shop	London
Steve Royal	Django Swing Page website, UK
Norbert Ruecker	Germany
Howard Rye	UK
Fred Sharp	USA
Nevill L Sherburn	Swaggie Records, Australia
Ken Smith	Red Lick Records, Wales
Karel Srpska	Jazzova, Prague
Henk Suerink	*Quintette* magazine, Holland
Ray Templeton	British Film Institute, London

Ed Zawadski — Prague

The efforts of the following people were also of great value to this work:

the late Eric Townley	UK
the late Emmanuel Ugge	President, Hot-Gramophone Club of Prague, 1934–48

I must also make special mention of the pioneering works by Max Abrams (*The Book of Django*), Ted Cherrett (*The Genius that was Django*) and Ian Cruickshank (*Django's Gypsies*), which have been in constant use throughout this research.

In compiling his original discography, Charles Delaunay credited the following people, who must be recognized in this new work: John Bajo, André Clergeat, Eddie Crommelin, Christian D'Angleterre, Ivan Deputier, Chris Evans, Harold Flakser, André Francis, Jean-Paul Guiter, Arthur Kinnear, René Ramel and Dietrich Schulz-Köhn.

In compiling his Fremeaux Intégrale CD series, Daniel Nevers credits the following people, who must also be recognized in this new work: Jean-Claude Alexandre, Alain Antonietto, Jean-Christophe Averty, Bernard Bassie, Philippe Baudoin, Olivier Brard, Jacques Bureau, Henri Chenut, Dominique Cravic, Jean-Pierre Daubresse, Ate van Delden, Alain Delot, Ivan Deputier, Yvonne Derudder, Claude Fihman, Iwan Fresart, Gérard Gazers, Jean-Paul Guitier, Freddy Haederli, Marcelle Hervé, Philippe Lafargue, Claude Laval, Ann LeGrand, Joss Linsen, Jacques Lubin, Maurice Malandry, Pierre Moglier, Robert Pernet, Jean Portier, René Ramel, Jean-Claude Rey, Gérard Roig, Didier Roussin, Anne Secheret, and Jean-Jacques Staub.

In addition to the books listed in the bibliography, the following were also consulted:

Olivier Bard and Daniel Nevers, *Le Jazz en France: Jazz and Hot Dance Music Discography*, Selection 3, Paris, 1991
Dave Clarke, *Penguin Encyclopaedia of Popular Music*, Penguin, 1986
Robert Cole, *A Traveller's History of Paris*, Windrush Press, 1994
Charles Delaunay, *New Hot Discography*, Criterion, NYC, 1948
Albert Goldschmidt, *Paris und Umgeborg*, Grieben, 1930
Les Guides Bleus: Paris, Hachette, 1931
Musique Adresse Universelle, Office Générale de la Musique, Paris, 1931
Stanley Sadie (ed.), *New Grove Dictionary of Music*, Macmillan, 2001
Brian Rust, *Jazz Records 1897–1942*, various editions, principally the third
Statesman's Yearbook, Macmillan, various editions
Paul Vernon, *Ethnic and Vernacular Music on Record 1898–1960*, Greenwood Press, 1995

The catalogues of the following record companies were also consulted: Charly (UK); Classics (France); EPM (France); Fremeaux (France); Prestige (USA); Red Lick Records (UK) and Vestapol (UK/USA), as were the following magazines and journals: *Ballroom and Band* (UK) 1934–35; *BMG* (UK) 1934–53; *Bulletin du Hot-Club de France* in *Jazz-Tango*, 1934–36; *Disques* (France) 1937–39 and 1946–48; *L'Edition Musicale Vivante* (France) 1930–34; *The Era* (UK) 1938–39; *The Gramophone* (UK) 1935–41; *Hot News* (UK) 1935; *Hot Revue* (Belgium) 1945–47; *Jazz* (Czechoslovakia) 1946–47; *Jazz Hot* (France) 1938–53; *Jazz Information* (USA) 1939; *Jazz Journal* (UK) 1948–51; *Jazz-Tango-Dancing/Jazz-Tango* (France) 1932–36; *Melody Maker* (UK) 1934–53; *Paroles de Musique* (France), 1935; *Quintette* (Holland) 1997–2001; *Radio Times* (UK) 1938–48; *Rhythm* (UK) 1938–39; *The Stage* (UK) 1938–39; *Swing Music* (UK) 1935–36. I also acknowledge the many references to Django Reinhardt and his associates on the Internet.

I wish to thank my editor at Ashgate, Rachel Lynch, for her unfailingly patient counsel, and the staff at Bookcraft Ltd, especially copy editor Sara Peacock, for their help and expertise in all matters editorial and typographical. Finally, though perhaps most importantly of all, my utter and heartfelt thanks go to my wife Judy Ebner for her continued support, understanding and tolerance, and also for her very able assistance in translations.

A contextual bio-discography 1910–1953

Hôpital Lariboisière, Paris **Sunday 26 January 1908**

The birth of Stéphane Grappelli.

Flach aux Corbias (Raven's Pond)
Liberchie, near Charleroi, Belgium **Sunday 23 January 1910 at c. 10.00pm**

The birth of Jean Reinhardt, *aka* Jean-Baptiste Reinhardt, *aka* Django Reinhardt.
For a reproduction of the birth certificate see Delaunay, page 213.
For details of Django Reinhardt's life until 1928, see Delaunay and Nevers, notes to Fmx FA301.

Paris **Tuesday 12 March 1912**

The birth of Joseph Reinhardt.

Paris **Monday 2 June 1919**

'L'Orchestre Scrap Iron Jazzerinos' records ten titles for Compagnie Gramophone du Française.
They are thought to be an African-American group, possibly drawn from James Reese Europe's 369 Hellfighters Band.
See Rust for details.

London **Monday 11 August 1919**

The Times reports that 'A Nigger Jazz Band' (*sic*) has appeared at Buckingham Palace before King George V and Queen Mary, adding that the personnel included Sidney Bechet and Arthur Briggs.

London **November 1920**

Billy Arnold's Novelty Jazz Band records two titles for the Columbia Graphaphone Company.
See Rust for details.

Paris **December 1921**

Billy Arnold's Novelty Jazz Band arrives in Paris.

Paris **January 1922**

'Mitchell's Jazz Kings' record for Pathé. Musicians include William 'Crickett' Smith (Arthur Briggs' uncle) and Dan Parrish.
See Rust for details of this and subsequent sessions.

Paris **July 1923**

'Billy Arnold's Novelty Jazz Band' records one title for Pathé as the 'Novelty Jazz Band'.

'Orchestre Pollard's Six' records two titles for Pathé. Musicians probably include Arthur Briggs.
See Rust for details.

Paris **July and November 1924**

'Orchestre Billy Max', *aka* 'Orchestre Stricken', records for Compagnie Gramophone du Française.

Hayes, Middlesex **Thursday 19 February 1925**

Jack Hylton and his orchestra record for the Gramophone Company. Musicians include Noel 'Chappie' d'Amato.
See Rust for details of this and subsequent sessions.

Berlin **July 1925**

Sam Wooding and his orchestra record eight titles for Vox. Musicians include Maceo Edwards and John Mitchell.
See Rust for details.

Paris **1926**

Photographer André Schaeffner publishes *Le Jazz* (Editions Claude Aveline).

New York **Tuesday 29 September 1926**

Eddie Lang and Joe Venuti record together for the first time, for Columbia (matrix numbers 142697–8).
See Rust for details of this and subsequent sessions.

Paris or environs **1927**

Django Reinhardt marries Mlle Baumgartner.

Berlin **January 1927**

'Arthur Briggs Savoy Syncops Orchestra' records for Clausophon.
See Rust for details of this and subsequent 1927/28 Berlin sessions for Clausophon, Polydor and Vox.

New York **Monday 10 January 1927**

Lloyd Scott and his orchestra record three titles for Victor. Musicians include Fletcher Allen and Dicky Wells.
See Rust for details.

London **Monday 27–Tuesday 28 June1927**

'Charles Remue and his New Stompers Orchestra' record fourteen titles for Edison Bell. Musicians include Stan Brenders.
See Rust for details.

Paris — July 1927

'Orchestre The Playboys' (*sic*) record two titles for Pathé.
'Probably an American band.' (Rust)

Berlin — Wednesday 28 September 1927

The 'New York Tanzorkestra' records two titles for Homokord (matrix numbers M19450–1). Musicians include André Forster, *aka* Andy Foster.
See Rust for details.

Paris — 1928

The first records by Louis Armstrong are made available in France on the Columbia BF series.

Paris — Monday 23 January 1928

Django Reinhardt's 18th birthday.

Hayes, Middlesex — Friday 27 January 1928

'Leon Abbey and his orchestra' record two unissued sides for the Gramophone Company. Musicians include Fletcher Allen.
See Rust for details.

Paris — Wednesday 20 June 1928

L'Accordéoniste Jean Vissade

Jean Vaissade (*sic*) (acc); Django Reinhardt (bjo); unknown (possibly [?] Baiz or [?] Coeffier) (slide whistle).
Engineer: M F C. Alexander

001 BT 4115-1 **Ma Régulière** (fox-trot) {2.56}
[***78*** Gr K-5469] [***LP*** Pat C054 10395/6] [***CD*** Fmx FA301]

002 BT 4116-1 **Griserie** (waltz) {2.43}
[***78*** Gr K-5454] [***LP*** Pat C054 16001; Swi 8420267]
[***CD*** Fmx FA301; Swi SW 8419]

003 BT 4118-1 **Parisette** (one-step) {2.39}
[***78*** Gr K-5454] [***CD*** Fmx FA301; Swi CDSW8419]

004 BT 4119-1 **La Caravane** {2.44}
[***78*** Gr K-5469] [***CD*** Fmx FA301]

BT 4117 remains untraced. There were believed to be a further six titles recorded at this session and subsequently destroyed; one of these may have been BT 4117.

Paris — c. June 1928 (see notes)

Jean Vissade

Jean Vaissade (*sic*) (acc); Django Reinhardt (as 'Jiango Renard') (bjo); Francesco Cariolato (xyl).

005 ID 999 **Amour De Gitane** (valse) {3.05}
[*78* Ideal 8543] [*CD* Fmx FA301]

006 ID 1000 **Aubade Charmeuse** (valse) {2.45}
[*78* Ideal 8544] [*CD* Fmx FA301]

007 ID 1001 **Mome La Gratiche** (valse) {2.47}
[*78* Ideal 8545] [*CD* Fmx FA301]

008 ID 1002 **L'Ondee** (valse) {2.37}
[*78* Ideal 8546] [*CD* Fmx FA301]

009 ID 1003 **La Plus Belle** (valse) {2.46}
[*78* Ideal 8547] [*CD* Fmx FA301]

010 ID 1004 **Déception D'Amour** (valse) {3.03}
[*78* Ideal 8548] [*CD* Fmx FA301]

Django reportedly received 500 francs for playing on these sessions.
All 'Ideal' recordings are acoustic.
'These recordings evidently took place from July to October 1928, despite the consecutive numbers of the recordings, as well as the matrices. On Ideal 8547/8548 the numerals in the wax (inscribed backwards) appear to indicate respectively 19 9 28 (evidently September 19, 1928) and 31 7 28 (evidently July 31 1928).' (Abrams)

Paris — c. June 1928

L'Orchestre Alexander

Maurice Alexander (acc); probably Django Reinhardt (bjo); unknown (traps).

011 H 848-B Parisette {2.20}
[*78* Henry 848] [*CD* Fmx FA301]

Paris — c. June 1928

Lud Gluskin records for Pathé. Musicians include Maurice Cizerone.
See Rust for details of this and subsequent sessions.

Paris — Sunday 24 June 1928

The franc is devalued from 19 US cents to 3.92 US cents, in order to adjust the national debt. This move causes hardship among low-income French workers.

Paris — c. September–October 1928

MM (Victor) Marceau, Accordéoniste Virtuose

Victor Marceau (acc); Django Reinhardt (as 'Jeangot') (bjo); Erardy (whistle).

012 H-966-A **Miss Columbia** (marche américaine) {2.10}
[*78* Henry 966] [*CD* Fmx FA301]

013 H 966-B **Au Pays De L'Hindustan** (fox-trot) {2.37}
[*78* Henry 966] [*CD* Fmx FA301]

014 H 968(A) **Moi Aussi** {2.42}
[*78* Henry 968] [*CD* Fmx FA301; Swi 8419]

015 H 968(B) **Tarragone** {2.46}
[*78* Henry 968] [*CD* Fmx FA301]

Paris c. September–October 1928

Chaumel, acc. par l'Orchestre de M. Alexander

[?] Chaumel (vcl) acc. probably by Maurice Alexander (acc); probably Django Reinhardt (bjo).

016 H962-A **Sur La Place De L'Opéra**
[*78* Henry 962]

017 H962-B **E Viva La Carmencita**
[*78* Henry 962]

'Henry' recordings are acoustic.
This is possibly the 'Chabel' that Django Reinhardt told Charles Delaunay he first recorded with.

Paris Thursday 1 November 1928

English dance bandleader Jack Hylton reportedly visits the club 'La Java' in Belleville, and offers Django Reinhardt a contract to play in his orchestra. However, current research indicates that Hylton and his orchestra were touring Germany at this time, and it seems unlikely that he would have been in Paris on 1 November. The most likely time frame for this scenario, if indeed it ever took place, is spring of 1928, when Hylton was definitely in Paris.

Paris Friday 2 November 1928

A fire in Django's caravan badly burns his hand.
See Delaunay and Nevers for details.

Paris Thursday 22 November 1928

Maurice Ravel's *Boléro* is makes its public debut.

Buenos Aires c. late 1928

The group 'Les Loups', featuring Oscar Alemán, record for Victor.

Paris January 1929

'Ray Ventura et ses Collégiens' record two titles for Columbia. Musicians include Roger Grasset and Gaston Lapeyronnie.
See Rust for details.

Buenos Aires Monday 14 January 1929

The group 'Trio Victor', featuring Oscar Alemán, record for Victor.

Paris **Wednesday 23 January 1929**

Django Reinhardt's 19th birthday.

Paris **Saturday 23 February 1929**

'Ray Ventura et ses Collégiens' record for two titles for Odéon. Musicians include Philippe Brun, Roger Grasset, Gaston Lapeyronnie, Stephen Mougin and Alex Renard.
See Rust for details.

Paris **Tuesday 12 March 1929**

'Eddie South and his Alabamians' record for Compagnie Française du Gramophone (matrix numbers BN-318–19, engineered by S E Tunn). Musicians include (possibly) Arthur Briggs and Stirling Conaway.
During this time, Eddie South was appearing at the Plantation Club, 58 rue Notre Dame de Lorette, 9e.
See Rust for details.

Paris **Tuesday 12 March 1929**

Jean Cocteau, accompanied by 'L'Orchestre Dan Parrish', reads two examples of his Dadaist poetry, 'La Toison D'Or' and 'Les Voleurs D'Enfants', released as an 80rpm coupling on French Columbia. Musicians include William 'Crickett' Smith (tpt).

Le Moulin de la Galette, Paris **April 1929**

'Gregor et ses Gregorians' record ten titles for Edison Bell records (matrix numbers 88853–62). Musicians include Pierre Allier, Stéphane Grappelli, Gaston Lapeyronnie, Stéphane Mougin, Sylvio Schmidt and Michel Warlop.

Paris **Thursday 16 May 1929**

'Ray Ventura et ses Collégiens' record four titles for Odéon. Musicians include Philippe Brun, Roger Grasset, Gaston Lapeyronnie and Stéphane Mougin.
See Rust for details.

Paris **July 1929**

The publication of the first issue of *Review de Jazz*, which current research indicates to be the first regular publication devoted to jazz anywhere in the world,

> [which] had as its ambition to be used as [a] union between editors, the heads of orchestras and the musicians. Created on the initiative of Gregor and his musicians, it had as collaborators Stephen Mougin, Philippe Brun, Stéphane Grappelli and Hughes Panassié. (Pascal Anquette, *Music in France*, Ministère des Affaires Etrangères).

Paris **Saturday 27 July 1929**

The resignation, due to ill health, of Premier Poincaré, ushering in a period of instability presided over by a series of short-lived cabinets.

Paris **Friday 27 September 1929**

'Ray Ventura et ses Collégiens' record three titles for Odéon. Musicians include Philippe Brun, Roger Grasset, Gaston Lapeyronnie and Stéphane Mougin.
See Rust for details.

Paris **Saturday 19 October 1929**

'Ray Ventura et ses Collégiens' record for Odéon. Musicians include Philippe Brun, Roger Grasset, Gaston Lapeyronnie and Stephen Mougin.
See Rust for details.

Paris **December 1929**

'Gregor et ses Gregorians' record for Columbia Records. Musicians include Philippe Brun and Michel Warlop.

New York City **Friday 20 and Monday 30 December 1929**

'King Nawahi's Hawaiians' record for Columbia. Musicians include Harry Volpe.

Paris **1930**

Django Reinhardt and pianist Stephen Mougin begin playing together.

Paris **c. January 1930**

Stéphane Grappelli appears in the film short *Gregor et ses Gregorians.*
See film file for details. The entire film appears on ***DVD*** MOE 001.

Small Queens Hall, London **Friday 10 January 1930**

Philippe Brun first records with Jack Hylton and his orchestra.
See Rust for details of this and subsequent sessions.

London **Tuesday 14 January 1930**

Lou Abelardo records four unissued titles for Decca. Musicians include Alan Ferguson.
See Rust for details.

Paris **Thursday 23 January 1930**

Django Reinhardt's 20th birthday.

Paris **March 1930**

The magazine *Review de jazz* ceases publication.

Paris **April 1930**

Production begins on Jean Cocteau's first film *Le Sang d'un poète.*

Paris **Wednesday 30 April 1930**

The National Workman's Insurance Law is finally passed, following many years of debate. It protects nine million workers by ensuring benefits in the case of sickness, old age and death. A 3 per cent contribution from workers' salaries and an equal amount from the employers finance it.

Paris **May 1930**

'Gregor et ses Gregorians' record two titles for Columbia. Musicians include Alex Combelle, (possibly) Guy Paquinet, Sylvio Schmidt and Michel Warlop.

'Ray Ventura et ses Collégiens' record two titles for Compagnie Française du Gramophone.

London **Wednesday 16 July 1930**

'Spike Hughes and his Orchestra' record for Decca. Musicians include Alan Ferguson.
See Rust for details of this and subsequent sessions.

London **Tuesday 19 August 1930**

'Phillip Lewis and his Orchestra' record for Decca. Musicians include Alan Ferguson.
See Rust for details of this and a subsequent session.

London **Thursday 25 September 1930**

'Creighton and Laughton', popular duettists, record for Decca. Musicians include Alan Ferguson.
See Rust for details.

London **Thursday 11 December 1930**

'Noble Sissle's Orchestra' record four titles for English Columbia (matrix numbers 10968–71). Musicians include Arthur Briggs and Frank 'Big Boy' Goudie.
See Rust for details.

Paris **Friday 23 January 1931**

Django Reinhardt's 21st birthday.

London **c. March 1931**

Eddie South and his Band appear at the Cafe Angles, Leicester Square.

Toulon **Spring 1931**

Django appears at the 'Café de Lion', where he meets Emil Savitry, and at the 'Coq Hardi', where he is seen by Jean Cocteau. Savitry introduces Reinhardt to jazz via his record collection. This reportedly included selections by Louis Armstrong (probably Columbia BF series issues), Joe Venuti and Ed Lang (probably French Odéon issues) and Duke Ellington (probably French Brunswick issues).
See Delaunay, pages 47–8.

Paris **Thursday 7 May 1931**

The International Colonial Exposition opens at the Bois de Vincennes.

Grand Théâtre, Toulon Friday 29 May 1931

Louis Vola et son Orchestre du Lido de Toulon

Louis Vola (acc, sb); Django Reinhardt (g); [?] Doubraire (p); Jules Pouzalgues, (vln); unknown (tpt; tbn; saxes; vln; dms).
Engineer: Ernest Gower

018 OG 762-1 **Canaria** {2.35}
[***78*** Gr K-6542] [***CD*** Fmx FA301]

019 OG764-1 **C'Est Une Valse Qui Chante** (valse) {3.04}
[***78*** Gr K-6339] [***CD*** Fmx FA301]

As above, vocal by Lixbot, without tpt, tbn, saxes, vln or dms.

020 OG 765-1 **Carinoso** {2.53}
[***78*** Gr K-6542] [***LP*** Pat C054 16001; Swi SW8420267]
[***CD*** Fmx FA301, Swi CDSW8419]

Five further titles, believed not to feature Django, were also recorded at this session. The earliest known matrix recorded by Gower in Toulon, OG750, was made two days earlier, on 27 May.

Palm Beach, Cannes Summer 1931

The Louis Vola orchestra, featuring Django, plays a summer season.

Paris June 1931

Paul Doumer assumes presidency of France.

Paris Saturday 31 October 1931

The closure of the International Colonial Exposition.

Paris late 1931

The formation of the University Jazz Club, from which developed the Hot Club de France.

Paris December 1931

Le Jazz et le disque: essai critique et historique by Arthur Hoeree is published in the December edition of *L'Edition musical vivant.* Among the records discussed are: Gram K5952 'Moanin' Low' by Jack Hylton 'avec un excellent chorus de trompette Ph. Brun' (*sic*), Pathé X96.046 'Walkin' My Baby Back Home' by Billy Arnold, and numerous recordings by Louis Armstrong, Duke Ellington, McLennon's Jazz Devils, the Mound City Blues Blowers, Red Nichols, Luis Russell and others.

Cannes 1932

Django's involvement in the film *Clair De Lune.*
No copy of the film has ever been found. See Delaunay, page 218, and the notes to Fmx FA301 for photographic evidence.

Brussels **1932**

Robert Goffin publishes *Aux frontières du jazz* (Editions du Sagittaire).

Paris **Wednesday 20 January 1932**

The première of Jean Cocteau's first film, *Le Sang d'un poète.*

Paris **Saturday 23 January 1932**

Django Reinhardt's 22nd birthday.

New York **Tuesday 2 February 1932**

Garland Wilson records two titles for Okeh (matrix numbers 405134–5).
See Rust for details.

Brussels **Monday 21 March 1932**

Willie Lewis records one title for the Belgian branch of the Gramophone Company Ltd (matrix number ON695, engineered by S E Tunn).
See Rust for details.

Paris **Friday 6 May 1932**

President Doumer is assassinated by a Russian émigré named Gourgoulov. Albert LeBrun becomes president. The May elections give the left-wing alliance a majority.

London **Friday 1 July 1932**

George Formby, accompanied by a section of the Jack Hylton orchestra, records for Decca. Musicians include Noel 'Chappie' d'Amato and Philippe Brun.

Paris **Thursday 22 December 1932**

Django begins a season at 'Le Boîte à Matelot'.
See Delaunay and Nevers for details.

Paris **July 1932**

Jazz-Tango-Dancing magazine notes the release of two records by the Belgian group 'The Radiolans':

'Southern Lullaby'/'Who Taught You That' (Decca F272)
'The Blue Duke'/'Shake Your Hip' (Decca F273).

Personnel: Gus DeLoof (tpt); Bauduin (tpt); Josse Breyre (tbn); Tielmans (tbn); David Bee (sax, cl); Fud Candrix (ts); Lauwers (sax); Lievens (pno); Leo Serluippens (dms); Chas Dolne (gtr).

Saint-Jean-de-Luz **July 1932**

'Brick Top et toute sa troupe (chanteurs et musiciens) doivent débuter dans un establissement de Biarritz ou de St Jean De Luz.' (Unsigned, *Jazz-Tango-Dancing*)

Paris **August 1932**

Hughes Panassié reviews Robert Goffin's book *Aux frontières du jazz* in *Jazz-Tango-Dancing*. *Jazz-Tango-Dancing* also enthusiastically reviews Les French Boys: 'China Boy'/ 'Some Of These Days' (Salabert 3166); André Ekyan (sax); Jean Thiland (piano); Didier Mauprey (bjo); Charlie Barnes (dms).

Paris **October 1932**

The first announcement, in *Jazz-Tango-Dancing*, of the establishment of the Hot-Club:

Jazz-Tango-Dancing
est hereux de vous
announcer la fondation du
HOT-CLUB
5 Rue de L'isly–Paris
Telephone: EUROPE 35–54
Les renseignements supplémentaires
seront publiés dans le prochain numéro

Paris **November 1932**

An article in *Jazz-Tango-Dancing* explains the philosophy, rules and goals of the newly formed Hot-Club.

Garland Wilson records four titles for French Brunswick, accompanying singer Nina Mae McKinney on one selection.

Brussels **November 1932**

Willie Lewis and his Orchestra and Gus DeLoof appear at 'Le Pinquin' club.

Paris **December 1932**

Manuel Pizzaro's Tango Orchestra and Tom Waltham's Jazz Orchestra appear at Le Claridge in Paris.

N J Canetti begins hosting a 30-minute radio show on Petite Parisien Radio, at 7pm on Sunday nights, featuring jazz records.

Paris **c. Thursday 22 December 1932**

Maceo Jefferson records one unissued title for Salabert. Musicians include Arthur Briggs, Peter Duconge, Frank 'Big Boy' Goudie and Freddy Johnson.

Paris **Thursday 22 December 1932**

Django appears at Boîte à Matelot.
See Delaunay, pages 57–8.

Cannes **January 1933**

'Orchestra Jazz Vola' appears at the Casino Municipal.
See Delaunay, page 61.

Paris **January 1933**

The first Hot-Club news page appears in *Jazz-Tango-Dancing*.

Paris **Monday 23 January 1933**

Django Reinhardt's 23rd birthday.

Paris **Monday 30 January 1933**

Garland Wilson, introduced by Jacques Bureau, appears in a broadcast on 'Radio L.L.' at 9.00pm. He plays 'Blues In B Flat' and 'Nobody's Sweetheart'.

Paris **Tuesday 31 January 1933 at 9.00pm**

Three *Films nègres inédits* are presented at Cinéma Falguière, 12 rue Armand-Moissand, Paris 15e:

St Louis Blues with Bessie Smith;

Black and Tan Fantasy with Duke Ellington and his Orchestra;

I'll Be Glad When You're Dead You Rascal You, a 'Betty Boop' animated short, directed by Max Fleischer and featuring film of Louis Armstrong and his Orchestra. Nina Mae McKinney and Garland Wilson provide live music, and a public debate on the subject of 'Hot Jazz' is conducted, led by N J Canetti and Hughes Panassié.

Paris **late January/early February 1933**

'Gregor et ses Gregorians' appear at the Olympia Théâtre. The personnel, reported in *Jazz-Tango-Dancing*, is as follows: Michel Emer and Roger Allier (directors); Stéphane Grappelli (pno); Michel Warlop (vln); Pierre Allier, [?] Pico, [?] Naudine, [?] Wladimir (brass); [?] Tharaud, Alex Combelle, [?] Lamory, André Ekyan [saxes]; [?] Feldman (gtr); Roger Grasset (sb); [?] McGregor (dms).

Paris **Wednesday 1 February 1933**

The first concert promoted by the Hot-Club, given by Freddy Johnson and Garland Wilson, is staged at Boîte à Musique.

Paris **Tuesday 1 March 1933**

A meeting of the Hot-Club de France at the Galerie D'Art Contemporain in the Boîte à Musique record shop at 135 blvd Raspail at 9.00pm.

Salle Chopin, Paris **Tuesday 14 March 1933**

Mademoiselle Eliane de Creus, du Théâtre Daunou.
Orchestre sous la direction de Jef de Murel (1)
L'Orchestre du Théâtre Daunou, dir. Jef de Murel (2)

Eliane de Creus (vcl) (1); Jean Sablon (vcl) (2) acc. by Faustin Jean-Jean (tpt); Léon Ferreri (tpt, tbn and vln); Roger Jean-Jean; (as, cl); possibly Paul Jean-Jean (ts, cl); Russell Goudey (as, bs); Michel Warlop (vln); Django Reinhardt (gtr); Michael Emer (pno, arr); possibly Henry Bruno (sb); Max Elloy (dms).

As above, without vocals (3).
Engineer: S E Tunn

021 OPG 639-1 **Y En N'A Pas Deux Comme Moi** (1) {3.11}
[***78*** Gr K-6862] [***CD*** Fmx FA301]

022 OPG 640-1 **Ah! La Beguine! [unissued]**

023 OPG 640-2 **Ah! La Beguine!** (2) {2.44}
[***78*** Gr K-6861] [***CD*** Fmx FA301]

024 OPG 641-1 **Si J'Aime Suzy [unissued]**

025 OPG 641-2 **Si J'Aime Suzy** (3) {2.19}
[***78*** Gr K-6861] [***LP*** Pat C054 16001] [***CD*** Fmx FA301]

Same date and location

Elaine de Creus et Jean Sablon

De Creus and Sablon (vcl); Django Reinhardt (gtr); Michel Emer (pno); Max Elloy (dms).

026 OPG 642-1 **Parce Que Je Vous Aime [unissued]**

027 OPG 642-2 **Parce Que Je Vous Aime** {3.18}
[***78*** Gr K-6863] [***LP*** HD CHD134; Swi 8420267]
[***CD*** Fmx FA301; Gal GALE419; Swi CDSW8419]

028 OPG 643-1 **Si J'Aime Suzy [unissued]**

029 OPG 643-2 **Si J'Aime Suzy** {2.51}
[***78*** Gr K-6863] [***LP*** HD CHD 134; Swi 8420267]
[***CD*** Fmx FA301; Gal GALE419; Swi CDSW8419]

All tunes recorded at this session were featured in the Operetta *Dix-neuf ans*, starring Eliane de Creus and Jean Sablon, playing at Théâtre Danou. See also numbers 036 and 037.
See also Delaunay, pages 60–1.

Paris — Sunday 19 March 1933

Guérino et son Orchestre Musette

Guérino (acc. and vcl); Pierre Pagliano (vln); possibly Django Reinhardt, Lucien Gallopain (gtrs); Pierre 'Baro' Ferret (gtr solo); 'Tarteboule' (sb); unknown (vcl).

030 KI5902-1 **Brise Napolitaine** {2.44}
[***78*** Od 250.418] [***CD*** Fmx FA301]

031 KI5906-1 **Vito** {2.27}
[***78*** Od 250.420] [***CD*** Fmx FA301]

032 KI5905-1 **Gallito** {2.56}
[***78*** Od 250.418] [***CD*** Fmx FA301]

033 KI 5907-1 **Ne Sois Pas Jalouse** {2.54}
[*78* Od 250.420] [*CD* Fmx FA301]

034 **Ensemble**
[*78* Od 250.419]

035 **Rêve A Printemps**
[*78* Od 250.419]

Odéon 250.419, probably from the above session, and possibly featuring Django Reinhardt, currently remains unfound. However, some discographers dispute the presence of Django Reinhardt on any recording from this session.

Paris — Wednesday 29 March 1933

The Hot-Club de France presents a 'Programme Spécial dans le Galerie d'Art Contemporain de la Boîte à Musique, 135 Boulevard Raspail' featuring Russell Goudey, Arthur Briggs, Freddy Johnson and Fred Elizalde at 9.00pm.

Columbia Studios, Paris — Monday 3 April 1933

Jean Sablon

Jean Sablon (vcl) acc. by Leone Ferreri (pno, vcl); Michael Emer (cel, vcl); Django Reinhardt (gtr, vcl) (1) Léon Ferreri or Michael Warlop (vln, vcl); Michel Emer (pno, vcl); Django Reinhardt (gtr, vcl); Max Elloy (dms, vcl); Eliane de Creus or Mireille (vcl) (2).
Engineer: Georges Cailly

036 CL 4257-1 **Le Même Coup** (1) {3.10}
[*78* Col DF1191] [*LP* WRC SH368] [*CD* Fmx FA301]

037 CL 4258-1 **Je Suis Sex-Appeal** (2) {2.53}
[*78* Col DF1191] [*CD* Fmx FA301; Gal GALE419]

Both these tunes are from *Dix-neuf ans*; see also numbers 021–029.

Paris — May 1933

The Hot-Club de Paris reports, in *Jazz-Tango-Dancing*, the existence of regional Hot-Clubs in Belgium (Anvers, Brussels), Egypt (Cairo), France (Bordeaux, Cannes, Lille, Marseilles, Nancy), Holland (Amsterdam, Rotterdam), Switzerland (Geneva, Neufchâtel, Zurich).

Paris — c. May 1933

Louis Vola records four titles for Compagnie Française du Gramophone. Personnel unknown.
See Rust for further details.

Paris — Wednesday 17 May 1933

At an unreported location (possibly Galerie d'Art Contemporain) the Hot-Club de Paris presents a concert by the following group: Arthur Briggs (tpt); Frank 'Big Boy' Goudie (ts and tpt); Peter Duconge (as and cl); Freddie (*sic*) Johnson (pno); Juan Fernandez (sb); Bill Taylor (dms); Moeco (*sic*) Jefferson (gtr).

Titles performed include 'China Boy'; 'Nobody's Sweetheart'; 'St Louis Blues'; 'Chinatown'; 'I've Found A New Baby'; 'Sweet Sue'; 'Sheik Of Araby' and others.

Paris **Wednesday 31 May 1933**

Freddy Johnson, Peter Duconge, Frank 'Big Boy' Goudie, Charlie Johnson, Juan Ferndandez, Billy Taylor and Sterling Conaway appear on Paris 'Radio L.L.'. Titles broadcast include 'Sheik Of Araby'; 'I Found A New Baby'; 'I've Got Rhythm'; 'Rockin' Chair'; 'Nobody's Sweetheart' and 'Stormy Weather'.

Paris **June 1933**

Ultraphone records advertises the release of three records by Gregor et ses Gregorians:

AP1005 'Fit As A Fiddle' / 'Young And Healthy'
AP1007 'Wheezy-Anna' / 'Ev'ry Day's A Lucky Day'
AP1008 'Daisy' / 'Vladivostock'

The Allier brothers leave Gregor et ses Gregorians.

Paris **Monday 19 June 1933**

The French government grants political asylum to Leon Trotsky.

Paris **Friday 30 June 1933**

Alberta Hunter, accompanied by the Freddy Johnson Orchestra ('un nouvel orchestra de 12 musiciens noirs'), appears in concert at the Salle Chopin theatre at 9.00pm. For the likely personnel of this group, see the entry for Sunday 29 October 1933.

Paris **July 1933**

The renamed 'Bulletin Mensuel du Hot-Club Français' newsletter appears in *Jazz-Tango-Dancing* for the first time as a wholly separate section with its own logo.

Saint-Jean-de-Luz **July 1933**

Gregor et ses Gregorians begin a season at La Pergola.

Paris **Saturday 8 July 1933**

'Freddy Johnson, Arthur Briggs and their all Star Orchestra' record five titles for French Brunswick (matrix numbers 6458–62bkp). Musicians include Sterling Conaway, Juan Fernandez and Frank 'Big Boy' Goudie.
See Rust for details.

Paris **Wednesday 19 July 1933**

Marlene Dietrich, accompanied by 'Freddy Johnson et son Jazz' records for Compagnie Gramophone du Française. Musicians include Arthur Briggs, Freddy Johnson and Juan Fernandez.
See Rust for details.

Paris **Thursday 27–Saturday 29 July 1933**

Duke Ellington and his orchestra appear at the Salle Pleyel. The concerts are reported upon in depth in *Jazz-Tango-Dancing* by Hughes Panassié.

French Brunswick release eight sequentially numbered 78rpm records by the Ellington orchestra.

Paris **August 1933**

Ultraphone Records advertises the release of a further selection by Gregor et ses Gregorians: 'Going! Going! Going!' / 'Do Love Me' (SU5004).

Paris **September 1933**

Jazz-Tango-Dancing reviews 'Freddy Johnson, Arthur Briggs et Their All-Star Orchestra' (*sic*); Brunswick 500.278.

Paris **October 1933**

Jazz-Tango-Dancing reviews 'Freddy Johnson and His Orchestra'; Brunswick A.500.277.

Paris **October 1933**

Compagnie Française du Gramophone announces the release of 'Le Hot Jazz' records:

K6941–3	Louis Armstrong
K6944–8	Duke Ellington
K6949	Henry Allen
K6950	McKinney's Cotton Pickers
K6951	Mound City Blue Blowers.

Comments on the recordings in the adverts written by Hughes Panassié.

Paris **Saturday 14 October 1933**

'Freddy Johnson and His Harlemites' record four titles for French Brunswick (matrix numbers 6574–6). Musicians include Arthur Briggs, Sterling Conaway and Juan Fernandez.
See Rust for details.

Salle Pleyel, Paris **Sunday 29 October 1933 at 9.00pm**

A 'Unique Gala d'Art Nègre' is presented, featuring the screening of three short films: *Black and Tan Fantasy* (Duke Ellington), *I Heard* (Don Redman) and *Minnie the Moocher* (Cab Calloway). These last two films are both 'Betty Boop' animated shorts directed by Max Fleischer and incorporating film of the artists. There is also a presentation of the film *Emperor Jones* starring Paul Robeson.

Live performance by Freddy Johnson and his Harlemites with Arthur Briggs. *Jazz-Tango-Dancing* reported that the Johnson orchestra personnel were as follows: Arthur Briggs, Bobby Jones and Theodore Brock (tpts); Herbert Fleming and Henry Burns (tbns); Booker Pittman, Alfred Pratt, Roy Butler and Cle Sadler (saxs); Billie Taylor, Juan Fernandez and Sterling Conaway (rhythm section), and that the titles played were 'The Sheik Of Araby', 'Dinah', 'Sophisticated Lady', 'Harlem Bound', 'Tiger Rag', 'un violent' 'I've Got Rhythm' and 'un interminable' 'St Louis Blues'.

Paris **November 1933**

The group 'Ferrari et son Ensemble', featuring Oscar Alemán, record for Sedoem.

Jazz-Tango-Dancing reviews Eddie South et son Orchestre's 'Gotta Go' / 'My! Oh My!' (Gram K.7029).

Paris **Friday 10 November 1933**

Freddy Johnson and His Harlemites record two titles for French Brunswick (matrix numbers 6645–46bkp). Musicians include Arthur Briggs, Sterling Conaway and Juan Fernandez.
See Rust for details.

At the Théâtre Revue Musicale, 132 blvd de Montparnasse, at 9pm, the Hot-Club presents a concert featuring: Freddy Johnson (pno); Alix Combelle (ts); Noël Chiboust (tpt); Michel Warlop (vln) and [?] McGregor (dms). Titles performed include: 'Nobody's Sweetheart', 'Some Of These Days', 'I've Got Rhythm', 'Dinah', 'Tiger Rag', 'Confessin'', 'Play, Fiddle, Play', 'You Rascal You', 'Willow, Weep For Me' and 'China Boy'.

Paris **December 1933**

Garland Wilson records four titles for French Brunswick (matrix numbers 5747–50bdp).
See Rust for details.

Paris **Friday 8 December 1933**

At the Théâtre Revue Musicale, the Hot-Club de Paris presents a concert featuring Arthur Briggs and Garland Wilson. Titles performed include 'Dinah', 'Blues In B Flat', 'Black And Tan Fantasy', 'China Boy', 'I Can't Give You Anything But Love', 'Chinatown', 'Some Of These Days', 'Mood Indigo', 'Nobody's Sweetheart', 'But What Can I Do Now I'm In Love?', 'I've Found a New Baby' and 'Tiger Rag'.

Paris **Monday 18 December 1933**

At the Salle Adler, the Hot-Club de Paris presents 'Festival Big Boy' featuring Frank 'Big Boy' Goudie (tpt/cl); [?] Masse (gtr); Sigismund Beck (sb) and [?] McGregor (dms).

The death of Jacques Rosenburg, age 29, is reported in *Jazz-Tango-Dancing*. Rosenburg was the jazz record reviews editor of *Jazz-Tango-Dancing* and a director of the Paris offices of the Campbell-Connolly publishing company.

Côte d'Azur — Winter 1933–34

As a member of the André Ekyan orchestra, Django tours the Côte d'Azur accompanying Jean Sablon.

Columbia Studios, Paris — Tuesday 16 January 1934

Jean Sablon acc. M André Ekyan et son Orchestre Jazz

Sablon (vcl) acc. possibly by Gaston Lapeyronnie, George Hirst (tpts); Maurice Cizeron, André Ekyan (as); Andy Foster (cl, as); Eugène d'Hellemes (tbn); Stéphane Grappelli (vln); Michel Emer (pno); Django Reinhardt (gtr); Roger Grasset (sb); Maurice Chaillou or Max Elloy (dms).
Engineer: Georges Cailly

038 CL 4661-1 **Le Jour Ou Je Te Vis** (The Day You Came Along) {3.08}
[*78* Col DF1406] [***LP*** HD CHD 134, WRC SH368] [***CD*** Fmx FA301, Gal GALE419, Swi 8419]

039 CL 4661-2 **Le Jour Ou Je Te Vis** [**unissued**]

040 CL 4662-1 **Un Sous Dans La Poche** [**unissued**]

041 CL 4662-2 **Un Sous Dans La Poche** [**unissued**]

042 CL 4663-1 **Prenez Garde Au Grand Méchant Loup** (Who's Afraid Of The Big Bad Wolf?) {2.31}
[***78*** Col DF1406] [***CD*** Fmx FA301; Gal GALE419]

043 CL 4663-2 **Prenez Garde Au Grand Méchant Loup** [**unissued**]

044 CL 4664-1 **Pas Sur La Bouche** {2.29}
[***78* unissued**] [***CD*** Fmx FA301]

This is the first time that Django Reinhardt and Stéphane Grappelli record together.

Paris — Tuesday 23 January 1934

Django Reinhardt's 24th birthday.

Paris — Sunday 4 February 1934

Django Reinhardt's first reported public appearance, at the Salle Lafayette. The Hot-Club-sponsored band, known as the 'Orchestre Sigismund Beck' featured the following personnel: Frank 'Big Boy' Goudie (tpt); Freddy Johnson (pno); Django Reinhardt (reported as 'Jungo Rheinart' by *Jazz-Tango-Dancing*) (gtr); Sigismund Beck (sb); Billy Taylor (dms). The tunes played were 'I've Got Rhythm', 'Dinah', 'Some Of These Days', 'China Boy' (piano solo by Johnson), 'Little Joe', 'Sweet Georgia Brown' ('with a piano–guitar duet'), 'Blues In B Flat' (trumpet solo), 'Nobody's Sweetheart' ('Rheinart is enthusiastically applauded and there is a wonderful chorus by Beck'), 'I've Found a New Baby' ('the best solo by Rheinart'), 'I Can't Give You Anything But Love', 'Tiger Rag', 'St Louis Blues', 'China Town' and 'Japanese Sandman'.

Jungo Rhienart. On peut que lui, ce fut la révélation de la soirée ... C'est un musicien très curieux, dont le style ne ressemble a aucun autre connu. Ceci n'a pas empêché le public de la comprendre très bien, et d'applaudir ses solos. Ce guitariste blanc procède par petites phrases étranges, bizarrement construites selon les ressources d'une extraordinaire fantaisie; phrases qui n'ont l'air de rien, et sont d'un délicatesse, d'une finesse, d'un tact qui laissent les auditeurs ahuris. Chacun sait que les solos de guitare (a part celui de 'Knocking A Jug' et quelques autres) sont souvent insipides, mais ce n'était vraiment pas le cas pour ceux-la!

En contrastant avec le style de Big Boy, fort, violent, direct, la legerété, la fraîcheur de celui de Rheinart, paraissaient délicieuses. Nous connaissons maintenant à Paris un grand improvisateur de plus. Cette richesse d'invention ne nuit d'ailleurs pas la solitude de son rythme dans les accompagnements, loin de la! De plus, Rhienart est un garçon charmant, qui semble apporter dans sa vie cette même fantaisie légère qui illuminasses solos: jugez-en; il a élu domicile dans une roulotte, ce qui lui permet de voir du pays sans bouger de chez lui.

... Nous avons eu qu'a déplorer l'absence, sur la scène, du frère de Rheinart et de notre ami Arthur Briggs, tous deux malades. (Jacques Bureau, *Jazz-Tango-Dancing*, February 1934)

Jungo Rheinart. He was the revelation of the evening. He is a very strange musician, whose style is like no other that I know. This hasn't prevented the public from understanding him very well and applauding his solos. This white guitarist proceeds in strange little phrases, put together oddly according to the resources of an extraordinary fantasy; phrases that don't seem to be anything, and have a delicacy, a finesse, a tact that leave his listeners flabbergasted. Everyone knows that guitar solos (apart from the one in 'Knocking A Jug' and a few others) are often insipid, but that really wasn't the case with these!

In contrast with Big Boy's loud, violent, direct style, Rheinart's had a delicious lightness and freshness. Now we have a great improviser in Paris as well. This richness of invention doesn't harm the solitude of his rhythm in the accompaniments elsewhere, far from it! What's more, Rheinart is a charming lad, who seems to have in his life this same fantasy light that illuminates his solos: judge for yourselves; he has chosen to live in a caravan, which lets him see the country without leaving home.

... We could only deplore the absence on stage of Rheinhart's brother and our friend Arthur Briggs, who were both ill.

Salle Chopin, Paris — Tuesday 6 February 1934

Germaine Sablon et L'Orchestre Michel Warlop

Sablon (vcl) acc. by Noël Chiboust (tpt); Marcel Dumont, Isidore Bassard (tbn); André Ekyan (cl, as); Amédée Charles (as); Alix Combelle (ts); Charles Lissée (as, bs); Stéphane Grappelli (pno); Django Reinhardt (gtr); Roger Grasset (sb); [?] McGregor (dms); Michel Warlop (arr, vln).

Engineer: S E Tunn

045 OPG 1296-1 **Un Jour … Sur La Mer** {3.16}
[***78*** Gr K-7193] [***CD*** Fmx FA301]

046 OPG 1297-1 **Ici L'On Pêche** {3.22}
[***78* unissued**] [***CD*** Fmx FA301]

Location and engineer as above — Monday 26 February 1934

047 OPG 1297-2 **Ici L'On Pêche** {3.27}
[***78* unissued**] [***CD*** Fmx FA301]

048 OPG 1298-1 **Toboggan** [**unissued**]

049 OPG 1298-2 **Toboggan** {2.44}
[***78*** Gr K-7193] [***CD*** Fmx FA301]

050 OPG1362-1 **Celle Qui Est Perdue** {2.34}
[***78*** Gr K-7238] [***CD*** Fmx FA301]

Paris — Tuesday 6–Monday 12 February 1934

Premier Daladier faces uproar in the Chamber of Deputies; demonstrations by all political parties erupt on the Place de la Concorde. Police attempt to stop demonstrators from reaching the Palais Bourbon and serious rioting ensues. Through the night of 6th/7th the rioting continues sporadically, then re-ignites on the morning of the 7th and involves wholesale looting, burning, running battles between several different factions and some gunfire, resulting in a number of deaths. Following a lull on the 8th, on which date a coalition cabinet is formed, rioting again erupts on the 9th, most notably in the area of Belleville. On the 12th the Socialists lead a general strike, bringing out more than a million workers. The Daladier government resigns as a result.

Paris — Saturday 27 February 1934

Freddy Johnson departs Paris for Holland.

Bal des Elèves de l'Ecole Centrale, Paris — Saturday 3 March 1934

A concert by the 'Black Jazz Orchestra', promoted by the Hot-Club de France.

> It was the living end when André Ekyan, Jungo [*sic*] Reinhardt, his brother and Al Romans [*sic*] joined Big Boy's [Goudie] band … it was delirium incarnate, delirium that lasted into the night. (Unsigned, *Jazz-Tango-Dancing* April 1934, quoted in Delaunay).

> The Black Jazz Orchestra included Goudie and Garland Wilson. Students received a 10-francs discount, and 'in case of a taxi-shortage, transportation would be available all night'. The audience heard, among other tunes, 'Tiger Rag', 'Dinah' and 'Some Of These Days', plus vocals by Alberta Hunter. (Abrams)

Salle Chopin, Paris Friday 16 March 1934

Michel Warlop et son Orchestre

Pierre Allier, Maurice Moufflard, Noël Chiboust (tpt); Marcel Dumont, Isidore Bassard (tbn); André Ekyan (cl and as); Amédée Charles (as); Alix Combelle (ts); Charles Lissée (as, cl and bs); Stéphane Grappelli (pno); Django Reinhardt (gtr); Roger Grasset (sb); [?] McGregor (dms); Michel Warlop (vln, arranger and conductor).
Engineer: S E Tunn

051 OPG 1415-1 **Presentation Stomp** {3.03}
[***78*** Gr K-7314] [***LP*** El (G) 83035; FELP154; HCLP120; HMV CLP1249; OCLP7529; Pat C054 16001] [***CD*** Cls 703; Fmx FA301]

052 OPG 1415-2 **Presentation Stomp [unissued]**

Same location and date

Germaine Sablon et L'Orchestre Michel Warlop

053 OPG 1416-1 **Je Ne Suis Pas Un Ange** {3.14}
[***78*** Gr K-7238] [***CD*** Fmx FA301]

054 OPG 1416-2 **Je Ne Suis Pas Un Ange [unissued]**

055 OPG 1417-1 **La Chanson Du Large** {3.18}
[***78*** Gr K-7256] [***CD*** Fmx FA301; Swi 8419]

056 OPG 1417-2 **La Chanson Du Large [unissued]**

HMV CLP1249 mistitled as 'Paramount Stomp'. The same LP also included OLA1995, 'Paramount Stomp', correctly titled.

London April 1934

Coleman Hawkins appears at the London Palladium theatre in a show called *In Town Tonight*. *Melody Maker* reports that the names posted on his dressing room were 'Coleman and Hawkins'.

Columbia Studios, Paris AM; Wednesday 11 April 1934

Jean Sablon and Trio

Sablon (vcl) acc. by André Ekyan (cl); Alec Siniavine (pno); Django Reinhardt (gtr).
Engineer: Georges Cailly

057 CL 4807-1 **Je Sais Que Vous Etes Jolie** {3.01}
[***78*** Col BF 404; ***DF 1506*** (F; E) 4191M] [***LP*** HD CHD134; WRC SH368] [***CD*** Fmx FA302; Gal GALE419]

058 CL 4808-1 **Par Correspondance** {2.36}
[***78*** Col BF 404; ***DF 1506*** (F; E) 4191M] [***LP*** WR(E) SH368] [***CD*** Fmx FA302]

London PM; Wednesday 11 April 1934

Jean Sablon, accompanied by Django Reinhardt, André Ekyan and Alec Siniavine, arrives by air from Paris to appear at the 'Monseigneur' club, Piccadilly, London for approximately three weeks. The same evening, he also appears in 'Cosmopolitan Cabaret', a BBC London-regional radio broadcast.

> Sablon had just arrived from Paris by air, bringing with him a pianist, guitar player and clarinetist. There was really no need to have gone to all the expense of bringing these musicians over, as they did nothing that warranted it. However, Sablon certainly made up for them. He was well worth the trip, and sang in a delightfully easy style several numbers in French and one, 'Mimi', in English. (Unsigned, *Melody Maker*, 21 April, 1934)

This would appear to be Django Reinhardt's first radio broadcast.
See Delaunay, pages 62–3, and page 223 for a photo of the musicians at the airport, ready for departure.

London Sunday 22 April 1934

A *Melody Maker* concert featuring Coleman Hawkins is cancelled at the last minute.

Salle Chopin, Paris Saturday 12 May 1934

Germaine Sablon acc. par Michel Warlop et son Orchestre

Germaine Sablon (vcl) acc. by Pierre Allier, Noël Chiboust, Maurice Mouflard (tpts); Isidore Bassart, Marcel Dumont (tbns); Amédée Charles, André Ekyan (as, cl); Alix Combelle (ts); Charles Lissée (bs, as); Michel Warlop (vln, ldr); Stéphane Grappelli (pno); Django Reinhardt (gtr); Roger Grasset (sb); [?] McGregor (dms).
Engineer: Ernest Gower

059 OPG 1572-1 **Tendresse-waltz** {3.05}
[*78* Gr K-7305] [*CD* Fmx FA302]

060 OPG 1573-2 **J'ai Besoin De Toi** {3.21}
[*78* Gr K-7479] [*CD* Fmx FA302]

Same location and date

Michel Warlop et son Orchestre

Personnel as last without Sablon.

061 OPG 1574-1 **Blue Interlude** {3.18}
[*78* Gr K-7314] [*CD* Cls 703; Fmx FA302]

062 OPG 1574-2 **Blue Interlude** [**unissued**]

Publicis Studios, Paris — August 1934

Django Reinhardt (1) / Trio Django Reinhardt (2) / 'Essais Django' (Django Tests) (Fremeaux)

Django Reinhardt (gtr), Joseph Reinhardt (gtr) (1); Django Reinhardt (gtr), Joseph Reinhardt (gtr), Juan Fernandez (sb) (2).

063 **Tiger Rag** (1) [**unissued**]

064 **Tiger Rag** (2) {2.19}
[*78* private acetate] [*LP* Vo 500064] [*CD* Cls 703; Fmx FA302]

065 **After You've Gone** (2) {2.11}
[*78* private acetate] [*LP* Vog 406505] [*CD* Cls 703; Fmx FA302]

066 **Confessin'** (2) {2.36}
[*78* private acetate] [*LP* Vog 406505] [*CD* Cls 703; Fmx FA302]

Delaunay's 1961 discography lists 'Tiger Rag' as being *without* Fernandez, then mentions two un-named titles *with* Fernandez. In his revised, 1988 discography he lists two takes of 'Tiger Rag', as detailed above, and specifically names the other two titles, but no copy of the first take of 'Tiger Rag' has ever been recovered and it may never have existed. Tests 064–6 survived because Delaunay took possession of them during the 1930s, and used them several times in his regular radio broadcasts.
See Delaunay, page 65.

Chez Florence, Paris — *c.* August/September 1934

Rehearsals by the Quintette for the Odéon recording take place.
See Delaunay, pages 66–7.

Dorchester Hotel, London — September–November 1934

Alberta Hunter performs and records in London. Musicians include Noel 'Chappie' d'Amato.
See entry under Jack Jackson and his Orchestra in Rust for details of recordings.

Odéon Studios, Paris — September 1934

Delaunay's Jazz

Stéphane Grappelli (vln); Django Reinhardt (gtr solo); Joseph Reinhardt, Roger Chaput (gtrs); Louis Vola (sb); Bert Marshall (vcl) (1).

067 1071 **I Saw Stars** (1) {2:41}
[*78* Od **unissued**] [*LP* Vog 500740] [*CD* Cls 703; Fmx FA302; JSP 341; Swi CDSW8419]

068 1072 **Confessin'** {2:46}
[*78* Od **unissued**] [*LP* Vog 500740] [*CD* AA24; Cls 703; Fmx FA302; JSP 341; Swi CDSW8419]

See Delaunay, pages 67–8.

Paris October 1934

Louis Armstrong records eight titles for Brunswick on his first visit (matrix numbers 1478–84, including alternate takes).
See Rust for details.

Paris Monday 1 October 1934

Eliane de Creus et ses Boys

Despite being listed in numerous previous Django Reinhardt discographies, this session, while featuring Michel Warlop, Michel Emer and probably Roger Grasset, does *not* include Django Reinhardt.
The following example from the session is included in the Fremeaux re-issue set to prove this point:

OLA 10 **La Rumba Da Boum** {3.16}
[***78*** Gr K-7395] [***CD*** Fmx FA302]

Paris November 1934

President Doumergue's government fails; a coalition is formed by Flandin.

'L'Orchestre H. Mollois', broadcasts on Radio-Paris; the featured musicians are [?] Bassart (tbn); Roger Chaput (gtr); R Debrienne (pno); [?] Herner (ts); [?] Lambert (as); H Mollois (sax); Maurice Mouflard (tpt); Louis Vola (sb).

Review of Gr K-7314 'Presentation Stomp' / 'Blue Interlude' by Michel Warlop. 'Avec Blue Interlude, Michel Warlop présente un echantillion remarquable de violon hot dominant de ses arabesques sinueuses la belle pâte sonore de l'ensemble. Et Presentation Stomp constitute, dans le domaine de l'agitation syncopée frénétique, un spécimen qui aurait sa place, sans discussion possible, ou cours d'une de ces nuits de Harlem, tant vantées par les fanatiques du hot américain.' (Unsigned, *L'Edition Musical Vivant*, November 1934)

André Ekyan et son Orchestre, in residence at Du Bœuf Sur Le Toit, are featured in *Jazz-Tango-Dancing*. The personnel includes Léo Detemple (pno); André Ekyan (ts); Emile Feldmann (gtr); Andy Foster [*aka* André Forster] (ts); Maurice Geigas (tpt); Raymond Guitard (ts); Jerry Mengo (dms).

Warlop's 'Presentation Stomp' is reviewed in *Jazz-Tango-Dancing*. Django Reinhardt is referred to in the text as 'Jungo Reinhardt'.

Jazz-Tango-Dancing lists the following bands in residence in Paris: Orchestre Jazz Goudie at the Coliseum, Orchestre Willie Lewis and Orchestre Vola at Le Florence, Orchestre Freddy Taylor at Villa d'Este.

The publication of Hughes Panassié's book *Le Jazz hot*.

Paris Friday 9 and Saturday 10 November 1934

Louis Armstong and his Orchestra appear at the Salle Rameau.

Salle Chopin, Paris — Tuesday 13 November 1934

Aime Simon-Girard acc. par Michel Warlop et son Orchestre (1)
Germaine Sablon acc. par Michel Warlop et son Orchestre (2)

Aime Simon-Girard (1) or Germaine Sablon (2) (vcl) acc. by Pierre Allier, Maurice Mouflard (tps); Marcel Dumont (tbn); André Ekyan (as, cl); Amédée Charles (as); Alix Combelle (ts); Charles Lissée(bs); Michel Warlop (vln, ldr); Stéphane Grappelli or Alain Romans (pno); Django Reinhardt (gtr); Roger Grasset (sb); Maurice Chula (dms).
Engineer: George W Deacon

069 OLA 148-1 **Cocktails Pour Deux** (Cocktails For Two) (1) {3.07}
[*78* Gr K-7374] [*CD* Fmx FA302]

070 OLA 149-1 **Deux Cigarettes Dans L'Ombre** (Two Cigarettes In The Dark) (2) {3.07}
[*78* Gr K-7373] [*CD* Fmx FA302]

071 OLA 149-2 **Deux Cigarettes Dans L'Ombre** (2) [**unissued**]

072 OLA 150-1 **L'Amour En Fleurs** (Love In Bloom) (2) {3.01}
[*78* Gr K-7374] [*CD* Fmx FA302]

073 OLA 151-1 **Je Voudre Vivre** (2) {2.44}
[*78* Gr K-7373] [*CD* Fmx FA302]

London — Saturday 17 November 1934

Vive le Hot!

Parisian music! Vivid words, conjuring up pictures of grinding accordions, of lusty washerwomen singing on rooftops, of swarthy apaches and exotic cocottes [*sic*] swing to the tune of a turgid tango … Beautiful visions these – but ten years behind the times. For Paris is fast becoming a hotbed of hot music!

Within an hour of my arrival I was in the midst of a veritable aural orgy. By my side was Pierre Nourry whose Hot Club de France flourished long before the English Rhythm Circle movement ever began. I was hustled along to the maisonette of Henri Bernard. An amazing young man, this. With typical gallic enthusiasm he has amassed a library of records that could hardly be rivalled in the States. Yet he cannot speak a word of English; has never been to England or America and started collecting less than six years ago!

Chiboust, a fine trumpet player, can be heard in one or two Maurice Chevalier records. An embryonic Bix, still waiting for his big break …

Then there is a brilliant young guitarist, Jungo Reinhart [*sic*]. He wanders though France in a caravan: a true Gypsy genius. When they can reach him they sometimes bring him to a recording studio … recently he made several titles with an orchestra formed for Columbia by André Ekyan, the great French clarinettist.

But Reinhart cares little for the vagaries of city life. On he roams through the woodlands of France, perhaps playing some favourite Lang masterpieces on his ancient portable gramophone, or improvising on his own guitar to a silent world.

Back in Paris the musical contingent does not share this precious freedom. The fetters of commercialism have even gripped Spencer Williams. This great coloured veteran of jazz, famous composer of *Basin Street Blues, Shimme-Sha Wobble, I Ain't Got Nobody* and innumerable hits of the last thirty years, is now resident in Paris, where I found him hard at work on some new popular songs for the English masses …

Arthur Briggs, another Parisian Harlemite, doughtily hits his top C's at the Chantilly, whilst his former partner, Freddy Johnson, scores new triumphs far away in Holland. And most important of all, there has been a coloured band playing in Paris which has excited audiences all over Europe – Willie Lewis and his Entertainers, who, at the time of which I am writing, played nightly *Chez Florence* [*sic*]. This place lies in a side turning of the Montparnasse district. The entrance promised nothing more than a typical Paris *boite de nuit*, with its neon letters and low-roofed, over-smart decorations. Inside, a languid crowd shuffles round the dance floor.

But in an instant this dull preliminary atmosphere is forgotten. Our attention is fixed on the bandstand. There stands a gaunt figure, very dark-skinned and grave of face, playing a saxophone. You are introduced. So this is Willie Lewis, the charming and polite *chef d'orchestre* of Europe's leading coloured unit.

A word whispered in Willie's ear, and the dry routine of commercial numbers will be forsaken. Choruses of the 'good ol' good ones' follow each other hell-for-leather; the strong rhythm section swings out. Already you can almost believe yourself in Harlem … There, in the corner, is fat Bobby Martin, the trumpet player with a Bubber Miley style and a boisterous personality that stirs even this *blasé* crowd from its lethargy. John Mitchell and Ted Fields work vigorously on the guitar and drums.

Next to Nelson Kincaid, the first alto, is Jerry Blake, an elegant tenor and clarinetist who told me about the discs he had made recently with Bennie Moten's band across the pond. Listen to him in *Lafayette*. This first-class swing man, one-time member of Redman's outfit, shares the general Harlem admiration for the great Little Don.

At the back there, almost hidden by his string bass and his sousaphone, is June Cole, who told me of the good old days he spent with Henderson's band back in 1928 and '29. Cole is still as great a bassist as ever. Then there was an outstanding pianist, Herman Chittison. After an hour of super-swinging, the boys laid down their instruments to go through their specialty act; for not only are they fine instrumentalists, but clever harmony singers and comedians as well.

The jaded Parisian crown to whom the music was of little importance, were at once captivated by this novelty act. If only the fans could frequent

> this expensive establishment nightly, there would be applause for the swinging as well as the singing. But one mustn't despair. Willie Lewis has an increasing circle of admirers in this gay city, for rhythmic music is in greater demands than ever before. And that is the Paris I have found in this year of grace 1934. Hot records swarming in the catalogues, and fans swarming to the Hot Club, with one increasing purpose – the propagation of the newest musical art in a country where accordions, washerwomen and tangos are fast losing their hold ... *Vive le Hot*! (Leonard G Feather, *Melody Maker*)

Feather is presumably referring to the Jean Sablon session of 11 April 1934, *qv*.

Paris **Wednesday 28 November 1934**

Louis Armstrong and his orchestra broadcast on Radio Poste Parisien.

Holland **Thursday 29 November 1934**

Freddy Johnson records four titles with Lex Van Spal and Orchestra for Decca (matrix numbers AM124–7).
See Rust for details.

Switzerland **November/December 1934**

Louis Armstrong and his Orchestra appear in concert; the itinerary is as follows:

Friday 30 November	Zurich
Sunday 1 December	Geneva
Monday 2 December	Lausanne
Tuesday 3 December	Berne

London **December 1934**

> **A Record Fans Should Hear**
>
> Fud Candrix, Belgium's super hot tenor player, is getting together a band of Continental stars for recording. The record, or records, will not be marketed commercially, but will only be obtainable on a subscription basis. Here is a chance for the fans. The record will cost no more than 2/6 – not much to gamble. If you want to know what Fud plays like ask anybody who has spent a holiday in Belgium recently. He is hotter than the hottest. (Unsigned, *Ballroom and Band*)
>
> All the good pianists, of course, are not in the States. On the Continent there is Freddy Johnson, a swell orchestral player. He feeds his men well and by sending his band gets the best out of them. But he gets very scared of an audience and so is not at his best when playing solo. (Garland Wilson, *Ballroom and Band*)

Paris **December 1934**

Jazz-Tango-Dancing changes its name to *Jazz-Tango*, and is launched with a redesigned front cover.

L'Ecole Normale de Musique, Paris — Sunday 2 December 1934

Django Reinhardt, Stéphane Grappelli, Joseph Reinhardt, Roger Chaput and Louis Vola appear at a concert organised by the Hot-Club de France's secretary Pierre Nourry. Django's name is spelled 'Djungo' and the Quintette do not officially appear as 'Quintette du Hot-Club de France'. Enthusiastic response to this concert leads to the immediate booking of a further concert on 16 February 1935. The 'Hot-Club Magazine' section of the December issue of *Jazz-Tango* announces this as follows:

> A very hot programme for Sunday evening, 2 December, from 10.00pm until perhaps 12.30am. Here are the details of the programme:
>
> Under the direction of Jungo Reinhardt, a quartet of ultra-hot strings: Jungo Reinhardt, guitar; Joseph Reinhardt, guitar; Stephan Grapelli, violin; VOLA, contrabasse. Between other pieces, we expect them to play 'Confessin'', 'After You've Gone', 'Tiger Rag' ...
>
> An executive of the Ultraphone company was present, and he agreed to record the group. (Abrams)

See Panassié, *Douze années de jazz*, page 141 and *Le Jazz hot*, page 419 for further details.
See Delaunay, page 68, and page 221 for a reproduction of an original poster for this concert.

Pathé Studios, Paris — Wednesday 12 December 1934

Patrick et son Orchestre de Danse

(under the leadership of Guy Paquinet ['Patrick'])
Gaston Lapeyronnie, Alphonse Cox, Noël Chiboust (tpts); Guy Paquinet, Pierre Deck, René Weiss (tbns); André Ekyan, Charles Lissée (cl, as); Andy Foster (cl, as, bs); Alix Combelle (ts); Jean Chaboud, (pno); Django Reinhardt (gtr); Louis Pecqueux (sb); Maurice Chaillou (dms, vcl) (1); Roger Chomer (vibes). Unknown vocal trio (2) arr. by Jean Chaboud.
Engineer: Eugène Ravenet

074 CPT 1700-1 **From Now On** (2) {3.02}
[***78*** Pat PA-468] [***CD*** Cls 703; Fmx FA302]

075 CPT 1702-1 **I Saw Stars** (1) {3.01}
[***78*** Pat PA-468] [***LP*** Swi 8420267] [***CD*** AA24; Cls 703; Fmx FA302; Swi CDSW8419]

Pathé Studios, Paris — Monday 17 December 1934

Same personnel and engineer as 12 December.

076 CPT 1701-1 **Black Panther Stomp** {2.49}
[***78*** Pat PA-467] [***CD*** Cls 703; Fmx FA302]

077 CPT 1703-1 **Okay Toots** (2) {2.43}
[***78*** Pat PA-466] [***CD*** Cls 703; Fmx FA302]

078 CPT 1704-1 **When My Ship Comes In** (2) {3.05}
[*78* Pat PA-466] [*CD* Cls 703; Fmx FA302]

079 CPT 1705-1 **My Carolina Hideaway** {2.37}
[*78* Pat PA-467] [*CD* Cls 703; Fmx FA302]

Note that although matrix numbers 1701 and 1702 appear out of sequence, the recording dates are, nonetheless, correct.

Paris — Wednesday 26 December 1934

to Monsieur Pierre Nourry, 15 Rue du Conservatoire, Paris
from Societe Ultraphone Française, 46 rue de la Bienfaisance, Paris 8e

Dear Sir,
I shall not attempt to conceal that I am somewhat taken aback by the exorbitant demands of the musicians in your quintet.

Perhaps you are unaware that the normal fee currently paid to first-class jazz soloists never exceeds 150 francs for each three hour session at which six sides are generally made.

On that basis the demands of the three supporting musicians far exceed the usual fees. Naturally I am not speaking of Grappelli.

The most favourable conditions I can contemplate are as set out below:

For the three accompanists (two guitarists and a double-bassist). An outright payment of 30 francs per side.

For Grappelli, an outright payment of 50 francs per side.

For Reinhardt, a royalty of 5 per cent and 50 francs royalty advance on each side recorded.

In view of the probable commercial value of the suggested recordings, you will understand that I cannot commit my company to paying fees that mean there would be no profit even when five hundred records have been produced.

I rely on you to give your artists a more realistic idea of the fees they can expect to receive.

Yours Faithfully,
Society Ultraphone Française, Caldairou

(Delaunay archives)

Ultraphone Studios, Paris — between Thursday 27 and Monday 31 December 1934

Django Reinhardt et le Quintette du Hot-Club de France (Oriole)/ Hot-Club of France (Royale)/Djungo Reinhardt and the Quintette of the Hot-Club de France (Supraphon)/Djungo Reinhardt et le Quintette du Hot-Club de France avec Stéphane Grappelly (Ultraphone)

Stéphane Grappelli (vln); Django Reinhardt (gtr solo); Joseph Reinhardt, Roger Chaput (gtrs); Louis Vola (sb).
Engineer: Willy Kuhn

080 P 77161 **Dinah** (Fox Trot) {2:33}
[***78*** DA17-1; JD 8004; Od D286044; Or LV100, LB1000; Roy 1753; Supra B-22642; Tel A-1959; **Ultr AP 1422**, B-14286; Var 8377] [***25cm LP*** Or MG10019] [***EP*** Or 7045; Sup SUK35615] [***LP*** Pac LDP D6272; Vog DPO5, COF03, 500740] [***CD*** AA24; ABM 1194; Cas MACD132; Cly DIG12; Cls 703; Dig CO3506; Ea EABCD71; Fmx FA302; Hab 111200; JSP 341; Kaz EUKCD913; LE JA5138, 5267; Mil 74321308652; Music CD6048; QED71; Recall SMCD307]

081 P 77162 **Tiger Rag** {2:33}
[***78*** DA17-5; JD 8003; Or LV101, LB1001; Roy 1753; Tel A-1959; **Ultr AP 1423**, B-14287; Var 8380] [***25cm LP*** Or MG10019] [***LP*** Pac(F) LDP D6272; Vog 500740, COF03] [***EP*** Or 7045; Sup SUK35615] [***CD*** AA24; ABM 1194; Cls 703; Cly DIG12; Ea EABCD71; Fmx FA302; JSP 341; LE AJA5138; Music 6048; QED71; Recall SMCD307; Vog 668003-1]

082 P 77163 **Lady Be Good** {2:53}
[***78*** JD 8003; Or LV100, LB1000; Roy 1754; Supra B-22642; **Ultr AP 1422**, B-14286;Var 8376] [***25cm LP*** Or MG10019] [***LP*** Pac(F)D6272; Vog 500740, COF03] [***EP*** Or 7045; Sup SUK35615] [***CD*** AA24; ABM CD1194; Cas MACCD132; Cls 703; Emp RAJCD808; Fmx FA302; JSP 341; Kaz EUKCD913; LE AJA5138, 5267; QED71; Recall SMDCD307; Vog 668003-1]

083 P 77164 **I Saw Stars** {2:28}
[***78*** Or LV101, LB1000, **Ultr AP 1423**, B-14287]
[***25cm LP*** Or MG10019]
[***LP*** Pac(F) D6272; Vog 500740, COF03] [***EP*** Or 7045; Sup SUK35615]
[***CD*** AA24; ABM CD1194; Cls 703; Cly DIG12; Fmx FA302; HD CDHD234; JSP 341; LE JA5138, 5267; QED71; Retro RZCD7002; Vog 668003-1]

See Panassié, *Douze années de jazz*, pages 142–3 for a first-hand account of this session.
Initial pressings for these couplings are reported to have been 500 each.

Paris — early 1935

Django begins a regular engagement at the 'Stage B' club in Montparnasse.

Jean Bérard is appointed head of Compagnie Gramophone du Française.

Paris — January 1935

'Django Reinhardt (for that is the correct spelling of his name) is comparable to the best American instrumentalists.' (*Jazz-Tango*, January 1935)

N J Canetti reviews Panassié's *Le Jazz hot* in *Jazz-Tango*.

The final Hot-Club newsletter appears as an integral part of *Jazz-Tango.*

London Saturday 5 January 1935

Melody Maker reviews Hughes Panassié's *Le Jazz Hot*, largely in favourable terms.

Columbia Studios, Paris Monday 7 January 1935

Jean Sablon

Sablon (vcl) acc. by Garland Wilson (1) or Alec Siniavine (2) (pno); Django Reinhardt (gtr).
Engineer: Georges Cailly

084 CI 5176-1 **The Continental** [**unissued**]

085 Cl 5176-2 **The Continental** (1) {2.56}
[***78*** Col DF 1672 (E, F)] [***LP*** HD CHD134; WR(E) SH368]
[***CD*** Fmx FA302; Gal GALE419; LE JA5167]

086 CI 5178-1 **Un Baiser** [**unissued**]

087 CI 5178-2 **Un Baiser** [**unissued**]

088 Cl 5178-3 **Un Baiser** (1) {3.16}
[***78*** **Col DF 1714** (E, F), 4178-M, 100001] [***CD*** Fmx FA302]

089 Cl 5179-1 **La Dernière Bergère** (2) {3.02}
[***78*** **Col DF 1714** (E, F), 4178-M, 100001] [***LP*** WRC SH368]
[***CD*** Fmx FA302; Gal GALE419]

Django Reinhardt does not play on Matrix 5177.

London Friday 18 January 1935

Valaida Snow records two titles for Parlophone; musicians include Alan Ferguson. See Rust for details of this and subsequent sessions.

Paris Wednesday 23 January 1935

Django Reinhardt's 25th birthday.

Paris Thursday 31 January 1935

The Quintette appear at the 'Gala du Disque et du Radio' exhibition.

Paris February 1935

Review of Stéphane Grappelli, Django Reinhardt and the Quintette du 'Hot-Club', 'I Saw Stars' / 'Tiger Rag' (Ultr AP 1423) and 'Dinah' / 'Lady Be Good' (Ultr AP 1422).

> Here are the first recordings from guitarist Django Reinhardt and Stephane Grappelly, accompanied, as we understand from the label, by the quintette(?) of the Hot-Club. Do you want to know my sincere impression of these four sides? They are far from being ordinary. 'I Saw Stars' is even excellent; unfortunately the instrumental combination offered is a little fatiguing after a while.

Django Reinhardt reveals himself on these four recordings as a truly exceptional guitarist, as much for his technique as for his style. Let's not forget that the guitar is from all viewpoints a very ungrateful [*sic*] instrument and exclusively reserved for rhythmic accompaniment in jazz orchestras. If it is possible, as Panassié said 'to play hot on any instrument' – and I am absolutely of the opinion that it is – it is undeniable that the melodic resources of the guitar are quite slim; meagre, I would say, in thinking about the sound of the guitar. Django consistently uses "all the strings" of his instrument – I must say – in deploying a swing of surprising intensity.

Stéphane Grappelly himself finds 'hot' phrases of a more pleasant equilibrium. His choruses are very well constructed, but he is on the other hand frankly handicapped by the sonority of his instrument, which comes through on the recordings as slightly shrill and sharp. There is no doubt that he is a better 'hot' violinist than Michel Warlop, Sylvio Schmidt or even perhaps Joe Venuti, but his sonority erodes some of the pleasure one experiences on hearing his beautiful and genuine flights of rhythm. Of these four sides, 'I Saw Stars' is in my opinion the most successful, while 'Tiger Rag' should not have been issued in this form. From a technical point of view, the recording almost loses the playing of the double bass – Vola, I believe – and mutes the solo guitar passages. Perhaps the slightly sharp sound of the violin is equally a fault of the recording, but this is not clear.

Let's hope that Django Reinhardt, Stéphane Grappelly with the quinette – but why the devil do they say 'quintette'? – it makes it more rich, but if there is only a trio accompanying them, one does not need to arouse in the listener the suspicion that on top of the small, specific technical problems, the recording conjured away two instruments – will do a new series of recordings, still more successful and putting plainly in evidence the incontestable value of the musicians' interpretations. (J Emi, *Jazz-Tango*)

The Hague — Monday 4 February 1935

Coleman Hawkins records eight titles for Dutch Decca (matrix numbers AM148–51 and 153 including alternates).
See Rust for details.

Paris — Tuesday 5 February 1935

Le Petit Mirsha

Le Petit Mirsha (vcl) acc. by Michel Warlop's Orchestre (unknown personnel, probably including Alec Siniavine (pno); Django Reinhardt (gtr) (1).
Mirsha (vcl) acc. by Alec Siniavine (pno); Django Reinhardt (gtr) (2).

090 OLA 300-1 **Maman Ne Vend Pas La Maison** (1) [**unissued**]

091 OLA 301-1 **Petit Homme C'est L'Heure De Faire Dodo** (1) [**unissued**]

092 OLA 302-1 **Vieni, Vieni** (2) {2.53}
[***78*** Gr K-7464] [***CD*** Fmx FA302; Swi SW 8419]

Théâtre des Champs-élysées, Paris Tuesday 5 February 1935

The Quintette participate in the 'Gala du Disques et Radio'.
See Delaunay, page 74.

Columbia Studios, Paris Saturday 9 February 1935

Léon Monosson acc. par L'Orchestre Alain Romans du Poste Parisien et son Ensemble

Monosson (vcl) acc. by Alex Renard (tpt) (1); Michel Warlop, Sylvio Schmidt or Stéphane Grappelli (vln); Alain Romans (pno, celeste, ldr); Django Reinhardt (gtr); possibly Lucien Simoens (sb).
Engineer: Georges Cailly

093 CL 5220-1 **Deux Cigarettes Dans L'Ombre** (Two Cigarettes In The Dark) {3.16}
[*78* Col DF 1690] [*CD* Fmx FA302]

094 CL 5221-1 **Tout Le Jour, Toute La Nuit** (Night and Day (*sic*)) (1) {3.20}
[*78* Col DF 1690] [*CD* Fmx FA302; Swi SW 8419]

L'Ecole Normale de Musique, Paris Saturday 16 February 1935

The Quintette du Hot-Club de France play their second concert.
See Delaunay, page 68, and page 222 for a reproduction of a poster for this event.

Chambre du Commerce, Nancy Wednesday 20 February 1935

The Quintette appears in concert. Also on the bill are the 'Hot Serenaders', a local band.

Salle Chopin, Paris Friday 22 February 1935

Le Petit Mirsha acc. par Michel Warlop et son Orchestre

Le Petit Mirsha (vcl) acc. by Noël Chiboust or Pierre Allier (tpt); Marcel Dumont (tbn); André Ekyan, Charles Lissée (as); Alix Combelle (ts); Alain Romans (pno); Django Reinhardt (gtr), Roger Grasset (sb) (1 as above; 2 without Chiboust or Allier).
Engineer: George W Deakin

095 OLA 330-1 **Maman Ne Vend Pas La Maison** (1) [**unissued**]

096 OLA 330-2 **Maman Ne Vend Pas La Maison** (1) {3.28}
[*78* Gr K-7464] [*CD* Fmx FA302]

097 OLA 331-1 **Petit Homme C'est L'Heure De Faire Dodo** (2) {3.38}
[*78* Gr K-7437] [*CD* Fmx FA302]

Salle Playell, Paris Saturday 23 February 1935

Coleman Hawkins, an orchestra lead by Arthur Briggs and Freddy Taylor, and the Quintette de Hot-Club du France appear in concert. In addition to items detailed in the review below, Hawkins reportedly play 'Avalon', 'Blue Moon', 'Sweet Sue', 'Hands Across The Table', 'After You've Gone', 'I Wish I Were Twins' and 'Some Of These Days'. Briggs and the orchestra play 'St Louis Blues' and 'Dinah'. The QHCF (described as a quartet at this event) play 'Tiger Rag' and two other, unidentified, tunes. Freddy Taylor, accompanied by the Quintette, sings 'Grabbin' Blues' and 'You Rascal You', and performs a dance.

> Over 1200 people attended Coleman Hawkins special concert at the Salle Playell on Saturday, and a great reception was given to the 'World's Greatest Saxophonist' by French hot fans. The concert was organized by the Hot Club de France, and, while not as financially successful as some of the other concerts given by this club, was a much-appreciated event from the fans point of view.
>
> Hawkins was supported by a mixed white and coloured band consisting of Castor McCord (tenor sax), Fletcher Allen and Peter Duconge (altos), Noël Chiboust (trumpet), Billy Taylor (drums), Reinhardt, jun. [*sic*] (guitar), Beck (string bass) and Arthur Briggs leading on trumpet.
>
> Later, this orchestra gave place to a string quartet directed by the violinist Stephan Grappelly, and the extraordinary guitarist Django Reinhardt. The three pieces given by this little ensemble were perfect and brought the house down.
>
> My personal opinion is that a tenor saxophone, even as played by the incomparable Hawkins, is not an instrument with which to hold a crowd of people, but there is no doubt about it, that Hawk gave of his best, his most successful items being 'The Day You Came Along', 'If I Could Be One Hour With You' and 'I Got Rhythm'.
>
> Despite the individual brilliance of the artists – particularly of Briggs in his solos – the supporting band was poor.
>
> As a matter of interest, the gross receipts of this concert were given to me as 18,000 francs. This sounds a lot but should be compared with the following sums netted at previous hot concerts in Paris; Duke Ellington 70,000 francs; Freddy Johnson 35,000 francs; Cab Calloway 27,000 francs; and Louis Armstrong 40,000 francs. (N J Canetti, *Melody Maker*, w/e 2 March 1935)

See Panassié *Douze années de jazz* for a first-hand account of this concert.
See Delaunay, page 75, and page 228 for a reproduction of a poster for this event.

Paris **March 1935**

Django Reinhardt's engagement at 'Stage B' ends and he joins Freddy Taylor and his Swing Men From Harlem at La Villa d'Este. Freddy Taylor and his Swing Men From Harlem record two titles for Ultraphon, also issued in the United Kingdom on Levy's Oriole label (matrix numbers 77285–6). Musicians include Fletcher Allen, Oscar Alemán and Eugène d'Hellemes.
See Rust for details.

'Blue Drag' (matrix 77285) issued on Royale 1778 is incorrectly credited as 'Freddy Taylor and the Quintet of the Hot Club of France'.

Paris — March 1935

The premier edition of *Jazz Hot*, separate from its inclusion in *Jazz-Tango-Dancing*, appears, featuring an article on Coleman Hawkins, reviews of Ultraphone AP 1422 and 1423 and a full-page Ultraphone advert for AP 1422, 1423, 1443 and 1444.

London — March 1935

> Another swell tenor man I met on the Continent was Big Boy Goudie who made a few records with Freddy Johnson. He has been in Paris a long time and wants to stay there always. He likes the atmosphere and plays with outfits with which he can swing when he wants to. He comes from the States, but when he hears from people like Babe Rusin that hot playing is not so popular there, he just wants to stay where he is. (Don Barrigo, tenor saxophonist with the Lew Stone orchestra, *Ballroom and Band*)

Paris — Saturday 2 March 1935

Coleman Hawkins acc. par Michel Warlop et son Orchestre avec Arthur Briggs

Coleman Hawkins (ts) acc. by Arthur Briggs (tpt solo); Noël Chiboust, Pierre Allier (tpts); Guy Paquinet (tbn); André Ekyan, Charles Lissée (as, cl); Alix Combelle (cl, ts); Stéphane Grappelli (pno); Django Reinhardt (gtr); Eugène d'Hellemmes (sb); Maurice Chaillou (dms).
Engineer: George W Deakin

098 OLA 346-1 **Blue Moon** {3.14}
[*78* El EG3537; Gr B-8388, **K-7455**, X-4497; Vi JA-860, A1419]
[***LP*** Pat C054 16001] [***CD*** Cls 602; DRG 8493; Fmx FA302;
HD CDHD230; JSP 344; Swi CDSW8403]

099 OLA 346-2 **Blue Moon [unissued]**

100 OLA 347-1 **Avalon** {3.01}
[*78* El EG3537; Gr B-8388, **K-7572**, X-4496] [***LP*** HD CHD 165;
LE AJA5054; Pat C054 16001; Vi LPM 1100] [***EP*** RCA EPC1100-2]
[***CD*** AA 24; BGO CD249; Cas PIESD233; Cly DIG12; Cls 602;
DRG 8493; Fmx FA302; HD CDHD165, CDHD230; JSP 344;
Kaz EUKCD913; LE CDAJA5138; QED 71; Swi CDSW8403]

101 OLA 347-2 **Avalon [unissued]**

102 OLA 348-1 **What A Difference A Day Made** {3.21}
[*78* Gr B-8494, **K-7455**, X-4497; Vi JA-860] [***LP*** Pat C 054 16001]
[***CD*** BGO CD249; Cls 602; DRG 8493; Fmx FA302; HD CDHD230;
JSP 344; Swi CDSW8403]

same date, location and engineer

Coleman Hawkins acc. par D Reinhardt and S Grappelli

Hawkins (ts), Stéphane Grappelli (pno); Django Reinhardt (gtr).

103 OLA 349-1 **Star Dust** {3.10}
[***78*** El EG3695; Gr B-8420, HN-4476, **K-7525**, X-4496; Vi A1419, DC15] [***25cm LP*** HMV DLP1055] [***LP*** HMV OCLP7529, HMV FELP154, HMV HCLP120; Pat C054 16001; Vi LPM1100] [***EP*** RCA EPC 1100-1] [***CD*** BGOCD249; Cls 602; DRG8493; Fmx FA302; HD CDHD230; JSP 344; Swi CDSW8403]

Pathé Studios, Paris — Monday 4 March 1935

Patrick et son Orchestre de Danse

Alex Renard, Gaston Lapeyronnie, Noël Chiboust (tpts); Guy Paquinet, Pierre Deck, René Weiss (tbns); André Ekyan (as, cl); Andy Foster (as, cl, bs); Maurice Cizeron (as, fl, cl); Alix Combelle (ts, cl); Jean Chabud (pno); Django Reinhardt (gtr solo); Joseph Reinhardt (gtr); Louis Pecqueux (sb); Maurice Chaillou (dms and vcl).
As above with Stéphane Grappelli and Michel Warlop (vlns), 'Hildegarde' [Hildegarde Sell] (vcl) (1).
Engineer: Eugène Ravenet

104 CPT 1841 **Hands Across The Table** {3.06}
[***78*** Pat 530] [***CD*** Cls 703; Fmx FA302]

105 CPT 1842 **We Were So Young** {3.12}
[***78*** Pat 530] [***CD*** Cls 703; Fmx FA302]

106 CPT 1843 **From You** {2.53}
[***78*** Pat 537] [***LP*** Swi SW8420267] [***CD*** Cls 703; Fmx FA302; Swi SW 8419]

107 CPT 1844 **Darling Je Vous Aime Beaucoup** (1) {3.17}
[***78*** Pat 538] [***CD*** Cls 703; Fmx FA302]

Paris — Tuesday 5 March 1935

Lina d'Acosta acc. by Oscar Alemán and pianist C. Riso, records for Pathé.

Ultraphone Studios, Paris — Tuesday 5 or Wednesday 6 March 1935

Django Reinhardt et le Quintette du Hot Club de France (Brunswick, European Decca)/Quintet of Hot Club of France (US Decca)/Stephane Grappelly And His Hot Four (UK Decca)/ Hot Club of France Quintet (Royale)/Djungo Reinhardt and the Quintet of the Hot Club de France (Supraphon)

Stéphane Grappelli (vln); Django Reinhardt (gtr solo); Roger Chaput, Joseph Reinhardt (gtrs); Louis Vola (sb).
As above, with Jerry Mengo (vcl) (1).
Engineer: Willy Kuhn

108 P 77240 **Lily Belle May June** (1) {3:15}
[***78*** Br 81304; De F-6351, 23004; Poly A-197; **Ultr AP 1444**]
[***LP*** Pac LDP D6272; Vog 500740, CLD745] [***CD*** AA24; Cls 727;
Fmx FA303; JSP 341; QED71]

109 P 77241 **Sweet Sue, Just You** (1) {2:52}
[***78*** Or LV104, LB1004; Roy 1780; **Ultr AP 1444**] [***25cm LP*** Or 10019]
[***LP*** Pac LDP D6272; Vo 500740, CLD745] [***CD*** AA24; ABM 1194;
Cas PIESD 233; Cls 727; Fmx FA303; JSP 341; QED71; Vog 668003-1]

110 P 77242 **Confessin'** {2:53}
[***78*** JD 8005, DA17-8; Or LV102, LB1002; Supra B-22639;
Ultr AP 1443, B-14289; Roy 1788] [***25cm LP*** Or MG10019]
[***LP*** Pac LDP D6272; Vog 500740, CLD745] [***CD*** AA24; ABM 1194;
Cls 727; Fmx FA303; JSP 341; LE JA5138, 5267, QED71]

111 P 77243 **The Continental** (1) {2:38}
[***78*** Or LV102, LB1002; **Ultr AP 1443**, B-14288]
[***25cm LP*** Or MG10019] [***LP*** Pac LDP D6272; Vog 500740, CLD745]
[***CD*** AA24; ABM CD1194; Cls 727; Cly DIG12; Fmx FA303; JSP 341;
LE AJA5138; QED71]

Pathé Studios, Paris — Friday 8 March 1935

Patrick et son Orchestre de Danse

Alex Renard, Noël Chiboust, Gaston Lapeyronnie (tpts); Guy Paquinet ['Patrick'] (tbn, ldr, arr); Pierre Deck, René Weiss (tbn); André Ekyan (as, cl); Andy Foster (as, cl, bs); Maurice Cizeron (cl, fl, as); Alix Combelle (ts); Stéphane Grappelli, Michel Warlop, Sylvio Schmidt (vlns); Jean Chabaud (pno); Roger Chomer (vibes); Django Reinhardt, Joseph Reinhardt (gtrs); Louis Pecqueux (sb); Maurice Chaillou (dms); Hildegarde [Hildegarde Sell] (vcl).
Louis Palex (arr. of CPT1857).
Engineer: Eugène Ravenet

112 CPT 1857 **Miss Otis Regrets** {3.03}
[***78*** Pat 537] [***CD*** Cls 703; Fmx FA303]

113 CPT 1858 **Waltzing With A Dream** {3.19}
[***78*** Pat 538] [***CD*** Cls 703; Fmx FA303]

London — Saturday 9 March 1935

A New Hot Magazine

Hibbs launches 'Swing Music'

When Leonard Hibbs recently edited the 'Short Survey of Modern Rhythm' for Brunswick, he did not realise the enormous interest that would be taken in it. Now, as a result of a vast number of enthusiastic letters received from hot fans, he has decided to make an even more ambitious bid to satisfy their needs.

He is producing a monthly magazine, called 'Swing Music', which is to cater for hot fans and, at the same time, is to serve as a means of binding the Rhythm Club movement more closely together. Every branch of hot music will be gone into in this magazine, and among other attractive features scheduled by Editor Hibbs is a serial autobiography of his Decca days by Spike Hughes.

This magazine, as its go-ahead editor points out in his exploitation matter, is to be an auxiliary to *Melody Maker* rather than a competitor, and, in not being hampered so much by considerations of space, should do a great deal for the Rhythm Club Movement, apart from general interest of the venture. (Unsigned, *Melody Maker*)

Paris — Thursday 21 March 1935

A 'Gala de l'Université Des Annales' concert is held at the Salle Gaveau featuring Josephine Baker, Arthur Briggs, Willie Lewis and Bobby Martin.

Paris — April 1935

'La Villa d'Este continues its matinées and evening with great success. The Freddy Taylor orchestra is always simply remarkable. This formation gives the greatest satisfaction in every formula (hot, sweet, attractive, vocal, etc).'
'Vola is always at Claridges with a very danceable jazz formation.'
'At Bœuf sur le Toit, André Ekyan has been replaced by an orchestra under the direction of Leon Abbey.' (Unsigned, *Jazz-Tango*)

Jazz-Tango reviews Patrick et son Orchestre (Pathé PA408) and Michel Warlop et son Orchestre (Gramophone K7441) without mentioning Django Reinhardt.

Paris — April 1935

The second issue of *Jazz Hot* reports that Django Reinhardt is a member of Freddy Taylor's band at Villa d'Este, and gives the following personnel: Charlie Johnson (1st ts); Freddy Taylor (2nd ts, leader); Chester Lanier (as, bs); Fletcher Allen (ts, arr); John Ferrier (pno); Django Reinhardt (gtr); Delhemme (*sic*) (sb, tuba); William Diener (*sic*) (dms). Ultraphone AP 1434 and 1444 are reviewed in the same issue.

London — April 1935

Sensation On Strings

Just how much these Frenchmen know about hot music has, until recently, been a bit of a mystery. We were all aware that France has many distinguished critics of *le hot*, but there has always been some question as to whether the Frenchman's knowledge of this subject was practical as well as academic. It is comparatively easy to write and talk about it; but playing it was another matter.

Four records have just come to light which prove incontestably that Frenchmen can produce first class hot music. They are played by Django Reinhardt's Hot Club Quintet, an all-string outfit. And they are not only sensationally surprising in the highest degree, but represent something original, yet completely satisfying, in the art of hot rhythm.

The most remarkable thing about these French discs is that there is no aping of Venuti or of Lang. These boys have the style, the technique, the personality, the tone and attack, and above all the sense of hot playing, to enable them to dispense with all imitation. Every side is just grand swing music from start to finish. Even the weakest of the four, *Tiger Rag*, has many exciting moments whilst *Dinah*, *Lady Be Good* and *I Saw Stars* are a joy in every way.

Collectors should be sure to get hold of these records (made by Ultraphone), if only to see that my enthusiasm is warranted. I don't think my critical reputation is in any danger. (Leonard Hibbs, *Swing Music*)

Paris **April 1935**

The magazine *Jazz Hot* (No. 2) features an article on Coleman Hawkins.

London **April 1935**

Review of Coleman Hawkins with the Ramblers, 'I Wish I Were Twins' (Decca F5457):

Here is the complete vindication of everything I said about the 'Hawk'. The Ramblers have got what it takes, and, as a result, they give 'Hawk' what he needs, and help him make one of the best records of his we have heard for a long, long, time. He *swings* here. The record is not very well recorded, but, nevertheless, is one that everybody should hear. It opens with a subdued orchestral passage.

Then 'Hawk' takes a chorus, followed by some nice brass work; then 'Hawk' again. And that's all; not an epic, but certainly a worth-while effort. (Unsigned, *Hot News*)

Watcha Say, Folks?

Garland Wilson greets all his friends and gives some news about Paris conditions

This is one pleasure that I didn't expect to ever have again, writing for all my friends in England, I mean; for when I left for France a month or two ago I thought that was just a step towards home. I certainly didn't expect to be able to get back to all you folks again.

Paris, of course, always has two or three first-class bands. One of the best is Freddy Taylor's at the Villa d'Este. One or two of Louis' old boys are with him, the line up being Charlie Johnson, trumpet; Fletcher Allen, tenor; Chester Lanier, alto; Sterling Conaway, guitar; Jose Riestra, bass, William Diemer, drums and John Ferrier, piano.

Arthur Briggs is at Stage B with a swell band with Django Reinhardt on guitar, and Stephane Grappelly on piano, though the latter sometimes plays fiddle. These two boys were in the Ultraphone records made for the Hot Club of France. Django is a swell player but you must hear him in person to appreciate him properly … . Django loves Ed Lang but Louis is his real master … . I heard him accompany Louis in 'The Day You Came Along' at the Hot Club in Paris. It was just one of those things!

Willie Lewis is packing the Chez Florence as usual. He has a real fine outfit, with Bobby Martin on trumpet; Jerry Blake, clarinet; June Cole, bass; Ted Fields, drums; John Mitchell, guitar; and, until recently, Herman Chittison, piano. Willie, of course, plays alto. (Garland Wilson, *Hot News*)

possibly Ultraphone Studios, Paris — *c.* April 1935

Freddy Taylor and his Swing Men from Harlem

Taylor (tpt, vcl); Charlie Johnson (tpt); Chester Lanier (cl, as, bs); Fletcher Allen (cl, ts, arr); John Ferrier (pno); Django Reinhardt (gtr); Eugène d'Hellemes (sb); William Diemer (dms).

114 Viper's Dream [unissued]

115 Blue Drag [unissued]

116 Swanee River [unissued]

117 How Come You Do Me Like You Do? [unissued]

Paris — April 1935

Freddy Taylor and his Orchestra

Freddy Taylor (tpt, vcl, ldr); possibly Charlie Johnson (tpt); Chester Lanier (cl, as, bs); Fletcher Allen (cl, ts, arr); Django Reinhardt or Oscar Alemán (gtr); Eugène d'Hellemmes (sb); William Diemer (dms).

118 K-169 **Swanee River** {3.03}
[***78* unissued**] [***CD*** Fmx FA303]

119 Mama Don't Allow [unissued]

120 Blue Drag [unissued]

121 How Come You Do Me Like You Do? [unissued]

There is some confusion arising from the above two sessions. Delaunay lists the first in his original (1961) and subsequent (1981) discographies, but they remain unfound. More recently, the sides from the second session were recovered in Paris, but some doubt exists as to whether the guitar player is Django Reinhardt or Oscar Alemán. Although the two sessions appear to be similar enough to be considered as perhaps different information about the same material, Daniel Nevers points out that Delaunay lists the pianist John Ferrier as appearing on the first, while there is no pianist evident on the second. Furthermore, Delaunay lists 'Viper's Dream', which does not appear in the second session, supplanted by 'Mama Don't Allow'. The three remaining titles from the second session await reissue. It is possible that the second session was made for the Odéon Company, since they used a K prefix for Paris-based recordings.

Ultraphone Studios, Paris c. mid-April 1935

Pierre Lord

Pierre Lord (vcl) acc. by Stéphane Grappelli (vln); René Ronald (pno); Django Reinhardt (gtr); as above, with Louis Vola (sb) (1).
Engineer: Willy Kuhn

122 P 77333 **Simplement** {3.09}
[*78* Ultr AP 1485] [*CD* Fmx FA303]

123 P 77334 **Smoke Gets In Your Eyes** (Fumée Aux Yeux) {2.47}
[*78* Sup B-22638; **Ultr AP 1478**, B-14291] [*CD* Fmx FA303]

124 P 77335 **Cocktails Pour Deux** (Cocktails For Two) (1) {3.07}
[*78* Ultr AP 1478] [*CD* Fmx FA303]

Ultraphone Studios, Paris late April 1935

Stephane Grappelly and His Hot Four (UK Decca)/Hot Club of France Quintet (US Decca)/Django Reinhardt et le Quintette du Hot Club de France avec Stephan Grappelly (Oriole, Ultraphon)/ Djungo Reinhardt and the Quintet of the Hot Club de France with Stephan Grappelly (Supraphon)

Stéphane Grappelli (vln); Django Reinhardt (gtr solo); Roger Chaput, Joseph Reinhardt (gtrs); Louis Vola (sb).
Engineer: Willy Kuhn

125 P 77351 **Blue Drag** {2:51}
[*78* Or LV103, LB1003; Roy 1778; Tel A-1958, A-1958-522; **Ultr AP 1479**, B-14290] [*LP* Pac LDP D6272; Vog 500740, COF03, DP05] [*CD* AA 24; ABM MCD1194; Arc SOL517; Avid AMSC648; Cls 727; Fmx FA303; Hab 111200; HD CDHD234; JSP 341; LE JA5138; Mil 74321308652; QED 71; Retro RZCD7002; Vog 668003-1]

126 P 77352 **Swanee River** {3:01}
[*78* JD DA17-1; Or LV103, LB1003; Tel A-1958; **Ultr AP 1479**, B-14290; Var 8378] [*LP* Pac LDP D6272; Vog 500740] [*CD* AA24; ABM CD1194; Arc CASTEL810562, SOL517; Avid AMSC648; Cls 727; Fmx FA303; JSP 341; LE AJA5138; QED71; Retro 7002; Vog 668003-1]

127 P 77353 **Ton Doux Sourire** (The Sunshine Of Your Smile) {2:53}
[*78* JD DA17-2; Or LV104, LB1004; Roy 1807; **Ultr AP 1484**, B-14288; Var 8380] [*LP* Pac LDP D6272; Vog 500740, COF03] [*CD* AA24; Cls 727; Fmx FA303; JSP 341; Retro 7002; QED71]

128 P 77354 **Ultrafox** {3:19}
[*78* De F-6150, Y-5205, 23003; JD DA17-3; Pol A-197; Roy 1785; Sup B-22639; **Ultr AP 1484**, B-14289; Var 8376] [*25cm LP* Lon(A) LL1344] [*LP* OB OLD12; Pac LDP D6272; Vog 500740]

[***EP*** De(E, F) DFE 6366] [***CD*** Arc SOL517; Cas MACCD132; Cls 727; Fmx FA303; JSP341; HD CDHD206; Kaz EUKCD913; LE AJA5138; QED71; Retro RZCD7002]

Matrix 77354, Supraphon B-22639, issued as 'Ultraphon–Rhythm–Fox-Trot'.

Paris — Tuesday 23 April 1935

Willie Lewis records four titles for Pathé (matrix numbers CPT1983–6). Musicians include June Cole.
See Rust for details.

Paris — May 1935

The Flandin government is overthrown when it attempts to use dictatorial power to rescue the falling franc. A new government headed by Laval replaces it.

London — May 1935

Article about QHCF by Hughes Panassié entitled 'Red Hot Strings' appears in *Hot News*.
See Cherrett, page 116 for a reproduction of this article.

Paris — May 1935

Reviews of 'Django Reinhardt avec le Quintette du Hot Club de France et Stéphane Grappelly' 'Blue Drag' / 'Swanee River' (Ultr AP 1479) and 'Ton Doux Sourire' / 'Ultra-Fox' (Ultr AP 1484).

> *Blue Drag* is the best recording to date of the Reinhardt–Grappelly quintette. On it, Stephane Grappelly shows himself as particularly inspired, and if the guitar accompaniment were not a little too strong during his chorus, I would be inclined to find it perfect.
>
> Reinhardt improvises a magnificent chorus and Vola holds forth with brio. *Swanee River* benefits from a meticulous recording, but hardly lends itself to the strongly limited possibilities of the quintette; the chorus played in unison by the guitars is torture for the ears despite the vigorous bass of Vola. Grappelly seems to me less at ease in fast pieces.
>
> The choice of 'Ton Doux Sourire' was hardly suitable for a *Hot* interpretation. Yet Django Reinhardt miraculously succeeded in playing upon this dull theme one of the better guitar choruses, with admirable warmth and sincerity.
>
> Stephane Grappelly gets off lightly in playing, note by note, the refrain on *Ton Doux Sourire*. *Ultra-Fox* is a relatively unsuccessful recording of the quintette. I didn't manage to find quality; perhaps it is the last recording of a long and tiring session. That could explain in part the lack of brio and rhythm on this side. I would not, however, like to end this column without indicating the brilliant success of the Reinhardt–Grappelly quintette's recordings in England. Produced by the enterprising house of Levy on the Oriole label and sold at a high price for that country, they are already in

the hands of every English jazz lover. English critics can't stop extolling the qualities of this ensemble, comparing Reinhardt and Grappelly, respectively, to Eddie Lang and Joe Venuti. Congratulations to this likeable quintette for this success, which helps encourage the appreciation of our jazz musicians. Very rarely have French jazz recordings been issued in England, even more rarely have they obtained a positive welcome there. (J Emi, *Jazz-Tango*)

Pathé Studios, Paris — Friday 17 May 1935

Germaine and Jean Sablon

Germaine and Jean Sablon (vcls) acc. by André Ekyan (cl); Alec Siniavine (pno); Django Reinhardt (gtr); Louis Vola (acc) (1), (sb) (2).
Engineer: George W Deakin

129 OLA 520-1 **Un Amour Comme Le Notre** (1) {2.59}
[*78* Gr K-7517] [*CD* Fmx FA303; Gal GALE419]

130 OLA 521-1 **La Petite Ile** (2) {2.50}
[*78* Gr K-7517] [*CD* Fmx FA303]

Ultraphone Studios, Paris — mid–late May 1935

Nane Cholet

Nane Cholet (vcl) acc. by Stéphane Grappelli (vln); René Ronald (pno); Django Reinhardt (gtr); Louis Vola (sb) (1).
As above, without Ronald or Vola (2).
Engineer: Willy Kuhn

131 P 77373 **Si J'avais Eté** (1) {3.00}
[*78* Ultr AP 1314] [*CD* Fmx FA303]

132 P 77374 **Fièvre** (Moonglow) (2) {3.18}
[*78* Ultr AP 1314] [*CD* Fmx FA303]

Paris — May/June 1935

Alix Combelle et son Orchestre

Combelle (ts, cl); Stéphane Grappelli (pno); Django Reinhardt (gtr solo); Joseph Reinhardt (gtr); Louis Vola (sb); Jerry Mengo (dms). Acetates

133 **What A Difference A Day Made** {2.27}
[*78* **unissued**] [*CD* Fmx FA303]

134 **The Sheik Of Araby** {2.17}
[*78* **unissued**] [*CD* Fmx FA303]

Abrams suggests these recordings may have been made as auditions for Ultraphon. Some discographers dispute the presence of Django Reinhardt on the above session.

Paris **May/June 1935**

The third issue of *Jazz Hot* reports that Oscar Allemand (*sic*) has replaced Django Reinhardt in Freddy Taylor's band at Villa d'Este.

Paris **early summer 1935**

Strikes in France hamper the production of gramophone records.

London **June 1935**

> I came back from Paris last week where I had the pleasure of hearing the excellent orchestra of Freddy Taylor and his swing men from Harlem. Django Reinhardt, the famous guitarist, has joined the band … . Willie Lewis's band made some records for Pathe, I believe. Willie's boys do not seem to play so hot as when they were at the Pinguin Club in Brussels, three years ago. Willie would gladly come to the International Exposition, but I do not know if arrangements are settled about it yet. (Carlos de Radzitzkey, *Hot News*)

London **June 1935**

Review of Django Reinhardt (solo gtr) and the Quintet of the 'Hot Club de France' with Stephane Grappelly (vln): 'Tiger Rag' /'I Saw Stars' (Oriole LV100; 3s. 6d.) and 'Dinah' /'Lady Be Good' (Oriole LV101; 3s. 6d.)

> Anybody who thinks that swing music can only come out of America or England is going to have the shock of his life on hearing these four recordings by five French artists. In fact, in spite of their comparatively high cost I can think of only one thing that can prevent them from becoming the sensational successes they deserve to be throughout this country, and that is that they are French Ultraphone recordings which have been bought by the ever enterprising Levy's branches at 94 Regent Street and High Street Whitechapel (London), Keith Prowses's larger branches, and possibly some of the larger London stores.
>
> The best inkling I can give you of what the combination sounds like is to describe it as a cross between the earlier Venuti's Blue Four and Brunswick's Spirits of Rhythm, but such a description is not only too broad to be of much value, but so underestimates the outfit's capabilities, that it gives you little idea of its cleverness. It not only has technical ability and an understanding of our music second to none, but an originality that is most refreshing after the plagiarisms which occur with nauseating regularity in the work of even the more creative jazz artists.
>
> Take for a start the playing of Django Reinhardt. Here we have a guitarist with a technique which has to be heard to be believed, but that is only one aspect of his attractions. A superficial hearing is all that is necessary to enable one to realize that in him we have an artist who not only has ideas of his own, but good ones. I don't think it is an exaggeration to say that even Ed Lang had not such a host of material up his sleeve, or the knack of

sustaining one's interest so grippingly by being able to twist his phrases about in such an unexpected and intriguing manner.

Then there is Stephane Grappelly, the violinist, who, if he is not quite so original as Reinhardt, is a good deal more than a budding Venuti.

These two artists being the featured soloists naturally are the first to attract attention, but the support that they are given is hardly less noteworthy. Supplied by two Spanish guitars (Joseph Reinhardt, Django's brother, and Louis Vola) and string bass (Roger Chapet) [*sic*] this accompaniment is an inspiration which few soloists get, and if these records are in any way a fair sample of the sort of thing our brother musicians in France are turning out, we in both England and America will have to look to our laurels. (Edgar Jackson, *The Gramophone*)

London June 1935

Django Reinhardt masterpieces released by Levy's on Oriole

Thanks to the initiative of Swing Music, which drew attention two months ago to the sensational Django Reinhardt 'hot string' records just issued in France, English fans will now be able to secure these discs at a far lower price than was originally anticipated.

Messrs Levy's, ever on the look-out for a chance to introduce new talent in swing music, have now prepared a supply of special pressings for Oriole release ('Dinah' and 'Lady Be Good'; 'Tiger Rag' and 'I Saw Stars'). Both these records are available at 3/6d each.

Rhythm Club secretaries are advised to draw up a list of members who want copies, as the dispatch of a large quantity at once will mean that there should be little or no postage and packing charge. At all events, no real fan should miss these grand titles, which are unquestionably the most fascinating hot records of the year. (Leonard Hibbs, *Swing Music*)

Salle Wagram, Paris Tuesday 4 June 1935

The Quintette appear in a concert promoted by the Club du Faubourg. The concert also features pianist Michel Stern, Al Romans, Michel Warlop and Arthur Briggs.

Salle Rameau, Paris Friday 13 June 1935

Jean Tranchant, accompanied by the Quintette, appears in concert.

Salle Playell, Paris Monday 16 June 1935

Jean Tranchant, accompanied by the Quintet, appears in concert.

Pathé Studios, Paris Monday 16 June 1935

Patrick et son Orchestre

Gaston Lapeyronnie, Noël Chiboust, Alex Renard (tpts); Guy Paquinet (tbn, dir, vcl) (2); Pierre Deck, René Weiss (tbns); Maurice Cizeron (cl, fl, as); André Ekyan (as, cl); Charles Lissée (as, cl, bs); Charles 'Coco' Kiehn (as, ts); Stéphane

Grappelli, Michel Warlop, Sylvio Schmidt (vlns); Jean Chaboud (pno); Django Reinhardt (gtr); Louis Pecqueux (sb); Maurice Chaillou (dms, vcl) (1); Roger Chomer (vbs).
Engineer: Eugène Ravenet

135 CPT2142 **You And The Night And The Music** (*arr. Louis Palex*) (1) {2.54}
[*78* Pat 667] [*CD* Cls 727; Fmx FA303]

136 CPT2143-1 **I Get A Kick Out Of You** (*arr. Walter Paul*) (1) {3.13}
[*78* Pat 669] [*CD* Cls 727; Fmx FA303]

137 CPT2144-1 **Seagulls** {2.46}
[*78* Pat 668] [*CD* Cls 727; Fmx FA303]

138 CPT2145-1 **Anything Goes** (*arr. Walter Paul*) {2.31}
[*78* Pat 669] [*CD* Cls 727; Fmx FA303]

139 CPT2146 **Easter Parade** (1) {3.12}
[*78* Pat 667] [*CD* Cls 727; Fmx FA303]

140 CPT2147-1 **I'm Gonna Wash My Hands Of You** (*arr. Stan Bowsher*) (2) {2.24}
[*78* Pat 668] [*CD* Cls 727; Fmx FA303]

London — Saturday 22 June 1935

Sidney Lipton, in his relentless bid for premier honours, has decided to make yet another change in his band which he hopes will result in an improvement in the rhythm section.

On July 5 Jack Llewellyn starts with him as a guitarist.

We had heard him and found him a brilliant player, and all who have heard him since are astounded at his all round ability on the instrument.

Guitar lovers will doubtless have their ears glued to their receivers when Sidney Lipton's band broadcasts from Grosvenor House on the next occasion, with Jack featured as a soloist as he undoubtedly will be. (Unsigned, *Melody Maker*)

Ultraphone Studios, Paris — late June 1935

Django Reinhardt et le Quintette du Hot-Club de France avec Arthur Briggs and Stéphane Grappelli (Brunswick, European Decca)/Stephane Grappelly and His Hot Four (UK Decca)/Quintet of the Hot Club of France (US Decca)/Hot Club of France Quintet (Royale, Varsity)

Arthur Briggs (tpt solo); Alphonse Cox, Pierre Allier (tpts); Eugène d'Hellemes (tbn); Stéphane Grappelli (vln); Django Reinhardt (gtr solo); Joseph Reinhardt, Pierre 'Baro' Ferret (gtrs); Louis Vola (sb).
Engineer: probably Willy Kuhn

141 P 77434 **Avalon** {2:50}
[***78*** Br A81074; DeF-6077, Y-5204, 23002; Pol A-142; Roy 1780; **Ultr AP 1512**; Var 8379] [***LP*** Pac LDP D6272; Vog 530187] [***CD*** Cls 727; Fmx FA303; JSP 341; Vog 668003-1]

142 P 77435 **Smoke Rings** {2:50}
[***78*** Br 81304; De F-6531; JD 8005; Roy 1788; **Ultr AP 1512**; Var 8379] [***LP*** Vog 530187] [***CD*** AA24; Cly DIG12; Cls 727; Fmx FA303; HD CHD234; JSP 341; LE AJA5138; Music CD6048; QED71; Vog 668003-1]

Ultraphone Studios, Paris — late June 1935

Stephan Grappelli et le Quintette du Hot-Club de France, avec Django Reinhardt (Brunswick, European Decca, Ultraphon)/ **Stephane Grappelly and His Hot Four** (UK Decca)/**Quintet of Hot Club of France** (US Decca)
Stéphane Grappelli (vln); Django Reinhardt (gtr solo); Joseph Reinhardt, Pierre 'Baro' Ferret (gtrs); Louis Vola (sb).
Engineer: probably Willy Kuhn

143 P 77440 **Clouds** {3:11}
[***78*** Br A81187; De F-6406, Y-5178, 23002; Poly A-142; Tel A-1960; **Ultr AP 1511**] [***LP*** Vog 530187, COF03, DP05] [***CD*** ARC Arc 810562, SOL517; Cls 727; Fmx FA303; Gal GALE435; HD CDHD234; JSP 341; QED71; Vog 668003-1]

144 P 77441 **Believe It, Beloved** {3:10}
[***78*** Br A81187; De F-6406, Y-5178; Pol 624076; Tel A-1860; **Ultr AP 1511**] [***LP*** Vog 530187, COF03] [***CD*** Cls 727; Fmx FA303; Gal GALE435; JSP 341; QED71]

Salle Rameau, Paris — Sunday 30 June 1935

The Mills Brothers, supported by the Quintette of the Hot Club of France and Freddy Johnson and his Harlemites, appear in concert.

London — July 1935

> The meeting of … the Portsmouth and Southsea Rhythm Club … of June 6 was one which will be remembered by all for a long while. Garland Wilson was appearing in Portsmouth with Jack Payne, and, thanks to enterprising committee men, it was arranged for him to pay a visit during the meeting. The news spread quickly and a record attendance was registered. The meeting began in the normal way by Mr Cassell [*sic*], who was followed by Mr J. Jarvis reciting discs from his own collection, and this proved very interesting. But all the while there was a feeling of suppressed excitement which broke loose when Garland appeared. In his inimitable style he rendered: 1. 'Honeysuckle Rose'; 2. 'The Way I Feel'; 3. 'I Wish That I Were Twins'; 4. 'Song Of The Bayou'; 5. 'Black And Tan Fantasy'; 6. 'I'll Take The South'.

> In 2 the sincerity was remarkable; in 3 the swing was swell; in 5 'colossal' was the only word to apply to the performance. Wild enthusiasm would have held Garland at the piano all night, but his time was all too short, and applause still followed him when he left. (Mr Sherrington, club secretary, *Swing Music*)

Salle Lafayette, Paris — Friday 5 July 1935

The Hot-Club de France offers a free concert by the Quintette. It is a well-attended event, and many new members joined the Hot-Club as a result.

Paris — Sunday 7 July 1935

The Quintette play a concert at Salle Hertz (Lafayette).

London — Saturday 13 July 1935

> That the two brilliant records of the Quintet of the Hot Club de France issued over here by Levy's wold prove popular was a foregone conclusion, and further examples of the art of this talented combination will be forthcoming in the near future.
>
> An item of even greater news for the fans is that Morris Levy is bringing the boys over in the autumn to appear in vaudeville. More important still, they will give some musician's concerts on the lines of those which they have already given so successfully in Paris.
>
> That Morris is well qualified to sponsor such a venture is beyond doubt as, apart from his well-known gramophone activities, he has launched the careers of such prominent artists as Denny Dennis and Beryl Orde.
>
> The Quintet, of course, is under the inspired leadership of Django Reinhardt, whose wonderful and highly original guitar playing is something really new to jazz, and it is of interest to know that this fine artist is a gipsy by predilection, as he lives in a caravan just outside Paris.
>
> Equally interesting is Stephane Grappelly, a truly terrific fiddle player with original and worth-while ideas, and he and Django receive more than adequate support from the rest of the bunch, Roger Chaput and Joseph Reinhardt on guitars and Louis Vola on bass.
>
> A strong feature of the performances of this quintet is then intensely musical quality of its renderings, which, with the grand swing generated, makes its records absolutely unique. (Unsigned, *Melody Maker*)

Paris — Saturday 27 July 1935

The government presses for, and is granted, emergency powers to produce a policy of financial retrenchment. The subsequent reduction of state salaries brings strong protest and a great deal of public disorder.

Ultraphone Studios, Paris — July/August 1935

Frank 'Big Boy' Goudie avec Section Rythmique

Frank Goudie (tpt) (1), (ts) (2), (cl) (3); Stéphane Grappelli (pno); Django

Reinhardt (gtr solo); Joseph Reinhardt (gtr); Sigismund Beck (sb); Jerry Mengo (dms).

Engineer: H Schuller

145 P 77468 **I've Found A New Baby** (1, 2, 3) {2:40}
[***78*** Tel A-1961, A-1961-523; **Ultr AP 1527**] [***LP*** Vog 530187]
[***CD*** Cls 727; Cly DIG12; Fmx FA303; JSP 341; Vog 668003-1]

146 P 77469 **St Louis Blues** (1, 2) {3:01}
[***78*** Supra A-22638; Tel A-1961, A-1961-523; **Ultr AP 1527**, B-14291]
[***LP*** Vog 530187] [***CD*** Cls 727; Fmx FA303; JSP 341; Vog 668003-1]

Paris — July/August 1935

The fourth issue of *Jazz Hot* reports that Stéphane Grappelli is appearing with Lud Glykson's orchestra at Casino de la Foret, Paris-Plage-Touquet, and that Django Reinhardt is appearing with Marco's orchestra at Saint-Jean-de-Luz.

In the same issue, Ultraphone advertises AP 1551 and 1512, and re-lists AP1422, 1423, 1443, 1444, 1479 and 1484. AP 1479 and 1484 are reviewed.

London — August 1935

> We deeply regret to announce the death, on July 18 last, of Mr. J.J. Levy.
>
> Mr. Levy was a pioneer in every sense of the word. One of the first record dealers in Europe, he was also the first to sell records on a stall in an open London market. This being the year 1900–1901. From small beginnings, his store grew until it became the largest record shop in Europe. During the last years of his life there were always more than 100,000 records in stock in the Whitechapel shop alone. Imagination boggles the mind when one tries to assess the number of records that he must have sold in his lifetime.
>
> But it is one thing to have a large record store, and quite a different thing to have one as unique as the one he founded and which will now be carried on by his son.
>
> The name Levy's has always been a famous one for swing music lovers as being the one shop in Europe where you can be sure to get the record you want. The first Ellington records ever issued in this country were issued by Levy's; and more recently this shop has shown its keenness by issuing the Django Reinhardt records.
>
> But we must not forget that Levy's are also famous for their enormous collection of foreign records. Discs can be obtained in every recorded language. And they were the first to make available to amateurs a private recording service comparable in every way to professional work.
>
> Many thousands of words more could be written about the achievements, the musical associations and the ambitions that have grown out of the foresight and enthusiasms of Jack Levy, but now we can only join with the Gramophone Industry, for which he did so much in our homage to one

who has passed away, and our deep sympathy with the loved ones he leaves behind. (Unsigned, *Swing Music*)

Paris c. August 1935

Arthur Briggs (tpt); Stéphane Grappelli (vln); Django Reinhardt (gtr); unknown (pno); Louis Vola (sb).

146a Bright Eyes {2.53} [**unissued**]

Despite some reports to the contrary, this recording does exist. Its origin, however, remains obscure. See items 169–72 for a possible alternative recording date and origin.

Columbia Studios, Paris August 1935

Jean Sablon

Sablon (vcl) acc. by Stéphane Grappelli (pno); Django Reinhardt (gtr).

147 CL5487-1 **Cette Chanson Est Pour Vous** [**unissued**]

148 CL5487-2 **Cette Chanson Est Pour Vous** [**unissued**]

149 CL5488-1 **Darling Je Vous Aime Beaucoup** [**unissued**]

150 CL5488-2 **Darling Je Vous Aime Beaucoup** [**unissued**]

151 CL5489-1 **Dernière Chanson** [**unissued**]

Ultraphone Studios, Paris Tuesday 20 August 1935

Alix Combelle et le Quintette du Hot-Club de France

Combelle (ts, cl); Stéphane Grappelli (pno); Django and Joseph Reinhardt (gtrs); Louis Vola (sb).

152 P 77522 **Crazy Rhythm** {2:30}
[***78*** Roy 1778; **Ultr AP 1544**; Var 8378] [***LP*** Vog 530187] [***CD*** AA24; Cls 714; Cly DIG12; Fmx FA303; JSP 341; Music CD6048; QED71]

153 P 77523 **The Sheik Of Araby** {2:36}
[***78*** JD 8004, DA1706; Roy 1807; **Ultr AP 1544**] [***LP*** Vog 530187] [***CD*** Cls 714; Fmx FA303; JSP 341]

Casino Handorff, Laren, The Netherlands Monday 26 August 1935

Coleman Hawkins records seven titles for Dutch Decca (matrix numbers AM177–80 including alternates).
See Rust for details.

Aux Nuit Bleues Cabaret, Paris September 1935

The first regular nightclub engagement for the Quintette, billed as 'Django Reinhardt, Stéphane Grappelly and their Virtuosos' (*sic*). (Abrams)

London **September 1935**

Review of Eddie South and his Orchestra: 'Gotta Go'/'My! Oh My!' (HMV BD193; 1s. 6d.)

> One of the most astonishing things about the Negro race is how few violinists it has produced. Although it boasts a veritable host of supreme players of all other instruments (at least supreme as exponents of the Negro's particular type of music) it has, in fact, produced only one fiddler of note – Eddie South.
>
> These two records of Eddie South are bound to arouse considerable controversy. Brilliant violinist as he is – and you may accept my word that as a classical exponent he is not to be sneered at – he is not what I could call a swing player. There are occasions when he even descends to 'chopping' his quavers – the first thing the legitimate player is taught *not* to do in dance music – and, in spite of all we know of the Negro's inherent instinct for rhythm, one does not have to study very deeply either South's playing or that of his orchestra realize that he sees little if any more in swing than the old-time jazz idiom is now as *démodé* as the bustle.
>
> Yet in spite of this corniness (there is no other word for it) there is something in the music which this coloured musician gives on these records that commands attention. Even if he played with a less supreme confidence one could hardly fail to recognize his abundant technique. One may like or dislike these performances according to one's lights, but even those who may find reason to criticize will be grateful to H.M.V. for having issued the disc. For one thing, no collector who takes any interest in the history of jazz could consider his library in any way complete without at least one record by the only Negro jazz fiddler of repute – Eddie South, the (as he styles himself) 'Dark Angel of the Violin'. (Edgar Jackson, *The Gramophone*)

Paris **September 1935**

André Ekyan and his Orchestra record four titles for Ultraphon (matrix numbers 77524–7). Musicians include Pierre Allier, Sigismund Beck, Alix Combelle, Roger Chaput, Léo Detemple, Charles Lissée and Jerry Mengo. See Rust for details.

'Freddy Taylor has left for America to recruit new musicians for the formation of a new orchestra which will tour Holland.' (Unsigned, *Jazz-Tango*)

Ultraphone Studios, Paris **Monday 2 September 1935**

Django Reinhardt et le Quintette du Hot-Club de France avec Stéphane Grapelly (Brunswick, European Decca, Ultraphon)/**Stephane Grappelly and His Hot Four** (UK Decca)/**Quintet of Hot Club of France** (US Decca)/**Hot Club of France Quintet** (Royale)

Stéphane Grappelli (vln); Django Reinhardt (gtr solo); Joseph Reinhardt, Pierre 'Baro' Ferret (gtrs); Louis Vola (sb).

154 P 77537 **Chasing Shadows** {2:57}
[***78*** Br A81206; De F-6002, Y-5120; Roy 1798; **Ultr AP 1547**] [***25cm LP*** Lon LL1344] [***LP*** HD CHD165; OB OLD12; Vogue 530187, COF03] [***CD*** AA24; Arc SOL517; Cls 727; Fmx FA303; Gal GALE435; HD CDHD165; JSP 341; Kaz EUKCD913; OB DOLD12; QED71; Vog 668003-1]

155 P 77538 **I've Had My Moments** {2:56}
[***78*** Br A81206; De F-6150, Y-5205; JD DA17-4; Roy 1798; **Ultr AP 1547**; Var 8377] [***25cm LP*** Lon LL1344] [***LP*** LE AJA5267; OB OLD12; Vog 530187, COF03] [***EP*** De DFE 6366] [***CD*** AA24; Arc SOL517; Cls 727; Cly DIG12; Fmx FA303; JSP 341; LE AJA5138, 5267; OB DOLD12; QED71]

156 P 77539 **Some Of These Days** {2:22}
[***78*** De F-6002, Y-5210, 23004; Pol A-230; **Ultr AP 1548**] [***LP*** Vog 530187, COF03, DP05] [***CD*** AA24; Arc SOL517; Cls 739; Cly DIG12; Ea CD71; Fmx FA303; Gal GALE435; HD CDHD165, 234; JSP 341; Music CD6049; OB DOLD12; QED 71; Vog 668003-1]

157 P 77540 **Djangology** {2:54}
[***78*** Br A-81047; De F-6077, Y-5204, 23003; Poly A230; **Ultr AP 1548**] [***25cm LP*** Lon LL1344] [***LP*** HD CHD165; OB OLD12; Vog 530187, COF03, DP05] [***CD*** AA24; Arc CASTEL810562, SOL517; Cas MACCD132; Cls 739; Cly DIG12; Dig CO3507; Fmx FA303; HD CDHD165; JSP 341; Kaz EUKCD913; LE JA5138, 5267, Music CD6048; OB DOLD12; QED71; Recall SMCD307]

Nane Cholet

Nane Cholet (vcl) acc. by Stéphane Grappelli (vln); Emil Stern (pno); Django Reinhardt (gtr); Jean Tranchant (vcl) (1).

158 P 77541 **Ainsi Soit-il** {2.52}
[***78*** Ultr AP 1552] [***CD*** Fmx FA303]
159 P 77542 **Les Quatre Farceurs** (1) {2.42}
[***78*** Ultr AP 1552] [***CD*** Fmx FA303]

Some discographers believe this is the first session on which Django uses a Maccaferri guitar.
Probably the same session as above.

Polydor Studios, Paris — Monday 2 or Friday 6 September 1935

Nitta Rette et son trio 'Hot'

Nitta (Nina?) Rette (vcl); Stéphane Grappelli (vln); Emil Stern (pno); Django Reinhardt (gtr).
Engineer: Rudolph Hamburger

160 1968-3/1hpp **Points Roses** [**unissued**]

161 1968-3/2hpp **Points Roses** [**unissued**]

162 1968-3/3hpp **Points Roses [unissued]**

163 1968-3/4hpp **Points Roses** {2.48}
[***78*** Pol F-524108] [***LP*** Pol 2489 188] [***CD*** Fmx FA304]

164 1969-4/1hpp **Un Instant D'Infini [unissued]**

165 1969-4/2hpp **Un Instant D'Infini [unissued]**

166 1969-4/3hpp **Un Instant D'Infini [unissued]**

167 1969-4/4hpp **Un Instant D'Infini** {3.27}
[***78*** Pol F-524108] [***LP*** Pol 2489 188] [***CD*** Fmx FA304]

168 1970-hpp **Mon Cœur Reste Près De Toi** {3.08}
[***78*** Pol F-524111] [***LP*** Pol 2489 188] [***CD*** Fmx FA304]

This session is out of sequence on Fremeaux.

Paris Thursday 12 September 1935

The situation of French mechanical performing rights companies is re-thought at a special meeting of representatives of various publishing companies (SACEM, BIEM, Francis Salabert and others), so that each previously independent performing rights company comes under one umbrella organization, with consequently greater industry control over the collection and dissemination of funds.

London Saturday 14 September 1935

> **Venuti's Rival**
> ***Remarkable Hot Fiddling by Stephane Grappelly in French Record***
> Django Reinhardt and Hot Club Quintet (augmented with brass section) with Stephane Grappelly [*sic*]: 'Avalon'/'Smoke Rings', French Ultraphone (AP1512), *soon to be issued by Levy's on Oriole (October 1)*
>
> When the first four sides by the Hot Club Five were released, I was probably one of a very small minority not over-impressed. To be sure, there was at least one exceptional chorus in *Dinah*, and some particularly astonishing guitar virtuosity on each disc, but still I could not see what the tremendous uproar or acclaim was about.
>
> Now that I have been over here for a few weeks I can see at least one good reason for their success; the fact that no British group has half the invention or momentum of this hitherto obscure Quintet. There really is a certain swing to all of the records they have made, together with some fiddle playing altogether astonishing for a European.
>
> It is Grappelly who is the real star of the band, even more so than the amazing gipsy Django Reinhardt. His fiddle playing has a bite and vitality, which places it in a class of its own, for there is little copying, for once, of Venuti's tricks and clichés.
>
> His tone has a vibrancy that reminds more of the golden days of Eddie South than any other fiddle star. Grappelly's phrasing is always near

perfection, and his technique more than ample. Hughes Panassié is right when he places him among the finest swing fiddlers anywhere.

Avalon is played at a good fast tempo, and contains samples of violin playing at its best. Reinhardt would be magnificent except that single-string guitar pyrotechnics are bound to become fatiguing in the long run.

The added brass section, which features Arthur Briggs on trumpet, is more than adequate, and fits in surprisingly well with the stringed ensemble.

Nothing could be more surprising than to find *Smoke Rings* made into something palatable. Outside of an 'arranged' introduction, which must be one of the most horrible interludes in recorded dance music, the interpretation is of an astonishingly high calibre; astonishing because it has taste, swing, imagination and is played by genuine Frenchmen (part of the brass excluded). Grappelly is really magnificent.

Levy's are also issuing on Oriole, *Swanee River* and *Blue Drag* by the same combination [*sic*]. Each has its points, and considering the fact that there is no other group remotely like it, should be listened to with considerable humility by both British and American musicians. (John Hammond, *Melody Maker*)

The record under discussion, while scheduled for release on Oriole, was never issued by them.

Swing on Strings
Django Reinhardt and His Hot Club Five

The Swing enthusiasts on the continent have lately brought to light a small orchestra which makes a big effort to get away from the stereotyped. The Quintet of the Hot Club of France has demonstrated once and for all that swing on strings is not some fantastic vision which occasionally walked abroad in the Lang-Venuti discs, but a very real proposition.

The Hot Club Quintet was formed last October for the entertainment of members of the Club and for concerts. Before entering the French Ultraphone catalogue, the Quintet made two trial recordings for another company which, for commercial reasons, were rejected.

The personnel of the orchestra is as follows: Stephane Grappelly (violin), Django Reinhardt (guitar), Joseph Reinhardt (guitar), Roger Chaput (guitar), and Louis Vola (string bass). A singular combination, it will be agreed, but at the same time distinctive and homogeneous.

The star men in the outfit are Grappelly and Django Reinhardt, who has played with his brother Joseph for a long time, of course [*sic*].

Comparison with Venuti is inevitable, so suffice it to say that the musical line of the latter is much more easy and flowing, his tone on the higher notes a little more sure and pleasing, although there is not much to choose between the two in this respect. On the other hand, Grappelly, fortunately, shows but little inclination to pass the border line of lyricism and embark on feats of technical ingenuity.

Grappelly also plays a fine swing piano, which may be heard in several records by house bands and other outfits assembled merely for recording, as also may Django Reinhardt on guitar. Grappelly is particularly good in a chorus of *There'll Be Some Changes Made*, a solo record on French Ultraphone by Frank 'Big Boy' Goodie, the well-known tenor player, who now plays, in addition, trumpet and clarinet.

The other soloist is Django Reinhardt, on guitar. Along with his brother Joseph he has led in the past a Bohemian sort of life, travelling where the fancy took him and making music after the fashion of that recorded on a few old Armstrong records which he had in his possession. This was his only acquaintance with jazz.

His playing is all the more wonderful when you realize that he suffers from a serious and formidable handicap – his inability to use the last two fingers of his left hand owing to paralysis. Hence his solos are for the most part one string.

His work on solo guitar combines swing with a high degree of musicality. The musician in him is evident when one listens to the delicate, smoothly-fusing graduations of light and shade in his work. Django has an exemplary command over the limited dynamics of a solo instrument. This strikes one in most of his solos.

His improvisation and phrasing contrast magnificently with those of Grappelly. Whereas the latter plays short, detached, compact phrases, and but rarely embarks on a more flowing style, each one of Django's phrases inevitably leads up to and merges with the following.

In his second chorus of *Dinah*, and also of *Blue Drag*, we find several examples of the manner in which one phrase flows into and is inextricably bound up with the next.

What are we to say of the other three members of the Quintet? To appreciate them fully one must hear them in the flesh.

The discs are, for the most part, under-recorded and the rich 'juicy' harmony of the guitars does not always come through. Yet the work of Joseph Reinhardt and Roger Chaput on guitars is in every detail all that is required. And the bass playing of Louis Vola is musical and unobtrusive.

Whether the string bass ought to be used as a solo instrument is a debatable point. Vola plays an averagely good solo in the relatively poor version of *Tiger Rag* by the quintet, but is more interesting in *Swanee River*, where he improvises a chorus while Django Reinhardt plays the melody.

Finally, a word about the wonderful verve, precision and swing which characterize the performances of this band when heard in the flesh. It is impossible to convey an impression of those masterly on three guitars at the end of eight-bar phrases, in bridge passages, and at the introduction to solo choruses.

The rhythm section works like one man, even in the final 'all-in' choruses – a proof that the intuition of the various members must be highly developed. It is unobtrusive when the solo demands, and it underlines equally well.

Most of the members of the Quintet play regularly in separate outfits. Let us hope they can be brought together for an early visit to England and that here they will be accorded a fitting reception. (R Kelly, *Melody Maker*)

See Cruickshank, page 111, for a facsimile of the original article.

Paris — late September 1935

Expiration of the contract between Ultraphone and the QHCF.

Polydor Studios, Paris — late September 1935

Arthur Briggs

Briggs (tpt) acc. by Stéphane Grappelli (vln); unknown (pno); Django Reinhardt (gtr); possibly Louis Vola (sb).

169 Tiger Rag [unissued]

170 Sweet Georgia Brown [unissued]

171 Who [unissued]

172 There'll Be Some Changes Made [unissued]

Matrix numbers 1950–2HPP (at least) are believed to belong to this session, but the relation of matrix to title remains unknown. Item 146a may possibly belong to this session.

Ultraphone Studios, Paris — c. Friday 27 September 1935

Bruce Boyce avec Django Reinhardt et Stéphane Grappelly

Boyce (vcl) acc. by Stéphane Grappelli (pno); Django Reinhardt (gtr) (1) or Grappelli only (2).
Engineer: W Holdt

173 P77574-1 **Run, Mary, Run** (1)/**Oh, Didn't It Rain** (2) {2.37}
[***78*** Ultr 512467] [***CD*** Fmx FA303]

Reverse of Ultraphone 512457, 'Wade In De Water' (*sic*), features Grappelli on piano, but Reinhardt is not present.

Polydor Studios, Paris — Monday 30 September 1935

Quintette du Hot-Club de France avec Django Reinhardt et Stéphane Grappelly (European issues)/Stephane Grappelly and his Hot Four (UK Decca)

Stéphane Grappelli (vln); Django Reinhardt (gtr solo); Joseph Reinhardt, Pierre 'Baro' Ferret (gtrs); Louis Vola (sb).
Engineer: Rudolph Hamburger

174 2009-HPP **St Louis Blues** {3.27}
[***78*** Br 505280, 500604, A-9945, A-82559; **De F-5824** (E, F); Y-062,

F-9019, 23032] [***25cm LP*** Br LPB 86018] [***LP*** De Ecl ECM2051]
[***CD*** Cas MACCD132, PIESD233; CC CD2010; Cls 708; Fmx FA304;
Gal GALE435; HD CDHD206; JSP 344; Kaz EUKCD913;
LE AJA5267; OB DOLD12; QED 71]

175 2010-HPP Chinatown, My Chinatown {2.55} [**unissued**]

Paris — September/October 1935

Jazz Hot (No. 5) features articles on Alix Combelle and André Ekyan and reviews Ultraphone AP1511 and 1512.

Paris — October 1935

Alix Combelle forms a new group to play at the 'Jeunesse' club in Paris. The personnel includes: Pierre Allier (tpt); Léo Detemple (pno); Charles Lissée (as, cl); [?] Marion (dms); Jerry Mengo (vcls); Lucien Simoens (sb).

London — October 1935

Reviews of Quintette of the Hot Club of France: 'Confessin' / 'The Continental' (Oriole LV102, 3s. 6d.); 'Blue Drag' / 'Swanee River' (Oriole LV103, 3s. 6d.)

> To start a rush for these it is only necessary to say that they are the same sort of thing as *Tiger Rag, I Saw Stars, Dinah* and *Lady Be Good*, which were reviewed on page 29 of the June *Gramophone*, and with which the combination made its English debut.
>
> The quality of recording is slightly different, and shows Grappelly to even better advantage, displaying his excellent tone to fine effect, and proving that there is justification for the opinion voiced by competent critics of this country that he is the equal of Venuti. Django Reinhardt is still the same wizard of the guitar.
>
> The records are not stocked by all retailers, but can be ordered through any gramophone dealer, or obtained direct from Levy's Sound Studios, 94, Regent Street, London, W.1.
>
> They are worth every penny of the 3s. 6d. charged for them. (Edgar Jackson, *The Gramophone*)

London — October 1935

Reviews of Quintet of the French Hot Club: 'The Continental'/'Confessin'' (Oriole LV102, 3/6); 'Swanee River'/'Blue Drag' (Oriole LV103, 3/6)

> Before I review these records I have been asked by the makers to remind you that they can be obtained from any Keith Prowse store; or to order from any other record dealer; or direct from Levy's at 96, Regent Street, London W.1.
>
> Of the first two sides, '*Confessin'*' is the better. A charming introduction by Reinhardt leads into Grappelly's solo. He is much more rhythmic than the others here. The background is rather dull, I think. When it is Reinhardt's turn to take a solo, he also is outstanding. But these two solos

are so full of swing and ideas that the record becomes essential without being completely satisfying. 'The Continental' has much more attack and bite but lacks the great beauty of these two solos.

Both of the other sides are simply swell. Much the best work by the French boys that has generally been released over here. '*Swanee*' is gloriously fast and the sentiment has been knocked clean out of it for all time. The tempo is not rock steady throughout but the fire in their fingers is undiminished. To the end. '*Blue Drag*' is OK. One point arises out of these discs. It is that this group as a group still lacks something in slow numbers. The soloists get right into the music but the ensemble does not seem to *feel* the music as they should. (Unsigned, *Swing Music*)

Coleman Hawkins (with the Ramblers): 'Some Of These Days'/'After You've Gone' (Decca F5581, 1/6)

This record strikes a final blow at the Ramblers. If Hawkins playing as he does here, cannot swing them, then no power on earth will ever make them think in terms of jazz music. Hawkins is inspired and gets me so much that I can now play both sides without even hearing the local band. '*After You've Gone*' is taken at its original slow tempo. Hawk just closes his eyes and ears of his mind and he plays. It almost seems that the very fact that a record was even made was coincidence or accident. The unlucky part of the accident (which of course supports the theory of the accident) is that the Ramblers were there at all. (Unsigned, *Swing Music*)

Polydor Studios, Paris — October 1935

Stephane Grappelly and his Hot Four (English-language issues)/
Quintette du Hot-Club de France (French-language issues)

Stéphane Grappelli (vln); Django Reinhardt (gtr solo); Joseph Reinhardt and Pierre 'Baro' Ferret (gtrs); Louis Vola (sb).
Engineer: Rudolph Hamburger

176 2035-HPP **Limehouse Blues** {3.08}
[***78*** Br A-884, A-82504, 500016, 505279; **De F-5780** (E, F); 23021; Od 0284865; Pol 580016] [***25cm LP*** Br LPB 86018]
[***LP*** De Ecl ECM2051] [***EP*** BT LP28052; De DFE6366] [***CD*** Cls 708; Dig CO3506; Fmx FA304; Gal GALE435; HD DCHD234; JSP 344; LE AJA5267; OB DOLD12]

177 2036-1/2HPP **I Got Rhythm** {2.54}
[***78*** Br A-9884, A-82504; **De F-5780** (E, F); Od 0284865]
[***25cm LP*** Br LPB 86018] [***LP*** De Ecl ECM2051; LE AJA5070, 5117, 5267; Met MTM12] [***EP*** De DFE6366] [***CD*** ABM 1194; Cls 708; Fmx FA304; Gal GALE435; JSP 344; LE AJA5267; OB DOLD12]

178 2037-HPP **Chinatown, My Chinatown** {2.54} [**unissued**]

Polydor Studios, Paris — Sunday 13 October 1935

André Pasdoc acc. par L'Orchestra Vola (1)
Yvonne Louis acc. par L'Orchestra Vola (2)

André Pasdoc (vcl) (1); Yvonne Louis (vcl) (2); Stéphane Grappelli, Michel Warlop (vlns); Django Reinhardt (gtr solo) (2); Joseph Reinhardt (gtr); Louis Vola (acc) (1), (sb) (2).
Engineer: Rudolph Hamburger

179 2038 HPP **Pourquoi, Pourquoi?** (1) {2.54}
[***78* unissued**] [***CD*** Fmx FA304]

180 2039 HPP **Vivre Pour Toi** (1) {3.14}
[***78* unissued**] [***LP*** Pol 512467] [***CD*** Fmx FA304]

181 2040 HPP **Mirages** (Chasing Shadows) (2) {2.55}
[***78* unissued**] [***LP*** Pol 512468] [***CD*** Fmx FA304]

Matrix 2038 HPP may not feature Django Reinhardt.

Hilversum, Holland — Monday 14 October 1935

Coleman Hawkins, accompanied by Freddy Johnson on piano, broadcasts for 30 minutes (9.40pm–10.10pm) on Hilversum Radio. They play 'I'm In The Mood For Love', 'Unconventional' (with vocal by Johnson) and 'Sweet Sue'.

Columbia Studios, Paris — Friday 18 October 1935

Jean Sablon

Jean Sablon (vcl) acc. by Stéphane Grappelli (vln); Django and Joseph Reinhardt (gtrs); Alec Siniavine (pno) (1); Louis Vola (sb).
Engineer: Georges Cailly

182 CL 5487-1 **Cette Chanson Est Pour Vous** {3.14}
[***78*** Col DF1487 (E, F)] [***CD*** Fmx FA304; Gal GALE419; Swi CDSW8419]

183 CL 5488-1 **Darling Je Vous Aime Beaucoup** (1) {3.10}
[***78* Col DF 1487** (E, F), 4222-M] [***LP*** Swi SW8420267]
[***CD*** Fmx FA304; Gal GALE 419; Swi CDSW8419]

184 CL5489-1 **Dernier Chanson** [**unissued**]

Polydor Studios, Paris — Monday 21 October 1935

Stephane Grappelli and his Hot Four (Quintette du Hot-Club de France) (Brunswick, European Decca)/Stephane Grappelly and His Hot 4 (US Decca)

Stéphane Grappelli (vln); Django Reinhardt (gtr solo); Joseph Reinhardt, Pierre 'Baro' Ferret (gtrs); Tony Rovira (sb).
Engineer: Rudolph Hamburger

185 2079-HPP **I've Found A New Baby** {3.02}
[*78* Br 505278, 500613, Br A-9987; **De F-5943** (E, F), 23031]
[*25cm LP* De 123998] [*LP* Aff BOX107; De Ecl ECM2051;
LE AJA5070; OB OLD12] [*CD* AA24; Cas MACCD132; Cls 708;
Dig CO3507; Fmx FA304; HD CDHD234; JSP 344; Kaz EUKCD913;
LE AJA5267; Music CD6048; OB DOLD12; QED71]

186 2080-1/2HPP **It Was So Beautiful** {2.49}
[*78* Br 505278, 500613, A-9987; **De F-5943** (E, F)] [*25cm LP* De 123998]
[*LP* De Ecl ECM2051; LE AJA5070; OB OLD12] [*CD* Cls 708;
Fmx FA304; Gal GALE435; HD CDHD234; JSP 344; Mil 74321308652;
OB DOLD12]

187 2081-HPP **China Boy** {2.59}
[*78* Br 505280, 500016, 500604, A-9943; **De F-5824** (E, F), F-49019,
Y5202, 23031; Pol 580016] [*25cm LP* Br LPB 86018]
[*LP* De Ecl ECM2051; LE AJA5070; OB OLD12]
[*CD* Cas MACCD132; Cls 708; Fmx FA304; Gal GALE435;
HD CDHD206; JSP 344; Kaz EUKCD913; OB DOLD 12]

188 2082-HPP **Moon Glow** {2.59}
[*78* Br A-9909; **De F-5381** (E, F), 23031] [*LP* De Ecl ECM2051;
E AJA5070; OB OLD12] [*CD* Avid AMSC648; Cls 708; Fmx FA304;
Gal GALE435; HD CDHD234; JSP 344; OB DOLD12]

189 2083-HPP **It Don't Mean A Thing** {3.01}
[*78* Br A-9909; **De F-5831** (E, F); 23032] [*LP* Ecl ECM2051;
LE AJA5070; OB OLD12] [*CD* Avid AMSC648; Cas MACCD132;
Cls 708; Dig CO3506; Fmx FA304; Gal GALE435; JSP 344;
Kaz EUKCD913; OB DOLD12]

London Saturday 26 October 1935

N J Canetti's Paris Letter

The new winter season has opened in the best possible manner; all the theatres and music halls are full and a big new theatre – the Alhambra – has just opened and seems to be very successful. It is obvious that with so much renewed activity in the entertainment world dance orchestras will find plenty of work and the unemployment among professional musicians will diminish rapidly.

Here are the principal clubs which have just re-opened:

At the Florence, Willie Lewis and his Orchestra, coloured entertainers, have just resumed. The orchestra has just been augmented by none other than Benny Carter, who has been in France for several weeks.

Benny Carter has introduced some American arrangements but up to the moment the band has not had the opportunity to use them. He is playing mostly alto sax and clarinet, but from time to time plays a very fine trumpet solo.

Benny seems very happy to be in Europe, and arrangements have been made for him to make some records for Polydor–Brunswick, accompanied by an all-star orchestra. These will, of course, appear in England under the Decca label.

At the Villa d'Este Freddy Taylor has returned from American with a number of new musicians, amongst whom is Coleman [*sic*], trumpet, formerly with Fletcher Henderson. In his orchestra is also the marvellous guitarist Oscar Allemand [*sic*], known mostly among professionals and connoisseurs … .

Freddy Taylor is more in form than ever, and the Villa d'Este is full each evening.

A new club, called 'Les Nuites Blues', has opened in Montmartre with the Reinhardt-Grappelly quintet. A smart crowd gathers there each night to hear the 'musical sensation of the season', this string quintet, which until recently has only been known to hot fans.

Apropos the Quintet, I would point out that it accompanied Larry Adler at his appearance at the Alhambra. Larry Adler, completely unknown in Paris, made such a sensation in his fortnight at the Alhambra that he was re-engaged for a further fortnight, and for this second engagement he asked the quintet to accompany him, thus giving Reinhardt and Grappelly the chance of being heard by the general public.

It was very favourably received, and Larry Adler's gesture was much appreciated by the French musicians. Arrangements are being made to produce Adler with the Quintet in a big concert at the Salle Pleyel in December.

A new radio station has just been opened, 'Radio Citie'. This belongs to a big evening paper, 'L'Intransigient', and seems likely to become one of the most important in France. The entertainment is under my direction and I hope to be able to give it a good impetus.

The inaugural concert saw a number of stars at the microphone, among them being Larry Adler, Pills and Tabet (two very famous French duetists), Isa Kramer (the American singer), the Grappelly Reinhardt quintet, Herman Chittison and other French artists not so well known in England.

Arrangements have been made to broadcast the best night club orchestras each night, and on alternate Sunday nights you may hear the 'Chez Florence' and the 'Villa d'Este'; on Fridays, 'Les Nuites Blues' and La Coupole'; on Mondays the 'Boeuf sur la Toit' and the 'Bagdad'.

Also every Wednesday evening, from 11.00–12.30 there will be a special 'Harlem Evening' when the best hot records will be broadcast. Each week also there will be a special half-hour for unissued hot records. I will be happy to have the opinion of English readers, especially as regards the dance music side of the programmes. Letters should be addressed to me at 'Radio Citie', 1 boulevard Haussmann, Paris. (N J Canetti, *Melody Maker*)

Paris — Wednesday 30 October 1935

Lina d'Acosta, accompanied by Oscar Alemán, records for Pathé.

London — Saturday 2 November 1935

Decca Executive Change

On Thursday of last week Alex Kraut severed his connection with the Decca Company, and as a result Harry Sarton is now recording manager in charge of the whole of this enterprising concern's British output.

Harry, of course, is no stranger to the game, as he has been the guiding spirit behind the Brunswick issues for a long time, and he brings to the job the ripe experience of a businessman combined with a knowledgeable enthusiasm for all that is best in modern rhythmic music.

Moreover, Harry has shown himself to be keenly interested in the Rhythm Club movement, which he has always been ready to help in any way possible, and many are the exciting recitals he has put over from time to time.

Coincident with this felicitous appointment comes the important news that, starting with the December list, the Decca company will be issuing discs by the Quintet of the Hot Club de France, a combination which has, in a very short space of time, set the fans by their ears. (Unsigned, *Melody Maker*)

Studio Albert, Paris — Saturday 23 November 1935

Garnet Clark and his Hot Club's Four

Garnet Clark (pno); Bill Coleman (tpt, vcl) (1); George Johnson (cl, as); Django Reinhardt (gtr); June Cole (sb).
Engineer: Georges Cailley

190 OLA 730-1 **Rosetta** {2.38}
[***78*** Gr K-7618] [***LP*** Pat C054 16001; Swa S1307] [***CD*** BGO CD249; Cls 739; DRG 8493; Fmx FA304; JSP349]

191 OLA 731-1 **Stardust** {2.30}
[***78*** Gr JK-2823, **K-7645**, X-4593] [***LP*** Pat C054 16001]
[***CD*** BGO CD249; Cls 739; Dig CO3506; DRG8493; Fmx FA304; JSP349]

192 OLA 731-2 **Stardust [unissued]**

193 OLA 732-1 **The Object Of My Affection** (1) {2.44}
[***78*** Gr K-7618] [***LP*** Pat C054 16001; Swa S1307] [***CD*** BGO CD249; Cls 739; DRG8493; Fmx FA304; JSP349]

OLA733-1, 'I Got Rhythm', is a piano solo by Garnet Clark.
See Panassié, *Douze années de jazz*, page 172 for comments on this session.

London **November/December 1935**

Review of Freddie Taylor and his Swing Men from Harlem: 'Viper's Dream'/ 'Blue Drag' (Oriole LV105, 3/6). Personnel: Freddie Taylor and Charlie Johnson (tps); Fletcher Allen (ts); Chester Lanier (as); Sterling Conway [*sic*] (gtr); Jose Riestra (sb); William Diemer (dms); John Ferrier (pno).

> '*Viper's Dream*' is not an incentive so much as a musical description of an accomplished fact. It is a pleasant arrangement in the blues tradition with a soft swing. It says in simple restrained music that we were told in words in '*Minnie The Moocher*', that hectic daughter of '*Willie The Weeper*'.
>
> '*Blue Drag*' is a lovely record with the same soft swing beautifully arranged for two trumpets and an inspired solo by the tenor man. (Unsigned, *Swing*).

London **December 1935**

Review of Coleman Hawkins with The Ramblers: 'Netcha's Dream'/ 'What Harlem Is To Me' (Decca F5775, 1s. 6d.)

> Compared with the bright *After You've Gone* and *Some Of These Days* which last September resulted so successfully from Hawkins' tie-up with The Ramblers, these two new performances are sadly disappointing.
>
> Both are presented as Blues and pretty poor Blues idiom it is at that – coarse and forced, and in the case of *What Harlem Is To Me* almost at times degenerating into 6/8 measure.
>
> The cause of the trouble seems to be that the band, instead of being used, as it was, purely as an accompaniment to Hawkins has been called upon to play a much more prominent part in the proceedings. It even has the honour of dealing at times with the more important matters of the moment while Hawkins is left to amuse himself with a subsiduary part which the arranger kindly gave him to pass the time away, and this appears to have so impressed it with its importance that it has become brassy and commonplace.
>
> It also seems to have impressed Hawkins, who plays about as poorly as he could. Or is it that his finesse has little chance against the blatancy of what is taking place around him? (Edgar Jackson, *The Gramophone*)

L'Ecole Normale de Musique, Paris **Friday 6 December 1935**

The Hot-Club de France presents a concert by Garnet Clark and his Orchestra. Musicians include Pierre Allier, Roger Chaput, Georges Marion and Jerry Mengo.

Columbia Studios, Paris **Saturday 7 December 1935**

Jean Sablon, avec acc. d'Orchestre

Jean Sablon (vcl) acc. by Stéphane Grappelli (vln, pno); Django Reinhardt (gtr solo); Joseph Reinhardt (gtr); Louis Vola (sb).
Engineer: Georges Cailly

194 CL 5487-3 **Cette Chanson Est Pour Vous** {3.04}
[***78*** Col DF1847 (E, F)] [***LP*** WRC SH368] [***CD*** Fmx FA304]

195 CL 5518-1 **Rendez-vous Sous La Pluie** {2.34}
[***78*** **Col 1847** (E, F); 4222-M] [***LP*** WRC SH368] [***CD*** Fmx FA304; Gal GALE419]

Paris — Saturday 28 December 1935

The government orders all political 'leagues' to be disbanded. The bulk of them immediately re-emerge unaltered as political 'parties'.

Paris — 1936

Charles Delaunay publishes *Hot discographie* (Editions Jazz Hot).

London — January 1936

Review of Quintette du Hot-Club de France: 'The Sunshine Of Your Smile'/ 'Sweet Sue' (Oriole LV104, 3s. 6d.). Django Reinhardt (solo gtr), Joseph Reinhardt and Louis Volga [*sic*] (gtrs), Roger Chapet [*sic*] (sb; Stephane Grappelly (vln).

> With two choruses given over to the most commercial of crooners, a good deal of valuable time is wasted in *Sweet Sue*. But the rest is the quintette well up to its usual form with more of Django's almost incredible technique on his guitar, and Grappelly and his violin in fine fettle.
>
> The choice of Ray's ballad for the coupling may turn out to be a good commercial stunt, but that's about all there is to be said for it. This is not an attempt (I rather wish it had been) to make one of those noses at the tune which Wingy Manone made at *Isle of Capri* by swinging it. A semblance of rhythm is suggested by the maintenance of tempo, otherwise it is more like a ballad transcription.
>
> The treatment is original, in some ways possibly mildly ingenious, but it doesn't add anything to jazz or ballad music, or for that matter to the Quintette's reputation for ideas that are not only different, but good. (Edgar Jackson, *The Gramophone*)

Paris — January 1936

Adelaide Hall records two titles for Ultraphone accompanied by John Ellsworth and his Orchestra (matrix numbers P-77616, 77618). Musicians include Max Blanc, Maurice Chaillou and Christian Wagner.
See Rust for details.

Paris — Friday 17 January 1936

Willie Lewis and his Orchestra record six titles for Pathé (matrix numbers CPT2451–5). Musicians include Benny Carter and June Cole.
See Rust for details.

Paris **Wednesday 22 January 1936**

The downfall of the Laval government, largely as a result of unpopularity due to its non-committal attitude towards Italy during the Ethiopian crisis. A temporary government is formed under Albert Serrate.

Paris **Thursday 23 January 1936**

Django Reinhardt's 26th birthday.

Paris **Friday 24 January 1936**

Bill Coleman records two titles for Ultraphone (matrix numbers 77624, 77625). Musicians include Stéphane Grappelli and Joseph Reinhardt.
See Rust for details.

Cinema Coliseum, Barcelona **Wednesday 29 and/or Thursday 30 January 1936**

The Quintette, Benny Carter and the 'Orquestra de Hot Club de Barcelona' in concert.

Paris **Friday 31 January 1936**

Bill Coleman records four titles for Compagnie Française du Gramophone. (matrix numbers 849–52). Musicians include Oscar Alemán, Eugène d'Hellemmes and John Ferrier.
See Rust for details.

Musica Catalana, Barcelona **Friday 31 January and/or Saturday 1 February 1936**

The Quintette, Benny Carter and the 'Orquesta de Hot Club de Barcelona' in concert. Garnet Clark was originally advertised as appearing at both locations, but evidently did not appear.
See Delaunay, page 229, for a reproduction of the original contract.

Paris **January/February 1936**

The magazine *Jazz Hot* (No. 7) features an article on Bill Coleman.

Paris **February 1936**

Jean Tranchant

Jean Tranchant (vcl, pno); Stéphane Grappelli (vln); Django Reinhardt (gtr).
Programme radiophonique du 'Micro de la Redoute'
Announcer: Francie Lenne

197 2117 **Les Baisers Prisonniers** {2.49}
[***CD*** Fmx FA304]

198 2118 **Mon Bateau Est Si Petit** {2.11}
[***CD*** Fmx FA304]

199 2119 **Quand Il Est Tard** {3.40}
[***CD*** Fmx FA304]

200 2120 **Le Piano Mécanique** {2.41}
[***CD*** Fmx FA304]

201 2121 **Ici L'On Pêche** {3.21}
[***CD*** Fmx FA304]

Pathé Studios, Paris — Saturday 22 February 1936

Jean Tranchant, acc. par Michel Emer et son Orchestre

Jean Tranchant (vcl) acc. by Pierre Allier and possibly Alex Renard (tpts); Maurice Ciseron, André Ekyan, Charles Lissée, André Lamory (cl, saxes); Stéphane Grappelli, Michel Warlop (vlns); Michel Emer (pno, dir); Django Reinhardt (gtr); Louis Vola (sb); unknown (dms).
Engineer: Eugène Ravenet

196 CPT2428-1 **L'Amour En Voyage** {3.13}
[***78*** Pat PA805] [***CD*** Fmx FA304]

CPT2425–7, from the same session, do not feature Django Reinhardt.

168 Bd Malesherbes
(Jean Sablon's home), Paris, 17e — Saturday 29 February 1936

Jean Sablon et ses Amis (Jean Sablon and his Friends)

Jean Sablon (vcls, comments, pno); Django Reinhardt (gtr, speech, laughter); Sophie Zeigler (Naguine Reinhardt) (humming, speech, laughter) recorded on a French-made 'Soubitez' home recording machine belonging to Sablon.

202 **La Jambe En Bois** {0.57}
[***CD*** Fmx FA304]

203 **Miss Otis Regrets/Blue Drag No. 1** {4.51}
[***CD*** Fmx FA304]

204 **Blue Drag No. 2** {2.54}
[***CD*** Fmx FA304]

London — March 1936

Review of Stéphane Grappelli and his Hot Four: 'China Boy'/'St Louis Blues' (Decca F5824, 3s. 6d.) Django Reinhardt (solo gtr), Joseph Reinhardt and Louis Volga [*sic*] (gtrs), Roger Chapet [*sic*] sb; Stephane Grappelly (vln).

> I would like to send *St Louis Blues* to Handy. I would like to send it to heaps of people. I would like to send it to you, to all who love jazz, and even those who don't. It is so exquisitely charming.
>
> Grappelly does not appear until the last few bars. The greater part of the record is played by Django Reinhardt and it is a triumph for him. He tells in simple poetry everything that Handy must have felt and meant when he wrote this melody.

I might add that the performance is also a superlative example of guitar technique, that its phrases are jazz idiom at its best, that it swings and so on, but one mentions these things only when they are an end in themselves. Here they are a means to the end which is summed up in one word – Artistry. If you want to hear something really delightful, get this record.

You will not be disappointed in the coupling either. It is at least up to the combination's usual high standard. And that's saying something. (Edgar Jackson, *The Gramophone*)

Review of Freddy Taylor and his Swing Men from Harlem: 'Blue Drag'/'Viper's Dream' (Oriole LV105, 3s. 6d.)

Much has been written about Swing. More has been talked about it. Yet no one has so far managed to explain in words what it means.

Perhaps it doesn't matter. An ounce of practice is worth a ton of theory, and this disc is a ton of practice. From now onwards when anyone asks me what swing is, I shall play him these records.

One of the things he will learn is that Swing is anything but pep. It is something infinitely tender. If it is not exactly simple in itself, it is something that may come from the simplest music. In fact, it would seem that the more simple the music is made, the more chance has Swing to show itself. No one could say that the trumpet duet which opens *Blue Drag* is anything but simple. Exquisitely fascinating. (Edgar Jackson, *The Gramophone*)

London — March 1936

Review of Stéphane Grappelli and his Hot Four: 'St Louis Blues'/'China Boy' (Decca F5826, 1/6d)

Lack of space makes it impossible for me to say all the very rude things I have in mind. *'St Louis Blues'* has its points. The other is one of those great unplayables. It doesn't mean a thing. (Unsigned, *Swing*)

Polydor Studios, Paris — Thursday 12 March 1936

Yvonne Louis avec acc. d'Orchestre

Yvonne Louis (vcl); unknown (cl); Stéphane Grappelli and Sylvio Schmidt (vlns); Michel Emer (pno); Django Reinhardt (gtr); Louis Vola (acc); unknown (percussion).
Engineer: Rudolph Hamburger

205 2354HPP **Au Grande Large** {3.11}
[***78*** Pol 512648] [***LP*** Pol 2489 188] [***CD*** Fmx FA304]

Polydor Nos 512612, 512618 and 512619 recorded on the same day by 'André Tildy's Orchestre' may possibly feature Django Reinhardt, but they remain unfound. There is no evidence of Django's presence on the reverse side of Polydor 512648.

Paris — Saturday 21 March 1936

Willie Lewis records four titles for Pathé (matrix numbers CPT2611–14). See Rust for details.

Paris — Saturday 28 March 1936

Willie Lewis records two titles for Pathé (matrix numbers CPT2630–1). Musicians include Frank 'Big Boy' Goudie and Louis Vola. See Rust for details.

London — Saturday 28 March 1936

> **Record Of The Week**
>
> Recommended to all musicians irrespective of whether their particular instrument is featured: *'St Louis Blues' and 'China Boy'* by Stephane Grappelly and his Hot Four (Decca F5824). (Unsigned, *Melody Maker*)

London — April 1936

Review of Coleman Hawkins: 'Star Dust' (by Freddy Jenkins, Harlem Seven) (HMV B8420, 2s. 6d.).

> I wonder how many other artists have recorded in as many countries as Hawkins. America, England, Holland, and now here's one he made in France. If it is not a great record, it is nevertheless a pleasant one.
>
> It consists of three choruses. Reinhardt takes the second, Bean the first and last. Perhaps not the best work of either, but still attractive. Grappelly we know better as a violinist. Piano is obviously his second instrument, but he plays it adequately for the occasion.
>
> The record was made at the same session as Hawkins *Avalon* and *Blue Moon* (H.M.V. B8388) with Michel Warlop's Orchestra, hence Delhemme [*sic*]. When they sent me the personnel they told me the complete rhythm section was used in *Star Dust*, but I cannot hear any drums. If you can they were played by N. Chaillou. (Edgar Jackson, *The Gramophone*)

London — Wednesday 15 April 1936

Benny Carter and his Orchestra record three titles for Vocalion. See Rust for details of this and subsequent London sessions.

Polydor Studios, Paris — Friday 17 April 1936

Michel Warlop et son Orchestre

Alex Renard (tpt); Maurice Cizeron (as, fl, cl); Alix Combelle (ts); Michel Warlop (vln, dir); Emil Stern (pno); Django Reinhardt (gtr solo); Joseph Reinhardt (gtr); Louis Vola (sb).
Engineer: Rudolph Hamburger

206 2422-HPP **Cloud Castles** {3.10}
[***78*** Pol F512736] [***LP*** Pol 2489 188] [***CD*** Cls 739; Fmx FA304]

207 2423-HPP **Magic Strings** {3.25}
[***78*** Pol F512736] [***LP*** Pol 2489 188] [***CD*** Cls 739; Fmx FA304]

208 2424-HPP **Sweet Serenade** {3.10}
[***78*** Pol F512737] [***LP*** Pol 2489 188] [***CD*** Cls 739; Fmx FA304]

209 2425-HPP **Crazy Strings** {3.22}
[***78*** Poly F512737] [***LP*** Pol 2489 188] [***CD*** Cls 739; Fmx FA304]

210 2426-HPP **Novel Pets** {3.27}
[***78*** Pol F512738] [***LP*** Pol 2489 188] [***CD*** Cls 739; Fmx FA304]

211 2427-1/2HPP **Budding Dancers** {2.38}
[***78*** Pol F512738] [***LP*** Pol 2489 188] [***CD*** Cls 739; Fmx FA304]

Pathé Studios, Paris — Tuesday 28 April 1936

Willie Lewis and his Orchestra record two titles for Pathé (matrix numbers CPT2630–1). Musicians include Bill Coleman, Frank 'Big Boy' Goudie, John Mitchell and Louis Vola.
See Rust for details.

London — April–May 1936

'Benny Carter and his Orchestra' record eight titles for British Vocalion (matrix numbers S103–10).
Carter continues to lead studio groups in recording sessions throughout the summer of 1936.
See Rust for details.

Paris — Sunday 3 May 1936

Parliamentary elections give the Popular Front a majority in the Chamber of Deputies, paving the way for the events of 5 June, *qv*.

Studio Albert, Paris — Monday 4 May 1936

Quintette du Hot-Club de France

Stéphane Grappelli (vln); Django Reinhardt (gtr solo); Joseph Reinhardt, Pierre 'Baro' Ferret (gtrs); Lucien Simoens (sb); Freddy Taylor (vcl) (1).
Engineer: Georges Cailley

212 OLA 1057-1 **I'se A Muggin'** (1) {3.03}
[***78*** **Gr K-7704**; Vi JA-874] [***LP*** Aff BOX107; FELP 154; HCLP120; HMV CLP 1249; OCLP7529; Pat C05416001; Swa S1399; Swi SW8420267] [***CD*** Aff AFS 10035; Cls 739; Cly DIG12; Dig CO3507; DRG8493; Fla PASTCD9738; Fmx FA305; JSP 344; Mil 74321308652; Mos MD 6-190; Swi CDSW8413]

213 OLA 1057-2 **I'se A Muggin'** [**unissued**]

214 OLA 1058-1 **I Can't Give You Anything But Love** (1) {3.19}
[***78*** El EG3717; Gr B-8463, **K-7706**; Vi 40-0122, 68-0684, A-1204, JA856] [***LP*** Aff BOX107; HMV OCLP7529, CLP1249, FELP 154, HCLP120; Swa S1399; Swi 8420267] [***CD*** Aff AFS 10035; Avid AMSC648; Cls 739; Dig CO3507; Emp RAJCD808; Fla PAST CD9738; Fmx FA305; JSP 344; Mil 74321308652; Mos MD 6-190; Recall SDM307; Swi CDSW8413]

215 OLA 1058-2 **I Can't Give You Anything But Love** [**unissued**]

216 OLA 1059-1 **Oriental Shuffle** {2.37}
[***78*** El EG3776; Gr B-8479, **K-7704**, N-4469; Vi 26506, JA-874] [***25cm LP*** Vi AVLT6] [***LP*** Aff BOX107; HMV OCLP7529, CLP 1249, FELP154, HCLP120; OB OLD12; Swa S1399; Swi SW8420267; Vi LPM1100] [***EP*** HMV 7EGH1001; RCA EPC1100-3] [***CD*** Aff AFS 10035; Avid AMSC648; Cls 739; Cly DIG12; Dig CO3507; Fla PAST CD9738; Fmx FA305; HD HD206; JSP 344; JTD 102415; Mos MD 6-190; OB DOLD12; Swi CDSW8413]

217 OLA 1060-1 **After You've Gone** (1) {2.46}
[***78*** El EG3776; Gr B-8479, **K-7707**, N-4463; Vi 25511, Vi JA-874] [***25cm LP*** Vi AVLT6] [***LP*** Aff BOX107; HD 165; HMV OCLP7529, CLP1249, FELP154, HCLP120; OB OLD 12; Pat C054 16002; Swa S1305; Swi 8420267; Vi LPM1100] [***EP*** RCA EPC1100-3] [***CD*** Aff AFS 10035; ARC CASTLE 810562, SOL507; Avid AMSC648; CC CWNCD2010; Cls 739; Cly CDDIG12; Dig CO3506; DRG 8493; EMP RAJCD808; Fla PAST CD9738; Fmx FA305; HD CDHD165; JHR 73509; JSP 344; JTD 102415; LE JA5267; Mos MD 6-190; OB DOLD12; Swi CDSW8413]

218 OLA 1060-2 **After You've Gone** [**unissued**]

219 OLA 1061-1 **Are You In The Mood?** {2.46}
[***78*** **Gr K-7707**; Vi 26506, JA-910] [***25cm LP*** HMV FFLP1138] [***LP*** AFF Box107; HMV OCLP7529, CLP1249, FELP154, HCLP120; Swa S1305; Swi SW420267] [***CD*** Aff AFS 10035; Cls 739; Fmx FA305; JSP 344; JTD 102415; Mos MD 6-190; Swi CDSW8413]

220 OLA 1062-1 **Limehouse Blues** {2.43}
[***78*** El EG3717; Gr B-8463, **K-7707**; Vi A1204, JA-856, 25511, 68-0684] [***25cm LP*** HMV FFLP1138] [***LP*** Aff BOX107; HMV OCLP7529, CLP1249, FELP154, HCLP120; OB OLD12; Swa S1305; Swi SW8420267] [***EP*** HMV 7EGH1001] [***CD*** Aff AFS 10035; Arc SOL507; Avid AMSC648; Cls 739; Cly CD1048, DIG12; Emp RAJCD808; Fla PAST CD9738; Fmx FA305; Gal GALE 421; HD CDHD206; JH 73509; JSP 344; JTD 102415; Mos MD 6-190; Music CD6048; Swi CDSW8413]

Switzerland **Monday 4 May 1936**

Coleman Hawkins, accompanied by The Berries, records four titles for Swiss Pathé (matrix numbers BB1075–8).
See Rust for details.

Paris **Tuesday 5 May 1936**

Willie Lewis records four titles for Pathé (matrix numbers CPT2649–52). Musicians include Frank 'Big Boy' Goudie and Louis Vola.
See Rust for details.

London **Saturday 16 May 1936**

> The enterprising methods of Mr. D.M. Levy, of the famous Regent Street record store, have always kept him in the vanguard where swing music matters are concerned, and his latest effort to cater for the interests of jazz fans is one of the most interesting of recent times.
>
> He has arranged for Benny Carter to visit the premises on Tuesday next, May 19, so that fans who manage to go along to 96 Regent Street, London, on that day, after 6.30pm, will have a splendid opportunity of meeting this star in person at an informal gathering.
>
> Benny will be glad to autograph all copies of his new Vocalion Swing records. (Unsigned, *Melody Maker*)

Paris **May–June 1936**

The magazine *Jazz Hot* (No. 9) features an article on Benny Carter.

London **June 1936**

Review of Stéphane Grappelli and his Hot Four: 'It Was So Beautiful' / 'I've Found A New Baby' (Decca F5943, 1s. 6d.)

> Grappelly and his satellites make no attempt to deviate from their now well-known way of doing things, and candidly I would be one of the last to want them to. Ever since I first heard their records they have been an unending source of pleasure to me, and these two, in which they are well up to form, are no exception. Reinhardt remains the same wizard of the guitar, Grappelly is still Venuti's only rival, and a better accompaniment from available instruments could hardly be imagined.
>
> And if all that sounds trite, it's merely because I have said so often before everything else I would like to say. (Edgar Jackson, *The Gramophone*)

Paris **Wednesday 3 June 1936**

'Jazz Sam Castendet' record for Columbia. Musicians include Bert Marshall.

Paris **Friday 5 June 1936**

The Popular Front, under Leon Blum wins the elections and forms a cabinet comprising Socialists and Radical Socialists, with support from the Communist Party. In the days following, a large number of sit-down strikes occur throughout

France, leading to the introduction of a programme of social reform. The programme established the 40-hour working week, reorganized and ultimately nationalized the banking system, attempted to suppress Fascist groups, introduced workers' paid holidays, and instigated the arbitration of labour disputes.

These actions cause dismay among employers, which in turn leads to a redistribution of capital outside of France and marks the start of an inflationary cycle.

London Saturday 6 June 1936

Freddy Johnson The Piano-Playing Postman

Hot and Rhythm Clubs have sprung up all over the world in the last three years. A Federation even is planned! Swell! It's impossible, however, to speak of the oldest one – the Hot Club de Paris – without mentioning the name of Freddy Johnson.

Who is Mr. Johnson anyway? Well, once upon a time there lived in New York City a promising youngster, who had decided that his life's ambition was ... a job at the post office. To obtain such he even passed exams!

But, and as always there is a but, after having finished his studies, fate rapped at his door in the person of a coloured gent, name of Benny Carter. Mr. Carter, with a profound dislike of post-offices, persuaded Mr. Johnson to go all-pro and leave his former ideal alone. The latter yielded to his proposition. Result: St. Bureaucratius lost a future gem, the Biz-ness drew a winner!

Freddy rambled along in different bands, such as Billy Fowler's and Elmer Snowden's, and with people such as Rex, Tommy Ladnier, Benny Carter, Prince Robinson, Walter Johnson, Clarence Holiday and, last but not least, Jimmy Harrison, virtuoso of the trombone.

In 1927 or so he joined the Wooding orchestra, crossing 'the pond' to play in Paris. Several famous musicians were a part of that aggregation, such as Cheatum, the best trumpet player anywhere, and Tommy Ladnier, a swell get-off trumpeter. Saxes were Willy Lewis, Ralph James and Jerry Blake, now with Don Redman again. After some years the band broke up, Willy Lewis remaining in France with only a part of the original crew. This is the same band that Benny Carter joined not so long ago.

Wooding toured Europe in the winter of 1928–29, when it was so cold it was even freezing in Turkey, as Freddy told me. As a contrast, in the summer following, it was so hot that when Wooding made some records the wax melted!

In Paris, Johnson played a long time at Bricktop's with Arthur Briggs on trumpet, Herb Fleming on trombone, and others. Finishing there, he went to Holland, where he has stayed for the last two years, mostly leading his own band. At the moment he's playing with Harry Pohl, a Dutch musician. So much for history.

Freddy is an inexhaustible source of information. Unlike most American musicians he likes to tell you about the good old days in Harlem. Here's one of Freddy's anecdotes … about Benny Carter. One day Benny had taken a fancy to clarinet playing. His progress on that instrument was so astonishing that the following conversation could be heard in New York City;

Mr. A: 'Yesterday I've heard Benny Carter playing that clarinet. Some swingin' kid!'

Mr. B: 'Oh yeah? Well, that's nothing – you should hear him today!'

During his stay in Europe he made a bunch of records for the French Brunswick Company, some of which were issued in England on Decca. The first was a duet with Arthur Briggs on trumpet. Titles: *Crabbin' Blues* (a Johnson opus) and *Japanese Sandman*. In several records Spencer Williams – famous composer of hit-tunes and blues – sings.

His best titles with his band were *Foxy and Grapesy* – a collective improvisation – and *Sweet Georgia Brown* in a marvellous Johnson arrangement. Featured were Arthur Briggs, Pete Duconge a New Orleans man – and 'Big Boy' Goudie on tenor.

Later he recorded with an augmented orchestra *Sweet Madness*, *Harlem Bound*, the inevitable *Tiger Rag* and *I Got Rhythm*. The orchestra, all coloured, boasted a five-piece brass section, four saxes and the usual rhythm group, with Bill Taylor on drums. Stars were Herbert Flemming on trombone, whose style is somewhat like Bennie Morton's, and Booker Pittman, alto and clarinet player with Lucky Millender's orchestra in Nice in '33.

In Holland also four titles were recorded: *I Want To Dance*, *Harlem Hot Club Stomp*, *Jungle Fever* and *You Took Advantage Of Me*. The first two are certainly fine and have Goldsmith as trumpeter. This combination was a mixed one and the best available.

Freddy's piano playing is remarkable. He gets the best out of his musicians. He is a born leader who knows how to 'send' a band. In his solo playing a certain Teddy Wilson influence can be observed. Freddy has a great admiration for Theodore, and who, by the way, has not? Still, however, Mr. Johnson was clever enough to stick to his own personality. He does not copy Teddy.

His arrangements and compositions, such as *Harlem Bound* and *Sweet Madness*, are quite original. Living in America and having an opportunity to feature them, he would undoubtedly be in a class with the famous three musketeers: Henderson, Redman and Carter.

A most charming personality and a true musician. (H H Niesen Jnr., *Melody Maker*)

London — Saturday 13 June 1936

Josse Breyere, the Belgian Jack Teagarden, left Stan Brenders I.N.R., Broadcasting band on June 1. This is the sensational news which broke upon Belgian fans last week. After due enquiries at the I.N.R. offices it was made clear that Josse had asked to be allowed to break his present contract with Stan, as an offer had been made to him of a magnitude which he could hardly neglect.

Josse has gone over to Ray Ventura's Orchestra, the famous French combination, which is said to be going over to the States shortly.

It will be remembered that Ventura signed on Gus Deloof, Belgium's best trumpet player, about two years ago. Much regret will be felt in regard to Josse's departure, for he is not only a stalwart of Stan Brender's Orchestra, but also one of the finest trombone players on the continent.

Josse started his musical career with a military band, then went over to jazz not so long ago. Consistent and strenuous work brought him on top, and for many years he was a member of the late Louis de Vries Internationals, and of Jack de Vries and Fud Candrix's bands. (Unsigned, *Melody Maker*)

New York — Wednesday 24 June 1936

Frank Victor records two guitar duets for Decca. The accompanying guitarist is Harry Volpe.
See Rust for details of this and a subsequent session.

London — August 1936

Review of Quintette of the Hot Club of France: 'I Can't Give You Anything But Love' / 'Limehouse Blues' (HMV B8463, 1s. 6d.)

Grappelly and Reinhardt are two of the finest technicians in jazz, and they love to display their technique.

To say that in doing so they forgot to swing, however, would be nothing short of libel; nevertheless one has to take a broad view of jazz to get the utmost enjoyment from their playing. There is no doubt that while they swing in the broad sense of the word, their music has a Continental flavouring which has not been free from criticism in certain quarters. Of course it is inevitable. One's inherent feelings and the influence of one's environment in the days of one's development are bound to have their effect. It is not that one consciously wants to veneer everything with the characteristics of one's race; it is more difficult not to see everything through the spectacles of one's education. Probably neither Grappelly nor Reinhardt could eradicate this Continental strain (a feature which seems to be the love of flow'ry phrases [*sic*]) for the simple reason that, it being natural and not acquired, they probably do not and could not realize where it exists.

So what? Does it make their music any less enjoyable? Yes – if you judge everything by one narrow standard. But why do so?

Isn't it fairer and more sensible to take things at their face value? Surely the acid test of anything is whether it is good of its kind, provided, of course, that the kind has some merit.

I think the mistake so many of us make – and in saying 'us' I do not exclude myself – is that we are too slow in differentiating between a subject and the various practices of it. We blame, or as the case may be, praise the one for the other, and vice versa.

All of which is by way of amusing theorizing, and certainly not intended as a defence of the records, for the simple reason that they do not need any. You have probably heard many other records on Decca by the combination, so you will know what to expect. The group has not attempted to alter its style for the sake of doing something for a different company, and I at any rate am glad. I always enjoy the wizardry of Messrs. Grappelly, Reinhardt, and their satellites. It is always refreshing. (Edgar Jackson, *The Gramophone*)

Copenhagen **between 26 and 29 August 1936**

'Benny Carter and Kai Ewan's Orchestra' record four titles from the Danish branch of the Gramophone Company Ltd (matrix numbers OC435–6 and 450–1).
See Rust for details.

London **Monday 7 September 1936**

Garland Wilson records four piano solos for English Brunswick (matrix numbers TB2426–9).
See Rust for details.

Stockholm **Saturday 12 September 1936**

Benny Carter, accompanied by Swedish musicians, records two titles for Sonora records (matrix numbers 1879–80).
See Rust for details.

London **Autumn 1936**

An article by Andre Durand, 'The Hot Club Quintet' appears in *Swing*, Autumn 1936.
See Cruickshank, page 88 for a reproduction.

Paris **Thursday 1 October 1936**

to Revue du Jazz Hot

Dear Sir,
The Quintette of the Hot Club will be ready to record with a hot singer on Monday the 12. Inst. [*sic*]. The programme decided on would be: two pieces requested by the English Company:
'Nagasaki'
'Georgia'

The others have either been recorded already, or as regards 'Stringing The Blues' and 'Jazz me Blues' it is impossible to find the music: As regards 'West End Blues', which has been made celebrated by Louis Armstrong, nobody has ventured to do it since him; it is moreover too slow for the quintette.

The other pieces would be:
'Boston Tea Party'
'South Sea Island'
two compositions which have only just been published in America, and which are already indicated by our correspondents as being likely to have a great a success.

The last two sides would be the last two compositions of Django Reinhardt.

Yours faithfully,
Pierre Nourry.

Paris — Monday 12 October 1936

from J Bérard, Cie Française du Gramophone
to Rex Palmer, The Gramophone Company, Hayes, England

Dear Mr Palmer,

Hot Club de France

Following on your letter of the 12 September, I inform you that the session of the Hot Club of France will take place very shortly, on the usual terms. i.e., Frs. 500 per side – that is Frs. 3000 for the session of six titles – without royalty.

Unfortunately they cannot record all the titles you had asked for – we think that we can accept to do the recordings they propose to us,

Yours faithfully
J Bérard

Studio Albert, Paris — Thursday 15 October 1936

Quintette du Hot-Club de France

Stéphane Grappelli (vln); Django Reinhardt (gtr solo); Joseph Reinhardt, Pierre 'Baro' Ferret (gtr); Louis Vola (sb); Freddy Taylor (vcl) (1).
Engineer: Georges Cailley

221 OLA 1290-1 **Nagasaki** (1) {2.48}
[***78*** El EG 3882; Gr B-8518, **K-7843**; Vi 25558, JA-1012, 1078]
[***LP*** Aff BOX107; HMVOCLP7529, CLP1249, FELP154, HCLP120; OB OLD12; Pat C054 16002; Swa S1305; Swi SW8420267]
[***CD*** ABM 1194; Aff AFS10035; Arc SOL517; CC 2010; Cls 739; Cly DIG12; Emp RAJCD808; Fla PAST CD9738; Fmx FA305; HD CDHD165; JH 73509; JSP 344; JTD102415; LE AJA5138, 5267; Mos MD 6-190; Music CD6048; OB DOLD12; Swi CDSW8413]

222 OLA1290-2 **Nagasaki** (1) [**unissued**]

223 OLA 1291-1 **Swing Guitars** {2.23}
[***78*** Gr B-8532, **K-7898**; Vi 25601, JA-1119] [***25cm LP*** Vi AVLT6]
[***LP*** Aff BOX107; El E83035; HMV OCLP7529, CLP1249, FELP154, HCLP120; Pat C054 16002; Swa S1305; Swi 8420267]
[***EP*** HMV 7EGH1001] [***CD*** ABM 1194; Aff AFS10035; Arc SOL507; BGO CD366; Cls 739; Cly CD1048, DIG12; Dig CO3506; Fla PAST CD9738; Fmx FA305; Gal GALE421; HD CDHD234; JH 73509; JSP344; JTD 102415; LE AJA5267; Mos MD 6-190; OB DOLD12; Recall SMCD307; Swi CDSW8413]

224 OLA 1292-1 **Georgia On My Mind** (1) {3.13}
[***78*** Gr B-8532, **K-7790; Vi 26578, JA-1119**] [***25cm LP*** Vi AVLT6]
[***LP*** Aff BOX107; HMV OCLP7529, CLP154, FELP154, HCLP120; Pat C054 16002; Swa S1305; Swi SW8420267; Vi LPM1100]
[***EP*** RCA EPC1100-1] [***CD*** Aff AFS10035; Arc CASTEL810562, SOL507; Avid AMSC648; Cls 739; Cly DIG12; Dig CO3506; DRG 8493; Ea EABCD71; Emp RAJCD808; Fmx FA305; JH 73509; JSP 344; JTD 102415; Mos MD 6-190; Music CD6048; Swi CDSW8413]

225 OLA 1292-2 **Georgia On My Mind** [**unissued**]

226 OLA 1293-1 **Shine** (1) {2.54}
[***78*** El EG3918; Gr B-8534 (Au, E), **K-7898**; Vi 26578, A-1277, JA1363]
[***LP*** Aff BOX107; HMV OCLP7529, CLP1249, FELP154, HCLP120; HD CHD165; OB OLD12; Pat C054 16002; Swa S1305; Swi SW420267; Vi LPM1100] [***EP*** HMV 7EGH1001; RCA EPC1100-2]
[***CD*** ABM CD1194; Aff AFS 10035; Arc SOL507; Avid AMSC648; Cls 739; Cly DIG12; Emp RAJCD808; Fla PAST CD 9738; Fmx FA305; Gal GALE435; HD CDHD165; JH 73509; JTD102415; Mos MD 6-190; OB DOLD12; Swi CDSW8413]

227 OLA 1294-1 **In The Still Of The Night** {3.03}
[***78*** El EG3918; Gr B-8534 (Au, E), **K-7898**; Vi 26578, A-1277, JA1363]
[***LP*** Aff BOX107; HMV OCLP7529, CLP1249, FELP154, HCLP120; OB OLD12; Pat C054 16002; Swa S1305; Swi SW842067]
[***CD*** Aff AFS 10035; Cls 739; Fla PAST CD9738; Fmx FA305; JSP 344; JTD 102415; Mos MD 6-190; OB DOLD12; Swi CDSW8413]

228 OLA 1295-1 **Sweet Chorus** {2.42}
[***78*** El EG3882; Gr B-8518, **K-7845**; Vi 40-0122] [***LP*** Aff BOX107; HD CHD165; HMV OCLP7529, CLP1249, FELP154, HCLP120; OB OLD12; Pat C054 16002; Swa S1305; Swi SW8420267]
[***EP*** El (G) 41098; HMV 7EGH1002; 7EMQ12; (F) 7EGF650]
[***CD*** Aff AFS 10035; Cls 739; Cly DIG12; Dig CO3507; Fla PAST CD9738; Fmx FA305; GALE421; Hab 111200; HD CDHD165; JSP 344; JTD102415; LE AJA5138; Mos MD 6-190; OB DOLD12; Recall SMCD307; Swi CDSW8413]

Artists' fees for this session were £28 1s. 1d. It is not known how these funds were disbursed among the musicians.

Paris — Thursday 15 October 1936

Willie Lewis and his Orchestra record six titles for Pathé (matrix numbers CPT2900–5). Musicians include Arthur Briggs, Bill Coleman, Frank 'Big Boy' Goudie and Louis Vola.
Note that Vola also appears in the previously listed session, recorded on the same day, although the order in which sessions were conducted remains unknown.
See Rust for details.

Pathé Studios, Paris — Thursday 22 October 1936

Jean Tranchant avec Stéphane Grappelli et Django Reinhardt

Jean Tranchant (vcl, pno, celeste) (1); Stéphane Grappelli (vln); Django Reinhardt (gtr).
Engineer: Eugène Ravenet

229 CPT 2931-1 **Mademoiselle Adeline** (1) {2.11}
[***78*** Pat PA1042] [***LP*** Swi SW8420267] [***CD*** Fmx FA305; Swi SW 8419]

230 CPT 2932-1 **Le Roi Marc** {2.43}
[***78*** Pat 1042] [***LP*** Swi SW8420267] [***CD*** Fmx FA305]

Pathé Studios, Paris — Thursday 12 November 1936

Nane Cholet, acc. par Stéphane Grappelli et son Ensemble 'Hot and Sweet'

Nane Cholet (vcl) acc. by Stéphane Grappelli (vln); Emil Stern (pno); Joseph and Django Reinhardt (gtrs); Louis Vola (sb).
Engineer: Eugène Ravenet

231 CPT2969-1 **Terrain A Vendre** {2.30}
[***78*** Pat 1059] [***CD*** Fmx FA305]

232 CPT2970-1 **Ainsi Soit-il** {2.08}
[***78*** Pat 1059] [***CD*** Fmx FA305]

Willie Lewis also recorded three titles at this same session, two accompanying Jean Trenchant (matrix numbers CPT2966–8). Musicians include Frank 'Big Boy' Goudie and Louis Vola.
See Rust for details.

Kawasaki, Japan — Saturday 14 November 1936

from H A Strauss, Nipponophone Company Ltd
to F B Duncan, Gramophone Company, Hayes, England

Dear Mr. Duncan

Re: **Hot Club de France**

We refer to Mr Palmer's letter of June 22 and would like you to include an agreement with the Company in question on our behalf for the outright purchase of the following matrices:

AP1422 Dinah (matrix P77161)
AP1479 Swanee River (matrix P77352)
Blue Drag (matrix P77351)
AP1511 Clouds (matrix P77440)

At a payment of French Frcs. 400.– per matrix as per Mr. Thomas' letter to us of April 30 1936; this charge includes all copyright and artist royalties.

The agreement should give us the exclusive right to use those matrices for our territory for all times and should prevent the French owner of the matrices to ship the same matrices or records thereof into our territory.

Please take care that the matrices which are sent to us are copper matrices and not nickelled ones and that they are accompanied by a bill from you charging us for those matrices with the same charge you use for Columbia matrices.

Yours very truly
H A Strauss

Current research indicates that these masters were never released in Japan.

London — Saturday 14 November 1936

Guitarist for Glasgow

Guitarist Alan Ferguson, after finishing with Chalmers Wood at the Kelvin Hall, has started in a Glasgow job and is now to be found at the Locarno Club, where, of course, Chalmers Wood supplies the music.

The combination at the club has been altered to suit the rather 'intimate' character of the job, and consist of piano, violin, guitar and drums, the personnel being, respectively, Bobbie Rosenbloom, Johnnie McMeekin, Alan Ferguson and Jim McNeilage. (Unsigned, *Melody Maker*)

Zurich — Saturday 28 November 1936

The QHCF and Fletcher Allen and His Swing Men From Harlem (*sic*) appear without Django, who had taken to the road. The concert, entitled 'Jungle Night in Zurich', was organized by 'The Committee of Italian Students in Zurich'.

London — December 1936

Review of *Hot Discography* by Charles Delaunay

When Hilton R. Schelman produced his *Rhythm on Record* (Melody Maker Ltd, 7s. 6d.) most of us believed his unbelievably ambitious work would for long remain the leading reference work in the field of hot record personnels; but although it has been out less than a year it has already been improved upon by Charles Delaunay in his *Hot Discography*.

Hot Discography scores over *Rhythm on Record* in that it avoids the latter's one drawback – the giving of collective personnels for batches of records. Commencing way back in the early 1920 period it essays to list the recordings of each band, group of artists or solo artist in chronological order of the session dates (giving in many cases the matrix numbers), and so successfully has the author tackled his Herculean task that I have so far been unable to trace more than one or two minor omissions and inaccuracies.

Delaunay is a Frenchman, and although his work is written in English, it is published in France. So far no English agent has been appointed, and those desiring the book must writer directly to France. Orders should be addressed to 'Hot Jazz', 15, rue du Conservatoire, Paris 9e. The price is Frs. 20 (approximately 3s. 10d.) post free, which must be sent with order by means of International Money Order or banker's cheque. (Edgar Jackson, *The Gramophone*)

Prague, Czechoslovakia — Wednesday 2 December 1936

Jan Sima and his Orchestra record two titles for Ultraphone. Musicans include Joe Turner.
See Rust for details.

L'Ecole Normale, Paris — Thursday 10 December 1936

The Quintette, without Django, appear at 'La Gala du Jazz Française'.

Camden, New Jersey — Wednesday 23 December 1936

from R P Mitchell, RCA Manufacturing Inc.
to Rex Palmer, The Gramophone Company Ltd, Hayes, Mddx.

Dear Mr Palmer,
The release by Decca in this country of several recordings by the Quintette Of The Hot Club Of France has created considerable interest in this group. We would, therefore, appreciate your sending to us as promptly as possible, samples and shells of the following:
Both sides of B-8479
" " " B-8463
" " " K-7707
" " " K-7790

Yours very truly
R P Mitchell, Recording and Record Sales

France — 1937

Django Reinhardt is reported to have been involved in the making of the film *Naples au baiser du feu* (*Naples Kissed by Fire*), directed by Augusto Genini and starring Tino Rossi. No evidence can currently be found to support this theory.

London **Wednesday 20 January 1937**

Sidney Lipton and his Orchestra record for Decca. Musicians include Jack Llewellyn.

Paris **Saturday 23 January 1937**

Django Reinhardt's 27th birthday.

Paris **January–February 1937**

The magazine *Jazz Hot* (No. 14) features an article on Rex Stewart.

Paris **Saturday 6 February 1937**

The first meeting between Charles Delaunay and Jean Bérard, of Compagnie Gramophone du Française, to discuss Delaunay's proposal for a label dedicated to jazz, called 'Swing'.

Bérard, to Delaunay's apparent surprise, agrees to the proposal, offering technical facilities and allowing Delaunay and the Hot-Club to choose artists and repertoire.

Hayes, Middlesex **Tuesday 3 March 1937**

from International Artist's Dept, Gramophone Company, Hayes, Mddx
to M Jean Bérard, Cie Française du Gramophone, 9 Blvd Hausemann, Paris

Dear M. Bérard,

Hot Club of France

We shall be much obliged if you can arrange for the Quintette Of The Hot Club de France to record as many of the following titles as possible – without vocal refrain:

Solitude
In a Sentimental Mood
When Day is Done
Body and Soul
Rose Room
You're Driving Me Crazy
Ain't Misbehavin'
Smoke Rings
Miss Annabelle Lee
Hot Lips
Misty Morning
Running Wild

We should also like you to arrange for them to do Liszt's 'Liebestraum' No. 3 and 'A Little Love a Little Kiss' as slow swing numbers.

We would also like two guitar solos from Django Reinhardt, choice of titles to be left to the artist.

Please advise us how soon this recording can be arranged.

Yours very truly
[unidentifiable signature]
The Gramophone Company Ltd,
International Artists' Department.

Amsterdam — Monday 24 March 1937

'Benny Carter and the Ramblers' record four titles for Dutch Decca (matrix numbers AM368–71). Musicians include Coleman Hawkins.
See Rust for details.

Paris — March–April 1937

The magazine *Jazz Hot* (No. 15) features an article on André Ekyan.

Amsterdam — April 1937

The likely date for Coleman Hawkins' appearance in a short film made by the 'Poligon' company.
See Filmography for further details.

Paris — Wednesday 21 April 1937

Quintette Du Hot-Club de France (French issues)/**Quintette of The Hot Club of France** (all other Gramophone Company issues)

Stéphane Grappelli (vln); Django Reinhardt (gtr solo); Pierre 'Baro' Ferret, Marcel Bianchi (gtrs); Louis Vola (sb).
Engineer: Eugène Ravenet

233 OLA 1702-1 **Exactly Like You** {2:27}
[***78*** El EG6178; Gr AL-2436, **B-8629**, GW-1509, GY-333, JK-2332; Vi 26733] [***LP*** Aff BOX107; Pat C 054 16002; Swa S1305; Swi SW8420267] [***EP*** HMV 7EGH1003] [***CD*** Aff 10035; Arc SOL507; Avid AMSC648; BGO198; Cas MACCD132; CC 2010; Cls 748; Dig CO3507; Emp RAJCD808; Fla PASTCD9738; Fmx FA305; Gal GALE435; HD CDHD234; JH 73509; JSP 349; Kaz EUKCD913; Mil 74321308652; Mos MD 6-190; Recall SMDCD307; Retro RZCD7002; Swi CDSW8413]

234 OLA 1703-1 **Charleston** {2:50}
[***78*** Swi 2] [***LP*** Aff BOX107; Pat C054 16002; Swa S1305; Swi SW8420267] [***EP*** Aus 7EGW8505; El E40920] [***CD*** ABM 1194; Aff 10035; Arc SOL517; Best 9101; BGO366; Cas MACCD132; Cls 748; Fmx FA305; Fr DGF50; HD CDHD234; JSP349; Kaz EUKCD913; LE AJA5267; Mos MD 6-190; Recall SMCD307; Swi CDSW8413]

235 OLA 1704-1 **You're Driving Me Crazy** {2:52}
[***78*** El EG6088; **Gr B-8606**, GY-432, JK-2048, JO-16; Vi 26733]

[***LP*** Aff BOX107; Pat C054 16002; Swa S1305; Swi SW8420267] [***CD*** Aff 10035; Arc SOL507; BGO CD366; Cas MACCD132; CC 2010; Cls 748; Dig CO3507; Emp RAJCD808; Fla PASTCD 9738; Fmx FA305; HD CDHD206; JH 73509; JSP 349; JTD 102415; Kaz EUKCD913; LE AJA5267; Mil 74321308652; Mos MD 6-190; Recall SMDCD307; Swi CDSW8413]

236 OLA 1705-1 **Tears** {2:35}
[***78*** Gr B-8718 (E, In)] [***LP*** Aff BOX107; Pat C054 16002; Swa S1305; Swi SW8420267] [***CD*** Aff 10035; Avid AMSC648; BGO CD198; Cls 748; Dig CO3506; Fla PASTCD9738; Fmx FA305; Gal GALE421; Hab 111200; HD CDHD234; JSP349; JTD102415; Mos MD 6-190; Swi CDSW8413]

237 OLA 1706-1 **Solitude** {3:06}
[***78*** Gr B-8669; Vi 40-0124] [***LP*** Aff BOX107; HD CHD165; Pat C054 16002; Swa S1305; Swi SW8420267] [***CD*** Aff 10035; Avid AMSC648; BGO CD198; CC 2010; Cls 748; Dig CO3507; Emp RAJCD808; Fla PASTCD9738; Fmx FA305; Gal GALE435; HD CDHD165; JSP 349; JTD 102415; Mos MD 6-190; Recall SMDCD307; Swi CDSW8413]

Paris — Thursday 22 April 1937

Details as above.

238 OLA 1707-1 **Hot Lips** {3:02}
[***78*** El EG6560; **Gr B-8690**, GY-297, JK-2049] [***LP*** Aff BOX107; Pat C 054 16003; Swa S1306; Swi SW8420267] [***EP*** HMV 7EGH1003] [***CD*** Aff AFS 10035; Avid AMSC648; BGO198; Cls 748; Fla PASTCD9738; Fmx FA305; JSP349; JTD 102415; Mos MD 6-190; Swi CDSW8413]

239 OLA 1708-1 **Ain't Misbehavin'** {2:51}
[***78*** El EG6560, **Gr B-8690**, JK-2049; Vi 40-0123] [***LP*** Aff BOX107; BBC RED680; Pat C054 16003; Swa S1306; Swi SW8420267] [***CD*** Aff AFS 10035; Arc SOL507; BGO198; CC2010; Cls 748; Dig CO3506; Emp RAJCD808; Fla PASTCD9738; Fmx FA305; Gal GALE435; JH 73509; JSP 349; JTD102415; Mos MD 6-190; Recall SMDCD307; Swi CDSW8413]

240 OLA 1709-1 **Rose Room** {2:42}
[***78*** Gr B-8718 (E, In)] [***LP*** Aff BOX107; Pat C054 16003; Swa S1306; Swi SW8420267] [***EP*** HMV 7EGH1003] [***CD*** Aff AFS 10035; Arc SOL507; Avid AMSC648; BGO 198; CC 2010; Cls 748; Cly CD1048, DIG12; Dig CO3507; Fla PASTCD 9738; Fmx FA305; HD CDHD234; JH 73509; JSP349; JTD 102415; LE AJA5138; Mos MD 6-190; Recall SMDCD307; Swi CDSW8413]

241 OLA 1710-1 **Body And Soul** {3:24}
[***78*** Gr B-8598 (E, In)] [***LP*** Aff BOX107; Pat C054 16003; Swa S1306; Swi SW8420267] [***CD*** Aff AFS 10035; Avid AMSC648; BGO 198; Cls 748; Cly DIG12; Ea EABCD71; Emp RAJCD808; Fmx FA305; Gal GALE421; JSP349; JTD 102415; Mos MD 6-190; Swi CDSW8413]

242 OLA 1711-1 **When Day Is Done** {3:10}
[***78*** **Gr B-8669**, GW-297; Vi 40-0123] [***LP*** Aff BOX107; Pat C054 16003; Swa S1306; Swi SW420267] [***CD*** Aff AFS 10035; Avid AMSC648; BGO CD198; Cls 748; Emp RAJCD808; Fmx FA305; HD CDHD234; JSP349; LE AJA5138; Mos MD 6-190; Swi CDSW8413]
An unidentified band member produces an inadvertent cough at 0:57 on this master.

Salle Chopin, Paris — Friday 23 April 1937

The Hot-Club de France presents Coleman Hawkins in concert.

Paris — Monday 26 April 1937

Details as above.

243 OLA 1712-1 **Runnin' Wild** {2:52}
[***78*** El 6561; **Gr B-8614**, HN-2495; Vi 40-0124] [***LP*** Aff BOX107; HD CHD165; Pat C054 16003; Swa S1306; Swi SW8420267] [***CD*** Aff AFS 10035; Avid AMSC648; BGO CD198; Cls 748; Emp RAJCD808; Fmx FA305; Gal GALE435; HD CDHD165, 234; JSP349; JTD 102415; LE AJA5267; Mil 74321308652; Mos MD 6-190; Swi CDSW8413]

244 OLA 1713-1 **Chicago** {3:24}
[***78*** **Swi 2**] [***LP*** Aff BOX107; Pat C054 16003; Swa S1306; Swi SW8420267] [***EP*** Aus 7EGW8505; El E40920; HMV 7EGH1004] [***CD*** Aff AFS 10035; Arc CASTEL 810562, SOL507; BGOCD366; Cas MACCD132; CC 2010; Cls 748; Cly CD1048; Dig CO3507; Fmx FA305; Fr DGF50; HD CDHD234; JH73509; JSP349; JTD 102415; Kaz EUKCD913; Milan 74321308652; Mos MD 6-190; Recall SMDCD307; Swi CDSW8413]

245 OLA 1714-1 **Liebestraum No. 3** {3:17}
[***78*** Gr AL-2492, **B-8737**; Vi JA-1363, A-1277] [***LP*** Aff BOX107; Pat C054 16003; Swa S1306] [***CD*** Aff AFS 10035; Cls 748; Fmx FA305; Hab 111200; JSP 349; Mos MD 6-190]

246 OLA 1715-1 **Miss Annabelle Lee** {2:46}
[***78*** El EG6561; **Gr B-8614** (Au, B), HN-2495; Vi 40-0125] [***LP*** Aff BOX107; HD CHD165; Pat C054 16003; Swa S1306; Swi SW8420267] [***CD*** Aff AFS 10035; Avid AMSC648; BGO CD198; Cls 748; Dig CO3507; Fla PASTCD9738; Fmx FA305; HD CDHD165; JSP349; Mil 74321308652; Mos MD 6-190; Swi CDSW8413]

247 OLA 1716-1 **A Little Love, A Little Kiss** {3:16}
[***78*** **Gr B-8598** (E, In)] [***LP*** Aff BOX107; HD CHD165; Pat C054 16003; Swa S1306; Swi SW420267] [***CD*** Aff AFS 10035; Avid AMSC648; BGO CD198; Cls 748; Dig CO3507; Fla PASTCD9738; Fmx FA305; Gal GALE435; HD CDHD165; JSP349; Mil 74321308652; Mos MD 6-190; Swi CDSW8413]

248 OLA 1717-1 **Mystery Pacific** {2:19}
[***78*** El EG6088; Gr AL-2404; **B-8606**, GY-432, JK-2048, JO-15, K-8396; Vi 40-0125] [***LP*** Aff BOX107; Pat C054 16003; Swa S1306; Swi SW420267] [***CD*** Aff AFS 10035; Cas MACCD132, Cls 748; Cly DIG12; Fla PASTCD9738; Fmx FA305; HD CDHD206; JSP349; Kaz EUKCD913; Mil 7432308652; Mos MD 6-190; Music CD6049; Swi CDSW8413]

249 OLA 1718-1 **In A Sentimental Mood** {2:57}
[***78*** El EG6178; Gr AL-2436, **B-8629**, GW-1509, GY-333, JK-2332] [***LP*** Aff BOX107; Pat C054 16003; Swa S1306] [***CD*** Aff AFS 10035; Avid AMSC648; BGO CD366; Cls 748; Cly CD1048, DIG12; Dig CO3507; Fla PASTCD9738; Fmx FA305; HD CDHD206; JSP349; Milan 74321308652; Mos MD 6-190; Recall SMDCD307; Swi CDSW8413]

Paris Tuesday 27 April 1937

As above (1).
Stéphane Grappelli (2); Grappelli (vln solo) acc. by Django Reinhardt (gtr).
Django Reinhardt (3); Reinhardt (gtr solo).
Engineer: Eugène Ravenet

250 OLA 1719-1 **The Sheik Of Araby** (1) {3:02}
[***78*** Gr AL-2492, **B-8737**] [***LP*** Aff BOX107; Pat C054 16003; Swa S1306; Swi SW8420267] [***EP*** HMV 7EGH1003] [***CD*** Aff AFS 10035; Avid AMSC648; BGO CD198; Cls 748; DRG 8493; Fmx FA305; JSP349; Mos MD 6-190; Recall SMDCD307; Swi CDSW8413]

251 OLA 1738-1 **I've Found A New Baby** (2) {2.00}
[***78*** **unissued**] [***LP*** **Pat C054 16005**] [***CD*** DRG 8493; Fmx FA305; JSP904; Mos MD 6-190]

252 OLA 1739-1 **Improvisation No. 1** (3) {2:55}
[***78*** **Gr B-8587**; Vi A1182] [***25cm LP*** CHDD 580] [***LP*** Pat C054 16003; Swa S1306; Swi SW8420267] [***EP*** HMV 7EMF40] [***CD*** Aff AFS 10035; Cas PIESD233; Cls 748; Cly DIG12; DRG 8493; Fmx FA305; HD CDHD234; JSP 349; LE AJA5267; Mos MD 6-190; Recall SMDCD307; Swi CDSW8413]

253 OLA 1740-1 **Parfum** (3) {2:57}
[***78*** Gr B-8587] [***25cm LP*** CHDD 580] [***LP*** Aff BOX107;

Pat C 054 16004; Swa S1399; Swi SW8420267] [***EP*** HMV 7EMF40] [***CD*** Aff AFS 10035; Cas PIEDSD233; Cls 748; Cly DIG12; DRG 8483; Fmx FA305; JSP 349; Mos MD 6-190; Swi CDSW8413]

254 OLA 1741-1 **Alabamy Bound** (2) {2.49}
[***78*** Swi 21] [***LP*** Aff BOX107; Pat C054 16004; Swa S1399; Swi SW8420267] [***CD*** Aff AFS 10035; BGO366; Cas PIESD233; Cly DIG12; DRG8493; Ea EABCD71; Fmx FA305; Fr DGF50; Gal GALE435; JSP 349; Milan 74321308652; Mos MD 6-190; Swi CDSW8413]

See Panassié, *Douze années de jazz*, pages 189–96, for comments regarding the English HMV recording sessions.

Casino Handorff, Laren, The Netherlands — Tuesday 27 April 1937

Coleman Hawkins records eleven titles for Dutch Decca (matrix numbers AM376–81 including alternates).
See Rust for details.
Note the juxtaposition of this and the following entry.

Pathé Studios, Paris — Wednesday 28 April 1937

Coleman Hawkins and his All Star 'Jam' Band

Hawkins (ts); Alix Combelle (cl); Benny Carter (tpt); André Ekyan (as); Stéphane Grappelli (pno); Django Reinhardt (gtr); Eugène d'Hellemmes (sb); Tommy Benford (dms).
Engineer: Eugène Ravenet

255 OLA 1742-1 **Honeysuckle Rose** {2.44}
[***78*** Col GN 5039; Gr B-8574, SG-364; **Swi 1**; Vi 26219, A-1294] [***LP*** Aff BOX107; Ast LP20102; BBC REB698; LE AJA5054; Pat C054 16004; Swi 8420267] [***EP*** Aus 7EGW8505; El E40920; HMV 7EG8393, 7EMF236] [***CD*** Aff AFS 10035; Avid AVC533; BGO CD249; Cly DIG12; DRG8493; Ea EABCD71; Emp RAJCD808; Fmx FA305; Fr DGF50; HD CDHD230; LE AJA5054; Swi CDSW8403, 8413]

256 OLA 1743-1 **Crazy Rhythm** {2.59}
[***78*** Col GN 5039; Gr B-8754, SG-364; **Swi 1**; Vi 1294] [***LP*** Aff BOX107; Astan LP20102; BBC RED698; LE AJA5054; Pat C054 16004; Swi SW8420267] [***EP*** El E40920; HMV 7EG8393, 7EMF26] [***CD*** Aff AFS 10035; Avid AVC533; BGO249; Cas PIESD233; Cly DIG12; DRG 8493; Ea EABCD71; Emp RAJCD808; Fmx FA305; Fr DGF50; Hab 111200; HD CDHD230; LE AJA5054, 5117; Music CD6048; Swi CDSW8403, 8413]

257 OLA 1744-1 **Out Of Nowhere** {3.15}
[***78*** **Gr B-8812**, JK-2639, K-8511] [***LP*** Aff BOX107; BBC RED698; LE AJA5054; Pat C054 16004; Swi SW8420267] [***EP*** HMV 7EG8393]

[***CD*** Aff AFS 10035; Arc CASTEL810562; BGO CD249; Cly DIG12; Emp RAJCD808; Fla PASTCD7032; Fmx FA305; Fr DGF50; Hab 111200; HD CDHD230; LE AJA5054; Music CD6048; Swi CDSW8403, 8413]

258 OLA 1745-1 **Sweet Georgia Brown** {2.59}
[***78*** **Gr B-8812**, JK-2639, K-8511] [***LP*** Aff BOX107; Astan LP20102; BBC REB698; LE AJA5054; Pat C054 16004; Swi SW8420267] [***EP*** HMV 7EG8393] [***CD*** Aff AFS 10035; ARC CASTEL810562, SOL507; BGO CD249; Cly DIG12; DRG 8493; Ea EABCD71; Emp RAJCD808; Fla PASTCD7032; Fmx FA305; Fr DGF50; Gal GALE421; HDCDHD230; JH 73509; LE AJA5054; Music CD6048; Swi CDSW8403, 8413]

London — Spring 1937

Article by Hughes Panassié entitled 'How We Recorded For The Swing Label', relating to events in the spring of 1937, appears in *Jazz Express*, 12 December 1947. See Cherrett, page 31 for a reproduction of this article.

Paris — April/May 1937

The QHCF begin a lengthy engagement at Brick Top's 'Big Apple' nightclub. (Abrams)

The magazine *Jazz Hot* (No. 16) publishes an article on Alix Combelle.

Hilversum — Wednesday 26 May 1937

Coleman Hawkins records two titles for Dutch Decca (matrix numbers 382–3). See Rust for details.

Paris — Friday 28 May 1937

from Charles Delaunay
to The Gramophone Company, Hayes, Mddx

Dear Sir,
We suppose that you have heard the test pressings of the recordings we made recently with the Hot-Club de France Quintette. We thought it would be better to write to you concerning these recordings.

First of all, some musical or commercial reasons convinced us to leave aside a few titles that you had suggested: Smoke Rings had been recorded before by the Quintette, Star Dust was not quite suitable to the musicians and it was impossible to obtain from the French publishers the music of Misty Morning.

We can tell you without any exaggeration that the 18 sides recorded (instead of 17) are on the whole better than any of the Quintette's previous records, for their personality as well as for the inspiration. Concerning the two solo pieces by Django Reinhardt they are sensational pieces of music, which may be appreciated not only by jazz but by music lovers in general.

We want to let you know about recordings we have just supervised of Coleman Hawkins, for 'La Voix de son Maitre'.

The first records made with Hawkins in France were not so good, because the Gramophone Co in France imposed us to back up Hawkins with the Warlop gang, which was at that time on of the Co's exclusivities. We had this time more liberty, and had the chance to give the great musician a support worthy of him: Bennie Carter, André Ekyan (alto sax) and Alix Combelle (tenor sax), make the greatest saxophone section that can be heard in Europe. The result is that Hawkins and Bennie Carter play better in these records than they have done it since they have left the States.

These are certainly the best records made in Europe in the past year, and may be you would be interested in hearing them. On account of the results, Bennie Carter is quite willing to make special arrangements for eventual 'Saxophone Quartet' swing records, to be played by Hawkins, Ekyan, Combelle and himself. We think that this should be a unique experience.

We take this opportunity to point out that all the records ever supervised by the Hot-Club de France, such as Bill Coleman's, Garnet Clark's, Freddie Johnson's, Freddy Taylor's, are among the most successful records made in Europe, and we think that it could be interesting for you to give us the chance of having recorded some of the great musicians who are in Paris at present, such as Bill Coleman, Kaiser Marshall (the coloured drummer from Fletcher Henderson's band), Johnny Russell (who played a tenor sax in some of Bennie Carter's records), Roger 'Ram' Rameres (a great coloured piano player from Willie Bryant's band), Coleman Hawkins, Bennie Carter, etc …

Occasionally we wonder if you have heard Bill Coleman's records as we notice that they have not been released in England.

We should very much like to hear from you, to tell us your opinions concerning the above matters.

Sincerely yours
Charles Delaunay,
Hot-Club de France
15, rue du Conservatoire
Paris (9e)

Paris — Saturday 29 May 1937 (9.35pm–10.10pm GMT)

Le Quintet du Hot-Club de France

Stéphane Grappelli (vln); Django Reinhardt (gtr solo); Joseph Reinhardt, Pierre 'Baro' Ferret (gtrs); Louis Vola (sb); Django Reinhardt (gtr solo) (1).
BBC Jazz Show Programme 'Swing That Music'
(*announcer's comments:* {0.18})

259 **Pennies From Heaven** {1.43}
[**unissued**] [***CD*** Fmx FA305]

260 **Exactly Like You** {2.49}
[**unissued**] [***CD*** Fmx FA305]

261 **In The Still Of The Night** {2.13}
[**unissued**] [***CD*** Fmx FA305]

262 **Fat** {1.52}
[**unissued**] [***CD*** Fmx FA305]

263 **Improvised guitar solo No. 1** (1) {1.44}
[**unissued**] [***CD*** Fmx FA305]

264 **Improvised guitar solo No. 2** (1) {1.30}
[**unissued**] [***CD*** Fmx FA305]

This programme was recorded in England by jazz enthusiast Alan Turner, most probably on a machine known as a 'Recording Radiogram', first manufactured by the Dennis Parish Recording Studios of London in 1935. He was unable, for technical reasons, to capture the entire programme, which was broadcast in the following order: Announcer's comments, Quintette tuning up, 'Pennies From Heaven', 'Lady Be Good', 'Improvisation', 'Sweet Chorus', 'Exactly Like You', 'In The Still Of The Night', 'Fat', 'Improvisation No. 2', 'St Louis Blues', 'Bricktop'.
See also Cherrett, page 65.

'The Big Apple' Club, Paris — Sunday 13 June 1937

The Hot Club of France Quintet

Stéphane Grappelli (vln); Django Reinhardt (gtr solos); Joseph Reinhardt and Gusti Mahla (gtrs); Louis Vola (sb).
*CBS radio broadcast The Saturday Night Swing Club (*sic*); acetates*
Announcers: Paul Douglas, New York; Edward R Murrow, Paris
opening comments by Paul Douglas {0.48}
[***CD*** Fmx FA306]

265 *(announced by Edward Murrow)* **Djangology** {1.43}
[**unissued**] [***CD*** Fmx FA306]

266 *(announced by Edward Murrow)* **Limehouse Blues** {2.15}
[**unissued**] [***CD*** Fmx FA306]

267 *(announced by Edward Murrow as 'Break Up')* **Bricktop** {2.10}
(closing remarks by Murrow and Douglas made over the music)
[**unissued**] [***CD*** Fmx FA306]

See Delaunay, pages 87–9 for an account of the events of this night.

Paris — Saturday 19 June 1937

The Senate refuses Léon Blum's demands for emergency fiscal powers, and the cabinet resigns. The government is now reformed around Camille Chautemps of the Radical Socialists as premier and Blum as vice premier.

Paris June–July 1937

The magazine *Jazz Hot* (No. 17) features an article on Coleman Hawkins.

Pathé Studios, Paris Wednesday 7 July 1937

Dicky Wells and His Orchestra

Dickie Wells (tbn); Bill Dillard, Bill Coleman, Shad Collins (tpts) (1); Django Reinhardt (gtr solo); Richard Fullbright (sb); Bill Beason (dms); Bill Coleman (vcl) (2).
Engineer: Eugène Ravenet

268 OLA 1884-1 **Bugle Call Rag** (1) {2.40}
[***78*** Col GN 5038; Gr B-8799; **Swi 6**; Vi 26220] [***LP*** Aff BOX107; Pat C054 16004; Swi SW8420267] [***EP*** HMV 7EMF34]
[***CD*** ABM 1194; Aff AFS 10035; BGO CD249; Cly DIG12; DRG 8493; Fmx FA306; Fr DGF50; JH 73509; Music CD6048; Swi CDSW84213]

269 OLA 1885-1 **Between The Devil And The Deep Blue Sea** (1) {2.55}
[***78*** Col GN 5038; Gr B-8799; **Swi 6**; Vi 26220] [***LP*** Pat C054 16004]
[***EP*** HMV 7EMF34] [***CD*** Aff AFS 10035; DRG 8493; Fmx FA306; Fr DGF50]

270 OLA 1886-1 **I Got Rhythm** (1) {2.12}
[***78*** Col GN 5035; Gr B-8826, SG-20001; ***Swi 27***] [***LP*** Aff BOX107; Ast LP20102; Pat C054 16004; Swi SW8420267] [***CD*** Aff AFS 10035; Avid AMSC568; BGO CD249; Cas PIESD233; Cly CD1048, DIG12; DRG8493; Ea EABCD71; Fmx FA306; Fr DGF50; JH 73509; Music CD6048; Swi CDSW8413]

271 OLA 1887-1 **Sweet Sue** {3.08}
[***78*** Gr B-8763; SG-20002; **Swi 16**] [***LP*** Pat C054 16004]
[***CD*** Aff AFS 10035; Fmx FA306; Fr DGF50]

272 OLA 1888-1 **Hangin' Around Boudon** (2) {2.52}
[***78*** Gr B-8763; SG-20002; **Swi 16**; Vi 26617] [***LP*** Aff BOX107; Pat C054 16004; Swi 8420267] [***CD*** Aff AFS 10035; Arc CASTEL810222; BGO CD249; Cly DIG12; DRG 8493; Fmx FA306; Fr DGF50; Swi CDSW8413]

273 OLA 1889-1 **Japanese Sandman** {2.57}
[***78*** Col GN 5035; Gr B-8826, SG-20001; **Swi 27**] [***LP*** Aff BOX107; Pat C054 16004; Swi SW8420267] [***CD*** Aff AFS 10035; Arc CASTEL810562, SOL507; BGO CD249; Cly DIG12; DRG8493; Fmx FA306; Fr DGF50; Music CD6048; Swi CDSW8413]

Same session as above

André Ekyan – Solo de Saxophone

André Ekyan (as); Django Reinhardt (gtr).

274 OLA 1890-1 **Pennies From Heaven** {2:20}
[**78 Swi 4**] [***LP*** Pat C054 16004] [***CD*** Cls 748; Fmx FA306; Fr DGF50]

275 OLA 1891-1 **Tiger Rag** {2:32}
[**78 Swi 4**] [***LP*** Pat C054 16004] [***CD*** Cls 748; Fmx FA306; Fr DGF50]

Paris — Monday 12 July 1937

'Dicky Wells and his Orchestra' record six titles for Swing records (matrix numbers OLA1894–9). Musicians include Roger Chaput (who substituted for Django Reinhardt at short notice), Shad Collins and Bill Dillard.
See Rust for details.

London — Monday 12 July 1937

Eric Siday records two titles for Parlophone (matrix numbers CE8496–7).
See Rust for details of this and other, unissued, sessions.

The Hague — Monday 16 August 1937

Benny Carter records seven titles for Dutch Decca (matrix numbers 393–400). Musicians include Freddy Johnson and Bertie King.
See Rust for details.

Amsterdam — Wednesday 18 August 1937

Coleman Hawkins records four titles for Dutch Decca, issued on Panachord (matrix numbers 401–2 including alternates). Musicians include Freddy Johnson.
See Rust for details.

Hayes, Middlesex — Thursday 19 August 1937

from International Artists Department, Columbia Graphophone Cy, Hayes, Mddx
to Mr J Bérard Les Industrie Musicale et Electronique Pathé Marconi, Paris

Dear Mr Bérard,

Hot Club de France

Referring to our letter of March 10th and your acknowledgment of April 1st, will you please let us know whether you have yet discussed with Mr. Reinhardt if the following four titles, which his group recorded for Ultraphone, are subject to artists royalty and if the Ultraphone had the exclusive world rights for these recordings.

'Dinah'
'Swanee River'
'Blue Drag'
'Clouds'

As you know, the Nipponophone Company are anxious to obtain the mother shells and exclusive selling rights for Japan of these four recordings, and the last proposition you received from the Ultraphone Company was Fr.500 per mother and a possibility of a royalty payable to the artists.

This matter has been dragging on for some months now, and the Nipponophone Company are pressing for a definitive reply. Will you please, therefore, let us know what the position is and the definite price which we can put forward to our associates.

You will recall that nine Ultraphone records were dispatched to the Nipponophone Company and, apparently, no charge has been made for these. Were these presented by the Ultraphone Company as samples free of charge? If not, perhaps you will let us have your invoice covering these records and postage.

Thanking you,
Yours very truly
[unidentified signature]
Columbia Graphaphone Company Limited,
International Artists Department

EMI Studios, 3 Abbey Road, London NW8 **Saturday 21 August 1937**

Fats Waller records six titles for the Gramophone Company (matrix numbers OEA6383/6384, 6701–4). Musicians include Alan Ferguson and Len Harrison. See Rust for details.

London **September 1937**

Reviews of Quintette of the Hot Club of France: 'Mystery Pacific'/ 'You're Driving Me Crazy' (HMV B8606, 3s.); 'Body And Soul'/'Little Love, A Little Kiss' (HMV B8598, 3s.)

A Little Love finds the combination using its usual recipe, but the ingredients curdled in the mixing. The fundamental rhythm of this number doesn't seem to have found any reflection in the swing make-up of the combination and gets lost between a straight and a dance measure. Reinhardt goes all cadenza and lyrical in the intro, and first half of the chorus, and gets nowhere. The best part is Grappelly's violin in the second chorus. Playing quietly and easily, he finds some nice phrases, and for once doesn't seem to be repeating himself.

Body and Soul brings the group back to something nearer its true form. The interpretation is rhythmical, and the real Reinhardt with his amazing technique and ingenious embroidery comes up again. All round, very pleasant music of its kind, in spite of the unfortunate disturbance of a cough round about the twenty-third bar of the first chorus.

Mystery Pacific and *You're driving me crazy* are very different propositions. First mentioned is one of those flare-up descriptive pieces of a train ride, on the lines of Ellington's *Daybreak Express* (H.M.V. B6468) and in its way almost as clever. It opens up with the train starting off and gathering speed as its whistle blows, none the less interesting because it required some imagination to get such effects on a group of guitars and one fiddle. Reinhardt then wastes time practicing his beloved chords, but the flag waves again on reaching the usual mildly disguised choruses of *Tiger rag* which always seem to duty in numbers which call for something fast and exciting to convey an impression of movement.

I give the record four stars for being smart in its class, but of course it is only a stunt novelty and many will doubtless prefer the coupling, which presents the combination in a more conventional composition, but at the very top of its form. (Edgar Jackson, *The Gramophone*)

Paris — Thursday 9 September 1937

Philippe Brun et Son Orchestre

Philippe Brun (tpt); Stéphane Grappelli (pno); Django Reinhardt (gtr solo); Louis Gasté (gtr); Eugène d'Hellemmes (sb); Maurice Chaillou (dms).
Engineer: Eugène Ravenet

276 OLA 1950-1 **Whoa Babe** [**unissued**]

277 OLA 1950-2 **Whoa Babe** {2.38}
[**78 unissued**] [***EP*** Aus 7EGW8505] [***CD*** Cls 762; Fmx FA306; Fr DGF50; Swi SW 8419]

278 OLA 1951-1 **P.B. Flat Blues** {2.52}
[**78 unissued**] [***LP*** **KC107**] [***CD*** Cls 762; Fmx FA306; Fr DGF50; Swi CDSW8419]

The take of OLA 1950-1 is believed still to be in existence in a private collection.

Same session as above

Django Reinhardt

Reinhardt (gtr solo); Louis Gaste (gtr); Eugène d'Hellemmes (sb).

279 OLA 1952-1 **St Louis Blues** {2.39}
[**78** Gr SG-365, N-4450; **Swi 7**] [***LP*** Aff BOX107; Pat C054 16005; Swa S1399; Swi SW8420267] [***EP*** HMV 7EGH1004; 7EMF40] [***CD*** Aff AFS 10035; BGO CD366; Cls 762; Cly DIG12; Ea EABCD71; Emp RAJCD808; Fmx FA306; Fr DGF50; GALE421; Hab 111200; JSP901; Mos MD 6-190; Music 6048; Recall SMDCD307; Swi CDSW8413]

280 OLA 1953-1 **Bouncin' Around (Rhythm In G Minor)** {2.42}
[**78** Gr SG-365, N-4450; **Swi 7**] [***LP*** Aff BOX107; Pat C054 16005; Swa S1399; Swi SW8420267] [***CD*** Aff AFS 10035; BGO CD366; Cas PIESD233; Cls 762; Cly DIG12; Fmx FA306; Fr DGF50; JSP901; Mos MD 6-190; Swi CDSW8413]

Studio Albert, Paris — Wednesday 29 September 1937

Eddie South (1)
Trio de Violons (2)
Duo de Violons (3)
Michel Warlop and Stephane Grappelli (4)
Stephane Grappelli (5)

Eddie South (vln); Django Reinhardt (gtr); Wilson Myers (sb) (1).
Eddie South, Stéphane Grappelli, Michel Warlop (vlns); Django Reinhardt (gtr solo); Roger Chaput (gtr); Wilson Myers (sb) (2).
As (2), without Warlop (3).
Michel Warlop, Stéphane Grappelli (vlns); Django Reinhardt, Roger Chaput (gtrs) (4).
Stéphane Grappelli (vln); Django Reinhardt (gtr) (5).
Engineer: Georges Cailly

281 OLA 2145-1 **Eddie's Blues** (1) {3.05}
[***78*** Gr B-8778; **Swi 8**; Vi 26222] [***LP*** Aff BOX107; Pat C054 16005; Swa S1252; Swi SW8420267] [***EP*** HMV 7EG8361] [***CD*** Aff AFS 10035; BGO CD249; Cas PIESD233; Cls 707; Cly DIG12; DRG 8493; Fmx FA306; Fr DGF50; Gal GALE451]

282 OLA 2146-1 **Sweet Georgia Brown** (1) {2.43}
[***78*** Gr B-8778; **Swi 8**; Vi 26222] [***LP*** Pat C054 16005; Swa S1252; Swi 8420267] [***EP*** HMV 7EG8361] [***CD*** Aff AFS 10035; BGO CD249; Cls 707; Cly CD1048; DRG8493; Fmx FA306; Fr DGF50; Swi CDSW8413]

283 OLA 2147-1 **Oh! Lady Be Good** (2) {3.14}
[***78*** Swi 45] [***LP*** Aff BOX107; Pat C054 16005; Swa S1399; Swi 8420267] [***EP*** HMV 7EGH1004] [***CD*** Aff AFS 10035; BGO366; Cls 707; Cly CD1048, DIG12; Dig CO3507; DRG 8493; Ea EABCD71; Fmx FA306; Fr DGF 50; Gal GALE451; Mil 74321308652; Music CD6048, Swi CDSW8413]

284 OLA 2148-1 **Dinah** (3) {2.24}
[***78*** Swi 12] [***LP*** Aff BOX107; Pat C054 16005; Swa S1399; Swi SW8420267] [***EP*** HMV 7EGH1005] [***CD*** Aff AFS 10035; Cls 707; DRG8493; Fmx FA306; Fr DGF50; Mil 74321308652; Swi CDSW8426]

285 OLA 2149-1 **Daphne** (3) {2.58}
[***78*** Swi 12] [***LP*** Aff BOX107; Pat C054 16005; Swa S1399; Swi SW8420267] [***EP*** HMV 7EGH1005] [***CD*** Aff AFS 10035; Cly DIG12; DRG 8493; Fmx FA306; Fr DGF50; Milan 74321308652; Swi CDSW8426]

286 OLA 2150-1 **You Took Advantage Of Me** (4) {2.52}
[***78*** Swi 74] [***LP*** Aff BOX107; Pat C054 16005; Swa S1399;

Swi SW8420267] [***EP*** HMV 7EGH1005] [***CD*** Aff AFS 10035; Cls 708; Fmx FA306; Fr DGF50; Mil 7432108652]

287 OLA 1738-2(R) **I've Found A New Baby** (5) {2.33}
[***78*** Swi 21] [***LP*** Pat C054 16005; Swa S1399; Swi SW8420267] [***EP*** HMV 7EGH1004] [***CD*** Aff AFS 10035; BGC CD366; Cls 708; Fmx FA306; Fr DGF50; Gal GALE435; Mil 74321308652]

The recording date for this portion of the session is correct, despite the matrix numbers being out of sequence.

Paris — September–October 1937

The magazine *Jazz Hot* (No. 19) features an article on Eddie South.

Paris — Monday 4 October 1937

Alix Combelle records six titles for Swing records (matrix numbers OLA1955–60). Musicians include Roger Chaput, Bill Coleman, Jerry Mengo, and Wilson Myers.
See Rust for details.

The Hague — probably Sunday 10 October 1937

Quintette du Hot-Club de France

Stéphane Grappelli (vln); Django Reinhardt, Joseph Reinhardt, Eugène Vées (gtrs); probably Louis Vola (sb).

288 [probably] **Swing Guitars** (27 secs) and two other, unidentified and unfilmed fragments, with commentary {1.58 total}
[***CD*** FMX FA307] [***DVD*** MOE 001 ('Swing Guitars' only)]

This is part of a longer film that appears to be a documentary, possibly called *Swing Night*, or incorporating those words in the title. The Quintette's appearance is preceded by a clip of an unidentified white jazz group, which then leads into an introduction in Dutch, which, in translation, reads 'The hot "Quintette du Hot Club de France", under its leader Django Reinhardt, is the great attraction of the "Swing Night".'

The film then moves into a performance by a white group called the 'Swing Papas'.

All three bands are clearly performing on the same stage. There are cutaway shots to dancing couples, but there is no direct filmed evidence of any group playing with dancers in the same shot.

The film was originally made by the Dutch Poligon film company. The remaining two unidentified portions appear to have originally been part of a Dutch radio broadcast.

There is some disagreement about the date of these recordings. Daniel Nevers places them as '*c.* 6/11/37'. Delaunay mentions in the text of his book that the Quintette appeared 'as guests of honour at the amateur jazz band contest', giving the date as 31 October. However, in the 1981 edition of Charles Delaunay's

book, page 232, a photograph clearly taken at the same time as the film was made, and credited to Poligon, is dated by Delaunay as 10 October 1937. Since it seems unlikely that Poligon would have predated a photograph by 21 days, the date of 10 October seems the most feasible.
See Filmography for further details.

Hayes, Middlesex — c. mid October 1937

Inter-office memo: précis of letter received from Pathé-Marconi, Paris, dated Thursday 14 October 1937

> Re: **Hot club de France.**
> Further to our letter of 19 August. They have now got in touch with Django Reinhardt and got him to sign a stamped paper undertaking not to claim royalty for the Ultraphone recordings which the Nipponophone Co wishes to buy. This paper is enclosed in duplicate.
>
> They have also asked the Ultraphone Co. to confirm to them the price of Fr.500 per matrix which they gave them in January last. As the Ultraphone director is at present away, they will give us confirmation of this price – which they think will be maintained – at the beginning of next week.

The paper enclosed says that the records made by D Reinhardt and his artists for the Ultraphone Co. of 'Dinah', 'Swanee River', 'Blue Drag' and 'Clouds' are not subject to any artiste's royalty.

Paris — Monday 18 October 1937

Willie Lewis records six titles for Pathé (matrix numbers CPT3474–9). Musicians include Arthur Briggs, Frank 'Big Boy' Goudie and Wilson Myers.
See Rust for details.

Salle Gaveau, Paris — Wednesday 20 October 1937

The QHCF appear at a Hot-Club concert promoted by *Jazz Hot* magazine, beginning at 9.00pm; they play, at least, 'Bolero', 'Cavaliere', 'Rose Room' and 'Djangologie'.
See Delaunay, page 89.

Paris — November 1937

Extract from *Disques Swing* catalogue No.1 (text accompanying advert for Swing Sw. 2 by the Quintette Du Hot-Club De France).

> The reputation of the Quintette of the Hot-Club de France doesn't need to be made. It's the only European 'hot' orchestra that has gained the admiration of America, the country of jazz. The improvisations of Grappelli on violin and Django Reinhardt on the guitar overflow so much with the richest and most original ideas that it wouldn't be rash to suggest that *Chicago* and *Charleston* are two of this group's most beautiful recordings.

Paris Tuesday 12 November 1937

Bill Coleman, accompanied by Stéphane Grappelli, Joseph Reinhardt, Wilson Myers and Ted Fields (dms) records five titles for Swing records (matrix numbers OLA1974–9).
See Rust for details.

This is also the date, according to Abrams, that Grappelli and Reinhardt actually signed the recording contract with Decca.

Pathé Studios, Paris Tuesday 19 November 1937

Bill Coleman and his Orchestra

Bill Coleman (tpt); Frank 'Big Boy' Goudie (ts, cl) (1); Christian Wagner (cl, as); Emil Stern (pno); Django Reinhardt (gtr); Lucien Simoens (sb); Jerry Mengo (dms).
Engineer: Eugène Ravenet

289 OLA 1979-1 **I Ain't Got Nobody** {2.59}
[***78*** Swi 14] [***LP*** Aff BOX107; Pat C054 16005; Swa S1252; Swi SW8420267] [***CD*** Aff AFS 10035; Cly DIG12; BGO 249; DRG8493; Fmx FA306]

290 OLA 1980-1 **Baby, Won't You Please Come Home?** {2.56}
[***78*** Swi 14] [***LP*** Aff BOX107; Pat C054 16005; Swa S1252; Swi SW8420267] [***CD*** Aff AFS 10035; BGO CD249; Cly DIG12; DRG 8493; Ea EACD71; Fmx FA306; Fr DGF52; Swi CDSW8419]

291 OLA 1980-2 **Baby, Won't You Please Come Home?** {2.58}
[***78*** **unissued**] [***CD*** Fmx FA306; Fr DGF52; **Swing CDSW 8419**]

292 OLA 1981-1 **Big Boy Blues** (1) {3.24}
[***78*** **Swi 32**; Vi 26223] [LP Aff BOX107; Pat C054 16005; Swa S1252, S1308; Swi 8420267] [***CD*** Aff AFS 10035; BGO CD249; Cly DIG12; DRG 8493; Fmx FA306; Fr DGF52]

293 OLA 1982-1 **Swing Guitars** {3.04}
[***78*** **Swi 32**; Vi 26223] [***LP*** Pat C054 16005; Swa S1308] [***CD*** Aff AFS 10035; Cly DIG12; DRG8493; Fmx FA306; Fr DGF52]

Same date

Bill Coleman, Trompete Solo

Bill Coleman (tpt); Django Reinhardt (gtr).

294 OLA 1983-1 **Bill Coleman Blues** {2.45}
[***78*** Col GN 5059; **Swi 42**; Vi 27318] [***LP*** Aff BOX107; Pat C054 16005; Swa S1252; Swi SW8420267] [***CD*** Aff AFS 10035; BGO CD249; Cas PIESD23; Cly DIG12; DRG 8493; Fmx FA306; Fr DGF52; Hab 111200]

Paris Thursday 18 November 1937

The royalist group Les Cagoulards are raided by government authorities and quantities of weapons and munitions, as well as plans for the violent overthrow of the government, are confiscated.

Pathé Studios, Paris — Tuesday 23 November 1937

Eddie South

Eddie South (vln); Django Reinhardt (gtr); as above, with Paul Cordonnier (sb) (1).
Engineer: Eugène Ravenet

295 OLA 1984-1 **Somebody Loves Me** {3.25}
[***78*** Swi 31] [***LP*** Pat C054 16006; Swa S1252, S1370]
[***EP*** HMV 7EG8361, 7EGH1005] [***CD*** Aff AFS10035; Cls 707;
Fmx 306; Fr DGF52]

296 OLA 1985-1 **I Can't Believe That You're In Love With Me** (1) {3.14}
[***78*** Swi 31] [***LP*** Aff BOX107; Pat C054 16006; Swa S1252, S1370;
Swi SW420267] [***EP*** HMV 7EG8361, 7EGH1005] [***CD*** Aff AFS10035;
BGO CD249; Cls 707; Cly DIG12; DRG 8493; Fmx FA306; Fr DGF52;
Swi CDSW8426]

Same location and date

Eddie South and Stephane Grappelli

Eddie South, Stéphane Grappelli (vlns); Django Reinhardt (gtr).

297 OLA 1986-1 **Interprétation Swing du Première Mouvement du Concerto en Re Mineur de Jean-Sébastien Bach** {2.24}
[***78*** Swi 18] [***LP*** Aff BOX107; Pat C054 16006; Swa S1370;
Swi SW8420267] [***CD*** Aff AFS 10035; Cls 707; Cly DIG12;
Fmx FA306; Fr DGF52; Gal GALE451; Swi CDSW8446]

Pathé Studios, Paris — Thursday 25 November 1937

Quintette du Hot-Club de France

Stéphane Grappelli (vln); Django Reinhardt (gtr solo); Joseph Reinhardt, Eugène Vées (gtrs); Louis Vola (sb).
Engineer: Eugène Ravenet

298 OLA 1987 **Bricktop** {3.01}
[***78*** **unissued** *Swing* test] [***CD*** **Fmx FA306**; Fr DGF52; JSP904;
Mos MD 6-190]

299 OLA 1988 **Speevy** {2.50}
[***78*** **unissued** *Swing* test] [***CD*** **Fmx FA306**; Fr DGF52; JSP904;
Mos MD 6-190]

300 OLA 1989 **Cavalerie** [**unissued**]

301 OLA 1990-1 **Minor Swing** {3.13}
[***78*** Swi 23] [***25cm LP*** CHDD 580] [***LP*** Pat C054 16006; Swa S1370;
Swi SW8420267] [***EP*** HMV 7EGH1002, 7EMQ12, (F) 7EGF650]
[***CD*** ABM CD1194; Arc CASTEL 810562, SOL507; BGO CD366;
CC2010; Cls 762; Cly CD1182, DIG12; Dig CO3507; Fmx FA306;

Fr DGF52; Gal GALE421; Hab 111200; HD CDHD206; JH 73509; JSP904; LE AJA5267; Mil 74321308652; Mos MD 6-190; Music CD6049; Recall SMDCD307; Swi CDSW8446]

302 OLA 1991-1 **Viper's Dream** {3.12}
[***78*** Gr SG-367; **Swi 23**; Vi 26218] [***LP*** Swa S1370; Swi SW8420267] [***EP*** HMV 7EGH1006] [***CD*** BGO CD366; Cly DIG12; Cls 762; Ea EABCD76; Fmx FA306; Fr DGF52; Gal GALE421; Hab 111200; JSP904; Mos Md 6-190; Swi CDSW8246]

Matrix OLA1989 was reportedly destroyed accidentally in March 1939. A test pressing is believed to exist, but its current whereabouts are unknown.

Same location, date and engineer

Eddie South and Stéphane Grappelli

Eddie South and Stéphane Grappelli (vlns); Django Reinhardt (gtr).
As above, with Paul Cordonnier (sb) (1).

303 OLA 1992-1 **Fiddle's Blues** (1) {2.43}
[***78*** Swi 45] [***LP*** Aff BOX107; BBC RED680; Pat C054 16006; Swa S1370; Swi SW8420267] [***CD*** Aff AFS10035; Cls 737; DRG 8493; Fmx FA306; Fr DGF52; Mil 74321308652; Swi CDSW8426]

304 OLA 1993-1 **Improvisation sur le Première Mouvement du Concerto en Re Mineur de J-S Bach** {3.17}
[***78*** Swi 18] [***LP*** Pat C054 16006; Swa S1370] [***25cm LP*** CHDD 580]: [***CD*** Aff AFS 10035; Cls 737; DRG 8493; Fmx FA306; Fr DGF52; Gal GALE435; HD CDHD206]

Paris — November–December 1937

The magazine *Jazz Hot* (No. 20) features articles on André Ekyan, Dickie Wells and Swing records ('une nouvelle marque de disques').

London — Wednesday 1 December 1937

The date of commencement for the contract between the Quintette and MPM Entertainments on behalf of the Decca Record Company Ltd.
See Delaunay, page 233 for a reproduction of page 1 of this contract.

Pathé Studios, Paris — Tuesday 7 December 1937

Le Quintette du Hot-Club de France avec Michel Warlop

Stéphane Grappelli, Michel Warlop (vlns); Django Reinhardt (gtr solo); Joseph Reinhardt, Eugène Vées (gtrs); Louis Vola (sb).
Engineer: Eugène Ravenet

305 OLA 1994-1 **Swinging With Django** {2.48}
[***78*** **Swi 40**; Vi 27272 (A, Ca)] [***LP*** Aff BOX107; Pat C054 16006; Swa S1370; Swi SW8420267] [***EP*** HMV 7EGH1006] [***CD*** Aff AFS 10035; BGO CD366; CC 2010; Cls 762; Dig CO3507;

Fmx FA306; Fr DGF52; HD CDHD206; JSP 904; Mil 74321308652; Mos MD 6-190; Swi CDSW8426]

306 OLA 1995-1 **Paramount Stomp** {2.34}
[***78*** **Swi 40**]; Vi 27272 (A, Ca)] [***LP*** Aff BOX107; Pat C054 16006; Swa S1370; Swi SW8420267] [***CD*** Aff AFS 10035; BGO CD366; Cls 762; Fmx FA306; Fr DGF52; HD CDHD206; JSP 904; Mil 74321308652; Mos MD 6-190; Swi CDSW8426]

Salle de L'Ecole Normale de Musique, Paris — Friday 10 December 1937

Concert featuring Eddie South, Garnet Clark, Garland Wilson and Una Mae Carlisle.

Pathé Studios, Paris — Tuesday 14 December 1937

Le Quintette du Hot-Club de France, les Cuivres et les Cordes

Philippe Brun, Gus Deloof, André Cornille (tpts); Guy Paquinet, Josse Breyere (tbns); Michel Warlop, Paul Bartel, Joseph Swetschin (vlns); Django Reinhardt (gtr solo, arr); Joseph Reinhardt, Eugène Vées (gtrs); Louis Vola (sb) (1).
As above, without Warlop and Swetschin (2).
Engineer: Eugène Ravenet

307 X2LA 1996-1 **Boléro** (1) {4.03}
[***78*** **Gr L-1046**; Vi JB215] [***25cm LP*** CHDD 855] [***LP*** Aff BOX107; Pat C054 16006; Swa S1370; Swi 8420267] [***CD*** Aff AFS 10035; Cls 762; Cly DIG12; Fmx FA306; Fr DGF52; JSP 904; Mos MD 6-190; Swi CDSW8426]

308 X2LA 1996-2 **Boléro** (1) {3.55}
[***78*** **unissued**] [***LP*** **KC 109**] [***CD*** Fmx FA306; Fr DGF52; JSP 904; Mos MD 6-190]

309 X2LA 1997-1 **Mabel** (2) {4.00}
[***78*** **unissued**] [***CD*** **Fmx FA306**; Fr DGF52; JSP 904; Mos MD 6-190]

310 X2LA 1997-2 **Mabel** (2) {4.09}
[***78*** Gr L-1046] [***LP*** Pat C054 16006; Swa S1370] [***CD*** Aff AFS 10035; Cls 762; Fmx FA306; Fr DGF52; JSP 904; Mos MD 6-190]

A voice, probably Django's, can be heard issuing an instruction to play quietly (saying 'ssshhhhh') at 3.47 on this master.
The above four X2LA matrices are 30cm (12") diameter masters/pressings.

Same location, date and engineer

Quintette du Hot-Club de France

Stéphane Grappelli (vln); Django Reinhardt (gtr solo); Joseph Reinhardt, Eugène Vées (gtrs); Louis Vola (sb).

311 OLA 1998-1 **My Serenade** {2.58}
[***78*** Swi 77] [***LP*** Aff BOX107; Pat C054 16006; Swa S1370; Swi SW8420267] [***EP*** An 73007; HMV 7EGH1006]

[***CD*** Aff AFS 10035; Cls 762; Cly DIG12; Ea EABCD71; Fmx FA306; Fr DGF52; Gal GALE421; JSP 901; Mos MD 6-190; Swi CDSW8426]

Pathé Studios, Paris — Tuesday 21 December 1937

Michel Warlop et son Orchestre

Michel Warlop (vln); André Pico (tpt) (1); André Lamory, Jean Magnien (cl, fl); Charles Schaaf (cl, ts); Georges Paquay (fl) (1), (dms) (2); Pierre Zeppilli (pno); Django Reinhardt (gtr); Louis Vola (sb).
As above, without Pico (2).
Engineer: Eugène Ravenet

312 OLA 1999-1 **Serenade For A Wealthy Widow** (1) {3.12}
[***78*** Swi 28] [***LP*** Pat C054 16006; Swa S1370] [***CD*** Cls 762; Fmx FA307]

313 OLA 2000-1 **Taj Mahal** (2) {3.19}
[***78*** Swi 28] [***LP*** Pat C054 16006; Swa S1370] [***CD*** Cls 762; Fmx FA307]

314 OLA 2214-1 **Organ Grinder's Swing** (1) {2.33}
[***78*** Col GN 5044; **Swi 43**] [***LP*** Pat C054 16007]
[***EP*** HMV 7EGH1006] [***CD*** Cls 762; Fmx FA307]

Same location, date and engineer

Django Reinhardt – solo de guitarre

Django Reinhardt (gtr); Louis Vola (sb).

315 OLA 2215-1 **You Rascal You** {3.03}
[***78*** Swi 35] [***LP*** Pat C054 16007; Swa S1399; Swi SW8420267]
[***CD*** Aff AFS 10035; Cas PIESD233; Cls 762; Cly DIG12; Fla PASTCD9792; Fmx FA307; JSP 904; Mos MD 6-190; Swi CDSW8426]

Same location, date and engineer

Michel Warlop – solos de violon

Michel Warlop (vln); Django Reinhardt (gtr); Louis Vola (sb) (1).

316 OLA 2216-1 **Tea For Two** {3.12}
[***78*** Swi 13] [***LP*** Aff BOX107; Pat C054 16007; Swa S1399; Swi SW8420267] [***CD*** Cls 762; Cly DIG12; Fla PASTCD9792; Fmx FA307; Gal GALE421; Hab 111200; Swi CDSW8426]

317 OLA 2217-1 **Christmas Swing** (1) {2.47}
[***78*** Swi 13] [***LP*** Pat C054 16007; Swa S1399] [***CD*** ABM 1130; Cls 762; Cly DIG12; Fmx FA307; HD CDHD234]

Pathé Studios, Paris — Monday 27 December 1937

Stéphane Grappelly – solos de violon

Stéphane Grappelli (vln); Django Reinhardt (gtr).
Engineer: Eugène Ravenet

318 OLA 2218-1 **Stephen's Blues** {3.13}
[*78* Swi 69] [***LP*** Aff BOX107; Pat C054 16007; Swa S1399; Swi SW420267] [***CD*** Aff AFS 10035; Cls 708; Fla PASTCD9792; Fmx FA307; Gal GALE435; JSP 904; Mil 74321308652; Mos MD 6-190; Swi CDSW8426]

319 OLA 2219-1 **Sugar** {3.00}
[*78* Swi 69] [***LP*** Aff BOX107; Pat C054 16007; Swa S1400; Swi SW420267] [***CD*** Aff AFS 10035; Cls 708; Fla PASTCD9792; Fmx FA307; Gal GALE435; JSP 904; Mil 74321308652; Mos MD 6-190; Swi CDSW8426]

Same location, date and engineer

Django Reinhardt – solos de guitare

Django Reinhardt (gtr) (1).
As above, acc. by Stéphane Grappelli (pno) (2).

320 OLA 2220-1 **Sweet Georgia Brown** (1) {3.13}
[*78* Swi 35] [***LP*** Pat C054 16007; Swa S1400] [***EP*** HMV 7EMF40] [***CD*** Aff AFS 10035; Cls 762; Fmx FA307; JSP 904; Mos MD 6-190]

321 OLA 2221-1 **Tea For Two** (2) {2.47}
[*78* Swi 211] [***LP*** Pat C054 16007; Swa S1400] [***CD*** Aff AFS 10035; Cls 762; Fmx FA307; JSP 904; Mos MD 6-190]

Same location, date and engineer

Philippe Brun – solo de trompette

Philippe Brun (tpt); Stéphane Grappelli (celeste); Django Reinhardt (gtr).

322 OLA 2222-1 **Blues** {3.00}
[*78* Swi 54] [***LP*** Aff BOX107; Pat C054 16007; Swa S1400; Swi SW8420267] [***CD*** Aff AFS 10035; Cls 762; Cly DIG12; Fmx FA307; Swi CDSW8426]

There was believed to have been an un-numbered test of 'Easy Going' by Brun, Grappelli and Reinhardt made at this session, which was either lost or destroyed. See following session.

Pathé Studios, Paris — Tuesday 28 December 1937

Philippe Brun and his Swing Band

Philippe Brun, Gus Deloof, André Cornille (tpt); Josse Breyere, Guy Paquinet (tbn); Max Blanc, Charles Lissée (cl, as); Jacques Helian (ts); Alix Combelle (cl, ts); Stéphane Grappelli (pno); Django Reinhardt (gtr); Louis Vola (sb); Maurice Chaillou (dms).
Arr. by Deloof and Breyere.
Engineer: Eugène Ravenet

323 OLA 2223-1 **Easy Going** {2.58}
[***78*** Swi 26] [***LP*** Aff BOX107; Pat C054 16007; Swi SW8420267]
[***CD*** Aff AFS 10035; Cls 762; Fmx FA307; Swi CDSW8419, 8426]

324 OLA 2223-2 **Easy Going** [**unissued**]

325 OLA 2308-1 **College Stomp** {2.57}
[***78*** Swi 15] [***LP*** Aff BOX107; Pat C054 16024; Swi SW8420267]
[***CD*** Aff AFS 10035; Cls 762; Fmx FA307; Swi CDSW8426]

326 OLA 2308-2 **College Stomp** [**unissued**]

327 OLA 2309-1 **I Wonder?** [**unissued**]

328 OLA 2310-1 **Harlem Swing** {2.32}
[***78*** Swi 15] [***LP*** Pat C054 16007] [***CD*** Aff AFS 10035; Cls 762; Fmx FA307]

Same location, date and engineer

Philippe Brun 'Jam' Band

Philippe Brun (tpt); Alix Combelle (cl, ts); Michel Warlop (vln); Stéphane Grappelli (pno); Django Reinhardt (gtr); Louis Vola (sb); Maurice Chaillou (dms).

329 OLA 2311-1 **It Had To Be You** {2.41}
[***78*** Swi 44] [***LP*** Pat C054 16024] [***CD*** Aff AFS 10035; Cls 777; Fmx FA307]

Same date

Michel Warlop – solos de violon

Michel Warlop (vln); Stéphane Grappelli (pno); Django Reinhardt (gtr); Louis Vola (sb).

330 OLA 2312-1 **Sweet Sue (Just You)** {2.26}
[***78*** Col GN 5044; **Swi 43**] [***LP*** Aff BOX107; Pat C054 16007; Swa S1400; Swi SW8420267] [***CD*** BGO CD249; Cly DIG12; Cls 777; DRG 84213; Ea EABCD71; Fmx FA307; Swi CDSW8413]

probably Paris 1938

'Ray Ventura et ses Collégiens' appear in the film *Feux de joie*.
See Filmography.

New York 1938

Metronome magazine publishes an article entitled 'Is This The Best Small Swing Group?'
See Cruickshank, page 105 for a reproduction.

Paris 1938

Charles Delaunay publishes the revised edition of *Le Jazz hot* (Editions Jazz Hot).

London Saturday 1 January 1938

Big Party from France Coming to Town for Grappelly–Reinhardt 'M.M.' Concert.
All 3/6 tickets sold out

The *Melody Maker* concerts for musicians promoted by Leslie MacDonnell, principal of MPM Entertainments Corporation Ltd, at which the famous Quintette of the Hot Club of France will make its first British appearance, is rapidly selling out.

The concert does not take place until Saturday January 30, and with four weeks yet to go the 3s. 6d. Upper Circle seats have all been bought and no more are available at the price.

Curiously enough, there has been an even bigger demand for five-shilling seats, especially in the back of the stalls, where, by last Wednesday, there were only some five dozen more to be sold. Similarly, there was a big run on the five-shilling seats in the Dress Circle, and, in fact, the whole of the accommodation there has gone.

The upshot of all this is that the five shilling seats now left, apart from the few dozen in the stalls, are limited to the front rows of the upper circle, and all those who want five shilling seats will have to give their orders in at once, or else they will be disappointed.

To show what a great significance attaches to the concert beyond the shores of England, it is only necessary to announce that a large party from France is travelling to London especially to witness it, This party is organised by 'Le Jazz Hot', the French equivalent to the *Melody Maker*, under the direction of Mr. Pierre Nourry, who has done so much to publicise the Quintette internationally.

At the M.M. concert it is expected that the Quintet's own special compositions *Daphne*, *Brick Top*, *Minor Swing*, *Bolero* (*de Django*), *Mystery Pacific*, *Djangology* and *Swing Guitars* will be among the most individual items. (Unsigned, *Melody Maker*)

London Tuesday 4 January 1938

Eric Siday records 'Tiger Rag' for Parlophone (matrix number CE8883). See Rust for details.

Columbia Studios, Paris Wednesday 5 January 1938

Jacotte Perrier et le Quintette du Hot-Club de France

Jacotte Perrier (vcl) acc. by Stéphane Grappelli (vln); Django and Joseph Reinhardt (gtrs); Sigismund Beck (sb).
Engineer: Georges Cailly

331 CL 6502-1 **Les Salades De L'Oncle François** {2.11}
[***78*** Col DF2344] [***LP*** Swi SW8420267] [***CD*** Fmx FA307; Swi CDSW 8419]

332 CL 6502-2 **Les Salades De L'Oncle François** [**unissued**]

333 CL 6503-1 **Ric Et Pussy** {2.38}
[***78*** Col DF2344] [***LP*** Swi SW8420267] [***CD*** Fmx FA307]

334 CL 6503-2 **Ric Et Pussy** [**unissued**]

Paris Friday 14 January 1938

The Socialists resign from the cabinet following an attempted reorganization by Chautemps.

London Saturday 15 January 1938

Radio Citie May Broadcast 'M.M.'s' Grappelly Reinhardt Concert
Cambridge Theatre Nearly Sold Out

Needless to say, French dance musicians are very elated about the *Melody Maker* concert on Sunday, January 30, which is to result in Stephane Grappelly and Django Reinhardt with their Quintette making their first public appearance in England.

The Quintet has put French dance music well on the world map and naturally enough its countrymen are anxious that Britishers should realize, in person, that the claims made for the Famous Five are not the result on national bias.

The Hot Club of France is arranging a special party of its members to attend the concert, and it is expected that there will be quite a large contingent in the stalls.

Over and above this, however, there is quite a lot of excitement throughout France, so much so that the ambitious little broadcasting station Radio Citie has applied to the *Melody Maker* for permission to broadcast the concert on its wavelengths, and this permission has been granted.

Unfortunately, the strength of the station is not such that it can be picked up in England except in the south, and by very good sets, so it still remains that visitors who wish to hear the orchestra ... will have to depend on buying tickets, of which very few now remain.

The concert, of course, takes place at the Cambridge Theatre, Great Earl Street, near Cambridge Circus, at 2.30pm. (Unsigned, *Melody Maker*)

Paris or London Sunday 23 January 1938

Django Reinhardt's 28th birthday.

Paris Thursday 27 January 1938

Eddie South plays a 'Farewell Concert' at L'Ecole Normale de Musique, accompanied by Garland Wilson, with Adelaide Hall as special guest.
See 5 February entry for a report of this event.

London Saturday 29 January 1938

Sold Out

As foretold from the beginning by the 'M.M.', all seats for the Swing Concert for Musicians which the old paper is presenting this Sunday at the Cambridge Theatre at 2.30pm have now been sold, but there are still optimists who hoped to pay for the privilege of standing. There is very little accommodation in this respect, however.

Django Reinhardt arrived in London at the beginning of this week and has enjoyed himself hunting up the boys. His partner, Stephane Grappelly, and the rest of the Hot Club of France ... arrive on Friday. Intensive rehearsals are going on in the Sidney Leopold camp, and Claude Bampton's Blind Orchestra are hard at it, too.

They will all meet on Sunday morning next for a complete rehearsal of the show, and the curtain goes up at 2.30pm sharp, with Chappie D'Amato, our compere, in charge of the stage.

In every way it looks as though this will be the most spectacular concert yet staged by the 'M.M.' and certainly there could be no better theatre for the job than the Cambridge.

Unfortunately, it looks as though Radio Citie has abandoned its intention to broadcast the concert. The B.B.C., which was providing technical facilities, has informed the 'M.M.' of the cancellation, but no direct notification has been received. (Unsigned, *Melody Maker*)

Cambridge Theatre,
Great Earl Street, London WC1 Sunday 30 January 1938 at 2.30pm

The Quintette appear as the star attraction in the 'Swing Music Concert For Musicians', sponsored by the weekly British journal the *Melody Maker*. Also appearing on the bill are The Mills Brothers, Eric Siday, Reg Leopold and 'Frenchie' Sorrell, and Claude Bampton's Blind Orchestra. The compere was Noel 'Chappie' D'Amato. The Quintette play, at least, 'Mystery Pacific', 'Bolero', 'Swing Guitars' and 'Daphne'.

See 5 February entry for the *Melody Maker* report, Cherrett, pages 23–4 for a facsimile of the programme for this concert, and Cherrett, page 26, for another contemporary report. See also Delaunay, page 90.

Decca Studios, Upper Thames Street,
London EC4 Monday 31 January 1938

Quintette du Hot-Club de France avec Django Reinhardt and Stéphane Grappelli (French language issues)/**The Quintette of the Hot Club of France with Django Reinhardt (Guitar) and Stephane Grappelly (Violin)** (English and Australian issues)/**Quintet of Hot Club of France** (US Decca)

Stéphane Grappelli (vln); Django Reinhardt (gtr solos); Roger Chaput, Eugène

Vées (gtrs); Louis Vola (sb), (bowed sb) (4); Reinhardt (comments) (1); Louis Vola (comments) (2); band members (comments) (3).
Engineer: Arthur Lilley

335 DTB 3523-1 **Honeysuckle Rose** {2:53}
[***78*** Br 505269, A-81503; **De F-6639** (B, E, F, H), 538, 23066; Od 284393; Pol A-315] [***25cm LP*** De 124015] [***LP*** AoC ACL 1158; LE AJA5070; Meteor MTM12] [***CD*** Cls 777; Dig CO3507; Fmx FA307; Gal GALE421; HD CDHD206; JH JHR73509; JSP 342; LE AJA5267; Milan 74321308652; Music CD6048]

336 DTB 3524-1 **Sweet Georgia Brown** (1) {3:06}
[***78*** Br 505270, Br A-81603; De **F-6675** (B, E, F, H), F-9045, F-9428, Y-5227, 542, 23065; Od 284393; Poly 624076] [***LP*** AoC ACL1158; BT LP2636771; LE AJA5070; Met MTM12; Verve 8451501] [***CD*** Cls 777; Dig CO3507; Fmx FA307; JSP 342; LE AJA5267]

337 DTB 3525-1 **Night And Day** {2:40}
[***78*** Br 505271, A-82559, A-81436; **De F-6616** (E, F), F-6616, F-8068, Y-5212, 23067; Od 284537; Poly 624076] [***LP*** AoC ACL1158; HD CHD165; LE AJA5070] [***CD*** Avid AMSC648; Cls 777; Dig CO3506; Fmx FA307; Gal GALE421; HD HDCD165; JSP 342; LE AJA5267; Milan 74321308652; Recall SMDCD307]

338 DTB 3526-1 **My Sweet** (1, 2, 3) {2:55}
[***78* unissued**] [***CD*** Fmx FA307; **JSP 342**]

339 DTB 3526-2 **My Sweet** (1, 2, 3) {2:53}
[***78*** Br 505270, A-81685; **De F-6769** (E, F), 9428, 573, 89045] [***LP*** AoC ACL1158; LE AJA5070] [***CD*** Cls 777; DIG CO3506; Fmx FA307; Gal GALE421; HD CDHD206; Hab 111200; JSP 342; Recall SMDCD307]

340 DTB 3527-1 **Souvenirs** (4) {2:44}
[***78*** Br 505269; **De F-6639** (B, E, F, H), 538, 23065; Poly A-315] [***25cm LP*** De 124015] [***LP*** AoC ACL1158] [***CD*** Avid AMSC648; Cls 777; Fmx FA307; HD CDHD206; JSP 342]

341 DTB 3528-1 **Daphne** {3:08}
[***78*** Br A-81685; **De** (E) **F-6769** (E, F), 573, 23152; Od 284357] [***LP*** AoC ACL1158] [***CD*** Cls 777; Dig CO3507; Fmx FA307; Gal GALE421; HD CDHD234; JSP 342; LE AJA5267; Recall SMDCD307]

342 DTB 3529-1 **Black and White** (3) {3:03}
[***78*** Br A-81603; 1610; **De F-6675** (B, E, F, H), Y-5227, 542, 23067] [***LP*** AoC ACL1158; LE AJA5070] [***CD*** Cls 777; Fmx FA307; JSP 342; Mil 74321308652]

343 DTB 3530-1 **Stompin' At Decca** {2:32}
[***78*** Br(G) A-81436; A-82559; **De F-6616** (E, F) F-8086, Y-5212, 23066]

[***LP*** AoC ACL1158; HD CHD165] [***CD*** Avid AMSC648; Cls 777; Fmx FA307; Gal GALE435; HD CDHD165; JSP 342]

See Fremeaux, page 307, for a photo taken at the above session.

Decca Studios, Upper Thames Street,
London EC4 Tuesday 1 February 1938

Django Reinhardt – guitar solo

Django Reinhardt (gtr); Stéphane Grappelli (pno).
Engineer: Arthur Lilley

344 DTB 3531-1 **Tornerai (J'attendrai)** {2:30}
[**78 De F-6721**, Y-5262, 23079] [***LP*** De MOR530; HD CHD165] [***CD*** Avid AMSC648; Cls 708; Dig CO3507; Fmx FA307; HD CDHD165; JSP 342]

Same session

Django Reinhardt (guitar) and Stephane Grappelly (piano) (English-language issues)

345 DTB 3532-1 **If I Had You** {2:47}
[**78 De F-6721**, 23098] [***LP*** HD CHD165] [***CD*** Avid AMSC648; Cls 708; Ea EABCD71; Fmx FA307; HD CDHD165; JSP 342]

Same location, date and engineer

Stéphane Grappelli (European Decca)/Stephane Grappelly and His Hot 4 (US Decca)

Stéphane Grappelli, (vln) (1), (pno) (2); Django Reinhardt (gtr).

346 DTB 3533-1 **It Had To Be You** (1, 2) {2:51}
[**78 De F-7009**, 23079] [***LP*** De MOR530] [***CD*** Avid AMSC648; Cls 708; Fmx FA307; Gal GALE435; JSP 342; Recall SMDCD307]

347 DTB 3534-1 **Nocturne** (1) {3:12}
[**78 De F-7009**, 23098] [***LP*** AoC ACL1189] [***CD*** Cls 708; Fmx FA307; Gal GALE435; JSP 342]

London Saturday 5 February 1938

The French Quintet Staggers Swing Concert Audience
Ovations For Everybody

'They came, they were seen, they conquered.'

That, in brief, summarises the conclusions of the vastly exciting Swing Music Concert, staged by the *Melody Maker* for M.P.M. Entertainments Corporation Ltd., at the Cambridge Theatre, last Sunday afternoon.

The five French musketeers of modern dance music had been known here for some years through their records. We had become accustomed to their slick methods of writing, orchestrating and playing, but never having heard them in person, we had come to take everything for granted and, latterly, our record reviewers had ceased to rave about them.

It is probably true to say, therefore, that hardly any visitor at the concert was prepared for the real thrill we were all to get from this music.

The Quintet appeared twice; firstly to open Part 1 of the concert, and finally as the second of the three turns in Part 2.

The reception from the audience should have pleased them, but as it subsequently appeared, they are used to more demonstrative and voluble audiences in their own country, and the phlegm of the British crowd may, at first, have given them the impression that we're a tough lot over here.

They couldn't have thought this, however, when they took their final call. Salvoes of applause crashed over their deserving heads as they lined up in front of the tabs, grinning delightedly at their overwhelming success. If they had missed, during their playing, the familiar calls of the French 'cats' and the wild clapping after every solo passage, such as they get at home, they will now realize that the rapt attention paid every single note by their British audience was none the less flattering, and in its way, even more complimentary.

The Quintet is curiously static as it plays. The three guitarists, sitting in a widely spaced line with Django in the centre, hardly bat an eyelid. The maestro occasionally cocks an eyebrow in concentration or permits an enigmatic smile to pass across his face, but, except for an almost imperceptible rocking, there is no movement, no showmanship, no gallery play whatsoever.

Grappelly, standing, works to the mike with great skill and experience. Unobtrusively he moves to the flank when he is tacit, a polished, good-looking grave-faced sort of fellow who plays like an angel. Louis Vola, the bassist, was a personal hit with the spectators. Once or twice he amused them with a little byplay, but he had already endeared himself to all by his beautiful tone and technique.

What can one say of Reinhardt adequately to appraise his enormous talents? His command of the instrument, his own self-developed technique, the subtle nuances imparted to every note struck, the terrific fecundity of his musical imagination, all tended to exhibit him as one of the greatest guitarists of his day.

He is, quite obviously, the main inspiration of the Quintet, and, in himself, is almost even a justification of that egregious organization known as the Hot Club de France. In having produced Reinhardt, let alone the Quintet, the Hot Club might well be forgiven much of that humourless fanaticism which mars its outlook on jazz matters.

Django's partner, Stephane Grappelly, is in no way overshadowed, however. That beautiful tone of his, that facile technique, that delightful and moving phrasing, judged by all legitimate standards, are impeccable.

So is the whole Quintet. Orchestrally they are like the Mills Brothers in their musical finish and their grave deportment. Credit to both Vées and

Chaput, the two other guitarists, self-effacing machines who never take a solo bar but who provide a foundation for their two principles, which is uncanny in its accuracy, aptness and understanding.

Rhythmically? Well, that is another matter. The Quintet's music is an amazing reconciliation between the commercial and the extreme. Maybe it's good for dancing and maybe not. Who wants to dance to music which is as good as this? Who wants to dance to Ellington? If the Quintet doesn't play swing music it plays darned good music, and that's the last word on that.

Considering that there was no opportunity for a full dress-rehearsal, the work of the stage staff was admirable, intelligent and most co-operative. For this, sincere thanks to the Cambridge Theatre's own stage manager and to Dave Toff, of M.P.M, who was here, there and everywhere knocking routines into order. Also, a belated but none the less spontaneous tribute to Chappie D'Amato, who as the compere, coupled informality with polish, and wit with respect. If he had to do it for as living he would go places.

So to the French and British National Anthems, the post-mortems backstage, and the excited chatter all round the theatre, as the well-pleased audience departed homeward.

It appears that everyone was thoroughly delighted, and the 'M.M.' even more so, because we had a swell audience. (Mathison Brooks, *Melody Maker*)

London Saturday 5 February 1938

Eddie South Holds Audience Spellbound in Farewell Concert

While so much talk of violinists, of swing music concerts, and of the Hot Club de France is still in the air, it might be apposite to point out that the *Melody Maker* was not the only organization to unite these elements last week. On Thursday, the Hot Club de France presented Eddie South and his four-piece accompaniment in a farewell concert prior to his departure from Paris to play a four-week theatre engagement in Amsterdam.

So many imaginative stories have been circulated about the ardour of Continental swing fans that a description of the evening may surprise you. The reception was more enthusiastic than eclectic, and when Garland Wilson came on as an interpolated act, his high-speed demolition of *Tiger Rag*, complete with solo choruses by the drummer, had a much bigger hand than his excellent interpretation of the blues.

The Ecole Normale de Musique, a widc but shallow hall with a circular stage, shocking acoustics and no amplification, is scarcely the best place in which to appreciate Eddie South's genius. Yet, from the moment when he plunged into Lady Be Good, right through the long programme of items selected on the spot, and in most cases not even announced, I was spellbound by the magnitude of his technique and style. It is a double tragedy that he has not been able to reintroduce himself to the British public during his current tour, but he has also been met with a series of catastrophes in the shape of night clubs on the verge of bankruptcy, three illnesses in his family and other misfortunes. When his engagement in Holland ends he may be free to give a concert or two in England before returning to America. (Unsigned, *Melody Maker*)

London week of 14 February 1938

Django Reinhardt, Stéphane Grappelli and Charles Delaunay are guests of the No. 1 Rhythm Club.

Paris March 1938

Jazz Hot publishes the results of the Hot-Club poll for best jazz records of the previous year. The details are:

Le Grand Prix du Disque Hot 1937
Dickie Wells and his Orchestra, *Between The Devil And The Deep Blue Sea* (Swing 4).

The Best American Recordings Published in France in 1937
1st prize: Louis Armstrong and The Mills Brothers, *Darling Nelly Gray* (Brunswick 505097).
2nd prize: Fats Waller and his Orchestra, *You're Not The Only Oyster In The Stew* (Gram K.7861).
Joint 3rd prize: Jimmie Lunceford, *I'll See You In My Dreams* (Brunswick 500697); Duke Ellington, *In A Jam* (Brunswick 500677).

The Best Recordings Published in Europe in 1937
1st prize: Coleman Hawkins and his All-Star Jam Band, *Crazy Rhythm* (Swing 1).
Joint 2nd prize: Teddy Weatherford, *Weather Beaten Blues* (Swing 5); Eddie South, *Sweet Georgia Brown* (Swing 8).
3rd prize: Willie Lewis and his Orchestra, *Sweet Sue* (Pathé PA1030).

The Best Recordings by French Musicians in 1937
1st prize: Quintette du Hot-Club de France, *Chicago* (Swing 2).
Joint 2nd prize: André Ekyan, *Pennies From Heaven* (Swing 4); Django Reinhardt, *Saint-Louis Blues* (Swing 7).
3rd prize: Michel Warlop et son Orchestre, *Harlem Hurricane* (Columbia DF2040).

Review of Michel Warlop, 'Tea For Two'/'Christmas Swing' (Swing 13)

'*Tea for Two*' is one of Warlop's best records to date. The number is taken at a very slow tempo, extremely favourable for Warlop's delightfully melodic style. The first chorus in particular is full of charming ideas. I want to call your attention also to the first phrases of the second chorus, following the verse on which Django plays a highly original solo. Warlop begins with several chords in a manner reminiscent of Eddie South, but which is none the less personal, and, in any case, charming to the highest degree.

'Christmas *Swing*' is taken at an extremely fast tempo, which is usually less than favourable to hot improvisation, but in this particular instance, one must confess that Warlop manages it very well. In certain Hot Club concerts, he sometimes has played in a slightly unorganised way on very fast tempos, while here, he develops the theme in a logical, very coherent fashion, with long phrases some of which are very pretty in contour.

The use of a mute on these two sides gives Warlop's violin a very phonogenic sonority.

Warlop is accompanied by Django alone in '*Tea For Two*', by both Django and Vola on the reverse. Django's accompaniment is in the same imagination strain [*sic*] as on the Eddie South and Ekyan records already released by Swing. And his first chorus-solo in '*Christmas Swing*' is astounding. (Hughes Panassié, *Jazz Hot*)

Review of Bill Coleman and his Orchestra, 'I Ain't Got Nobody'/'Baby Won't You Please Come Home' (Swing 14)

These are two entirely improvised executions. '*I Ain't Got Nobody*' is clearly the better side. The number is certainly on of the best jazz themes and the musicians are generally very inspired on it. Bill Coleman is in great form. One feels his absolute mastery in the first chorus, so restrained and yet so full of ideas (ideas often so subtle that, as sometimes happens with Coleman, one doesn't get them all right off. Big Boy is splendid in the second chorus. He is one of those rare tenor saxes that don't copy Hawkins. On the contrary, he keeps to his old pure style and his trenchant tone with the slightest suspicion of the effeminate lisping of most Hawkins imitators. A direct style with extremely well constructed phrases. There are very few tenor saxes whom I place above 'Big Boy'. In the third chorus, Christian Wagner asserts himself as one of the best French clarinettists. He plays with a dirty, very effective growl, and is evidently inspired by the number, for his embroidery is full of pretty contours.

The last chorus is a very successful collective improvisation, the three musicians get together very well. Big Boy's part is particularly intelligent, and Bill Coleman charms me more than ever, notably by the inflected ascending note on the eight bar of the chorus.

The rhythm section is excellent, and Jerry Mengo plays better here than on Swing's recent Combelle disc. Django's time seems more marvelous than ever on this disc. What a musician!

'*Baby Won't You Please Come Home*' is also a very pretty theme, but, although the solos are agreeable enough, there is not as much inspiration in most of them. I like especially Wagner's alto solo, Big Boy's and Django's. The only bad thing about the record is the insipid, cliché coda, very badly played into the bargain. (Hughes Panassié, *Jazz Hot*)

Review of Philippe Brun and his Swing Band, 'College Stomp'/ 'Harlem Swing' (Swing 15)

> Here is the first record made by a 13 piece white European band which can stand up beside the records of the great white American orchestras. Which alone should make it an event in jazz history ... The brass section is entirely that of Ray Ventura, whose extraordinary worth we know well – it's by far the best in Europe ...
>
> 'College *Stomp*' is an arrangement by Philippe Brun of a simple and direct composition. Its style recalls the good old days, with clarinet ensemble in the upper register like in the old Fletcher Henderson records, and a blues chorus by its saxes and clarinets in unison answered by the brasses ...
>
> After a first part devoted to brass and clarinet ensembles, a classical 12 bar blues theme makes its appearance with two splendid trumpet choruses by Brun, in exemplary style, which stand out admirably and are played with rare force and precision. A little further, Josse Breyere on trombone and Max Blanc on alto take two choruses on the same theme, and the record finishes with a well carried-off ensemble.
>
> '*Harlem Swing*' is arranged in very good style by Gus Deloof. On this side. Combelle takes an impressively powerful chorus, perhaps his finest recorded to date. What swing! Django and Philippe Brun also have good solos but Philippe is somewhat overshadowed by a too strongly recorded sax accompaniment.
>
> What is particularly astounding is the ensemble swing which is as good on the part of the melodic section ... who would have believed that a European orchestra of this composition could have made so wonderful a record? (Hughes Panassié, *Jazz Hot*)

All Panassié reviews were originally translated by Walter E Schapp.

London — March 1938

Review of Quintette [*sic*] of the Hot Club of France, 'Rose Room'/'Tears' (HMV B8718, 3s.)

> Since last month I have heard, for the first time, this combination in the flesh. It was at a concert in London given last month mainly for musicians. One of these days I want to have a chat about to what extent one's critical views of records are influenced by having heard the artists 'in person'. I think it has a very big bearing on one's views, however unbiased one may try to be – but for the moment this question must wait.
>
> Taken all round, I am now inclined to think the Quintette's records seldom do it justice. For one thing I don't think they quite show the beauty of Grappelly's tone. He may not always reflect the breadth of melodic imagination of Eddie South, the rhythm of Venuti or the abandon of Stuff

Smith, but he has a delicacy of touch and an easy, impeccable technique, the subtleties of which the microphone does not always catch.

Also it is not enough to hear Reinhardt to realise his phenomenal technique. Wizardly as one may imagine him to be from the records, one needs to see the movement of his hands to realise the facility of his execution. And in saying that I am not allowing myself to be unduly impressed by the fact that nearly all he does with his left hand he does with two fingers ... though I am quite prepared to admit that every time I now listen to his records I see those first and second digits flashing nimbly up and down the fingerboard, and it certainly does add fascination to what I hear.

Also I think I have been inclined to underestimate Louis Vola. This big, grey-haired Frenchman means much more to the combination than its records suggest. He has a cleaner tone than the microphone seems ready to confess, and certainly an agility in execution which does not readily convey. These two new records of the Quintette are on much the same lines, and as good, as most of the many others we have been given lately, but to appreciate them fully I still think one needs to have heard the combination 'in the flesh'. (Edgar Jackson, *The Gramophone*)

Review of Quintet of the Hot Club of France, 'Night And Day'/'Stomping At Decca' (Decca F6616, 2s.)

Stomping at Decca is to my mind about the best swing record the combination has ever made – and not only because the Decca recording seems to suit it better than that of the French studios, in which its H.M.V. records are produced. (Edgar Jackson, *The Gramophone*)

Review of Coleman Hawkins (tenor sax) with Freddy Johnson (piano), 'Devotion'/'Lamentation' (Decca F6597, 2s.)

Hawkins has gone in for the Rudy Wiedoeft *Valse Vanité* type of writing. The only difference is that even in the parts that are not 'in tempo' one still senses the jazz idiom and the melodies are more captivating. So much for the composition. As regards performance, I can only repeat that to my mind Hawkins is not only the greatest tenor saxophone technician in existence, but one of the few who play with real feeling, even if at times he is inclined to display his emotions a trifle too frothily. (Edgar Jackson, *The Gramophone*)

Pathé Studios, Paris — Friday 4 March 1938

Ray Ventura et ses Collégiens

Philippe Brun, Gus Deloof, André Cornille (tpts); Guy Paquinet, Josse Breyere, (tbns); Max Blanc (cl, fl, as); John Arslanian (cl, b-cl, ts, bas, vcl); André Lluis (cl, as); Adrien Mareze (ts); Jean-Louis Jeanson, Roger du Hautbourg, Jean Pienet (vlns); Bob Vaz (pno); Django Reinhardt (gtr); Louis Vola (sb); André Taylor (dms); Jacques 'Coco' Aslan (timpani, vcl) (1); André Dassary (vcl) (2).

Arr. by Paul Misraki; dir. by Ray Ventura.
Engineer: Eugène Ravenet

348 CPT 3836-1 **Un Sourire En Chantant** (With A Smile And A Song) (2) {3.02}
[***78*** Pat PA1476] [***CD*** Cls 777; Fmx FA307]

349 CPT 3837-1 **Sifflez En Travaillant** (Whistle While You Work) (1) {3.03}
[***78*** Pat PA1476] [***CD*** Cls 777; Fmx FA307]

Paris — Saturday 5 March 1938

Fletcher Allen and his Orchestra record three titles for Swing Records (matrix numbers OSW20–2). Musicians include Pierre Allier, Marcel Bianchi, Alix Combelle, Pierre Fouad, Charles Lissée, Tony Rovira and Ray Stokes.
See Rust for details.

Pathé Studios, Paris — Monday 7 March 1938

Benny Carter and his Orchestra

Benny Carter (as) (1), (tpt) (2); Fletcher Allen (as); Alix Combelle (ts); Bertie King (ts) (1), (cl) (2); York de Souza (pno); Django Reinhardt (gtr); Len Harrison (sb); Robert Mommarche (dms).
Engineer: Eugène Ravenet

350 OSW 4-1 **I'm Coming, Virginia** (1) {3.01}
[***78*** **Swi 20**, 201; Vi 26221, Vi A-1286]
[***40cm 33rpm transcription*** OWI 133] [***LP*** Aff BOX107; Pat C054 16007; Swa S1252; Swi 8420267] [***CD*** Aff AFS 10035; BGO CD249; Cly DIG 12; DRG 8493; Fmx FA307; Swi CDSW8403, 8426]

351 OSW 5-1 **Farewell Blues** (1) {3.13}
[***78*** Col GN 5041; **Swi 36**; 201] [***LP*** Pat C054 16007; Swa S1252]
[***CD*** Aff AFS 10035; Fmx FA307]

352 OSW 6-1 **Blue Light Blues** (2) {3.04}
[***78*** **Swi 20**; Vi 26221, A-1286] [***LP*** Aff BOX107; Pat C054 16008; Swa S1252; Swi SW8420267] [***CD*** ABM 1194; Aff AFS 10035; Arc SOL507; BGO CD249; Cas PIESD233; Cly DIG12; DRG 8493; Fmx FA307; JH 73509; Swi CDSW8403, CDSW8426]

Paris — Tuesday 8 March 1938

Philippe Brun and his Swing Band

Philippe Brun, Gus Deloof, André Cornille (tp, ts); Guy Paquinet, Josse Breyere (tbns); Max Blanc, Charles Lissée (as); Noël Chiboust, Alix Combelle (ts); Stéphane Grappelli (pno); Django Reinhardt (gtr); Louis Vola (sb); Maurice Chaillou (dms).
Arr. by Guy Paquinet.

Engineer: Eugène Ravenet

353 OSW 7-1 **Bouncin' Around** {3.13}
[*78* Swi 54] [*CD* Cls 777; Fmx FA307; Swi CDSW 8419]

354 OSW 8-1 **Ridin' Along The Moscowa** {2.49}
[*78* Swi 34] [*CD* Cls 777; Fmx FA307; Swi CDSW 8419]

355 OSW 9-1 **Gotta Date In Louisiana** {2.46}
[*78* Swi 34] [*LP* Pat C054 16024] [*CD* Cls 777; Fmx FA307; Swi CDSW 8419]

356 OSW 10-1 **Gabriel Swing** {2.37}
[*78* Swi 26] [*CD* Cls 777; Fmx FA307; Swi CDSW 8419]

Same location, date and engineer

Philippe Brun 'Jam' Band

Philippe Brun (tpt); Alix Combelle (cl); Noël Chiboust (ts); Stéphane Grappelli (pno); Django Reinhardt (gtr); Louis Vola (sb); Maurice Chaillou (dms).

357 OSW 11-1 **Doin' The New Low Down** {3.11}
[*78* Swi 44] [*CD* Cls 777; Fmx FA307; Swi CDSW8419]

Paris — Wednesday 9th March 1938

Michel Warlop, accompanied by Garland Wilson, records one title for Swing. At the same session Wilson records five piano solos and one celeste solo.
See Rust for details.

Paris — Thursday 10 March 1938

The Chautemps government falls. Léon Blum unsuccessfully attempts to form a coalition government.

Paris — Friday 11 March 1938

Fletcher Allen and his orchestra play a concert at the Salle de L'Ecole Normale de Musique at 8.45pm. The advertising promises 'un *Jam Session* français avec Alix Combelle et Pierre Allier'.

Hilversum — Sunday 13 March 1938

Eddie South records four titles for Dutch Brunswick (matrix numbers AM750–4). Musicians include Paul Cordonnier and Tommy Benford.
See Rust for details.

London — c. mid-March 1938

Ray Ventura and his Collégiens pay a three-day visit to play a concert at the Odeon Theatre, Guildford, Surrey; broadcast on the BBC and record for Parlophone. Musicians include Philippe Brun, Gus Deloof, Guy Paquinet and Louis Vola.
See Rust for details of recordings.

Paris **Tuesday 15 March 1938**

Fletcher Allen records three titles for Swing records (matrix numbers OSW20–2). Musicians include Pierre Allier, Marcel Bianchi, Alix Combelle, Pierre Fouad, Tony Rovira and Ray Stokes.
At the same session, Pierre Allier et son Orchestre (musicians as above, without Allen) record a further two titles (matrix numbers OSW23–4).
See Rust for details.

Salle Gaveau, Paris **Thursday 17 March 1938**

The QHCF play two concerts with the comedian Fernandel, at 2.45pm and 5.00pm. The Quintet play, at least, 'Swing Guitars', 'Mystery Pacific', 'Bolero' and 'Daphne'.

London **April 1938**

Review of Quintette of the Hot Club of France, 'Honeysuckle Rose'/ 'Souvenirs' (Decca F6639, 2s.)

> If only for the technique and ingenuity of wizard Reinhardt, I find *Honeysuckle Rose* not only entertaining, but refreshing in spite of the countless records there have been made by the Quintette over the last year or two.
> *Souvenirs* has the added attraction of being a new and delightful little entr'acte sort of melody, which properly handled might well be built into a hit. (Edgar Jackson, *The Gramophone*)

Hilversum **April 1938**

Bobby Martin and his All-Star Orchestra record two titles for Dutch Brunswick. Musicians include Bill Coleman, John Mitchell and Ram Ramirez.
See Rust for details.

Paris **Sunday 10 April 1938**

A new government under Edouard Daladier is formed, with support from Blum. He devalues the Franc and successfully intervenes in threatened strike action.

Paris **Friday 22 April 1938**

Quintette of the Hot Club de France

Stéphane Grappelli (vln); Django Reinhardt (gtr solo); Joseph Reinhardt, Eugène Vées (gtrs); Roger Grasset (sb).
BBC Radio broadcast 'Swing Music From The Continent' 7.30pm–7.55pm GMT
Introduction {0.26}

358 **Djangology** {2.12}
[***CD*** Fmx FA307]

359 **Daphné** {0.39}
[***CD*** Fmx FA307]

Paris April/May 1938

Review of Quintette Du Hot-Club de France, 'Bolero'/ 'Mabel' (Columbia L1046)

Gramophone should be highly commended for going ahead and publishing this 12" record of Django Reinhardt's magisterial composition, the '*Bolero*', utilizing all the instrumentalists necessary to bring out its full value.

Django's 'Bolero' is not, strictly speaking, jazz music, but as Django is one of the world's great hot soloists, nothing he does can help but affect us.

Django is such a universally gifted musician that he is able to produce masterpieces in other domains than that of jazz. His '*Bolero*' pleases me infinitely. It is marked by that same spontaneity which is exhibited in everything Django does, and which is exactly what is so often lacking in many classical or modern symphonic works.

The extreme simplicity of the theme which is exposed on a rather uniform plan, serves as a base for tonal combinations. Without being very complicated, the harmonies are full and so intelligently divided among the different instruments that the whole of the record is set off in relief, which comes more from the tonal volume than from the movement of the melodic line. On the classical bolero rhythm extraordinarily animated by Django's guitar, the theme is taken up successively by the various instruments or instrumental sections which play it with a liveliness often absent from classical orchestras. The sonority of the flute is very appropriate to the atmosphere of the composition, and Paquinet's trombone solo is remarkably executed.

In short, the '*Bolero*' is a fine proof of Django's magnificent gifts as composer and also arranger, for he is responsible for the orchestration such a sensitive and ingenious fashion – and a further proof of his genius as a guitarist for the way he plays his solo in this number denotes a mastery and sureness which suffice to place a musician among the most important of his epoch.

Last remark on this '*Bolero*'; it is completely free from all the tra-la-la business so classical or modern composers escape. That's not the least of its qualities.

The reverse, '*Mabel*', is on the contrary, authentic jazz music, and in its field, noways inferior to the '*Bolero*' ... Outside of Grappelly's excellent chorus, it's in some way a concerto for guitar and orchestra. I've rarely heard Django play as well; he improvises with the most absolute ease, avoiding all clichés, using the most varied phrases, accumulating the richest finds from the point of view of both pure musicians swing. The record abounds with his playing, yet the end seems to come too soon, and we receive the very distinct impression that Django could have held us breathless for several minutes more without the slightest difficulty. In his first chorus, admire the originality of his break solo at the end of the middle part, and eight measures further on, note the marvellous nimbleness with which he executes that rapid rising figure. But beautiful as the first chorus is, I am even more enthusiastic about the whole latter part of the disc, while he dialogues with the brasses, weaving with unerring instinct in the margin of the fine arrangement he wrote himself. What luxury of nuance and ideas!

The brasses play splendidly. Beautiful, massive tone, intelligently phrased, plenty of swing in execution. The three trumpets are particularly remarkable for their attack and hot intonations in the last part of the record.

Please, don't anyone talk of plagiarism from '*Christopher Columbus*' as regards this arrangement. '*Christopher Columbus*' was built on a classical riff belonging to no one in particular, and anyone has the right to utilize it. The only thing is to use it intelligently. (Hughes Panassié, *Jazz Hot*)

Review of Dickey Wells and his Orchestra, 'Sweet Sue'/ 'Hangin' Around Boudon' (Swing 16)

'*Sweet Sue*' includes five choruses. Dickey Wells plays the first with his characteristic easy power. In the second, Bill Coleman, in great form, touches me more than ever with his extraordinary sensitiveness. Remark also the purity of his melodic style: the phrases of the last 8 bars, for example, strongly recall the melodic style of Louis Armstrong in 1927, the Louis of '*Struttin With Some Barbecue*' but, as Bill plays them very differently, one can easily miss the resemblance. For the 3rd chorus [the] return in force of Dickey Wells, and for the fourth Bill Coleman returns with a terrific chorus way out of this world. Then, the dialogue tightens up for the final chorus, Dickey Wells surges forth again but only takes 4 bars, giving way to Coleman for 4 bars in turn, and so on. Tension mounts, certain of Dickey's entries are seizing in their passion and violence. The only regrettable thing is that for the final 8 bars, both musicians content themselves by executing together a banal riff, instead of each continuing to improvise; it lets down the tension.

Django's guitar and Fullbright's bass are splendid. Unfortunately, the guitar was a little strongly recorded.

'*Hangin' Around Boudon*' is such a beautiful blues that I have no hesitation in saying that it's at least as good as '*Hot Club Blues*'. A word of explanation about the title: Boudon is a Montmartre cafe where colored musicians usually go before and after work.

Bill Coleman takes the first chorus in admirably limpid style. In the second, Django shows that he carries in him the same spirit of the blues as the great Negro musicians. In the third, Dickey Wells is as wonderful as in '*Dickey Wells' Blues*'. The fourth chorus is a dialogue between Bill Coleman, scat singing splendidly, and Dickey Wells, responding with muted trombone. The fifth is played by Dickey, still with a mute, on a poignant, confidential tone; it's the bluest chorus imaginable. The sixth and last chorus is perhaps the best of all: Bill Coleman throws forth a

> series of pathetic phrases, magnificently patterned and incisive, Dickey Wells, without mute this time, answers in all his beautiful power, improvising phrases which fit perfectly into those of the trumpet. This passage is 'out of this world'. It's the hottest, most moving music conceivable. (Hughes Panassié, *Jazz Hot*)

Review of Eddie South, Stéphane Grappelli and Django Reinhardt, 'Swing Interpretation Of The First Movement'/ 'Improvisation "Concerto In D minor" by J S Bach' (Swing 18)

> The title of the record leaves us in no doubt as to the spirit in which the recordings were made. Nevertheless, it is not entirely useless to begin with a little amplification. There is no pretension that Bach gains in being interpreted in jazz style, but it is a simple attempt to take advantage of the limitless resources of Bach's music and of the often asserted and more or less direct affinities between Bach and jazz, to try to interpret him in a new way which would bring out the contemporaneous and direct sides of both Bach and jazz music. From the point of view of classical execution of Bach, this record is meaningless, but from an objective viewpoint it's quite another matter.
>
> On the first side, Eddie South and Stéphane Grappelly have hardly, if at all, touched Bach's text. The modifications here are slight, and the whole value of the interpretation lies in the character of the execution. An execution full of guarded warmth in which Eddie South and Stéphane Grappelly have succeeded in allying all the joyous force of Bach's music to the spontaneities typical of hot jazz. The surprise provoked by this record arouses one to enthusiasm, for it is not based on any ambiguity. It is frank, and no troubled nor vulgar elements intrude. As beautiful as the violin part is, I think Django's is even more extraordinary. He has created, from [a] little scrap, the accompaniment from a rhythmical point of view, and although obliged to simplify the harmonies for a single guitar, he was able to furnish the essential base with astonishing precision and sureness.
>
> The second side is an improvisation. Bach's theme is only a frame on which Eddie South and Stéphane Grappelly create a series of strictly hot phrases which, because of the theme, are revealed in an entirely new light. Without losing any of their character, they seem to adapt themselves marvellously to the classical character of the theme, and Grappelly, who seems to be more at ease than Eddie South, exhibits a wonderful inventive gift. A light undulation towards the end of the record is only transitory and doesn't in any way tarnish the glory of this truly extraordinary recording. Django, on this side, allows full rein to his superb vitality and sends the two soloists with his habitual ardour. (Hughes Panassié, *Jazz Hot*)

All original translations by Walter E Schapp.

probably Paris c. April/May 1938

Quintette of the Hot Club of France

Stéphane Grappelli (vln); Django Reinhardt (gtr) (1),
As above, augmented by Joseph Reinhardt, Pierre Ferret (gtrs); unknown (possibly Lucien Simoens) (sb) (2).
Jazz Hot film soundtrack
Introduction {2.30}

360 J'attendrai (1) {1.27}
[***CD*** Fmx FA308] [***DVD*** MOE 001]

361 J'attendrai (2) {1.21}
[***CD*** Fmx FA308] [***DVD*** MOE 001]

This short film (duration 6:20) was made by an unknown British film company (possibly British Gaumont) as a promotional device for the 1938 visit to the UK by the quintet. The entire film is available on ***DVD*** MOE 001. See Filmography for further details.

London May 1938

Review of Quintette of the Hot Club of France, 'Liebestraum No. 3'/'Sheik of Araby' (HMV B8737, 3s.)

> This is where I go on strike. I flatly refuse to wrack whatever may be left in the place where I once had a brain to find new words to describe records which in all major respects are identical with records I have been attempting to describe for years.
>
> But being a generous little fellow, I'll give you something to talk about should these records happen to crop up as a topics of conversation. There is a quite amazing similarity between Liszt's *Leibestraum No. 3* and Spencer Williams jazz classic *Basin Street Blues.* If you don't believe me, play this record of *Leibestraum* to any jazz enthusiast, don't show him the label, and tell him it's *Basin Street Blues,* and I'll bet you get away with it. Then if you want to go further, you can start to find out where the similarity between the compositions lies. (Edgar Jackson, *The Gramophone*)

Paris May 1938

Léo Marjane acc. par Wal Berg et son Orchestre

Léo Marjane (vcl) acc. by Alex Renard (tpt); unknown (tpt, 3/4 saxes, cl, fl); Stéphane Grappelli, Michel Warlop, one unknown (vlns); Wal Berg or Pierre Spiers (pno); Django Reinhardt (gtr); Roger Grasset (sb); Jerry Mengo (dms). Arr. and dir. by Wal Berg.
Engineer: Eugène Ravenet

362 OLA2513-1 **Bei Mir Bist Du Schon** (in English) {2.51}
[***78*** Gr K-8112] [***CD*** Fmx FA308]

363 OLA2514-1 **Bei Mir Bist Du Schon** (in French) {2.44}
[***78*** Gra K-8113] [***CD*** Fmx FA308]

Hilversum — Wednesday 4 May 1938

Willie Lewis records six titles for Decca released on Panachord (matrix numbers AM482–7). Musicians include Arthur Briggs, Bill Coleman, Frank 'Big Boy' Goudie and Wilson Myers.
See Rust for details.

Salle de L'Ecole Normal, Paris — Friday 13 May 1938

A 'Hot-Club de France Jam Session' features Eddy Bruner, Alix Combelle, Albert Ferreri, Freddy Taylor, Stéphane Grappelli, Roger Chaput, Roger Grasset, Pierre Fouad, Gus Viseur et son ensemble and the Dupont-Durand quintet.

London — Friday 20 May 1938

Una Mae Carlisle records six titles for Vocalion (matrix numbers DR3654–9). Musicians include Alan Ferguson, Len Harrison and Bertie King.
See Rust for details.

Paris — Thursday 26 May 1938

Quintet of the Hot Club of France

Django Reinhardt (gtr); Stéphane Grappelli (vln); other musicians unidentified, but probably: Joseph Reinhardt, Eugène Vées (gtrs); Roger Grasset (sb).
BBC Radio programme 'Band Boomerang' 7.00pm–7.40pm GMT
Reported titles broadcast: 'Le Chant Du Mireur' (*sic*), 'Mabel', 'Chant De Guitare' (*sic*), 'Speevy', 'Black And White'.
No recordings are known to have survived.

Columbia Studios, Paris — Tuesday 31 May 1938

Larry Adler avec acc. d'orchestre 'swing' (French-language labels)/ Larry Adler (The Mouth Organ Virtuoso) (English-language labels)

Larry Adler (hca); Stéphane Grappelli (pno); Django Reinhardt (gtr solo, comment) (1); Joseph Reinhardt, Eugène Vées (gtrs); Roger Grasset (sb).
Engineer: Georges Cailley

364 CL 6716-1 **Body And Soul** {3.03}
[***78*** Col DB 5047, **DF 2427**, MC 5047] [***LP*** Pat C054 16008; Swa S1400] [***EP*** Col SEG7775] [***CD*** Cls 777; DRG 8493; Fmx FA308; HD CDHD234]

365 CL6716-2 **Body And Soul [unissued]**

366 CL 6717-1 **Lover Come Back To Me** {2.31}
[***78*** Col DF 2444] [***LP*** Pat C054 16008; Swa S1400] [***EP*** Col SEG7775] [***CD*** Cls 777; DRG 8493; Fmx FA308]

367 CL 6717-2 **Lover Come Back To Me** (1) {2.35}
[***78*** **Col DB 5037**, MC 5047; RZ G-23542] [***CD*** Fmx FA308]

368 CL 6718-1 **My Melancholy Baby** {3.12}
[***78*** Col DB 5047, **DF 2444**, MC 5047; Od 291032] [***LP*** Pat C054 16008; Swa S1400] [***EP*** Col SEG7775] [***CD*** Cls 777; Dig8493; Fmx FA308; HD CDHD234]

369 CL 6718-2 **My Melancholy Baby** [**unissued**]

370 CL 6719-1 **I Got Rhythm** {2.51}
[***78*** Col DF 2427] [***LP*** Pat C054 16008; Swa S1400] [***EP*** Col SEG7775] [***CD*** Cls 777; Fmx FA308]

371 CL 6719-2 **I Got Rhythm** {2.56}
[***78*** **Col DB 5037**, MC 5037; MZ 239; RZ G-23542] [***CD*** Aff AFS10035; Fmx FA308]

London June 1938

Review of Willie Lewis and his Orchestra, 'Basin Street Blues'/ 'Swing, Brothers, Swing' (Columbia FB1955, 2s); personnel probably Willie Lewis (alto) directing Jay Hayman (alto); 'Big Boy' Goudie (ten); Jack Butler, Bill Coleman (tmps); Billy Burns (trmb); Herman Chittison (pno); John Mitchell (gtr); Wilson Myers (sb); Ted Fields (dms).

> For those who may not keep so closely in touch with these matters may I remind you that Willie Lewis and his Orchestra are a coloured combination playing in Paris, where they have been for some considerable time now. You may remember they were relayed by the B.B.C. from the Poste Parisien studios last November, and have appeared in the Columbia supplements more than once.
>
> Willie Lewis, who has quite a good voice and a pleasing style, sings the first chorus of *Basin Street Blues*, after which there is a brass chorus, saxophone chorus and the usual ensemble to finish with. The choruses, scored on the straightforward block principle, are constructed of tuneful, rhythmical phrases, and the sections play confidently with a nice sense of style. All round a performance which, if it is not the last word in refinement, gets home on its honesty of intent.
>
> The attempt to tear up *Swing Brother Swing* at a much faster tempo shows the bands tendency towards roughness even more obviously, but this is to a great extent offset by a healthy enthusiasm and more than a suggestion of lift in the rhythm. The trumpet playing is pretty wild, but it's exciting – if you respond to that sort of thing. (Edgar Jackson, *The Gramophone*)

Review of Quintet of the Hot Club of France, 'Black and White'/'Sweet Georgia Brown' (Decca F6675, 2s.)

> This is positively the last time I shall agree to review a record by these French lads unless they do something different.

And yet, I don't know. It still seems to be a pleasing sort of noise and the skill is undeniable. (Edgar Jackson, *The Gramophone*)

Paris — Monday 13 June 1938

Eddie Bruner and his Orchestra record five titles for Swing records (matrix numbers OSW27–31). Musicians include Oscar Alemán, Tommy Benford, Noël Chiboust, Bill Coleman, Alix Combelle and Roger Grasset.

Polydor Studios, Paris — Tuesday 14 June 1938

Quintette du Hot-Club de France (French-language issues)/**The Quintet of the Hot Club of France with Django Reinhardt (Guitar) Stephane Grappelly (Violin)** (English-language issues)

Stéphane Grappelli (vln); Django Reinhardt (gtr solo, comment) (1); Joseph Reinhardt, Eugène Vées (gtrs); Roger Grasset (sb, bowed sb) (2).
Engineer: Rudolph Hamburger

372 4209-1/2HPP **Billet Doux** {2.52}
[***78*** **De F-7568** (E, F), De23263 (A, Ca); Od 286192]
[***LP*** De ECM 2051, LE AJA5070] [***CD*** Cas MACCD132; Cls 777; Fmx FA308; HD CDHD206; JSP 343; Kaz EUKCD913]

373 4210-HPP **Swing From Paris** (1, 2) {2.29}
[***78*** Br 505276; **De F-6899** (E, F), Y-5348; Od 286192]
[***LP*** De ECM 2051; LE AJA5070] [***CD*** Avid AMSC648; Cls 777; Fmx FA308; Gal GALE435; JA 157222; JSP 343; Mil 74321308652]

374 4210-1/2HPP **Swing From Paris** [**unissued**]

375 4211-HPP **Them There Eyes** {3.00}
[***78*** Br 505276; **De F-6899** (E, F), Y-5348, 573, 23262 (A, Ca)]
[***25cm LP*** De 123998] [***LP*** De ECM 2051; LE AJA5070]
[***CD*** Avid AMSC648; Cas MACCD132; Fmx FA308; Gal GALE435; HD CDHD165; JA 157222; JSP343; Kaz EUKCD913; LE AJA5267]

376 CBD4211-1/2HPP **Them There Eyes** [**unissued**]

377 4212-HPP **Three Little Words** {2.50}
[***78*** Br 505277, A-81901; **De F-6875** (E, F), Y-5270, 572, 23264 (A, Ca), 333016; Od 284778] [***LP*** De ECM 2051; HD CHD165; LE AJA5070]
[***CD*** Avid AMSC648; Cls 793; Fmx FA308; HD CDHD165; JA 157222; JSP 343; Mil 74321308652]

378 4212-1/2HPP **Three Little Words** [**unissued**]

379 4213-HPP **Appel Direct (Appel Indirect)** {2.58}
[***78*** Br 505277, A-81901; **De F-6875** (E, F), 572, 23261 (A, Ca), 333016; Od 286044] [***LP*** De ECM 2051; HD CHD165; LE AJA5070]
[***CD*** Cls 793; Fmx FA308; HD CDHD165; JA 157222; JSP 343; Kaz EUKCD913]

380 4213-1/2HPP **Appel Direct (Appel Indirect)** [**unissued**]

The possibility of take 4209-HHP existing is highly unlikely. Confusion arose over various record company's use of the ½ suffix on the matrix number. 'It is unlikely that [this] exists as such, under the matrix of 4209-HPP; probably there was only one take, regardless of the stamping' (Abrams). Decca 23261 issued as 'Direct Appeal'.

Hilversum — Tuesday 14 June 1938

Coleman Hawkins records eight titles for Dutch Decca, issued on Panachord (matrix numbers AM488–93 including alternates). Musicians include Freddy Johnson.
See Rust for details.

Moulin de la Galette, Paris — Thursday 30 June 1938

Quintette du Hot-Club de France

Stéphane Grappelli (vln); Django Reinhardt (gtr solo); Joseph Reinhardt and Eugène Vées (gtrs); Roger Grasset (sb).
Radio broadcast, Grand Nuit Du Jazz/Swing Night in Paris; acetates.

381 Medley: Daphne/Limehouse Blues/Swing Guitars {7.48}
[***CD*** Fmx FA308]

Same location and date

Valaida Snow (tpt, vcl); Django Reinhardt (gtr solo); Roger Grasset (gtr).
Acetates.

382 Medley: Bei Mir Bist Du Schon/St Louis Blues {2.45}
[***CD*** Fmx FA308]

Same location and date

Michel Warlop (vln); Django Reinhardt (gtr).

383 Sweet Sue (incomplete) {2.15}
[***CD*** Fmx FA308]

'Swing Night In Paris' also included performances by Jean Tranchant, Fletcher Allen and His Swing Men From Harlem, Pierre Allier's Swingsters, Chiboust–Bianchi's Gang, Alix Combelle Swing Band, Léo DeTemple Orchestra and the Dupont–Durand Quintette.

Paris — June/July 1938

Jazz Hot notes that the Quintette are in residence at 'Au Florence'.

Review of Quintette du Hot-Club de France, 'My Sweet'/'Sweet Georgia Brown' (Decca F9428)

> '*My Sweet*' is taken on a very fast tempo, just a little too much so. Nevertheless, Django and Grappelly manage to play as well as usual. For me the

best part of the record is Grappelly's entry and the phrases immediately following it. It is grand that Stéphane should have succeeded in playing so well on such a tempo.

I believe the Quintette could have done better with such a number as '*Sweet Georgia Brown*'. Certainly there are very good passages, but Django and Stéphane are less regularly inspired than in most of their recent discs. Under these conditions it is not surprising that this side should suffer in comparison with Eddie South's recording of the same tune. (Hughes Panassié, *Jazz Hot*)

Review of Benny Carter and his Orchestra, 'I'm Coming Virginia'/ 'Blue Light Blues' (Swing 20)

'*I'm Coming Virginia*' is a sax quartet arranged in that sparkling fashion of which Benny holds the secret. Note the richness of the effects obtained by using alternately unison and harmony during the performances.

There are three good solos, the first by Combelle, the second by Django, the third by Benny himself. The arranged parts are, however, the most sensational part of the disc.

'*Blue Light Blues*' is a quite different type of performance; Benny takes the trumpet, Bertie King the clarinet and all improvise from one end to the other. Although Benny is quite good on the trumpet, the best solos on this side are by Combelle and Fletcher Allen, both taking two choruses. Combelle invents some imaginative, broken phrases which makes his solo very different from those he has recorded up till now; as he is remarkably well recorded, his fine, full tone comes out very well. As for Fletcher Allen's solo, it is in a very original style and is like nothing I know: the style is a little breathless and capricious, with a melodic line that is sometimes unusual. A really fine solo.

There is a deplorable false start on this record: Benny starts off alone in a relatively slow tempo, and the rhythm section comes in a much faster pace, thus producing a queer effect. This rhythm section, apart from Django, is pretty weak. (Hughes Panassié, *Jazz Hot*)

Review of Stéphane Grappelli, 'I've Found A New Baby'/'Alabamy Bound' (Swing 21)

Grappelly has rarely played so magnificently on a record as in '*I've Found A New Baby*'. Some strange chords from Django as an introduction give Stéphane a springboard from which to attack the number in an entirely new way. Instead of an exposition of the theme in the first few bars, as it is almost always done, Stéphane invents a new melody and then, altering it little by little, launches out into an admirably warm and intelligent improvisation. It comes out in one flow – you feel that at the beginning of the disc – Grappelly has made a discovery and has wanted to exploit it quietly. (Hughes Panassié, *Jazz Hot*)

Review of Quintette du Hot-Club de France, 'Viper's Dream'/'Minor Swing' (Swing 22)

> The first disc by the Quintet to appear on Swing was very fine, but I believe that, on the whole, this new one is even better!
>
> The Quintette has achieved the amazing exploit of recording '*Viper's Dream*', which does not suffer in comparisons to Freddy Taylor's lovely record. Framed by this very lovely theme, in the record there are first two blues choruses by Django, then later by Grappelly. These, in my opinion, are the finest passages in the disc. I doubt if Django has recorded a finer solo than this; his melodic invention has incomparable sobriety and ease, and what grand inspiration! Grappelly's solo is also one of the best; it is nevertheless possible that many may not see this, it is so pure and transparent.
>
> '*Minor Swing*' is no less successful. The title gives a good description of the type of piece it is. It contains two fine solos by Django and Grappelly, both on top form. The simple theme leaves plenty of room for improvisation, and gives liberty of which Django and Grappelly make the best possible use. (Hughes Panassié, *Jazz Hot*)

England — **last week of June 1938**

The Quintette arrive in England to play a series of engagements arranged by 'Will Collins and Lew Grade Ltd, Theatrical and Vaudeville Exchange'.

London — **July 1938**

Review of Coleman Hawkins and his All Star Jam Band, 'Crazy Rhythm'/ 'Honeysuckle Rose' (HMV B8754, 3s.)

> As already stated, this is the first disc to be issued here from the French 'Swing' catalogue recently acquired by H.M.V. As far as Hawkins is concerned, both sides are grand examples of the playing of this brilliant swing virtuoso. There is also a nice chorus in *Crazy Rhythm* by Benny Carter. Looked at as a band, however, the combination is not quite so successful. There are moments when it is inclined to be messy, and Reinhardt's solo in *Honeysuckle Rose* has neither the brilliance nor the technique usually associated with this fine guitarist. However, the records are mostly Hawkins', who compensates in a great measure for such shortcomings as they may have. (Edgar Jackson, *The Gramophone*)

State Theatre, High Road, Kilburn, London NW6 — **probably Friday 1 July 1938**

Concert by the Quintette of the Hot Club of France.

Ardwick Hippodrome, Manchester — **Saturday 2–Monday 4 July 1938**

Concerts by the Quintette of the Hot Club of France with introductions and occasional vocals Danish entertainer Carola Merrild. English vocalist Donald Peers and comedian Albert Modley also appear.

See Cherrett, pages 53–4 for a contemporary report of one of these concerts.

> ... from behind the closed curtains comes the ripple of golden notes from a magical guitar; backed seconds later by a solid swinging lifting beat and the resonant biting attack of a rhythmic violin ... The curtains swing open to reveal the Quintet Of The Hot Club of France centre stage with ... a casual, swarthy figure hunched over a Macaferri guitar from which pours with an effortless fluency a cascade of rhythmic and incredibly melodious improvisations ... nonchalantly ... the little French gypsy sweeps into ... 'Limehouse Blues' ... Chromatic runs bubbling up from the bass and steaming up, unbroken, through three octaves; great chunky solid mounting sequences of octaves that bring the audience out of their seats – we still cannot believe it!! (Unsigned, quoted in Abrams)

The Gig Club, Bourne Hall, Wood Green, London N22 — Sunday 10 July 1938

Concert by the Quintette of the Hot Club of France.

Empire Theatre, Wood Green, London N22 — week beginning Monday 11 July 1938

The Quintette of the Hot Club of France appear in concert.

Trocadero, Elephant and Castle, London SE1 — week beginning Monday 18 July 1938

The Quintette of the Hot Club of France appear in concert.

Empire Theatre, Shepherd's Bush, London W12 — week beginning Monday 25 July 1938

The Quintette of the Hot Club of France appear in concert.

London — August 1938

Review of Dickey Wells and his Orchestra, 'Hangin' Around Boudon'/'Sweet Sue' (HMV B8763, 3s.)

> These are the second two sides to be issued here from the French 'Swing' catalogue.
>
> In *Hangin' Around Boudon* the boys play the 12-bar blues. There is a scat chorus by Bill Coleman which is neither particularly good nor particularly pleasant, but on his trumpet Coleman is the high spot of the proceedings. He has the tone and the technique and plays with real feeling. Wells, in consequence, is rather overshadowed and seems if only by contrast to lack personality. Still, his performance is nice so far as it goes, so is Reinhardt's, but Django seldom sounds at his best outside his own Hot Club Quintette.
>
> Sweet Sue is another succession of good solos by Coleman and Wells, who could have been heard to better advantage had the rhythm section not been quire so heavy. Bernstein's [*sic*] bass for all its brilliance is a little

too close to the microphone and so rather too string and not too clear. (Edgar Jackson, *The Gramophone*)

Review of Stan Brenders et L'Orchestra de Jazz de L'I.N.R., 'Big Chief "Swing It"'/'Growin' Old' (HMV F290, 3s); Brenders directing Ch Remue, Louis Billen (altos); J Demany (ten); A Saguet (ten, bar); P Hondt, R Chantrain, E Vanderborght (tmps); J Damon, G Van Camp (trmbs); J Ourwerx (pno); Chas Dolne (gtr); Tur Peeters (sb); Jos Aerts (ds).

This record has been sent to me at the instigation of the secretary of the Jazz Club of Belgium. Although recorded in Belgium it is pressed at the H.M.V. factory at Hayes and is available to English purchasers by order through any H.M.V. dealer.

I.N.R. stands for Institute National Belge de Radiodiffusion, of which the band is the official combination. It often broadcasts from I.N.R. but as the station transmits on only 15kw its reception is not good over here.

The record shows what the band really can do. It plays a rather florid style from full-blooded arrangements somewhat akin to the orchestrations Fletcher Henderson was writing for Goodman not so long ago, and its performances would not disgrace an American ensemble. Also it has its soloists, notably the clarinet, trumpet and tenor sax.

If this is a fair example of what is happening over there, Continental jazz is something which may soon have to be gauged by more than the work of the French Hot Club Quintette, Ray Ventura's boys and one or two other groups hitherto looked upon as the bright exceptions which prove the rule that, outside England, European dance musicians are not really swing minded. (Edgar Jackson, *The Gramophone*)

Trocadero Theatre, Elephant and Castle, London SE1 — probably Monday 1 August 1938

The Quintette are reported booked to appear in concert (*Melody Maker* 28 July), but the dates are unclear.

Empire Theatre, Hackney, London E8 — week beginning Monday 1 August 1938

The Quintette of the Hot Club of France appear in concert.

Metropolitan Theatre, unknown location, London — week beginning Monday 8 August 1938

The Quintette of the Hot Club of France appear in concert.
There were several Metropolitan Theatres operating in the London area at this time, but the specific venue for the week in question remains unconfirmed.

Empire Theatre, Glasgow — week beginning Monday 15 August 1938

In the *Performer* magazine of 11 August the Quintette are announced as appearing.

New Empress Theatre, Brixton, London SW16 — week beginning Monday 22 August 1938

In the *Performer* magazine of 18 August the Quintette are announced as appearing. Also on the bill were magician Chris Charlton and comedy duo Collinson and Dean.

Decca Studios, Broadhurst Gardens, London NW6 — Tuesday 30 August 1938

Quintette du Hot-Club de France (French-language issues)/**The Quintet of the Hot Club of France** (English-language issues)

Stéphane Grappelli (vln); Django Reinhardt (gtr solo); Joseph Reinhardt, Eugène Vées (gtrs); Roger Grasset (sb).

Engineer: Arthur Lilley or Arthur Haddy

384 DR 2878-1 **The Flat Foot Floogie** {2:54}
[***78*** Br 505267, A-81682; **De F-6776** (E, F), 9433] [***25cm LP*** De 124015] [***CD*** Avid AMSC648; Cls 793; Fmx FA308; JSP 342]

385 DR 2879-1 **Lambeth Walk** {2:45}
[***78*** Br A-81692; **De F-6776** (E, F), 9433, 23077] [***25cm LP*** De 124015] [***LP*** AofC ACL1158; LE AJA5070] [***CD*** Cls 793; CC 2010; Dig CO3506; Fmx FA308; HD CDHD206; JA 157222; JSP 342; LE AJA5070]

386 DR 2880-1 **Why Shouldn't I Care?** {2:47}
[***78*** De 23077] [***CD*** Cls 793; Fmx FA308; JSP 342]

London — September 1938

Review of Larry Adler, 'I Got Rhythm'/ 'Lover Come Back To Me' (Columbia DB5037, 3s.)

> Paul Holt's page in the *Daily Express* describes this as the hottest record of the month. Which just shows how opinions can differ. Larry Adler couples a phenomenal technique with a good deal more originality and style than most 'popular' artists playing freak instruments, and what the accompaniment is like you will know if you recognise the names of the players as being none other than the French Hot Club Quintette. But there, as far as swing goes, the records end. (Edgar Jackson, *The Gramophone*)

Review of Django Reinhardt and Stéphane Grappelli, 'If I Had You'/ 'Tournerai' (Decca F6721, 2s.)

> For all Reinhardt's technique playing about with the jazz idiom for the sake of recording guitar and piano duets has not resulted in much more than a reasonably insignificant music. [*sic*]
>
> Perhaps the fault is mainly that Grappelly is not quite the right type of accompanist for Reinhardt, who anyway seems to need the sonority of a bass if not a band. (Edgar Jackson, *The Gramophone*)

Review of Eddie South, 'Eddie's Blues'/ 'Sweet Georgia Brown' (HMV B8778, 3s.)

> This is, of course, the cue to start a long argument about the violin in the jazz; why it so seldom seems to be successful, whether it is due to the inherent characteristics of the instrument, the way it is too often used, or because there are such few good jazz fiddlers, and if the latter why?
>
> Fortunately for you, however, I have not the space, and anyway you will find the answers to most of the questions in these records.
>
> Eddie South is not only a fine violinist, but a fine jazz violinist, or if you prefer it not only a fine jazz violinist but a fine violinist. As regards jazz he shows the violin in a new light. If he is not greater than Venuti he is at any rate as great, and different, and in some ways I think he is better. South has the rhythm and adds soul to it. He has a greater sense of music *per se* as distinct from music for the sake of rhythm. Able through the passing of time to see Venuti in proper perspective I am forced to the opinion, while admitting his many great qualities, that rhythm was an end with him, whereas with South it is but a vehicle for something much more.
>
> And I hand it to Reinhardt for producing just the right accompaniments. It takes a real artist to know just when and how to keep himself subservient to the soloist, not to mention the feeling for rhythm when playing with swingsters such as Eddie South. One can hardly believe this is the same Reinhardt who played the aforementioned solos on Decca. The accompaniments sound so right, the solos artificial. (Edgar Jackson, *The Gramophone*)

Review of Coleman Hawkins and Freddy Johnson, 'Star Dust'/'Well, All Right Then!' (Vocalion S123, 3s.)

> The tragedy is that Hawkins, who is still head and shoulders and then some above all the rest has to trundle round the continent making odd records where and when he can, with no studio enterprising enough to provide him with a band. Not that I've anything against Freddy Johnson as a pianist, but the tenor sax is altogether too heavy and robust an instrument to be stood on the support of a piano, which merely sounds tinkly behind it and cannot provide the foundational strength or sonority it needs. (Edgar Jackson, *The Gramophone*)

Decca Studios, Broadhurst Gardens, London NW6 — Thursday 1 September 1938

Django Reinhardt

Django Reinhardt (gtr solo); Stéphane Grappelli (pno).
Engineer: Arthur Lilley or Arthur Haddy

387 DR 2903-1 **I've Got My Love To Keep Me Warm** {2:28}
[***78*** De F-6935 (E, F)] [***LP*** AofC ACL1189] [***CD*** Avid AMSC648; Cls 793; Fmx FA308; JSP 342; Mil 74321308652]

388 DR 2903-2 **I've Got My Love To Keep Me Warm** {2:22}
[*78* De F-6935 (E, F)] [*25cm LP* De 124015] [*CD* Fmx FA308; JSP 342]

389 DR 2904-1 **Please Be Kind** {2:43}
[*78* **De F-6828** (E, F), Y-5266] [*LP* AofC ACL1189] [*CD* Cls 793; Fmx FA308; JSP 342]

Palladium Theatre, Argyle Street,
London W1 — Tuesday 5 September 1938

The Quintette of the Hot-Club de France appear in concert.

Decca Studios, Broadhurst Gardens,
London NW6 — Saturday 10 September 1938

Django Reinhardt (solos) et S. Grappelli (French-language issues)/
Django Reinhardt and Stephane Grappelly (English-language issues)
Personnel and engineer as 1 September.

390 DR 2907-1 **Louise** {2:36}
[*78* **De F-6828** (E, F), Y-5266] [*25cm LP* De 124015]
[*LP* AofC ACL 1189] [*CD* Avid AMSC648; Cls 793; Dig CO3506; Fmx FA308; JSP 342]

Same location, date and engineer

Django Reinhardt (solos)
Django Reinhardt (gtr).

391 DR 2908-1 **Improvisation No. 2** {2:39}
[*78* De F-6935 (E, F)] [*LP* AofC ACL1189] [*CD* Cas PIESD233; Cls 793; Fmx FA308; JSP 342; LE AJA5138]

392 DR 2908-2 **Improvisation No. 2** {2:40}
[*78* **unissued**] [*CD* Fmx FA308; **JSP 342**]

London — Monday 12 September 1938

'Leonard Feather and Ye Olde English Swynge Band' (*sic*) record four titles for Decca. Musicians include Alan Ferguson, Len Harrison and Bertie King.

Chiswick Empire Theatre,
London W4 — Monday 12 to probably Saturday 17 September 1938

A week's residence by the QHCF as part of a variety programme. See Cherrett, page 20, for a facsimile of the original programme.

London — Thursday 22 September 1938

The 'West Indian Orchestra' record for Decca. Musicians include Bertie King.

Paris — Tuesday 27 September 1938

Willie Lewis records two titles for Decca (matrix numbers 4453–4hpp).
See Rust for details.

Paris — Wednesday 28 September 1938

Bill Coleman records two titles for Swing records (matrix numbers OSW43–4). Musicians include Tommy Benford and Wilson Myers.
See Rust for details.

London — September/October 1938

Article about Django Reinhardt in *Fretted Harmony* magazine No. 15, September/October issue.
See Cruickshank, page 105, for a reproduction of this article.

Paris — September/October 1938

Jazz Hot announces the availability of Delaunay's *Hot Discographie 1938*, priced at 30 FF.

Charles Delaunay reviews Roger Chaput's *Hot Guitars* instruction book in *Jazz Hot*.

Review of Michel Warlop et son Orchestre, 'Taj Mahal'/'Serenade For a Wealthy Widow' (Swing 28)

> *Taj Mahal* is easily the better side. Alongside a pretty flute accompaniment, Warlop improvises for a long while in the charming style so distinctly his own. Notice at the beginning of the record, Django's splendid playing, with exquisitely toned low notes placed here and there.
>
> The backing has some excellent passages, but the interest is not kept up so well. The rhythm section, apart from Django, seems pretty feeble, and certain ensembles by the trumpet and clarinets could have been more incisive. Warlop is not so inspired as on the reverse, but there is a very hot guitar solo. My admiration for Django increases daily. (Hughes Panassié, *Jazz Hot*)

London — October 1938

Review of Quintette of the Hot Club of France, 'Daphne'/'My Sweet' (Decca F6769, 2s.); 'Flat Foot Floogie'/'Lambeth Walk' (Decca F6776, 2s)

> *My Sweet* owes its loss of stars to an interruption which, if it is not vulgar is at least disturbing and unnecessary. The record suddenly stops in the middle. Then comes talk (in French) about somebody taking a solo, followed by a lot of laughter and some more talk about hotting it up. Apparently hotting it up means tearing it up. Anyway, it is an end of that poise and tunefulness which have always thought to be among the combination's most attractive features, and what follows is merely just bad hot playing. The other three sides are the Quintette's mixture as before with *Daphne* as the best record and *Floogee* as perhaps the weakest if only because this amusing bit of nonsense is both the most suitable tune for the style of treatment and, relying to a great extent on its ridiculous words, needs a vocal chorus. (Edgar Jackson, *The Gramophone*)

Review of Dicky Wells and his Orchestra, 'Between The Devil And The Deep Blue Sea'/'Bugle Call Rag' (HMV B8799, 3s.)

> *Between the Devil* may lack the final touch of grooming which would have enable it to be described as elegant, but it gets home because in having made no attempt to overset the confines of genuine jazz it has captured so much of what lies within them.
>
> In a way it may be said to have contradicted its fundamental intention. The obvious absence of any desire to produce a gallery fetcher has created a spirit of naturalness which has enabled the players to rise in many cases above their form and at times produce music which is almost thrilling its impression of inevitability. Bill Coleman plays better trumpet than I can remember having heard from him, Dicky Wells' trombone has not only the rhythm one associates with it, but an easy melodic line, and Reinhardt is happily content not to overwork his undeniable technique for the sake of it. The whole performance has the comfort of relaxation and if in the rhythm team the bass is the high spot instrumentally it still says much for the section that it swings along in a manner which entirely conceals the fact that such a valuable instrument as the piano is absent.
>
> But perhaps the real strength of the record is best realised on hearing its obverse. Compared with *Between The Devil*, *Bugle Call* is inclined to be forced and consequently at times awkward. Whatever its good points may be, and it is not without them, it lacks the easy naturalness of its coupling. (Edgar Jackson, *The Gramophone*)

Review of Una Mae Carlisle, 'Hangover Blues'/'Mean To Me' (Vocalion S198, 3s); Una Mae Carlisle (vocalist, pno); Bertie King (ten, cl); David Wilkins (tmp); Alan Ferguson (gtr); Len Harrison (sb); H. Schnieder (dms).

> *Hangover Blues* is easily Una Mae's best record to date. She sings it well – naturally but with personality and style. The fault of irregular tempo, which I have noticed in her piano playing when I have heard her on the air by herself, is corrected by the fact that she is held to tempo by the band and she plays the blues interestingly and tunefully with the authentic character with which she sings it. The accompaniment is excellent. David Wilkins and Bertie King have the feel for the blues and Len Harrison's bass is a concert in itself.
>
> *Mean To Me* fails, I feel, by the conception of the song. A haunting little melody, it seems to call for the melancholy which is inherent in it. Instead Una treats it satirically to which end she has revised the lyric. Still perhaps after all there is something to be said for the idea. It's a grand thing to be able to laugh at life. (Edgar Jackson, *The Gramophone*)

Paris **Saturday 1 October 1938**

The publication date of the main French Columbia–Gramophone–Pathé dealers' catalogue, which lists the following items as being available:

Larry Adler Columbia DF2366, 2427
Garnet Clark Gramophone K7645
Bill Coleman Gramophone K7705, 776
Coleman Hawkins Gramophone K7527
Quintette du Hot Club de France Columbia L1046 (described in the catalogue as 'Orchestre Symphonique'); Gramophone K 7704, 7706, 7707, 7898, 7790

The retail price for these items was 20FF.

Paris — Tuesday 4 October 1938

The Daladier government breaks ties with the Communist and Socialist parties, signaling the end of the Popular Front.

Hippodrome Theatre, Manchester — Monday 10–Friday 14 October 1938

The Quintette of the Hot Club of France appear in residence. The Monday show was performed without Django Reinhardt or Eugène Vées, who were suffering from what the *Melody Maker* described as 'passport irregularities'.

Paris — last week of October 1938

The Quintette of the Hot Club of France return to Paris.

Paris — October/November 1938

The Quintette of the Hot Club of France play dates at the Marignan and the ABC theatres in Paris.

Paris — Monday 7 November 1938

Ernst von Roth, a German diplomat, is shot outside the German Embassy on Rue de Lille by Herschal Grynszpan, a 17-year-old Jewish Pole who had recently been expelled from the Reich.

This action, and Roth's subsequent death two days later, was used as the excuse for 'Krystallnacht' on the night of 9/10 November, in which the Nazis launched a coordinated attack on Jewish people and property in Germany and Austria.

London — Thursday 10 November 1938

George Chisholm and his Jive Five record two titles for Decca. Musicians include Alan Ferguson.
See Rust for details.

Paris — Wednesday 30 November 1938

In protest at government measures that include the radical modification of the 40-hour week, workers call for a nationwide 24-hour strike. The government reacts by putting railways and other essential services under military orders coupled with threats of severe punishment for strikers. Many strike leaders are arrested and the strike movement collapses.

Paris — November–December 1938

Review of Eddie South, 'Somebody Loves Me'/'I Can't Believe That You're In Love With Me' (Swing 31)

> On *Somebody Loves Me*, Eddie South is accompanied by Django alone, while on the reverse Paul Cordonnier, a colored bass player, is added.
>
> Eddie's remarkable ease of expression is more evident than ever on *Somebody Loves Me*. One gets the impression that he is just practicing the five choruses to himself, so great is his relaxation.
>
> These choruses are all played in a different key, except for the fourth and fifth. Which are in the same key. It's impossible to try to point out all of Eddie's brilliant ideas in this beautiful improvisation. Nevertheless, I'd like to give special mention to a tremendous passage in the first chorus – the long phrase which runs from the sixteenth to the twenty-first measure. I have heard few things more impressive than this ravishing phrase, which is so rich musically and whose power and verve mark a musician of extraordinary gifts. It's hard to believe that such a phrase could be completely improvised. It's as astonishing as Benny Carter's subtle melodic line.
>
> Django's accompaniment is as fine as Eddie's work. His background work is supple, sonorous and intense, and his modulations are really a joy to the listener.
>
> A lot of people will probably feel that Eddie is playing sentimentally in the first chorus of *I Can't Believe That You're In Love With Me*. Nor will I attempt to deny it. But his playing has such spirit that I enjoy it even when it is sentimental. As a matter of fact, his interpretation grows hotter as the piece progresses. The beginning of the second chorus is much dryer, and with the third Eddie really starts to warm up, playing in the low register with a harsh power, while Django backs him up magnificently. Paul Cordonnier does a good job on bass. (Hughes Panassié, *Jazz Hot*)

Paris — December 1938

Willie Lewis records two titles for Pathé (matrix numbers CPT4471–2). Musicians include Fletcher Allen, Tommy Benford, Bill Coleman, Eugène d'Hellemes and Wilson Myers.
See Rust for details.

London — December 1938

Review of Quintet of the Hot Club of France, 'Appel Direct' / 'Three Little Words' (Decca F6785, 2s.)

> *Solos by Django almost all the way through both sides should be enough for anyone*
>
> Both of these sides are recent Paris recordings. *Appel Direct* is a dull tune. Reinhardt takes the first half of the record with a solid solo, and then Grappelly comes in and increases the tension, if not the swing, and Reinhardt winds up with a short solo (the tune is still dull).

> *Three Little Words* is taken at Duke's tempo – the ideal one. Grappelly plays and Django swings. Listen to his solo. Even if his attack and ideas are not quite so grand as those of Teddy Bunn, his two choruses here are stirring stuff. It is Grappelly who lacks grip on this record, which, if not one of the best by this group, makes very pleasant listening. (Unsigned, *Rhythm*)

Copenhagen — Monday 5 December 1938

Oscar Alemán records two guitar solos for the Danish branch of the Gramophone Company (matrix numbers 1085–6).
See Rust for details.

Oslo — Monday 5 December 1938

'Freddy Valier's String Swing', featuring guitarist Robert Normann, make four sides in the QHCF style.

L'Ecole Normale de Musique, Paris — Friday 9 December 1938

A concert featuring Josse Breyere, Philippe Brun, Roger Chaput, Al Ferreri, Pierre Foaud, Louis Gaste, Max Geldray, Charles Hary, Danny Polo, Joseph Reinhardt, Jean Storne and Louis Vola.

Paris — Wednesday 14 December 1938

'The Hot Club Swing Stars' record four titles for Swing records (matrix numbers OSW51–4). Musicians include Pierre Allier, Max Blanc, Philippe Brun, Roger Chaput, Noël Chiboust, Alix Combelle, Pierre Fouad, Maurice Moufflard and Louis Vola.
See Rust for details.

Coliseum, Paris — Friday 16 December 1938

The Quintette appear in 'Le Grande Nuit de Jazz'. Also on the bill are: Pierre Allier, Arthur Briggs, Philippe Brun, Eddie Brunner, Una Mae Carlisle, Noël Chiboust, Alix Combelle, Edgar Courence, Richard Day, Leo DeTemple, Max Geldray, Frank 'Big Boy' Goudie, George Johnson, Willy Lewis, Leo Marjane, The Manhatten Trio, Valaida, Michel Warlop and Garland Wilson.

Paris — 1939

Charles Delaunay publishes *Hot iconographie* (Editions Jazz Hot).

London — January 1939

Review of Dicky Wells and his Orchestra, 'Japanese Sandman'/ Trio of Trumpets, 'I Got Rhythm' (HMV B8826, 3s.)

> *Terrific stuff, this!*
>
> Dicky Wells plays a colossal first chorus behind which you can hear some not so good guitar from Django. Bill Coleman plays some grand stuff in the next passage. One of his very best – completely incomplete! Then, funnily enough, Django plays as well as he ever did. Maybe he was not quite

at home with the all-American rhythm trio. Last chorus consists of Coleman and Wells playing magnificently.

The Trio of Trumpets consists of Bill Dillard, Bill Coleman and Shad Collins and they are accompanied by Wells, Fullbright, Reinhardt and Beason. Each of the three takes a whole chorus and then the trio blows a terrific fanfare of a final chorus

In many ways, this is an extra-ordinary record and may well become one of the most popular of the year. Not to be missed. (Unsigned, *Rhythm*)

Review of Quintet of the Hot Club of France, 'Swing From Paris'/'Them There Eyes' (Decca F6899, 2s.)

The French boys are well on top of these tunes

Bass, and then bass and guitar, give out a familiar – non-jazz – riff which leads into an intriguing tune played first by Reinhardt in that nice, new simple way of his. Grappelly comes in and plays 'hot' without being as good as he can be. The record has a pleasant lift to it, the last third being devoted to repetitions of the opening riff.

Eyes is in fast tempo, Grappelly comes first and is followed two choruses in very hot style by Django. His playing is very swell indeed, and this solo would alone justify the record. After that, they both go to town and Django slips back into his old style in his excitement. (Unsigned, *Rhythm*)

Paris — **Monday 23 January 1939**

Django Reinhardt's 29th birthday.

Paris — **Monday 30 January 1939**

'Danny Polo and his Swing Stars' record six titles for Decca (matrix numbers 4859–64). Musicians include Oscar Alemán, Philippe Brun, Una Mae Carlisle, Alix Combelle, Jerry Mengo and Louis Vola.
See Rust for details.

London — **February 1939**

Review of Django Reinhardt, 'Improvisation'/Django Reinhardt and Stephane Grappelly, 'I've Got My Love To Keep Me Warm' (Decca F6935, 2s.)

Non-swing instramusic

Improvisation is a lovely guitar solo but not swing music. Reverse is in two parts. First a slow straight statement of the tune and second a fast chorus in hotter style. Each half swings in its own way and Reinhardt is always worth the money. Or nearly always. (Unsigned, *Rhythm*)

Paris — **February 1939**

Max Geldray records two titles for Swing records (matrix numbers OSW61–2). Musicians include Roger Chaput, Louis Vola and Michael Warlop.
See Rust for details.

Scandinavia — February 1939

The Quintette embark upon a tour. See Delaunay pages 95–6.

Oslo — Wednesday 8 February 1939

The QHCF play at Den Gamle Logen (Freemason's Hall). Robert Normann is in the audience.

Paris — February/March 1939

Review of Gus Viseur's Music, 'It Had To Be You'/ 'Wind And Strings' (Swing)

> Pannassié doesn't like the accordion. I don't like it either. But while listening to this new group I experience a pleasure comparable to that which Django's and Grappelly's Quintette gave me – I seem to discover in Viseur's renditions an intimate, delicate music in no wise similar to what you'd expect from an accordeon.
>
> And I can also see the vicious clique claims the Quintette is always the same thing rise up against this band. Space is lacking and it would be outside the scope of this article to try to restore them. But what I deplore is that it is always the same callow youths who believe themselves intelligent in condemning, with satisfaction, the Armstrongs and Hawkins, and in crowning the Goodmans and the Harry James's.
>
> This is not to deny the excellent qualities of these last, but to stigmatise a viewpoint which does more than any other to harm the true cause of jazz. I shall return later the this question, and give the little stinkers what's coming to them.
>
> One likes or one doesn't like the accordion, so be it. But if one approaches these renditions in good faith, one has to recognize a rare charm and delicacy which prove Gustave Viseur a real artist.
>
> I have no hesitation in saying that we have in him a musical phenomenon in the order of Django Reinhardt, about whom it becomes more and more necessary to write an article which will clear up certain points and combat the indifference and ill-will rendered him by the principal international critics, without waiting until he is dead before tossing wreaths in his direction.
>
> To get back to the disc, we can say that it contains another revelation in the person of Pierre Ferret whose guitar solos are so reminiscent of Django Reinhardt. (Charles Delaunay, *Jazz Hot*)

Paris — Thursday 9 March 1939

Gus Viseur, under the nom-de-disque 'Orchestre Musette Victor', records for Columbia. Musicians include Oscar Alemán, Tommy Benford and Eddie Bruner.

Polydor Studios, Paris — Tuesday 21 March 1939

Quintette du Hot-Club de France

Stéphane Grappelli (vln); Django Reinhardt (gtr solo); Joseph Reinhardt, Pierre 'Baro' Ferret (gtrs); Emmanuel Soudieux (sb).
Engineer: Rudolph Hamburger

393 4967-HPP **Hungaria** {2.46}
[***78*** **De F-7198**, Y-5580, 615] [***CD*** Avid AMSC648; Arc SOL517; Cls 793; Fmx FA308; JSP 343; Mil 74321308652]

394 4967-1/2HPP **Hungaria** {2.45}
[***78*** De F-7198] [***CD*** Fmx FA308; JSP 343]

395 4968 HPP **Jeepers Creepers** {3.13}
[***78*** Br 505275, A-82082; Col R 14124; **De F-7027** (E, F), 587] [***CD*** Avid AMSC648; Fmx FA308; JSP 343]

396 4968-1/2HPP **Jeepers Creepers** {3.13}
[***78*** De F-7027] [***25cm LP*** De 123998] [***LP*** Ast LP20102; Met MTM12] [***CD*** Cls 793; Fmx FA308; HD CDHD206; JSP 343; JA 157222]

397 4969-HPP **Swing '39 [unissued]**

398 4969-1/2HPP **Swing '39** {3.18}
[***78*** Br 505275, A-82082, A-82135; Col R 14124; **De F-7027** (E, F), 23262 (A, Ca), 587] [***25cm LP*** De 123998] [***LP*** De ECM2051; LE AJA5070] [***CD*** CC 2010; Cls 793; Fmx FA308; Gal GALE421; Hab 111200; JA 157222; Kaz EUKCD913; Recall SMDCD307]

399 CAX4970-HPP **Japanese Sandman** {2.39}
[***78*** De **F-7133**, Y-5450, 606, 23263 (A, Ca); Fo 606] [***CD*** Avid AMSC648; Cas MACCD132; CC2010; Cls 793; Dig CO3506; Fmx FA308; HD CDHD206; JA 157222; JH 73509; JSP 343; Kaz EUKCD913]

400 4970-1/2HPP **Japanese Sandman [unissued]**

401 4971-HPP **I Wonder Where My Baby Is Tonight?** {3.01}
[***78*** De F-7100] [***25cm LP*** De 123998] [***CD*** Cls 793; Fmx FA308; HD CD206; JSP 343]

402 4971-1/2HPP **I Wonder Where My Baby Is Tonight?** {3.07}
[***78*** **De F-7100**; Y-5408, 597, 23152; Od 284563, 283647, 283286] [***CD*** Fmx FA308; JSP 343]

Paris — Wednesday 22 March 1939

Same personnel, location and engineer as above.

403 4972-HPP **Tea For Two** {2.50}
[***78*** **unissued**] [***LP*** De (F) 115213A; **KC 109**] [***CD*** Fmx FA308; JSP 343]

404 4972-1/2HPP **Tea For Two** {2.51}
[***78*** **unissued**] [***LP*** De (F) 115123A] [***CD*** Arc SOL517; Avid AMSC648; Cls 793; Ea EABCD71; Fmx FA308; JA 157222; **JSP 343**]

405 4973-HPP C **My Melancholy Baby** {3.20}
[***78*** De 23261] [***CD*** Avid AMSC658; Cls 793; Fmx FA308; JA 157222; JSP 343]

406 4973-1/2HPP **My Melancholy Baby [unissued]**

407 4974-HPP **Time On My Hands** [**unissued**]

408 4974-1/2HPP **Time On My Hands** {2.40} [***78*** Br 505273; **De F-7100**, Y-5408, 597, 333016, 59019 Od D286347, D284363, 283286] [***25cm LP*** De 124015] [***CD*** Cls 793; Fmx FA308; HD CDHD206; JSP 343]

409 CA4975-HPP **Twelfth Year** {2.37} [***78*** Br 505272; **De F-7133**, Y-5450, 606, 23264 (A, Ca), 59023; Fo 606] [***25cm LP*** De 124015] [***CD*** Avid AMSC648; Cas MACCD132; Cls 793; Fmx FA308; HD CDHD165; JSP 343; Kaz EUKCD913; Mil 7432108652]

410 4975-1/2HPP **Twelfth Year** {2.40} [***78*** De F-7133] [***CD*** Fmx FA308; **JSP 343**]

411 4976-HPP **Hungaria** [**unissued**]

Oslo — Friday 24 March 1939

'Freddie Vallier and String Swing', featuring Robert Normann, record two titles in the QHCF style.

Paris — c. 1 April 1939

Duke Ellington and his orchestra arrive in Paris and are honoured at a party in the new offices of the Hot-Club de France.
See Delaunay for photo of this event.

Studio Albert, 61 rue Albert, Paris — Saturday 4 April 1939

Jean Sablon acc. par Wal Berg et son Orchestre

Jean Sablon (vcl) acc. by possibly Django Reinhardt (gtr solo) or probably Joseph Reinhardt (gtr solo); Pierre 'Baro' Ferret (gtr); Wal Berg or Emile Stern (pno); Emmanuel Soudieux (sb); Maurice Chalou or Jerry Mengo (dms).
Engineer: Georges Cailley

412 OLA 3017-1 **Sérénade Sans Espoir** (Penny Serenade) {3.10} [***78*** Gr K-8366] [***CD*** Fmx FA308]

Disagreement exists over the presence of Django Reinhardt on OLA3017. Aural evidence tends to support the theory that he was not present; however, for the sake of completeness it appears on Fremeaux and is included here.

Pathé Studios, Paris — Wednesday 5 April 1939

Rex Stewart and his Feetwarmers

Rex Stewart (cnt); Barney Bigard (cl, dms) (1); Django Reinhardt (gtr solo); Billy Taylor (sb).
Engineer: Eugène Ravenet

413 OSW 63-1 **Montmartre** {2.23} [***78*** HRS 1003; **Swi 56**] [***LP*** Aff BOX107; Pat C054 16008; Swa S1252; Swi SW8420267] [***EP*** Atl 523; Pat EA26] [***CD*** Aff AFS10035;

Arc CASTEL810252; Avid AVC530; BGO CD249; Cas PIESD233; Cls 793; Cly DIG12; DRG8493; Fmx FA309; Swi CDSW8426]

414 OSW 64-1 **Low Cotton** {2.59}
[***78*** HRS 1003; **Swi 203**] [***LP*** Aff BOX107; Pat C054 16008; Swa S1252; Swi SW8420267] [***EP*** Atl 523] [***CD*** Aff AFS 10035; BGO CD249; Cls 793; Cly DIG12; DRG 8493; Fmx FA309; Swi CDSW8426]

415 OSW 64-2 **Low Cotton [unissued]**

416 OSW 65-1 **Finesse** (Night Wind) (1) {2.19}
[***78*** Gr B-9154; HRS 1004; Pat PG 538, P 11062, **Swi 70**] [***LP*** Aff BOX107; Pat C054 16008; Swa S1252; Swi SW8420267] [***EP*** Pat EA26] [***CD*** Aff AFS10035; Avid AVC530; BGO249; Cls 793; Cly DIG12; DRG8493; Fmx FA309; Swi CDSW8426]

417 OSW 65-2 **Finesse [unissued]**

418 OSW 66-1 **I Know That You Know** {2.32}
[***78*** HRS 1004; Pat PG 538, P 11062; **Swi 70**] [***LP*** Aff BOX107; Pat C054 16008; Swa S1252; Swi SW8420267] [***EP*** Pat EA26] [***CD*** ABM 1194; Aff AFS 10035; BGO CD249; Cls 793; Cly DIG12; DRG8493; Fmx FA309; Swi CDSW8426]

419 OSW 66-2 **I Know That You Know [unissued]**

420 OSW 67-1 **Solid Old Man** (1) {3.02}
[***78*** HRS 1004; **Swi 56**] [***25cm LP*** CHDD 588] [***LP*** Aff BOX107; Pat C054 16008; Swa S1252; Swi SW8420267] [***EP*** Pat EA26] [***CD*** Aff AFS 10035; Avid AVC530; BGO CD249; Cls 793; Cly DIG12; DRG 8493; Fmx FA309; Swi CDSW8426]

421 OSW 67-2 **Solid Old Man [unissued]**

HRS 1003 and 1004 illegally issued as by Rex Stewart's Big Four and re-titled 'Improvisations In Ellingtonia'.
At the same session, Oscar Alemán, accompanied by John Mitchell and Wilson Myers, also records for Swing.
See Rust for details.

Paris April–May 1939

> … if most of the great musicians … belong to the epic beginnings of jazz this doesn't at all mean that new genius can't arise.
>
> Right here at hand, Django Reinhardt presents a similar case (and I hope no-one will read chauvinism into this – art knows no national frontiers).
>
> What aberration, what prejudice – or else, incompetence – have not most jazz critics of the entire world shown towards him. The very ones who had discovered him some years previously.

When his first records appeared, they all proclaimed it a miracle, and marvelled at his virtuosity and the imagination of his solos. Then as the discs of the QHCF successively appeared, not knowing what to say about them, they laid down the dictum that it was always the same sort of stuff – the same argument used by those who dislike the music of J S Bach.

It is possible not to like the guitar, guitar solos or Django's particular style, but through carping at the instrumentalist, they seem to have sacrificed the artist without ever suspecting that Reinhardt's personality lay elsewhere than in his guitar, and, just as they admired the marvellous trumpeter in Louis Armstrong for a long time without ever realizing that the man possessed the full genius of a new art, so today, they are completely misguided on the true meaning of Django's genius.

So I borrow from one of the leading musical personages in England, Mr. Constant Lambert, the following lines from the *Sunday Referee*, August 1937: 'Django undoubtedly is the most interesting figure in dance music since Duke Ellington and, like Ellington, he is not so much an arranger as a composer. He is far more than a purely executive artist, which is what distinguishes him from the average "swing" player who merely puts frills round some dull tune by somebody else.

'Reinhardt, with the collaboration of an excellent fiddler called Grappelly, works out at rehearsal his curious and individual pieces which may be roughly described as a mixture of Ellington and Ravel's "Bolero" with a slight touch of Satie thrown in … '

Ought we not to neglect the incompetent opinions of those who will never understand or who, unacquainted with his work, are unable to speak seriously about Django? For I can cite just as well the judgement of all the great musicians who have come into contact with him – Hawkins, Benny Carter, Eddie South, Dicky Wells or Bill Coleman – and who will tell you better than I ever could of Django's exceptional worth.

Their opinion counts much more with me than the insignificances of the scribers of *Down Beat*, *Melody Maker*, *Music* and other musical magazines (to which I would add *Jazz Hot* where not the signer of this article). (Charles Delaunay, *Jazz Hot*)

Paris **Friday 12 May 1939**

Oscar Alemán records four titles for Swing records (matrix numbers OSW68–71). Musicians include John Mitchell and Wilson Myers.
See Rust for details.

Polydor Studios, Paris **Monday 17 May 1939**

Quintette du Hot-Club de France (French-language issues)/**The Quintette of the Hot Club of France** (English-language issues)
Stéphane Grappelli (vln); Django Reinhardt (gtr solo); Joseph Reinhardt, Pierre 'Baro' Ferret (gtrs); Emmanuel Soudieux (sb).
Engineer: Rudolph Hamburger

422 5080-HPP **My Melancholy Baby** {2.46}
[***78*** Col R 14231; **De F-7198** (E, F), Y-5580, 615; Fo 615] [***CD*** Cls 813; Fmx FA309; JSP 343]

423 5081-HPP **Japanese Sandman** {3.05}
[***78*** Br 505274; **De 59006**; Poly 580017] [***CD*** Cls 813; Fmx FA309; JSP 343]

424 5082-HPP **Tea For Two** {3.12}
[***78*** Br 505279; **De F-7568** (E, F), 59006; Od 284773; Pol 580017] [***25cm LP*** De 124015] [***LP*** De MOR530] [***CD*** Cls 813; Fmx FA309; JSP 343]

425 5083-HPP **I Wonder Where My Baby Is Tonight?** {2.44}
[***78*** Br 505273; **De 59019**] [***LP*** De MOR530] [***CD*** Cls 813; JSP 343; Fmx FA309]

426 5084-HPP **Hungaria** {2.45}
[***78*** Br 505272; **De 59023**] [***LP*** De MOR 530] [***CD*** Cls 813; Fmx FA309; HD CDHD206; JSP 343]

Pathé Studios, Paris — Wednesday 24 May 1939

André Ekyan et son Orchestre

Frank 'Big Boy' Goudie (tpt, ts); André Ekyan (ts); Joe Turner (pno); Django Reinhardt (gtr); Lucien Simoens (sb); Tommy Benford (dms).
Engineer: Eugène Ravenet

427 OSW 72 **The Sheik** [{2.56}
[***78*** **unissued** *Swing* test] [***25cm LP*** HMV FELP 1120] [***CD*** Cls 813; Fmx FA309]

Same location, date and engineer

André Ekyan – Solo de Clarinet and Saxophone

André Ekyan (as); Django Reinhardt (gtr); Lucien Simones (sb).

428 OSW 73-1 **Dream Ship** {2.47}
[***78*** Swi 67] [***LP*** Pat C054 16008] [***CD*** Cls 813; Fmx FA309]

429 OSW 74-1 **I Can't Believe That You're In Love With Me** {2.18}
[***78*** Swi 67] [***LP*** Pat C054 16008] [***CD*** Cls 813; Fmx FA309]

Same date and engineer

André Ekyan et son Orchetra

Personnel as for OSW 72.

430 OSW 75 **Darktown Strutters Ball** {2.31}
[***78*** **unissued**] [***25cm LP*** **HMV FELP1120**] [***LP*** Pat C054 16008] [***CD*** Cls 813; Fmx FA309]

431 OSW 76 **Blues of Yesterdays** {2.33}
[**78 unissued**] [***25cm LP*** **HMV FELP1120**] [***LP*** Pat C054 16008]
[***CD*** Cls 813; Fmx FA309]

Matrix numbers OSW82 and OWSD83 are piano solos by Joe Turner accompanied by Benford.

London — Friday 26 May 1939

As a featured member of 'Jack Hylton and His Orchestra', Coleman Hawkins records two titles (matrix numbers OEA7953–4).
See Rust for details.

Paris — Sunday 28 May 1939

Frank 'Big Boy' Goudie and his Orchestra record five titles for Swing records (matrix numbers OSW77–81). Musicians include Tommy Benford, André Ekyan, Wilson Myers and Joe Turner.
See Rust for details.

Paris — c. spring 1939

Quintette du Hot-Club de France

Stéphane Grappelli (vln, announcements, speech); Django Reinhardt (gtr solo); probably Joseph Reinhardt, Pierre 'Baro' Ferret (gtrs); Emmanuel Soudieux (sb).
Radio broadcast; acetate.

432 **Tiger Rag** {2.17}
[***CD*** Fmx FA309]

Some discographers dispute the presence of either Reinhardt or Grappelli on this recording.

Paris — Wednesday 28 June 1939

'Freddy Johnson and his Orchestra' record six titles for Swing records. Musicians include Tommy Benford, Alix Combelle and Wilson Myers (matrix numbers OSW84–9).
See Rust for details.

Paris — Friday 30 June 1939

Quintette du Hot-Club de France

Stéphane Grappelli (vln); Django Reinhardt (gtr solo); Eugène Vées, Pierre 'Baro' Ferret (gtrs); Emmanuel Soudieux (sb).
Engineer: Ernie Gower

433 OPG 1719-1 **Stockholm** {2.45}
[**78** Swi 128] [***LP*** Aff BOX107; Pat C054 16009; Swa S1400;
Swi SW8420267] [***CD*** Aff AFS 10035; Cls 813; Fmx FA309;
Gal GALE421; Hab 111200; JSP 904; Mos MD 6-190;
Recall SMDCD307; Swi CDSW8426]

434 OPG 1720-1 **Younger Generation** {2.22}
[***78*** Swi 77] [***LP*** Aff BOX107; Pat C054 16009; Swa S1400; Swi SW8420267] [***CD*** ABM 1003; Aff AFS 10035; Cls 813; Fla PASTCD9792; Fmx FA309; JSP 904; Mos MD 6-190; Swi CDSW8426]

Same location, date and engineer

Django Reinhardt – solo de guitare

Django Reinhardt (gtr); Pierre 'Baro' Ferret (gtr); Emmanuel Soudieux (sb).

435 OPG 1721-1 **I'll See You In My Dreams** {2.29}
[***78*** Swi 211] [***LP*** Aff BOX107; Pat C054 16009; Swa S1400; Swi SW8420267] [***CD*** Aff AFS 10035; Cas MACCD132, PIESD233; Cls 813; Cly DIG12; Fla PASTCD9792; Fmx FA309; HD CDHD234; JSP 904; Kaz EUKCD913; LE AJA5267; Mos MD 6-190; Swi CDSW8426]

Django Reinhardt – solos de guitare

Django Reinhardt (gtr).

436 OPG 1722-1 **Echoes of Spain** {3.05}
[***78*** Swi 65] [***LP*** Aff BOX107; Pat C054 16009; Swa S1400; Swi SW8420267] [***EP*** HMV 7EGH1002, 7EMF40, 7EMQ12, (F) 7EGF650] [***CD*** Aff AFS 10035; Cls 813; Fla PASTCD9792; Fmx FA309; JSP 904; Mos MD 6-190; Swi CDSW8426]

Same location, date and engineer

Stéphane Grappelly – solos de violon

Stéphane Grappelli (vln); Django Reinhardt (gtr).

437 OPG 1723-1 **Out of Nowhere** {3.13}
[***78*** Swi 199] [***LP*** Pat C054 16009; Swa S1400] [***CD*** Cls 708; Fmx FA309; JSP 904; Mos MD 6-190]

438 OPG 1724-1 **Baby** {2.36}
[***78*** Swi 199] [***LP*** Pat C054 16009; Swa S1400; Swi SW8420267] [***CD*** Cls 708; Fmx FA309; Gal GALE435; JSP 904; Mil 74321308652; Mos MD 6-190; Swi CDSW8426]

Same location, date and engineer

Django Reinhardt – solo de guitare

Django Reinhardt (gtr solo).

439 OPG 1725-1 **Naguine** {2.25}
[***78*** Swi 65] [***LP*** Aff BOX107; Pat C054 16009; Swa S1400; Swi SW8420267] [***CD*** Aff AFS 10035; Cls 813; Cly DIG12; Fla PASTCD9792; Fmx FA309; Gal GALE421; JSP 904; Mos MD 6-190; Recall SMDCD307]

On the same day as the above session, as members of 'Louis Bacon and his Orchestra', Freddy Johnson, Roger Chaput and Tommy Benford record five titles for the Swing label (matrix numbers OSW 90–4).

England **last week of July 1939**

The Quintette (Reinhardt, Grappelli, Ferret, Vées and Soudieux) arrive for a lengthy tour arranged by 'Will Collins and Lew Grade Ltd., Theatrical and Vaudeville Exchange'.

Empire Theatre, Hackney, London E8 **week beginning Tuesday 1 August 1939**

The Quintette of the Hot Club of France appear in concert.

Metropolitan Theatre, unknown location, London **week beginning Tuesday 8 August 1939**

The Quintette of the Hot Club of France appear in concert. There were several Metropolitan Theatres operating in London at this time; the specific venue remains unconfirmed.

State Cinema, Kilburn, London NW6 **Monday 14 August 1939**

The Quintette of the Hot Club of France appear in concert.

Empire Theatre, Glasgow **week beginning Tuesday 15 August 1939**

The Quintette of the Hot Club of France appear in concert.

BBC Television Studios, White City, Wood Lane, London W12 **Wednesday 16 August 1939**

The Quintette of the Hot Club of France appear on BBC television at 9.00pm. The *Radio Times* describes it thus:

> **'Quintette du Hot Club de Paris'**
> **With Django Reinhardt, Stephane Grappelly, Beryl Davis**
> *titles to be performed*
> Signature tune
> Djangology
> Hungaria
> Minor Swing
> Wishing (vocal)
> The Man I Love (guitar solo accompanied by the piano)
> Don't Worry 'Bout Me (vocal)
> Deep Purple
> Running Wild
> Presentation by Eric Fawcett

This is the broadcast date. Since the Quintette were in Glasgow at the time of the broadcast, the performances were clearly filmed at an earlier time during this British tour. No evidence can currently be found of the programme's survival, but it is not precluded.

Berlin, London, Paris — Sunday 20 August 1939

The Polish crisis, which will lead to the declaration of war, begins.

State Cinema, Kilburn, London NW6 — Tuesday 22 August 1939

The Quintette of the Hot Club of France appear in concert.

Decca Studios, Broadhurst Gardens,
London NW6 — Friday 25 August 1939

Django Reinhardt et le Quintette du Hot-Club de France avec Stéphane Grappelli (French-language issues)/The Quintet of the Hot Club of France with D Reinhardt and Stephane Grappelly (English-language issues)

Stéphane Grappelli (vln, pno) (1); Django Reinhardt (gtr solo); Joseph Reinhardt, Eugène Vées (gtrs); Emmanuel Soudieux (sb); Beryl Davis (vcl) (2).
Engineer: Arthur Lilley or Arthur Haddy

440 DR 3861-1 **Undecided** (2) {2:29}
[*78* Br 505268, 505271; **De F-7140** E, F), 616, 59018; Od 284997; Pat 20172] [***LP*** AofC ACL1189] [***CD*** Cls 813; Fmx FA309; JSP 342]

441 DR 3862-1 **H C Q Strut** {2:56}
[*78* Br 505267; Col R 14231; **De F-7390** (E, F); (B, E, H, Sw), 606, 59045; Od 264997] [***LP*** AofC ACL1158; LE AJA5070]
[***CD*** Arc SOL517; Avid AMSC648; Cls 813; Dig CO3506; Fmx FA309; Hab 111200; JA 157222; JSP 342]

442 DR 3863-1 **Don't Worry About Me** (1, 2) {2:56}
[*78* Br 505268; **De F-7140**, 59018; Pat 20172] [***LP*** AofC ACL1189]
[***CD*** Arc SOL517; Avid AMSC648; Cls 813; Fmx FA309; JSP 342]

443 DR 3864-1 **The Man I Love** (1) {3:10}
[*78* **De F-7390** (B, E, H), 59045] [***LP*** AofC ACL1189] [***CD*** Arc SOL517; Cls 813; Fmx FA309; Gal GALE421; Hab 111200; JSP 342]

Delaunay originally noted that pressings of Decca F7390, matrix DR3862, showed takes (1) and (2), further noting that no difference between the two pressings had been discovered. The Dutch pressing of 441 shows a second take number (2) after the matrix number, but the recording is take 1; (2) was probably a Dutch engineer's allocated remastering number. Abrams notes the existence of a take 2, but refers to it as 'the same as take 1'.
Beryl Davis was the featured vocalist with the Oscar Rabin band.

London — Saturday 26 August 1939

Reinhardt, Grappelly and Co. Here Again

At the gigantic State Theatre, Kilburn, last week, the Quintette of the Hot Club of France scored their second triumph in this country when they commenced a second tour of England by appearances at this movie house.

Ably compered by young Beryl Davis, daughter of the Rabin guitarist

Harry Davis, the opening announcement was made from behind the curtain and brought a terrific welcoming applause, which swelled even higher as the curtain went up on the swinging white-coated Hot Club Five.

Opening tunes were *Djangology* and *Hungaria*, which were beautifully played, only to be surpassed by Reinhardt's *Minor Swing*, which the fiddler built up to a tremendous climax, and revived memories of the Quintet's great *Melody Maker* concert at the Cambridge Theatre in January 1938.

Beryl Davis did a couple of slow tunes, *Wishing* and *Don't Worry About Me*, which one could not connect in any striking way to the Hot Club style of jazz, and did a very plaintive and winning treatment of *The Man I Love*.

The Quintette came back strongly with an arrangement of *Deep Purple* and encored with a fast, enthusiastic *Running Wild*, which brought much palm-pelting as the curtain dropped. This group of Frenchmen is consistently interesting in the restricted style to which it is forced by its actual instrumentation. Grappelly showed that he is still one of the sweetest hot fiddlers in the world, and his romantic tone and thoughtful interpretation out him in a class by himself in European music.

Next week the Quintette is working at the Trocadero Cinema, Elephant and Castle, with a provincial tour to follow. They will be here when Ray Ventura and his twenty-three musicians come over for their stage tour, and will swell the numbers of top-notch French musicians working in England to twenty-eight. (Unsigned, *Melody Maker*)

London **Sunday 3 September 1939**

On hearing that war has been declared (at 11.00am GMT), Django leaves immediately for France. The rest of the Quintette follow, except for Grappelli, who will stay in London for the duration of the war.
See Delaunay, Nevers.
The QHCF were scheduled to play a concert on Tuesday 5 September at the State Theatre, Kilburn, London, NW6, which was cancelled.
Concerts booked for the following venues were also cancelled:

4 September	Shakespeare Theatre, Liverpool
5 September	London Palladium
13 September	Chiswick Empire, London
18 September	Tivoli Theatre, Aberdeen

See Delaunay, pages 98–9.

Paris **Sunday 3 September 1939**

As a result of the declaration of war on Germany, theatres in Paris close, only to re-open the following day.

London **mid-September 1939**

Stéphane Grappelli begins a residence with Hatchett's Swingtette, under the direction of Arthur Young, at Hatchett's Restaurant, Piccadilly.

New York **Tuesday 19 September 1939**

In a recent Frankie 'Half-Pint' Jaxon disc, *Callin' Corrine* (Decca 7619), there's a pleasant surprise in the presence of Barney Bigard's fine blues clarinet. This was Barney's first appearance on any non-Ellington disc in a long time, unless you consider the records made in Paris by some of Duke's men un-Ellingtonian. The first of these, incidentally, has arrived – *Solid Old Man – Montmartre* by Rex Stewart's Feetwarmers (Swing No. 56), with Bigard, Django Reinhardt, and Billy Taylor. Rex was in fine fettle and Django effectively subdued on the first side, a pretty blues. Barney did emergency duty on drums as well as playing clarinet. *Montmarte* is a rather fancy side, and less interesting. *Finesse, I Know That You Know* and *Low Cotton*, also waxed by the quartet, are still to be released.

A letter from Charles Delaunay, written from an army training camp in France, has just been received in New York. The second edition of *Hot Discography*, Delaunay writes, has been exhausted; no more copies will be available. Bad news, which confirms our determination to publish as much record information as space will allow. Delaunay's discography was a result of remarkable efforts, but it's no more than a groundwork for a really definitive history of jazz records. From time to time *Jazz Information* will hunt down some of the flaws in the 1938 Discography. We invite collectors, particularly, to stop hoarding the various bits of odd information in their possession. Perhaps, by putting these obscure scraps of news, personnels, rarities, opinions and theories into print, where they will be seen and discussed, we can help build the foundation for an accurate and complete hot discography. (Unsigned, *Jazz Information*, Vol. 1, No. 2)

London **October 1939**

Review of Quintet of The Hot Club of France, 'Hungaria'/'My Melancholy Baby' (Decca F7198, 2s.)

In clearly pointing out at the start of *Melancholy Baby* that this number was inspired by Mendelssohn's *Songs Without Words*, Django Reinhardt naively puts himself in the place of people who live in glass houses. *Hungaria*, for which he and Grappelly are given credit on the label, is a far more exact copy of the Mercums-Caffard-Brunies *Angry*, which was a popular, hit some years ago.

However, these are perhaps minor matters. The important point is the records are well up to the Quintette's usual standard, especially *Melancholy Baby*, in which Django really excels himself. (Edgar Jackson, *The Gramophone*)

New York **Tuesday 17 October 1939**

United States Records, new big-time disc organization headed by Eli Oberstein, former Victor executive, announced its first release last week.

Shipments of records bearing the new Royale and Varsity labels was to have begun on October 12. New York dealers, however, were still awaiting their arrival on Monday (16) as *Jazz Information* went to press. The new discs should be available when this issue appears.

The first U.S. releases included, besides a number of sweet and popular titles, several records of interest to the swing fan. On the 75-cent Royale list, there are a pair of sides repressed from Ultraphone masters. These are Freddy Taylor's *'Blue Drag'* and Alix Combelle's *'Crazy Rhythm'*. Both were recorded in Paris in 1935. (Unsigned, *Jazz Information*, Vol. 1, No. 6)

New York **Tuesday 24 October 1939**

Review of 'Tiger Rag'/'Dinah' (Royale 1753)

Two sides from the first record date of the Quintet of the Hot Club of France, repressed from Ultraphone masters and now released for the first time in America. Without denying Django's evidently great talent, we must admit that these are pretty awful. Quite aside from the difficulties encountered by an all-string jazz orchestra, the amateur standing of the musicians, as far as Jazz is concerned, leads to fatal mistakes in tempo and rhythm – and the swing isn't here. (Unsigned, *Jazz Information*, Vol. 1, No. 7)

New York **Tuesday 7 November 1939**

Review of 'Sweet Sue'/'Avalon' (Royale 1780)

Royale reissues two French jazz records made in Paris in 1934. The only American musician on the disc is Arthur Briggs, who plays a trumpet solo on Avalon, which is hardly up to his reputation. Grappelly and Django play their usual music, and Jerry Mengo sings an unhappy vocal on the first side. (Unsigned, *Jazz Information*, Vol. 1, No. 9)

New York **Tuesday 14 November 1939**

Review of Alix Combelle and Freddy Taylor (Royale 1778)

Two sides recorded in Paris in 1935, and repressed from Ultraphone masters. On the label, Taylor's accompaniment is incorrectly credited to the Quintet of the Hot Club of France. Both sides are afflicted with French rhythm sections and arranging. The main interest comes from the tenor solos, on the first side by Combelle and on the second by Allen. Combelle's clarinet is inferior, and Taylor's muted trumpet undistinguished. (Unsigned, *Jazz Information*, Vol. 1, No. 10)

New York **Friday 24 November 1939**

The motives which lead American musicians so far afield are simple enough. Like most Americans they like to see the world, and they don't object to making their sightseeing a source of profit as well. Again, like most of us, many of them have sentimental, if indeed not familial, ties with the old country. Delving into more commercial incentives, a trip to Europe, even though it be for a week's engagement in some Paris dive, enables the boys to obtain work when, perhaps, they're unable to secure a suitable job at home. And on their return, they can be billed as 'Joe Doakes And His World Famous Orchestra, Just Back From A Triumphal European Tour'.

For the Negro musician, there is another reason, far more important than any of these. That is the almost complete absence, among the common people of Western Europe, of prejudice against the colored men. In Paris, Brussels, Amsterdam, or in any backwater town he can go where he chooses and with whom he chooses. This opportunity to escape the discrimination which still prevails even in the Northern U.S., is the magnet which attracts countless intelligent Negroes to Europe. It is this which induces many of them to give up their citizenship and raise their children as Frenchmen, Dutch or even Russian.

But even though he may remain abroad for several years, don't think there isn't a strong bond which holds the Negro to his America. In the summer of 1937, it was my privilege to hear Coleman Hawkins playing at the Negro Palace in Amsterdam. Accompanying him were Freddy Johnson, Negro pianist who has been in Europe since 1929 or earlier, and Maurice van Kleef, a Dutch drummer. The place was usually crowded with Dutch fans including all the leading musicians, some of whom occasionally sat in with the Trio. But most of the time, except for a piano chorus or two or maybe a drum break, Hawkins was out there alone, uncorking four or five choruses in a row to the plaudits of the crowd. Looking closely, I could see that Hawkins had but half an ear for his applause. Whenever he thought he'd hit on a good idea, he would turn toward Johnson and watch for Freddy's approval. The way the two men leaned on each other was almost pitiful. So, when, after three years or so abroad, Hawkins records such titles as 'What Harlem is To Me' and 'I Wanna Go Back to Harlem', you can bet your bottom dollar that these are not empty words or tunes.

At the height of his career, Hawkins accepted an offer to appear in London under Jack Hylton's sponsorship in 1934. For five years he remained abroad, leading various orchestras and recording in France, England, Holland, Denmark, Belgium and Switzerland. His first recordings abroad were solos backed by an English rhythm section. Moving to Holland, he recorded with the Ramblers, a competent full-size Dutch orchestra (Four of these sides are available on American Decca). Other Dutch recordings were made last year, with Benny Carter's orchestra and the Coleman Hawkins Trio (Johnson and Van Kleef).

A 1935 Paris session had Arthur Briggs on trumpet and a full orchestra of leading French instrumentalists. Two years ago, Hughes Pannassié had the idea of a recording orchestra composed solely of a sax section and a rhythm section – no brass. The idea, personnel, and the records themselves are all interesting, without being any more than that. With Hawkins on tenor was Alix Combelle, his able if erratic French imitator; the altos were Benny Carter and the fine French soloist André Ekyan. The rhythm section was composed of Django Reinhardt and Stéphane Grappelly from the H.C.F. Quintette. (Grappelly played piano on this occasion). D'Hellemes on bass and an old Jelly Roll Morton stalwart, Tommy Benford.

As Coleman Hawkins and his All Star Jam Band, they recorded 'Crazy Rhythm', 'Honeysuckle Rose', 'Out Of Nowhere' and 'Sweet Georgia Brown', for the Swing label. The first two sides are available here on Victor; the other two (on which Carter shifted to trumpet) were thought to be unfit to be issued in France, and appear only on HMV. 'Crazy Rhythm' is a succession of solos by each sax in turn at break-neck speed. Hawkins taking the last two choruses. Because of its undisciplined formlessness, it can be considered only as a tour de force. 'Honeysuckle Rose', on the contrary, is a fine Carter arrangement, with the Hawk filling in most of the solo spots.

As those of you who have heard him at Kelly's Stable must realize, five years abroad have done Hawkins no good. The adulation of critics and public has tended to bring out the exhibitionist in him, while playing as a featured soloist with inferior orchestras accustomed him to consider himself as the star, not as a fully integrated member of the band. His present habit of playing at random everything that comes into his head is directly attributable to the burden that fell on his shoulders as lone melody-man, with his trio, for over a year. All of which is not to say that Hawkins doesn't, at intervals, play as well as he ever did. (Walter E Schapp, *Jazz Information*, Vol. 1, No. 11)

New York **Friday 8 December 1939**

Although years in Europe have had a deleterious effect on Coleman Hawkins, they have produced some fine work from at least two jazzmen who merit the adjective great. I refer to Benny Carter and Eddie South.

Carter's stay abroad almost coincides with that of Hawkins; he left a year later and returned a year before. Benny traded Harlem for England in 1935, joining up with Willy Lewis' outfit which boasted such stars as Bill Coleman and Bobby Martin, trumpets; Herman Chittison, piano; and June Cole, bassist. Lewis' band, like many such colored combinations abroad, had the necessary instrumentalists but lacked the able arranging, and the orchestral drive, which are requisites for a really first-rate orchestra. The addition of Benny Carter wiped out any deficiency on the first score at least. Listen, for example, to Lewis' recording of 'Star Dust', which contains a saxophone ensemble of the sort only Benny can write.

The story of Carter's meandering in Europe, after his stay with Lewis, reads much like that of Hawkins. He led diverse combinations and produced recordings in England and all along the western periphery of the Continent. During 1936 there were several recording sessions for the new English Vocalion Swing series, with an all-star English combination including Tommy McQuater and Max Goldberg, trumpets; and Buddy Featherstonhaugh tenor sax. Some of these sides, but not the best, have appeared on American Brunswick. Benny is featured on almost any instrument you could name – trumpet, tenor and alto saxes, clarinet and piano – to say nothing of his services as vocalist, arranger, and usually composer as well. (It is wise to say nothing of his services as a vocalist). Although he had toyed with other instruments, he was still known chiefly as an alto saxophonist until he went abroad and cultivated his technique on trumpet, clarinet and tenor. The band doesn't swing, but when they get going on a slow number such as Benny's own lovely 'Nightfall' or 'Just A Mood', or his swell arrangement of 'These Foolish Things', the result (which cannot by any stretch of the imagination be called hot jazz) is nevertheless delightful, and indeed memorable music. On these discs, Benny's work on alto and especially clarinet is unsurpassable. Note how his clarinet style has changed since the days of the Chocolate Dandies' 'Dee Blues'; here his solos are played in low register, with a round, full tone. I am afraid, however, that his trumpet work will never compare to his mastery of tone and technique on the reed instruments.

The guitarist, on one of these English sessions, was none other than Bernard Addison, who was touring Europe at the time as accompanist with the Mills Brothers.

Leaving Great Britain, Carter recorded with Kai Ewan's Orchestra in Denmark (H.M.V.), and with the Ramblers at Laren in Holland. Not all of these are listed in [the] Discography. I have, for instance, a fine coupling by Benny Carter and the ramblers of 'Blue Rhythm' and 'New Swing Street' (Dutch Decca F42110). Both numbers were written by Dutch boys. Late in 1937, Carter led a combination, mostly English musicians including George Chisholm on trombone, at Scheveningen in Holland. At this time, the Hawk was playing in Amsterdam, and together with his pianist Freddy Johnson, he used to sit in on Carter's recording dates for English Vocalion.

In 1938, Benny switched his affection to Paris, where he was featured at 'Le Bœuf sur le Toit'. His recordings for the Swing label (issued here on Victor), 'I'm Coming Virginia' – 'Blue Light Blues', were made there with a mixed pickup band featuring Fletcher Allen, alto; Bertie King, clarinet; Alix Combelle, tenor and Django Reinhardt, guitar. Both Allen (who had his own band at another Parisian boite) and King are American Negroes, and both take good solos on 'Blue Light Blues'. Benny plays trumpet in 'Blue Light Blues' and alto in 'Virginia' and also 'Farewell Blues' (Swing 36), a fine waxing of a Carter arrangement, at the same session but issued too late for inclusion in [the] Discography. Benny is also featured on the Hawkins All-Star Jam band sides.

Benny returned to New York in May 1938, and soon formed his present orchestra. To understand why we have termed Hawkins' European venture a failure, and Carter's a success, you have only to compare their European recordings, and present work of their respective orchestras.

Both personal and musical factors enabled Benny to escape the pitfalls of instrumental virtuosity which ensnared the Hawk. The main safety valve, we think, was his arranging ability, which made him the heart of his bands, not merely the head. Then, too, his versatility was sensational enough to obviate the need for demonstrating a bewildering technique on any instrument.

In the case of Eddie South, we have one of our top-notch jazzmen whose best efforts on wax were recorded in Europe. Eddie, probably the greatest violinist of jazz, has a beautiful tone and an amazing technique on his instrument. The only thing he lacks is a purely hot temperament – he could be content playing semi-classical numbers. To get the best out of him, he must be supervised by a genuine hot addict. When Hughes Pannassié got him to record for the Swing label in Paris, 1937, he made his earlier work for Victor look sick. And even Venuti is put to shame by South at his best.

But first let's get the historical part straight. Eddie's first foreign venture was a Paris stand, in 1928. Two numbers from that period, 'Two guitars' and 'Doin' The raccoon', have been preserved on wax by French Gramophone. Eddie returned to Paris in 1937, to lead a band at the International Exposition. He brought with him as pianist David Martin; Martin's only recordings in France, however, were made with Alix Combelle, not South.

For his Swing session, South recorded two fine solos; 'Eddie's Blues' and 'Sweet Georgia Brown', choosing as his accompanists Django Reinhardt, who he idolizes, and the American bassist Wilson Myers. Myers, incidentally, is the 'Ernest Meyers' who played bass on the great New Orleans Feetwarmers date. He tells me that he learned the bull fiddle only the day before that memorable session, having been till then a guitarist.

Eddie joined with Stéphane Grappelly of the H.C.F. Quintette to produce what are likely to remain the greatest hot violin duets ever, 'Dinah' and 'Daphne'. Both of them know how to put a violin through its paces, and the entente between them, as when they answer each other's phrases in the final choruses, borders on the incredible. This same duet, with Django's backing, experimented with a Bach concert, filling one side of the record with a straight improvisation, the other with a swing interpretation. Finally, Michel Warlop, another leading French fiddler, was added, and the trio made 'Fiddle Blues' and 'Lady Be Good' (Swing 54).

South and Martin returned to the U.S. on the same boat as Carter, in May 1938. Since then Eddie has led his orchestra in various cities, but nothing has yet been done to rescue this great jazz violinist from comparative obscurity. (Walter E Schaap, *Jazz Information*, Vol.1, No.11)

Review of Hot Club of France Quintet, 'Ultrafox'/'Swanee River' (Royal 1785); 'Confessing'/'Smoke Rings' (Royal 1788)

More reissues from Ultraphone, these four sides by the Quintet are no more interesting than those already issued. Django, who is a better improviser than jazz musician, doesn't get much chance to show his talents, and Grappelly's fiddling is too prominent. The best side is Confessin', which is smooth and pleasant, in the popular vein. (Unsigned, *Jazz Information,* Vol. 1, No. 11)

New York — Friday 15 December 1939

Review of Hot Club of France Quintet, 'Chasin' Shadows'/'I've Had My Moments' (Royale 1798)

Django Reinhardt's long guitar solo in Chasin' Shadows is a masterpiece of its kind – wonderfully conceived and executed, played with matchless spirit and, of course, technique. The tune is sentimentally lovely, but Django's improvisations on it are genuinely memorable. Without falling into a discussion of the nature of jazz, we might suggest that the quality of his work, in spite of superficial resemblances, is much closer to the genius of the Spanish guitarists than to hot music. (Unsigned, *Jazz Information,* Vol. 1, No. 14)

New York — Friday 22 December 1939

Here we shall consider a group of Negro musicians who have become more fully integrated into the continental jazz scene. Most of these were veritable missionaries of jazz, preaching the new musical doctrine from the platforms of hundreds of cafes and 'dancings' scattered throughout every country in Europe. For the most part their solid bourgeois audience was horrified by what seemed to them raucous cacophony. Many of the musicians finally succumbed, and deserted hot music for the waltzes tangos and rumbas that the public demanded.

Others stuck it out, buoyed by the admiration shining in the eyes of a few rebellious students or of certain European musicians who were impressed by this new music, and by the evident joy with which it imbued its performers. One such was Arthur Briggs, a member of Noble Sissle's Orchestra. God alone knows how many countries Briggs has played in; it is doubtful if he himself can remember them all – and besides, some of them are no longer countries. Briggs gained a tremendous reputation abroad, and while he hardly rates 'second to Louis', as has often been claimed, he does show a remarkable resemblance, at times, to the great Armstrong. Usually, Briggs is leading a small mixed band of his own in some obscure spot, but most of his recordings have been made as featured soloist in some better known band. Together with Coleman Hawkins he played on a few sides by Michael Warlop's Orchestra, made in Paris, in 1935. A few months later he was featured in the H.C.F Quintette's record, recently issued here on Royale. Some of his recordings, however, were made while he was working regularly with Noble Sissle's and Freddy Johnson's orchestras. His solo on Johnson's 'Sweet Georgia Brown' (made for French Brunswick in 1933) is probably the peak of his recorded career, and can stand comparison with the work of the greatest trumpets. With Johnson on piano, he also waxed a few solos about this time.

Bobby Martin, who recently returned to this country, has had a somewhat similar career. Martin was featured in Sam Wooding's colored combination, which toured Europe way back in the twenties. He also played with Willy Lewis' aggregation at the time Benny Carter went over to join it.

A greater trumpet, however, than either of these, to my way of thinking, is Bill Coleman. Bill's style, his sharp, clear tone, remind one of a strangely sensitive Henry Allen; and indeed, the two played side by side with both Luis Russell and Don Redman. Coleman's first recorded solo was on the Cecil Scott 'Lawd Lawd', recently reissued by Bluebird. Going abroad with Lucky Millinder in 1933, Bill soon returned to the United States, where he was featured on a few Fats Waller discs. But after a year or so, he yielded again to the urge for travel; and this time he visited France only as a stepping-stone to such exotic places as Bombay and Cairo. As far as we know, he is till in Egypt. Much of the time, Coleman was lead trumpet with Willy Lewis. Other recordings abroad were with Garnet Clark in 1935 and with Dicky Wells and Alix Combelle in 1937. Under his own name he made a dozen or so sides with pick-up bands in France.

A fine reed man, Frank 'Big Boy' Goodie has been abroad more years than you could shake a baton at. Goodie strangely enough, really owes his nickname to his height; he stands well over six feet. A New Orleans boy, he still plays in the old style; and very well too. Generally he is featured on tenor sax, but he is also proficient on alto, clarinet and trumpet. Big Boy has recorded with Noble Sissle, Freddy Johnson, Willy Lewis and Bill Coleman. The Coleman recording of 'Big Boy Blues', a Swing disc, has been reissued by Victor. Under his own name, Goodie demonstrates his versatility on two Ultraphone sides 'St Louis Blues' and 'I Found A New Baby' (Ul AP-1527).

Fletcher Allen, a fine arranger and sax man, played with Lloyd Scott back in 1927. In Europe, he worked for a while with Freddy Taylor, and later organized his own outfit. At Benny Carter's session for Swing, Allen played second alto, taking the solo in 'Blue Light Blues'. With his own band, Allen recorded 'Swinging In Paris', 'Fletcher's Stomp' (Swing 29) and 'What'll I Do' (Swing 36).

Several rhythm men who participated in historic recordings have been knocking about Europe for the past several years. Both June Cole and Kaiser Marshall, bass and drums respectively with the old Fletcher Henderson outfit, found their way to the other side. Coles played for some time with Willy Lewis and also recorded with Garnet Clark. As far as I know, Marshall kept out of the recording studios while abroad; he returned home some time ago, and is now with Edgar Hayes' band. Another old-timer, Tommy Benford, known for his work with Jelly Roll Morton, was playing this year with Willy Lewis. Tommy handled the traps on Coleman Hawkins All-Star jam Band date. Wilson Myers, bassist for the New Orleans Feetwarmers, recorded abroad with Eddie South, Bill Coleman and Alix Combelle. Unlike most bassists Myers prefers to use the bow on his bass fiddle. It's really terrific to watch him bowing out fantastic breaks, his body doing contortionist tricks, while his face remains solemn as a preacher's.

But the number of pianists who played abroad is even more impressive. One reason for this is that the European 'boite' works on a limited budget, and the piano is the most satisfactory solo instrument. Garland Wilson, for example, became a standard fixture at 'Le Boeuf sur le Toit'. Wilson is a wonderful pianist, in the direct line of Fats Waller; while his style, not purely hot, is overburdened with changes of temp and the like, his touch is superb. He has recorded a whole string of solos for English Parlophone and Brunswick, French Brunswick, and Swing, also participating in a Danny Polo session.

Freddy Johnson has been away for over ten years now, long enough to learn Dutch (which is no mean feat). He is primarily a band pianist and arranger, and will readily admit that he can't play solos. His 1933 band in Paris might well be considered the best colored outfit ever assembled outside the U.S. Not many records made around that time can surpass 'Sweet Georgia Brown'. Later Johnson drifted to Holland, recording with Lex van Spell's Orchestra, Benny Carter and Coleman Hawkins' Trio. During the fall of 1937 and 1938 he played together with the Hawk in Amsterdam.

A very talented pianist was the unfortunate Garnet Clark. Clark waxed two sides with an Alex Hill band before leaving the States. In Europe, he recorded a solo of 'I Got Rhythm', and three sides with a small but choice band, for French Gramophone. Clark came to a tragic end, in an asylum.

Herman Chittison of Willy Lewis' Orchestra has the reputation of being the best pianist on the Continent for the last few years. For example, Freddy Johnson refused to take any solos at a Hot Club of France concert last spring, saying 'Hell, I'm no Chittison'. Chittison has recorded any number of solos for French Brunswick, and a few sides for the Swing label. When Armstrong came to France in 1934, Chittison was in the band that recorded with him. Chittison has also recorded with Willy Lewis, Eddie Brunner, and Bill Coleman; together with Coleman and Fletcher Allen, left Lewis at the beginning of the year to play in Egypt.

Europeans out to 'cherche la femme', musically speaking, could hear quite a bit American talent. For example, Valaida Snow, colored trumpet player, won herself a high reputation leading her own band in England and France. Una Mae Carlisle, the pretty little pianist, recorded with Danny Polo. And Adelaide Hall the 'Blackbirds' star, she of 'Creole Love Call' fame, even had her own night club in Paris.

Any number of musicians deserve a mention in our story, but we lack information about them. (Walter E Schaap, *Jazz Information*, Vol. 1, No. 15)

New York — **Friday 29 December 1939**

Review of Hot Club of France Quintet with Alix Combelle, 'The Sheik of Araby'/'Your Sweet Smile' (Royale 1807)

> Two reissues of Ultraphone masters made in Paris, 1935. Combelle, tenor sax star of the French Hot Club, and a competent follower of Hawkins, struggles vainly against a pathetic rhythm section, and unfortunately also plays clarinet without having enough command of the instrument. The coupling (originally issued as 'Ton Doux Sourie') is commercial. (Unsigned, *Jazz Information*, Vol. 1, No. 16)

London — **Friday 29 December 1939**

Stéphane Grappelli records for Decca with Arthur Young and Hatchett's Swingtette.

Paris — **Winter 1939/40**

Alix Combelle, André Ekyan, Jean Ferret, Charlie Lewis, Django Reinhardt and Emmanuel Soudieux form a group to play at 'The Jimmy's Bar' in Paris.

Paris — **1940**

Charles Delaunay publishes *De la vie du jazz* (Editions Jazz Hot).

Studio du Poste Parisien, Paris — **Friday 12 January 1940**

Gus Viseur et ses Potes

Gustave 'Gus' Viseur (acc); Django Reinhardt (gtr); probably Emmanuel Soudieux (sb) (1).
As above, with Philippe Brun (tpt) (2).
Radio broadcast, acetates.

444 Daphne (1) {2.21}
[***LP*** Vog 406505; **KC 109**] [***CD*** Fmx FA309]

445 It Had To Be You (2) {2.44}
[***LP*** Vog 406505; **KC109**] [***CD*** Fmx FA309]

Paris — **Tuesday 23 January 1940**

Django Reinhardt's 30th birthday.

Oslo — **Wednesday 14 February 1940**

'Oslo Swingklubb's Band with Jacques Butler' and 'Jacques Butler and His Swing Patrol', featuring Robert Normann, record one title each in the QHCF style.

Paris — **Thursday 15 February 1940**

Ray Stokes records four piano solos for Swing records (matrix numbers OSW100–3).
See Rust for details.

Studio Albert, Paris — Thursday 15 February 1940

Arthur Briggs and his Orchestra

Arthur Briggs (tpt); Christian Wagner (cl); Alix Combelle (as, ts); Ray Stokes (pno); Django Reinhardt (gtr); Tony Rovira (sb).
Engineer: Eugène Ravenet

446 OSW 95-1 **My Melancholy Baby** {2.51}
[***78*** Swi 72] [***LP*** Pat C054 16024] [***CD*** DRG8493; Fmx FA309]

447 OSW 96-1 **Braggin' The Briggs Pt. I** {3.06}
[***78*** Swi 205] [***CD*** Fmx FA309]

448 OSW 97-1 **Braggin' The Briggs Pt. II** {2.45}
[***78*** Swi 205] [***CD*** Fmx FA309]

449 OSW 98-1 **Sometimes I'm Happy** (2.40}
[***78*** **unissued**] [***LP*** Pat C054 16024] [***CD*** Fmx FA309]

450 OSW 99-1 **Scatterbrain** {2.17}
[***78*** Swi 72] [***LP*** Pat C054 16009] [***CD*** Fmx FA309]

Studio Albert, Paris — Tuesday 20 February 1940

Alix Combelle and his Swing Band

Alex Renard, Pierre Allier, Albert Piguilhem, Philippe Brun (tpts); Guy Paquinet (tbn); Alix Combelle (ts, speech, ldr); Charlie Lewis (pno); Django Reinhardt (gtr solo); Joseph Reinhardt (gtr); Marceau Sarbib (sb); 'H.P. Chadel' (Charles Delaunay) (dms).
Engineer: Eugène Ravenet

451 OSW 104-1 **Jumpin' At The Woodside** {2.54}
[***78*** Swi 93] [***LP*** Pat C054 16009] [***CD*** Cls 714; Fmx FA309]

452 OSW 105-1 **Week-End Stomp** {2.46}
[***78*** Swi 73] [***LP*** Pat C054 16024] [***CD*** Cls 714; Fmx FA309]

453 OSW 106-1 **Nerves And Fever** {3.21}
[***78*** **unissued**] [***CD*** **Cls 714**, Fmx FA309]

454 OSW 107-1 **Fast, Slow, Medium Tempo** {3.00}
[***78*** Swi 81] [***CD*** Cls 714; Fmx FA309]

455 OSW 108-1 **Panassié Stomp** {3.02}
[***78*** Swi 81] [***LP*** Pat C054 16024] [***CD*** Cls 714; Fmx FA309]

456 OSW 109-1 **Rock-a-bye Basie** {2.47}
[***78*** Swi 73] [***LP*** Pat C054 16024] [***CD*** Cls 714; Fmx FA309]

Studio Albert, Paris — Thursday 22 February 1940

Philippe Brun and his Jam Band

Philippe Brun (tpt); Guy Paquinet (tbn); Alix Combelle (cl); Charlie Lewis (pno); Django Reinhardt (gtr, speech) (1); Marceau Sarbib (sb); 'H.P. Chadel' (Charles Delaunay) (dms).

457 OSW 110-1 **Boogie Woogie Part 1** {2.51}
[*78* Swi 80] [*LP* Pat C054 16009] [*CD* Cls 813; Fmx FA309]

458 OSW 111-1 **Boogie Woogie Part 2** (1) {2.31}
[*78* Swi 80] [*LP* Pat C054 16009] [*CD* Cls 813; Fmx FA309]

459 OSW 112-1 **Blue Skies** {2.36}
[*78* Swi 190] [*LP* Aff BOX107; Pat C054 16009]
[*CD* Arc CASTEL10252; BGO 366; Cls 813; Fmx FA309]

460 OSW 113-1 **Stomp** {2.16}
[*78* Swi 190] [*LP* Pat C054 16009] [*CD* Cls 813; Fmx FA309]

The original studio recording sheet identifies these sides as by 'Alix Combelle et son Orchestre'.

London March 1940

Review of Quintet of the Hot Club of France, 'H.C.Q. Strut'/ 'Man I Love (The)' (Decca F7390, 2s.)

> *H.C.Q.* (Hot Club to you) *Strut* finds Reinhardt and Grappelly doing their usual stuff in their own particular way respectively on guitar and violin. They swing this pleasant melody easily and Reinhardt's wizardry technique is as obvious as ever.
>
> Although labelled as by the Quintet, The Man I Love is actually a duet by Reinhardt and Grappelly on piano [*sic*]. When they play 'in tempo' the music has quite the Ed Lang – Arthur Schutt touch. Still, that doesn't mean that the parts that are not 'in tempo' are unmusical. (Edgar Jackson, *The Gramophone*)

Studio Albert, Paris Friday 22 March 1940

André Ekyan – saxophone solo

André Ekyan (as); Django Reinhardt (gtr solo); Pierre 'Baro' Ferret (gtr); Emmanuel Soudieux (sb).
Engineer: Eugène Ravenet

461 OSW 114-1 **Rosetta** {2.25}
[*78* Swi 98] [*LP* Pat C054 16009] [*CD* Cls 831; Fmx FA310]

462 OSW 115-1 **Sugar** {2.37}
[*78* **Swi 98**, 202] [*LP* Pat C054 16009] [*CD* Cls 831; Fmx FA310]

463 OSW 116-1 **A Pretty Girl Is Like A Melody** {2.36}
[*78* Swi 194] [*LP* Pat C054 16009] [*CD* Cls 831; Fmx FA310]

464 OSW 117-1 **Margie** {2.12}
[*78* **Swi 194**, 202] [*LP* Pat C054 16010] [*CD* Cls 831; Fmx FA310]

Same location, date and engineer

Django's Music

Philippe Brun, Pierre Allier, Alex Renard, Al Piguilhem (tpts); André Ekyan (as); Guy Paquinet, Gaston Moat, Pierre Deck (tbns); Alix Combelle (bs); Charlie Lewis (pno); Django Reinhardt (gtr solo); Pierre 'Baro' Ferret (gtr); Emmanuel Soudieux (sb) (1).
As above, with André Ekyan (as) added (2).
Brun, Allier, Renard, Paquinet, Ekyan, Combelle, Lewis, Reinhardt, Ferret, Soudieux (3).
Brun, Renard, Combelle, Lewis, Reinhardt, Ferret, Soudieux (4).
Arr. by Django Reinhardt.

465 OSW 118-1 **Tears** (1) {2.45}
[**78** Swi 79] [***LP*** Pat C054 16010] [***CD*** Aff AFS 10035; Cls 831; Fmx FA310]

466 OSW 119-1 **Limehouse Blues** (2) {2.25}
[**78** Swi 82] [***LP*** Aff BOX107; Pat C054 16010] [***CD*** Aff AFS 10035; Cas PIESD233; Cls 831; Cly DIG12; Fla PASTCD9792; Fmx FA310]

467 OSW 120-1 **Daphné** (3) {2.48}
[**78** Swi 82] [***LP*** Pat C054 16010] [***CD*** Aff AFS 10035; Cls 831; Cly DIG12; Fla PASTCD9792; Fmx FA310]

468 OSW 121-1 **At The Jimmy's Bar** (4) {2.48}
[**78** Swi 79] [***LP*** Aff BOX107; Pat C054 16010] [***CD*** Aff AFS 10035; Cly DIG12; Cls 831; Fla PASTCD9792; Fmx FA310]

'At The Jimmy's Bar', Paris — c. March 1940

Django Reinhardt et L'Orchestre de Chez 'Jimmy'

Django Reinhardt (gtr solo) acc. by L'Orchestre de 'Jimmy'; Philippe Brun (tpt) (1); Charlie Lewis (pno); Pierre 'Baro' Ferret (gtr); Emmanuel Soudieux (sb); Pierre Fouad or 'H P Chadel' (Charles Delaunay) (dms).
Radio broadcast, 'Radio Citie'; acetates.

469 **Sweet Sue (Just You)** (1) {5.15}
[**unissued**] [***CD*** Fmx FA310]

470 **Appel Indirect** {5.03}
[**unissued**] [***CD*** Fmx FA310]

Paris — Friday 10 May 1940

Django and Naguine reportedly leave Paris for the South of France.

France — Sunday 12 May 1940

The 'Battle of France' begins as German troops cross the Meuse river.

London — **Saturday 25 May 1940**

Stéphane Grappelli records for Decca with Arthur Young and Hatchett's Swingtette.

Paris — **June 1940**

Philippe Brun and André Ekyan join the French armed forces.

Paris — **Monday 3 June 1940**

The Luftwaffe attack Paris, dropping an estimated 1,100 bombs.

Dunkirk — **Tuesday 4 June 1940**

The final day of the evacuation of the British Expeditionary Force.

Paris — **Friday 14 June 1940**

Paris falls; the German army conducts a victory parade along the Champs-Élysées. Meanwhile, from Bordeaux, General Charles de Gaulle escapes by air to England.

Paris — **Sunday 23 June 1940**

Adolf Hitler visits Paris for the first and only time.

London — **Tuesday 30 July 1940**

Stéphane Grappelli records for two titles for Decca as 'Stephane Grappelly and His Musicians' (matrix numbers DR4903–4). Musicians include Jack Llewellyn. See Rust for details.

Paris — **c. mid-August 1940**

Django and Naguine reportedly return to Paris.

London — **September 1940**

Arthur Young leaves Hatchett's Swingtette and is replaced by Dennis Moonan. Stéphane Grappelli continues to play with the group.

Oslo — **Thursday 12 September 1940**

'String Swing', featuring Robert Normann, record two titles in the QHCF style.

Paris — **Autumn 1940**

The Quintette begin a long engagement at the 'Club Normandie'.

Studio Albert, Paris — **Tuesday 1 October 1940**

Django Reinhardt et le Quintette du Hot-Club de France

Hubert Rostaing (cl, ts) (1); Django Reinhardt (gtr solo); Joseph Reinhardt (gtr); Francis Luca (sb); Pierre Fouad (dms).
As above, with Josette Dayde (vcl) (2).
Engineer: Eugène Ravenet

471 OSW 127-1 **Nuages** {3.16}
[**78 unissued**] [LP **KC109**; Swi 8420267] [***CD*** Cls 831; Fmx FA310; Gal GALE421; JSP 901; Mos MD 6-190; Rec SMDCD307]

472 OSW 128-1 **Rythme Futur** {2.37}
[***78*** Swi 83] [***LP*** Pat C054 16010] [***EP*** An 73006] [***CD*** Aff AFS 10035; Cls 831; Fmx FA310; JA 157222; JSP 904; Mos MD 6-190]

473 OSW 129-1 **Begin The Beguine** {2.50}
[**78 unissued**] [***LP*** Aff BOX107; **Pat C054 16010**] [***CD*** Aff AFS10035; Cas PIESD233; Cls 831; Cly DIG12; Fmx FA310; Gal GALE421; JSP 904; Mos MD 6-190]

474 OSW 130-1 **Blues** {3.08}
[***78*** Swi 83] [***LP*** Pat C054 16010] [***CD*** Cls 831; Fmx FA310; JA 157222; JSP 904; Mos MD 6-190]

475 OSW 131-1 **Cou-Cou** (2) {2.40}
[**78 unissued**] [***LP*** **Pat C054 16010** (extract only); Swi SW8420267] [***CD*** **Cls 831** (in full); Fmx FA310; JSP 904; Mos MD 6-190]

476 OSW 132-1 **Indécision** (Undecided) (1) {3.02}
[**78 unissued**] [***LP*** Pat C054 116010] [***CD*** Aff AFS 10035; Cls 831; Fmx FA310; JSP 904; Mos MD 6-190]

'Normandie' cinéma, Paris

The Quintette begin an engagement.
See Delaunay, pages 102–3.

Studio Albert, Paris — Monday 21 October 1940

Alix Combelle et son Orchestre

Aime Barelli, Christian Bellest, Pierre-Severin Luino (tpts); Eugène d'Hellemmes (tbn); Max Blanc, Marcel Coestier (as); Noël Chiboust, Alix Combelle (ts); Raymond Wrascoff (pno); Django Reinhardt (gtr); Francis Luca (sb); Pierre Fouad (dms).
Engineer: Eugène Ravenet

477 OSW 133-1 **Tel Quel** (En Plein Sur Le Nez) {3.11}
[***78*** Swi 93] [***CD*** Cls 714; Fmx FA310]

478 OSW 134-1 **Deux Pieds Gauches** (Two Left Feet) {2.50}
[***78*** Swi 85] [***CD*** Cls 714; Fmx FA310]

479 OSW 135-1 **Joyeuse Fumée** (Holy Smoke) {2.40}
[***78*** Swi 85] [***CD*** Cls 751; Fmx FA310]

480 OSW 136-1 **Tiger Rag** {2.45}
[***78*** Swi 84] [***LP*** Pat C054 16010] [***CD*** Cls 751; Fmx FA310]

481 OSW 137-1 **Quatre Tickets** {2.32}
[***78*** Swi 84] [***LP*** Pat C054 16010] [***CD*** Cls 751; Fmx FA310]

Studio Albert, Paris — Tuesday 22 October 1940

Noel Chiboust et son Orchestre

Aime Barelli (tpt); Max Blanc (cl, as); Noël Chiboust, Alix Combelle (ts); Raymond Wrascoff (pno); Django Reinhardt (gtr); Francis Luca (sb); Pierre Fouad (dms).
Arr. by Noël Chiboust.
Engineer: Eugène Ravenet

482 OSW 138-1 **Sérénade d'Hiver** (Winter Serenade) {2.39}
[*78* Swi 86] [*LP* Pat C054 16025] [*CD* Cls 831; Fmx FA310]

483 OSW 138-2 **Sérénade d'Hiver** [**unissued**]

484 OSW 139-1 **Le Sheik** {2.15}
[*78* Swi 86] [*LP* Pat C054 16010] [*CD* Cls 831; Fmx FA310]

485 OSW 139-2 **Le Sheik** [**unissued**]

486 OSW 140-1 **Noël Blues** {2.55}
[*78* Swi 97] [*LP* Pat C054 16010] [*CD* Cls 831; Fmx FA310]

487 OSW 141-1 **Margie** {2.18}
[*78* Swi 97] [*LP* Pat C054 16011] [*CD* Cls 831; Fmx FA310]

488 OSW 141-2 **Margie** [**unissued**]

489 OSW 142-1 **Bijou** {2.21}
[*78* Swi 119] [*CD* Cls 831; Fmx FA310]

Same location, date and engineer

Hubert Rostaing – Aime Barelli et Leur Orchestre

Aime Barelli, Christian Bellest (tpts); Hubert Rostaing (cl); Alix Combelle (ts); Raymond Wrascoff (pno); Django Reinhardt (gtr); Francis Luca (sb); Pierre Fouad (dms).
Arr. by Hubert Rostaing and Django Reinhardt.

490 OSW 143-1 **Indécision** (Undecided) {3.16}
[*78* Swi 87] [*LP* Pat C054 16011] [*CD* Cls 831; Fmx FA310]

491 OSW 144-1 **Oui, C'est Ça** {2.37}
[*78* Swi 87] [*LP* Pat C054 16011] [*CD* Cls 831; Fmx FA310]

Zurich — c. November 1940

Eddie Bruner and his Band record seven titles for Swiss Columbia.
See Rust for details.

Ciro's Club, Paris — December 1940

The Quintette appear in residence for an unspecified period of time.

Studio Albert, Paris Friday 13 December 1940

Quintette du Hot-Club de France Avec Alix Combelle

Hubert Rostaing (cl); Alix Combelle (cl) (1), (ts) (2), chimes (3); Django Reinhardt (gtr solo); Joseph Reinhardt (gtr); Tony Rovira (sb); Pierre Fouad (dms).
Engineer: Pierre Hamard

492 OSW 145-1 **Swing '41** (1) {3.05}
[***78*** Swi 85] [***LP*** Aff BOX107; Pat C054 16011; Swi SW8420267] [***CD*** Aff AFS 10035; Arc CASTEL810562; Cas PIESD233; Cls 852; Cly DIG12; Fla PASTCD9792; Fmx FA310; Gal GALE421; JA 157222; JSP 904; Mos MD 6-190; Recall SMDCD307; Swi CDSW8426]

493 OSW 146-1 **Nuages** (1) {3.17}
[***78*** **Swi 88**; Pat PN 44126; PG 532; P I1041] [***25cm LP*** CHDD 588] [***LP*** Aff BOX107; Ast LP20102; Met MTM12; Pat C054 16011; Swi SW8420267] [***EP*** An 73006; HMV 7EGH1002, 7EMF165, 7EMQ12, (F) 7EGF650] [***CD*** Aff AFS10035; Arc CASTEL810562, SOL507; Cas PIESD233; CC 2010; Cls 852; Cly CD1048, DIG12; Fla PASTCD9792; Fmx FA310; Hab 111200; JA 157222; JSP 904; Kaz EUKCD913; LE AJA5267; Mos MD 6-190; Swi CDSW8426]

494 OSW 147-1 **Pour Vous** (Exactly Like You) (1, 2) {3.05}
[***78*** Swi 118] [***LP*** Aff BOX107; Pat C054 16011] [***CD*** Aff AFS 10035; Cls 852; Cly DIG12; Fla PASTCD9792; Fmx FA310; JSP 904; Mos MD 6-190]

495 OSW 148-1 **Fantaisie Sur Une Danse Norvégienne** {2.30}
[***78*** **unissued** *Swing* test] [***LP*** Aff BOX107; **HMV FELP 236**; Pat C054 16011] [***CD*** Aff AFS 10035; Cls 852; Fmx FA310; Gal GALE421; JSP 904; Mos MD 6-190]

496 OSW 149-1 **Vendredi 13** (3) {3.01}
[***78*** Swi 123] [***LP*** Pat C054 16011] [***CD*** Aff AFS10035; Cls 852; Fmx FA310; JSP 904; Mos MD 6-190]

497 OSW 150-1 **Liebesfreud** {2.37}
[***78*** **unissued** *Swing* test] [***LP*** Aff BOX107; **HMV FELP 236**; Pat C054 160111] [***CD*** Aff AFS10035; Cls 852; Fmx FA310; JSP 904]

498 OSW 151-1 **Mabel** {3.16}
[***78*** Swi 137] [***LP*** Pat C054 16011] [***CD*** Cls 852; Fmx FA310; JSP 904; Mos MD 6-190]

499 OSW 152-1 **Petits Mensonges** (Little White Lies) {3.14}
[***78*** Swi 103] [***LP*** Aff BOX107; Pat C054 16011] [***CD*** Aff AFS10035; Cls 852; Cly DIG12; DIG CO3506; Fla PASTCD97972; Fmx FA310; JSP 904; Mos MD 6-190]

500 OSW 153-1 **Les Yeux Noirs** {2.11}
[***78*** **Swi 88**; Pat PG 532, PI 11041] [***LP*** Pat C054 16011]

[***EP*** HMV 7EGF941] [***CD*** Aff AFS10035; Cls 852; Fmx FA310; JA 157222; JSP 904; Mos MD 6-190]

501 OSW 154-1 **Sweet Sue** (Just You) {2.47}
[***78*** Swi 118] [***LP*** Aff BOX107; Pat C054 16011] [***CD*** Aff AFS10035; Cls 852; Cly DIG12; Dig CO3506; Emp RAJCD808; Fla PASTCD9792; Fmx FA310; Gal GALE421; Hab 111200; JSP 904; Mos MD 6-190; Rccall SMDCD307]

Studio Albert, Paris — Tuesday 17 December 1940

Personnel, engineer and label credits as above.

502 OSW 155-1 **Swing De Paris** (1) {3.00}
[***78*** Swi 176] [***LP*** Aff BOX107; HD CHD165; Pat C054 16011] [***CD*** ABM1003; Aff AFS 10035; Arc CASTEL10562; Cls 852; Cly DIG12; Dig MO3057; Fla PASTCD9792; Fmx FA310; HD CDHD165; JSP 902; Mos MD 6-190]

503 OSW 156-1 **Oiseaux De Iles** (1, 2) {2.47}
[***78*** Swi 103] [***LP*** Aff BOX107; Pat C054 16012] [***EP*** An 73007] [***CD*** Aff AFS10035; Cls 852; Cly DIG12; Fmx FA310; JSP 902; Mos Md 6-190; Recall SMDCD307]

504 OSW 157-1 **All Of Me** (2) {2.45}
[***78*** Swi 128] [***LP*** Aff BOX107; Pat C054 16012] [***CD*** Aff AFS10035; Cls 852; Cly DIG12; Emp RAJCD808; Fmx FA310; JSP 902; Mos MD 6-190; Recall SMDCD307]

Studio Albert, Paris — Wednesday 18 December 1940

Trio de Saxophone Alix Combelle

Alix Combelle (ts, ldr); Hubert Rostaing (ts, cl); Christian Wagner (cl, as); Django Reinhardt (gtr solo); Joseph Reinhardt (gtr); Tony Rovira (sb); Pierre Fouad (dms).
Arr. by Hubert Rostaing.
Engineer: Pierre Hamard

505 OSW 162-1 **Cascades** {2.51}
[***78*** Swi 117] [***CD*** Cls 751; Fmx FA311]

506 OSW 163-1 **Reflets** {2.47}
[***78*** Swi 117] [***CD*** Cls 751; Fmx FA311]

507 OSW 164-1 **Onze Heures Vingt** {3.18}
[***78*** Swi 96] [***LP*** Pat C054 16024] [***CD*** Cls 751; Fmx FA311]

508 OSW 165-1 **Sur Le Bords D'Alamo** (On The Alamo) {3.12}
[***78*** Swi 96] [***LP*** Pat C054 116012] [***CD*** Cls 751; Fmx FA311]

Same location, date and engineer

Christian Wagner et Son Orchestre

Personnel as above but without Joseph Reinhardt.

509 OSW 166-1 **Pour Terminer** {3.03}
[***78*** Swi 102] [***LP*** Pat C054 16012] [***CD*** Cls 852; Fmx FA310]

510 OSW 167-1 **Pour Commencer** {2.56}
[***78*** Swi 102] [***CD*** Arc CASTEL810222; Cls 852; Fmx FA310]

For reasons of space and ease of programming, Swing 102 appears out of chronological sequence on the Fremeaux release.

Same location, date and engineer

Pierre Allier et Son Orchestre

Pierre Allier (tpt solo, ldr); Jean Heutschel, Georges Wallez (tpts); André Cauzard (tbn); Hubert Rostaing (cl, as); Charles Lissée, Pierre Martineau (as, cl); Roger Allier (ts, bs); Paul Collot (pno); Django Reinhardt (gtr solo); Jean Belloni (tuba); Pierre Fouad (dms).
Arr. by Pierre Allier.

511 OSW 168-1 **Les Yeux Noirs** {2.56}
[***78*** Swi 108] [X***CD*** Cls 852; Fmx FA311]

512 OSW 169-1 **Begin The Beguine** {2.28}
[***78*** Swi 89] [***CD*** Cls 852; Fmx FA311]

513 OSW 170-1 **Swingin' The Blues** {2.11}
[***78*** Swi 89] [***CD*** Cls 852; Fmx FA311]

Same session

Pierre Allier (tpt); Charles Lissée (as); Hubert Rostaing (cl, as); Paul Collot (pno); Django Reinhardt (gtr solo); Pierre Fouad (dms).

514 OSW 171-1 **Petite Lili** {3.25}
[***78*** Swi 126] [***LP*** Pat C054 16012] [***CD*** Cls 852; Fmx FA311]

515 OSW 172-1 **Ninouche** (Minouche) {3.23}
[***78*** Swi 108] [***LP*** Pat C054 16012] [***CD*** Cls 852; Fmx FA311]

Salle Gaveau, Paris — Thursday 19 December 1940

The 'new' Quintette, including Hubert Rostaing, appear in concert at the 'Festival of French Jazz'.
See Delaunay, pages 103–4.

Salle Pleyel, Paris — Tuesday 24 December 1940

The Quintette, in the company of 'L'Orchestre Fred Adison', begin a week-long engagement at the 'Week of Screen Record and Radio Stars'.

Studio Albert, Paris Thursday 26 December 1940

Festival Swing

Christian Bellest (1st tpt solo); Pierre Allier (2nd tpt solo); Aime Barelli (3rd tpt solo); Pierre-Severin Luino (tpt); Guy Paquinet (tbn solo); Maurice Gladieu (tbn); Christian Wagner (cl solo); Max Blanc (as solo); Georges Jacquemont (1st ts solo), Noël Chiboust (2nd ts solo); Alex Combelle (ts, announcements); and Le Quintette du Hot-Club de France: Hubert Rostaing (cl); Django Reinhardt (gtr solo, announcement); Joseph Reinhardt (gtr); Tony Rovira (sb); Pierre Fouad (dms); Charles Delaunay (announcements and identification of musicians).
Engineer: Eugène Ravenet

516 2SW 173-1 **Festival Swing** {4.11}
[***78*** Swi 91] [***LP*** Pat C054 16012] [***CD*** Cas CASTEL810562; Cls 852; Fmx FA311; JSP 904; Mos MD 6-190]

This is a 30cm (12") master and pressing.

Same location, date and engineer

Django's Music

Personnel as above, without Delaunay.

517 OSW 174-1 **Stockholm** {3.12}
[***78*** Swi 95] [***LP*** Pat C054 16012] [***CD*** Cls 852; Fmx FA311]

Paris 1941

Charlie Lewis records eight titles at two sessions for Pathé (matrix numbers CPT5267–8; CPT 5322–7).
Matrix CPT5322 is titled 'Djangology/Bricktop'. Musicians include Sigismund Beck, Pierre Fouad and André Jourdan.

Paris c. early 1941

Louis Vola leaves for Argentina.

Paris c. late January 1941

Django Reinhardt begins an approximately six-month engagement at the 'Jane Stick' nightclub.
See Delaunay, page 104.

Paris Tuesday 23 January 1941

Django Reinhardt's 31st birthday.

Monte Christo Club, Paris February 1941

The Quintette appear in residence.

Salle Pleyel, Paris Sunday 2 February 1941

Django and the 'Grand Orchestre Swing' appear in concert.
See Delaunay, page 252, for a reproduction of a poster for this event.

Oslo — Tuesday 25 February 1941

'String Swing', featuring Robert Normann, record two titles in the QHCF style.

London — Friday 28 February 1941

Stéphane Grappelli records for Decca as 'Stephan Grappelly and his Musicians' (matrix numbers DR4902–3 and DR5403–6).
See Rust for details.

'The Avenue' Club, Paris — March 1941

The Quintette appear in residence for an unspecified period.

Columbia Studios, Paris — Wednesday 12 March 1941

Charles Trenet acc. by Django Reinhardt and the Quintette du Hot Club de France (English-language issues)/**Charles Trenet, Accompagné Par Django Reinhardt Et Le Quintette Du Hot-Club De France** (French-language issues)

Charles Trenet (vcl) acc. by Léo Chauliac (pno); Django Reinhardt (gtr solo); Joseph Reinhardt (gtr); Tony Rovira (sb); Pierre Fouad (dms).
Engineer: Eugène Ravenet

518 CL 7419 **Un Rien Me Fait Chanter** [**unissued**]

519 CL 7420-1 **La Cigale Et La Fourmi** {2.20}
[***78*** Col DCF 262, **DF 2886**, CQ 2225] [***LP*** Pat C054 10395/6]
[***EP*** Col SEG7619] [***CD*** Cls 852; Fmx FA311]

L'Imperatrice Club, Paris — Spring 1941

The Quintette appear in residence.

London — Wednesday 9 April 1941

Stéphane Grappelli records for Decca as 'Stephane Grappelly And His Quartet' (matrix numbers DR5579–82). Musicians include Jack Llewelyn.
See Rust for details.

Paris — Wednesday 16 April 1941

'Christian Wagner et son Orchestre' record two titles for Swing records (matrix numbers OSW210–11). Musicians include Noël Chiboust, Pierre Fouad, Charlie Lewis, Alex Renard, Hubert Rostaing and Tony Rovira.
See Rust for details.

Paris — Friday 25 April 1941

'Maceo Jefferson et son Orchestre' record four titles for Odéon (matrix numbers Ki-9194–7). Musicians include Aime Barelli, Christian Bellest, Noël Chiboust, Charlie Lewis and Guy Paquinet.
See Rust for details.

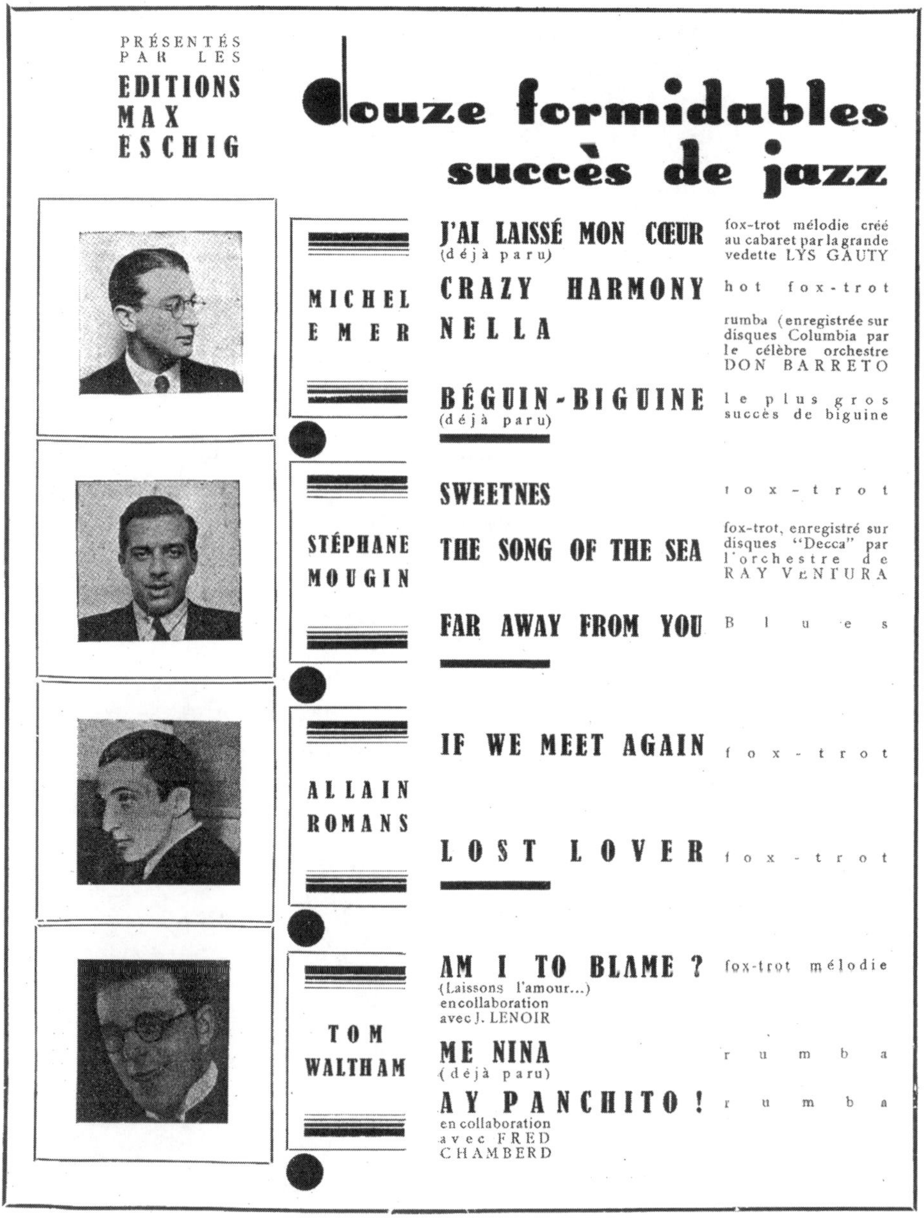

Advertisement for Editions Max Eschig, *Jazz-Tango-Dancing*, August 1932

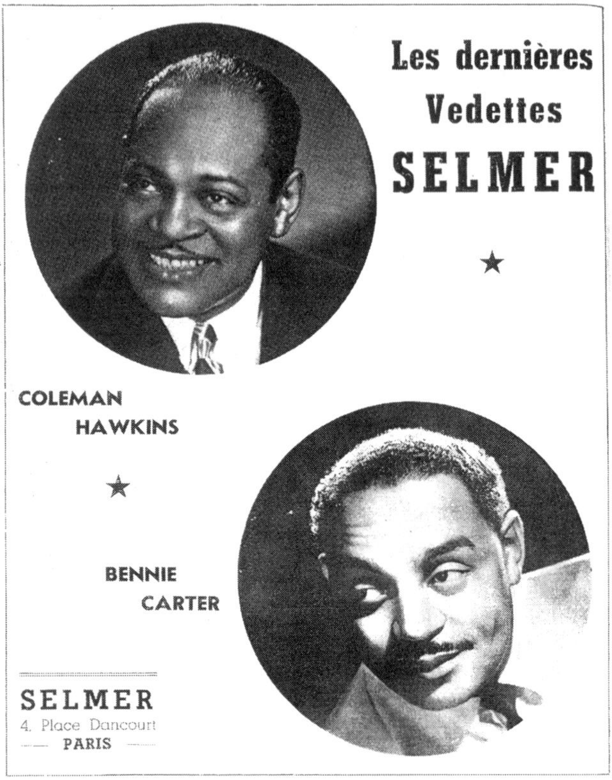

Advertisement for Coleman Hawkins and Bennie Carter, *Jazz Hot*

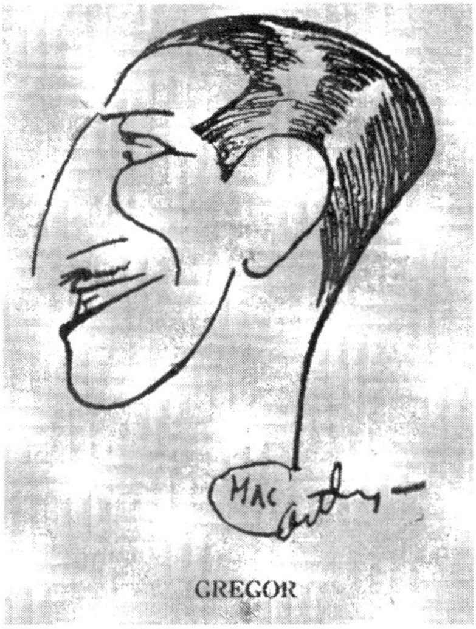

Gregor cartoon, *Jazz Tango*

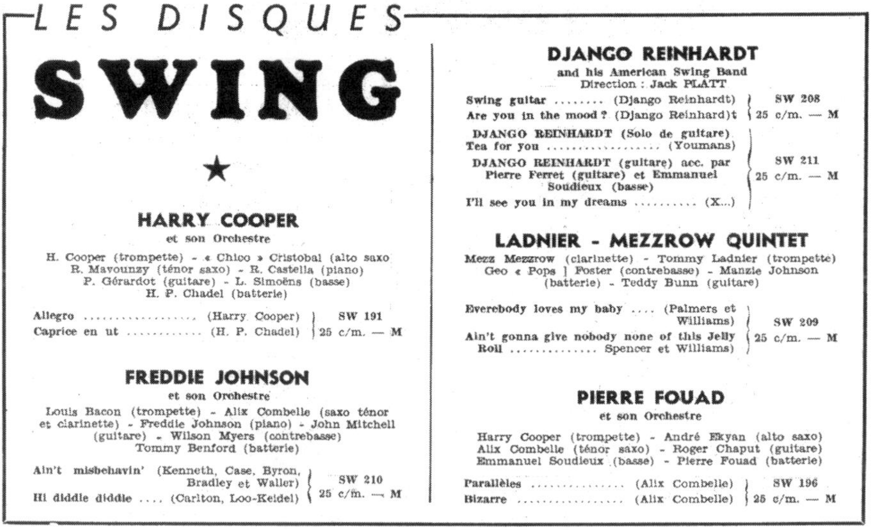

Advertisement for Les Disques Swing, *Jazz Hot*, May/June 1946

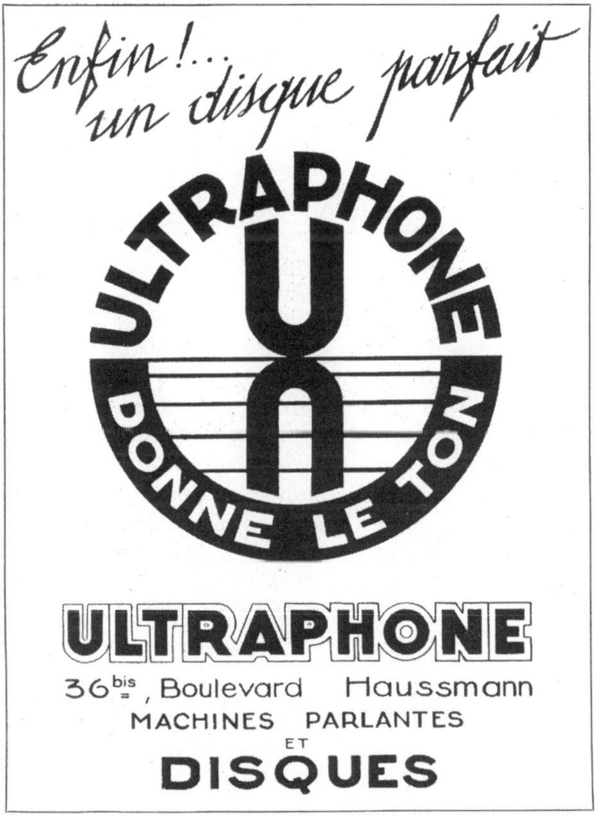

Advertisement for Ultraphone, *L'Edition musical vivant*

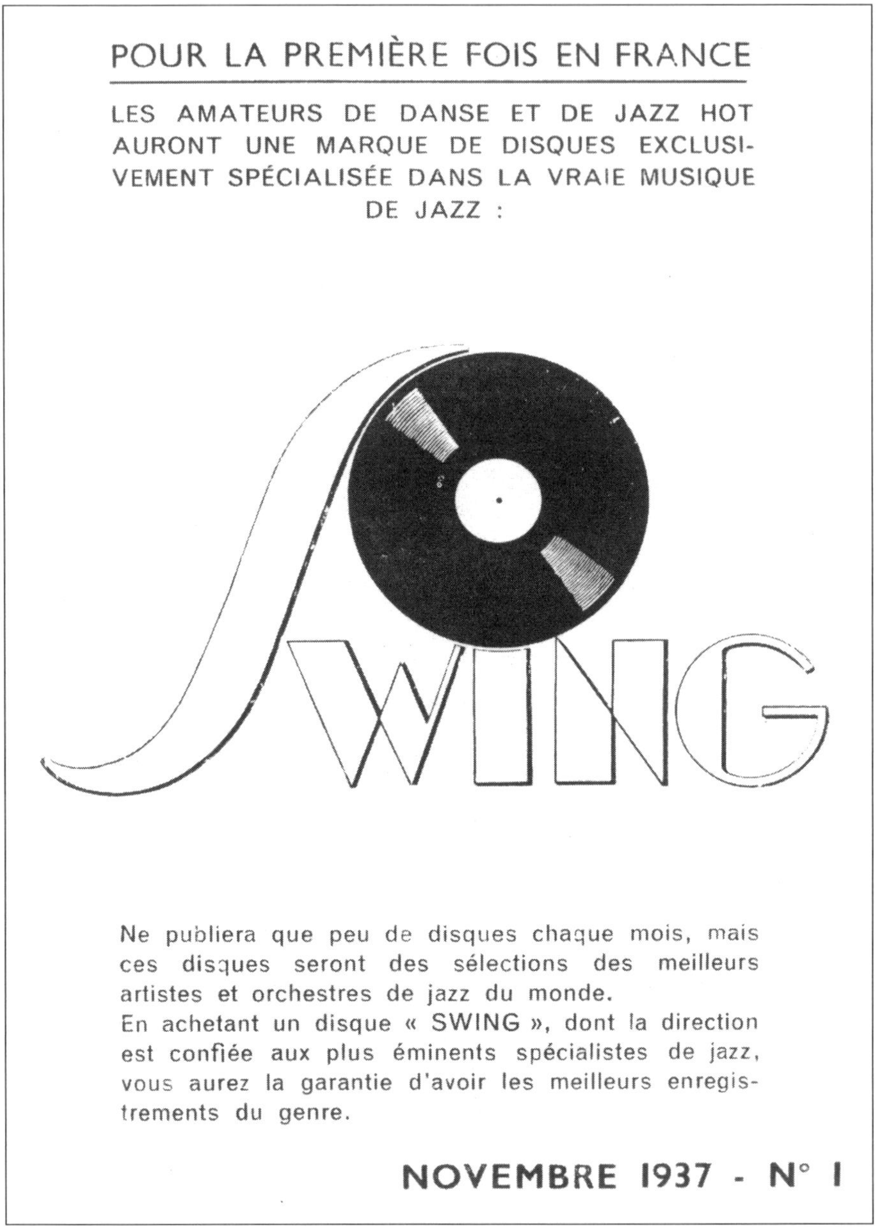

The first catalogue supplement of Swing records

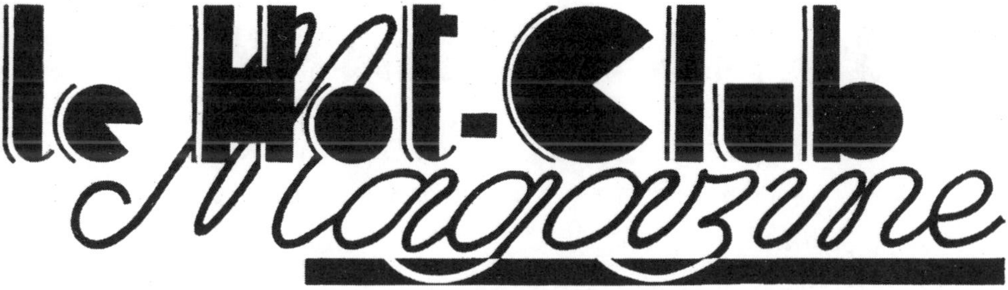

Announcement of the foundation of the Hot-Club, *Jazz-Tango-Dancing*, November 1933

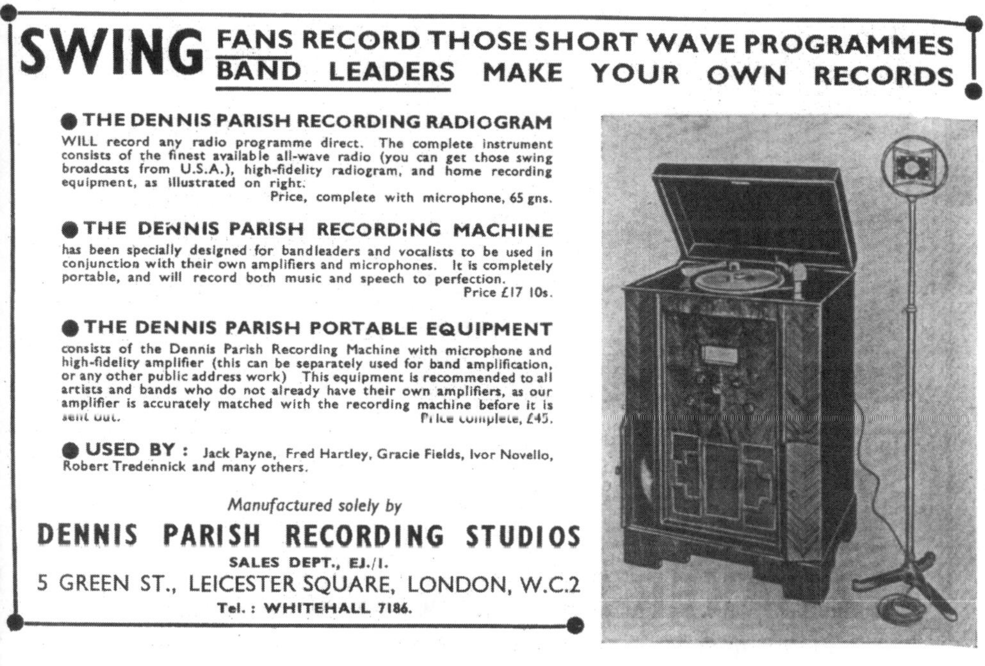

Advertisement for Dennis Parish Recording Studios, *Swing Music*, 1935

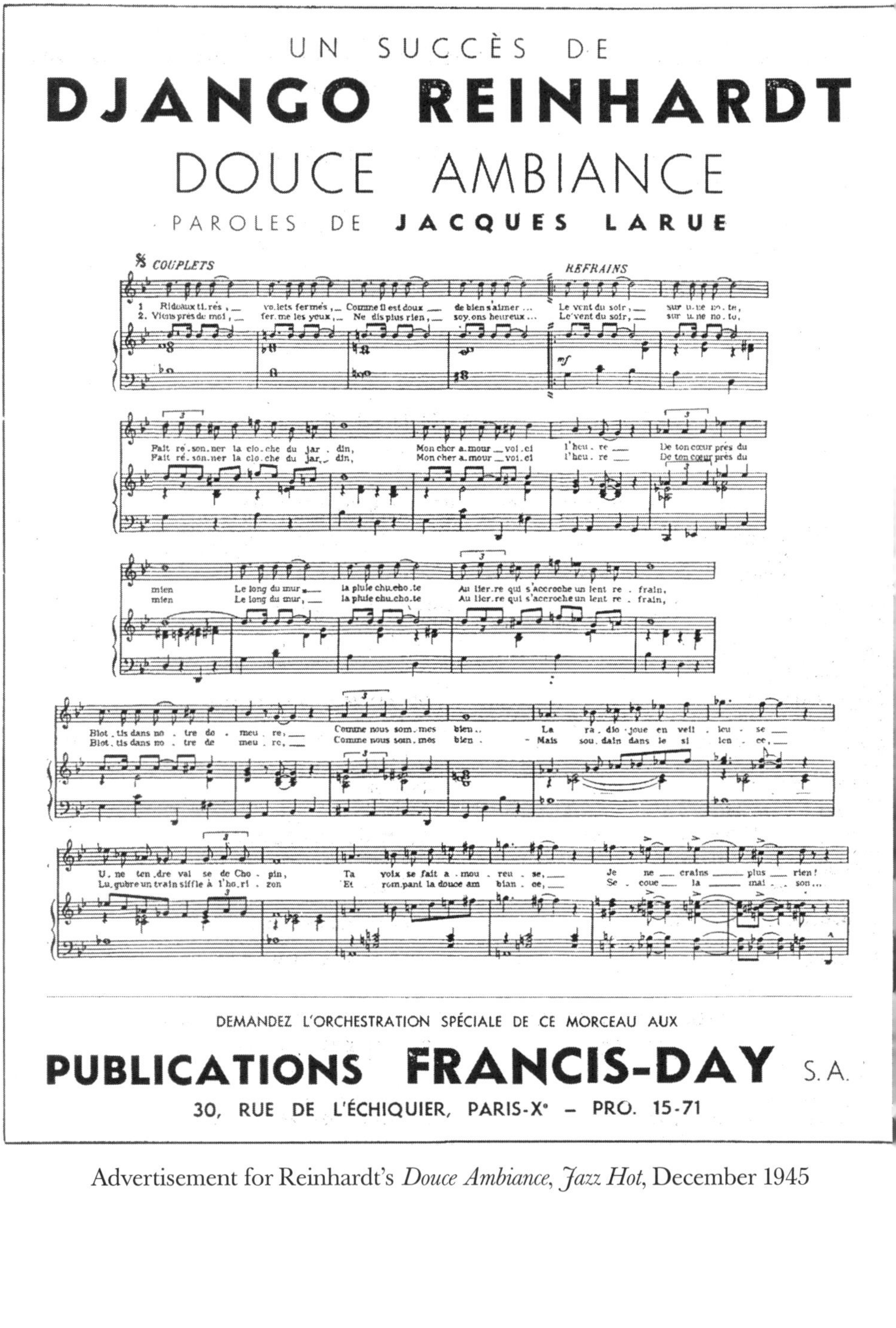

Advertisement for Reinhardt's *Douce Ambiance*, *Jazz Hot*, December 1945

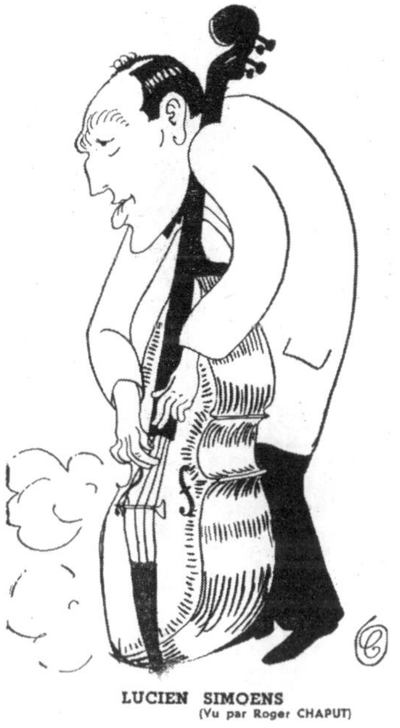

Cartoon of Lucien Simoens by Roger Chaput, *Jazz Hot*, January 1946

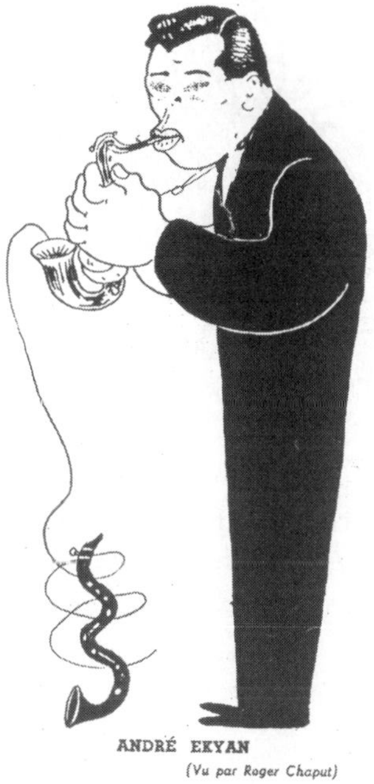

Cartoon of André Ekyan by Roger Chaput, *Jazz Hot*

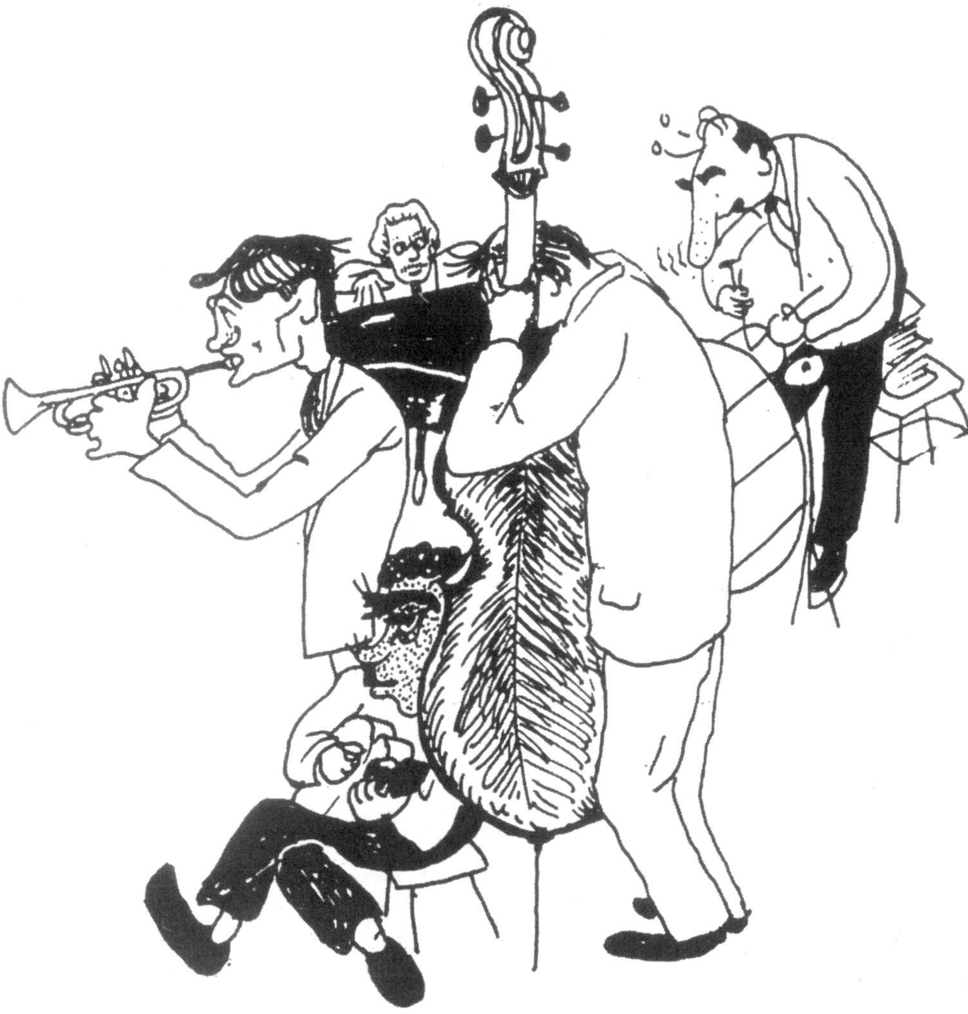

Cartoon of Bellest, Dieval, Fouad, J Reinhardt and Simoens by Roger Chaput, *Jazz Hot*, December 1947

Paris **Monday 30 April 1941**

'Sarrane Ferret et le Swing Quintette de Paris' record four titles for Odéon (matrix numbers Ki9202–5). Musicians include Pierre 'Baro' Ferret, Pierre Fouad and André Luis.

London **May/June 1941**

Stéphane Grappelli records ten titles with the 'Witley Court Music Box', a Surrey-based dance band organised within the Pinchin Johnson paint manufacturing company (matrix numbers CTP 11730–8 and 11751). Musicians include Noel 'Chappie' D'Amato. Titles include 'Sweet Sue', 'Some Of These Days', 'I Got Rhythm' and 'Crazy Rhythm'. The records, issued under the name of the 'Witley Court Music Box', were manufactured by the Gramophone Company Ltd, and issued under the Special Record logo, using a JH prefix. These were made for local, private distribution, and, as noted in the label, profits were donated to the Pinchin Johnson Spitfire Fund. Two issues on this label are reportedly by Django, although current information does not indicate what titles they were. They are likely to be known titles from Gramophone Company matrices.

Oslo **Wednesday 11 June 1941**

'String Swing', featuring Robert Normann, record two titles in the QHCF style.

Zurich **Thursday 19 June 1941**

Willie Lewis records twelve titles for Elite records (matrix numbers 1886–97). Musicians include Louis Bacon, Tommy Benford and June Cole.
See Rust for details.

Paris **Saturday 21 June 1941**

'Sarane Ferret et le Swing Quintette de Paris' record four titles for Odéon (matrix numbers Ki9229–32). Musicians include Pierre 'Baro' Ferre and Jean 'Matelo' Ferret.

Zurich **Friday 27 June 1941**

Willie Lewis records twelve titles for Elite records (matrix numbers 1920–31). Musicians include Louis Bacon, Tommy Benford and June Cole.
See Rust for details.

Paris **Thursday 21 August 1941**

Pierre Fabien shoots a German officer at the Barbes Metro station, signalling the beginning of violent action by the French Resistance.

London **September 1941**

Stéphane Grappelli records a further seven titles with the Witley Court Music Box (matrix numbers CRP2183–90). Titles include 'Truckin'', 'Lady Be Good', 'Japanese Sandman' and 'Dinah'.

'Normandie' Cinema, Paris — Monday September 1–Sunday September 14 1941

The Quintette appear in residence.

Studio Albert, Paris — Thursday 11 September 1941

André Ekyan (solo de saxophone alto)

André Ekyan (as); Django Reinhardt (gtr solo); Eugène Vées (gtr); Emmanuel Soudieux (sb); Pierre Fouad (dms).
Engineer: Eugène Ravenet

520 OSW 225-1 **Hungaria** {2.27}
[*78* Swi 127] [*CD* Cls 877; Fmx FA311]

521 OSW 226-1 **De Nulle Part** (Out Of Nowhere) {3.00}
[*78* Swi 127] [*LP* Pat C054 16012] [*CD* Cls 877; Fmx FA311]

Same session

Django Reinhardt et le Quintette du Hot-Club de France

Hubert Rostaing (cl); Django Reinhardt (gtr solo); Eugène Vées (gtr); Emmanuel Soudieux (sb); Pierre Fouad (dms).
Arr. by Hubert Rostaing and Django Reinhardt

522 OSW 227-1 **Dinette** (Dinah) {2.50}
[*78* Swi 146] [*LP* Pat C054 16012] [*EP* An 73007] [*CD* Cls 877; Fmx FA311; JSP 904; Mos MD 6-190; Recall SMDCD3207]

523 OSW 228-1 **Crépuscule** {3.00}
[*78* Swi 123] [*LP* Pat C054 16012] [*CD* Cls 877; Fmx FA311; JSP 904; Mos MD 6-190]

524 OSW 229-1 **Swing '42** {2.47}
[*78* Swi 137] [*LP* Pat C054 16012] [*EP* HMV 7EGF941] [*CD* Cls 877; Fmx FA311; JSP 904; Mos MD 6-190]

Olympia, Paris — Monday 15–Tuesday 30 September 1941

The Quintette appear in residence.

Studio Albert, Paris — Friday 26 September 1941

Festival Swing 1942 Part 1

Hubert Rostaing et son Orchestre Alex Caturegli, Alex Renard, Aime Barelli (tpts); Maurice Gladieu, Guy Paquinet (tbns); Hubert Rostaing (cl); Christian Wagner (as); Noël Chiboust, Georges Jacquemont (ts); Eugène Vées (gtr); Emmanuel Soudieux (sb); Armand Molinetti (dms).
Arr. by Hubert Rostaing.

Jam-Session Paul Collot (pno); Noël Chiboust (ts); Guy Paquinet (tbn); Christian Wagner (cl); Alex Renard (tpt); Eugène Vées (gtr); Emmanuel Soudieux (sb); Armand Molinetti (dms).

Gus Viseur et son Orchestre Gus Viseur (acc); André Luis (ts); Lucien Gallopian; Harry Kett (gtrs); Maurice Speilleux (sb).
Alix Combelle et son Orchestre Charles Suire, Jean Lemay, Christian Bellest (tpts); Jean-Louis Jeanson (tbn); Pierre Delhoumeau, Charles Lissée (cl, as); Gaston Etienne (cl, ts); Alix Combelle (ts); Henry Gauthier (pno); Joseph Reinhardt (gtr); Tony Rovira (sb); Jerry Mengo (dms).
Engineer: Eugène Ravenet

525 2SW 235-1 **Festival Swing 1942 Part 1** {2.25}
[**78** Swi X129] [***LP*** Pat C054 16012 (extract only)] [***CD*** Cls 877; Fmx FA311]

30cm (12") master and release.
Django Reinhardt does not play on this matrix, but it is included both on Fremeaux and in this work on the grounds of completeness.

Same location, date and engineer

Festival Swing 1942 Part 2

Aime Barelli et son Orchestre Alex Cauregli, Aime Barelli (tpts); Maurice Gladieu (tbn); Charles Hary (ts); Joseph Reinhardt (gtr); Emmanuel Soudieux (sb); Armand Molinetti (dms).
Michel Warlop Trio Michel Warlop (vln); Joseph Reinhardt (gtr); Emmanuel Soudieux (sb).
Dany Kane Quintette Danny Kane (hca); Willy Kett (vibraphone); Joseph Reinhardt (gtr); Emmanuel Soudieux (sb); Armand Molinetti (dms).
Django's Music Alex Caturegli, Christian Bellest, Aime Barelli (tpts); Maurice Gladieu, Guy Paquinet (tbns); Hubert Rostaing, Christian Wagner (cl, as); Georges Jacquemont, Charles Hary (ts); Django Reinhardt, Eugène Vées (gtrs); Emmanuel Soudieux (sb); Pierre Foaud (dms).
Arr. by Django Reinhardt

526 2SW235-2 **Festival Swing 1942 Part 2** {4.56}
[**78 unissued**] [***CD*** **Fmx FA311**; JSP 904]

30cm (12") master.

London — October 1941

Stéphane Grappelli records a further four titles with the Witley Court Music Box (matrix numbers CTP11796–9).

Moulin Rouge, Paris — Wednesday 1–Tuesday 14 October 1941

The Quintette appear in residence.

Oslo — Thursday 23 October 1941

'String Swing', featuring Robert Normann, record two titles in the QHCF style.

Théâtre ABC, Paris — Friday 31 October 1941

The Quintette appear in residence.

Buenos Aires late 1941–early 1942

'Oscar Alemán y su Quinteto de Swing' record for Odéon.

'Le Nid' Club, Paris early 1942

The Quintette appear in residence.

Paris Friday 2 January 1942

'Sarane Ferret et le Quintette de Paris' record four titles for Odéon (matrix numbers 93309–12). Musicians include Jean 'Matelot' Ferret and Pierre 'Baro' Ferret.

Paris Thursday 23 January 1942

Django Reinhardt's 32nd birthday.

London Tuesday 17 February 1942

Stéphane Grappelli, as 'Stephane Grappelly And His Quintet' records two titles for Decca (matrix numbers DR6685–6). Musicians include Noel 'Chappie' d'Amato.

Studio Albert, Paris Tuesday 31 March 1942

Hubert Rostaing et son Orchestre

Hubert Rostaing (cl, as); Aime Barelli (tpt); Noël Chiboust (ts); Paul Collot (pno); Eugène Vées (gtr); Django Reinhardt (bowed sb solo); Emmanuel Soudieux (sb); André Jourdan (dms).
Engineer: Pierre Hamard

527 OSW 261-1 **Première Idée D'Eddie** (Petit Pêche Mignon) {3.21}
[***78*** Swi 151] [***LP*** Pat C054 16013] [***CD*** Cls 877; Fmx FA311]

528 OSW 261-2 **Première Idée D'Eddie** [**unissued**]

Django Reinhardt plays bowed bass on OSW 261-1, not guitar.

Same location, date and engineer

Django's Music

Aime Barelli, Alex Caturegli, Pierre-Severin Luino (tpts); Maurice Gladieu, Pierre Remy (tbns); Hubert Rostaing (cl, as); Maurice Cizeron (fl, as); Christian Wagner (as); Noël Chiboust (ts); Paul Collot (pno); Django Reinhardt (gtr solo); Eugène Vées (gtr); Emmanuel Soudieux (sb); André Jourdan (dms).

529 2SW 262-1 **Nymphéas** {4.13}
[***78*** Swi X186] [***LP*** Pat C054 16013] [***CD*** Cls 877; Fmx FA311]

530 2SW 261-2 **Nymphéas** [**unissued**]

531 2SW 263-1 **Féerie** {3.43}
[***78*** Swi X186] [***LP*** Pat C054 16013] [***CD*** Cas CASTEL810562; Cls 877; Fmx FA311]

532 2SW 263-2 **Féerie** [**unissued**]

2SW 262-1 and 2SW 263-1 30cm (12") master and release; 2SW 261-2 and 2SW 263-2 30cm (12") master.

Same location, date and engineer

Django Reinhardt et le Quintette du Hot-Club de France

Hubert Rostaing (cl); Django Reinhardt (gtr solo); Eugène Vées (gtr); Emmanuel Soudieux (sb); André Jourdan (dms).

533 OSW 265-1 **Belleville** {2.31}
[***78*** Swi 162] [***LP*** Aff BOX107; Pat C054 16013] [***CD*** Cls 877; Cly DIG12; Fmx FA311; JSP 904; Mos MD 6-190; Recall SMDCD307]

534 OSW 266-1 **Lentement, Mademoiselle** {3.17}
[***78*** Swi 146] [***LP*** Aff BOX107; Pat C054 16013] [***CD*** Cls 877; Cly DIG12; Fmx FA311; JSP 904; Mos MD 6-190]

Salle Pleyel, Paris — Friday 3–Sunday 5 April 1942

Django appears in concert with Fud Candrix and his band.

Brussels — Thursday 16–Saturday 18 April 1942

Django plays at the Palais de Beaux-Arts accompanied by both Stan Brenders' Orchestra and Fud Candrix and his band.

Sobedi Studios, Brussels — Thursday 16 April 1942

Django Reinhardt

Django Reinhardt (gtr solos or vln solos) (1); Ivan de Bie (pno).

535 16189 **Vous Et Moi** (1) {3.11}
[***78*** Rythme D-5016] [***LP*** Poly 2344 146] [***CD*** Cls 877; Fmx FA311]

536 16190 **Distraction** {2.58}
[***78*** Rythme D-5016] [***LP*** Poly 2344 146] [***CD*** Cls 877; Fmx FA311]

537 16191 **Blues En Mineur** (1) {2.50}
[***78*** Oly 5017; **Rythme D-5017**; Sof 5017] [***LP*** Poly 2344 146] [***CD*** Cls 877; Fmx FA311]

538 16192 **Studio 24** {3.01}
[***78*** Oly 5017; **Rythme D-5017**; Sof 5017] [***LP*** Poly 2344 146] [***CD*** Cls 877; Fmx FA311]

Same location, date and engineer

Django Reinhardt et son Grande Orchestre [or] Fud Candrix et son Grande Orchestre

Maurice Giegas, Janot Morales, Lucien Devroye (tpts); Nic Frerar, Lou Melon (tbns); Bobby Naret, Lou Logist (cl, as); Victor Ingeveldt (ts, fl); Benny Pauwels (cl, ts); Fud Candrix (cl, ts); Ivan de Bie (pno); Django Reinhardt (gtr solo); Eugène Vées (gtr); Emmanuel Soudieux (sb); André Jourdan (dms).
Arr. by Fud Candrix.

539 16194 **Place De Brouckère** {2.50}
[*78* Rythme D-5030] [*LP* Poly 2344 146] [*CD* Cls 877; Fmx FA311]

540 16195 **Seul Ce Soir** {2.51}
[*78* Rythme D-5050] [*LP* Poly 2344 146] [*CD* Cls 877; Fmx FA311]

541 16196 **Mixture** {2.36}
[*78* Rythme D-5018] [*LP* Poly 2344 146] [*CD* Cls 877; Fmx FA311]

542 16197 **Bei Dir War Es Immer So Schön** {3.04}
[*78* Rythme D-5018] [*LP* Poly 2344 146] [*CD* Cls 877; Fmx FA311]

Sobedi Studios, Brussels — Friday 8 May 1942

Django Reinhardt – Stan Brenders et son Grand Orchestre de Danse

Paul d'Hondt, George Clais, Raymond Chantrain (tpts); Jean Damm, Sus Van Camp (tbns); Louis Billen, Jo Magis (cl, as); Jack Demany (ts, vln); Arthur Saguet (bs, ts, cl); Jeff Van Heerswingels (ts); John Ouwerx (pno); Django Reinhardt (gtr solo); Jim Van Der Jeught (gtr); Jean Douillez, Walter Feron, Emile Deltour, Chas Dolne (vlns), Arthur Peters (sb); Josse Aerts (dms); Jack Demany, Jean Douillez, Walter Feron, Emile Deltour, Chas Dolne (vcls).
As above, without the four violinists (1).

543 16218 **Divine Beguine** {2.54}
[*78* Rythme D-5026] [*LP* Poly 2344 146] [*CD* Cls 877; Fmx FA311]

544 16219 **Nuages** {4.06}
[*78* Rythme D-5500] [*LP* Poly 2344 146] [*CD* Cls 877; Fmx FA311]

545 16220 **Djangologie** {3.02}
[*78* Rythme D-5500] [*LP* Poly 2344 146] [*CD* Cls 877; Fmx FA311]

546 16221 **Eclats De Cuivres** (1) {2.59}
[*78* Rythme D-5024] [*LP* Poly 2344 146] [*CD* Cls 905; Fmx FA311]

547 16222 **Django Rag** (1) {2.34}
[*78* Rythme D-5025] [*LP* Poly 2344 146] [*CD* Cls 905; Fmx FA311]

548 16223 **Dynamisme** (1) {2.43}
[*78* Rythme D-5025] [*LP* Poly 2344 146] [*CD* Cls 905; Fmx FA311]

549 16224 **Tons D'Ebène** (1) {2.52}
[*78* Rythme D-5024] [*LP* Poly 2344 146] [*CD* Cls 905; Fmx FA311]

550 16225 **Chez Moi A Six Heures** (1) {2.42}
[*78* Rythme D-5024] [*LP* Poly 2344 146] [*CD* Cls 905; Fmx FA311]

16219 and 16220 30cm (12") master and release.
See Delaunay, pages 110–11.

France — Summer 1942

The Quintette spend a large part of the summer of 1942 touring and playing in the Côte d'Azur, Nice, Lyon, the Riviera and finally Algiers, North Africa, where the group breaks up.

See Delaunay pages 111–12.

Chicago, Illinois **Monday 15 June 1942**

Down Beat magazine erroneously reports the death of Django Reinhardt. 'The story, probably not an exclusive, gave *Down Beat* the reputation of being a magazine more than ten years ahead of its time.' (Abrams)

Buenos Aires **mid-1942**

'Oscar Alemán y su Quinteto de Swing' record for Odéon.

Paris **Wednesday 8 July 1942**

Pierre Fouad and his Orchestra record four titles for Swing records (matrix numbers OSW295–8). Musicians include Roger Chaput, Alix Combelle, Harry Cooper, André Ekyan and Emmanuel Soudieux.
See Rust for details.

London **Thursday 20 August 1942**

Stéphane Grappelli records for Decca as 'Stéphane Grappelly And His Quintet' (matrix numbers DR6930 and 3). Musicians include Noel 'Chappie' d'Amato.

London **Thursday 20 August 1942**

Melody Maker picks up the June *Down Beat* story, but believes it to be inaccurate.
See Cherrett, page 7 for a reproduction of the original article.

London **September 1942**

Remarks regarding an unspecified pre-war concert in London (possibly Manchester, 4 June 1938)

> Insistent were the demands for the personal appearances, in London, of the Quintette. Arrangements were made. Before thrilled audiences thronging the Capital's leading music halls played Django and his fellow musicians.
>
> To appease the inevitable commercial element among listeners, announcements and vocals were handled by Norwegian Carola Merrild. Disquietingly, the Quintette's brilliance was almost eclipsed by a quite different allure. Unperturbed, Reinhardt, white coated and detached, just played on. Smooth, suave, Grappelly stood smilingly before a separate microphone, lured bewitching melodies from his singing violin [*sic*]. Plump, bespectacled Vola plucked away at his sonorous bass while expressionless Joseph Reinhardt and Pierre Ferret plucked out a solid rhythmic background.
>
> The Quintette was, above all, original. Gratifying indeed the complete absence of any silver-tinselled gallery appeal. No vacuous baton wielder grinned toothily, waved his arms or juggled self-consciously. Almost exotic were the contrasted lightning effects. Swarthily handsome leader Reinhardt gleamed in the centre of an unwavering spotlight.
>
> To the strains of 'Djangology' the curtain slowly descended. (Laurie Henshaw, *BMG*)

Chicago Thursday 1 October 1942

Rumors that Django lives

London, England – Following printing of the American report of the death of Django Reinhardt, *Melody Maker*, the English counterpart of *Down Beat*, has been stormed with letters from readers who state positively that they have heard Reinhardt broadcasting very recently.

No definite station name has been given and at the present time it seems impossible to check further, but *Melody Maker*, itself, indicates a belief that Django is still alive. He is the famed guitarist whose work with the *Quintet of the Hot Club of France* is well known in America. (Unsigned, *Down Beat*)

Paris Wednesday 18 November 1942

Freddy Jumbo et son Orchestre record Django's composition 'Swing '42' for Polydor (Polydor 524.794, matrix 6135/2DRPP). Musicians include Robert Mavounzy.

Paris Wednesday 2 December 1942

'Sarane Ferret et le Quintette de Paris' record four titles for Odéon (matrix numbers Ki 9442–5). Musicians include Jean 'Matelot' Ferret and Lucien Simoens.

Paris 1943

Charles Delaunay publishes the third edition of *Hot discography* (Editions Jazz Hot).

Paris 1943

Joseph Reinhardt makes the following recordings, released on Belgian Decca:

Joseph Reinhardt et son Ensemble

Joseph Reinhardt (gtr); Gus Viseur (acc); Claude Laurence (André Hodier) (pno) and others, unknown.

ST711 Pam Pam [**78** De 9109]

ST712 Zazou [**78** De 9108]

ST 713 Fantastique [**78** De 9109]

ST 714 Ballade [**78** De 9108]

and, at a later date in the same year,

Joseph Reinhardt et son Ensemble

Joseph Reinhardt (gtr); Pierre Ferret (gtr); Claude Laurance (André Hodier) (vln); Emmanuel Souideux (sb); Gaston Leonard (dms); unknown (vcl).

ST970 J'attend L'Amour [**78** De 9132]

ST971 Un Peu De Rêve [**78** De 9133]

ST972 Douce Georgette [**78** De 9132

ST973 L'Oeil Noir [**78** De 9132]

Berlin **early 1943**

Django Reinhardt reportedly plays a engagement at the 'Femina Bar' on the Hohenstaufenstrasse. There is, however, disagreement about this (see Mazzoletti's *Il jazz in Italia* and the notes to Fremeaux FA316).

London **January 1943**

Article by Laurie Henshaw in *BMG* on Django Reinhardt.
See Cherrett, page 17 for a reproduction of this article.

Paris **Thursday 7 January 1943**

'Fredy Jumbo et son ensemble' record for Polydor. Musicians include Robert Mavounzy.

Paris **Thursday 14 January 1943**

Harry Cooper et son Orchestre record the Django Reinhardt composition 'Nuages' for Swing (Swing 155, matrix OSW312). The band includes Robert Mavounzy and Lucien Simoens.

London **Thursday 21 January 1943**

Stéphane Grappelli, as 'Stephane Grappelly And His Quintet' record two titles for Decca (matrix numbers DR7189–90). Musicians include Noel 'Chappie' d'Amato.

Paris **Saturday 23 January 1943**

Django Reinhardt's 33rd birthday.

Studio Pelouze, Paris **Wednesday 17 February 1943**

Django Reinhardt et le Quintette du Hot-Club de France

André Lluis, Gérard Leveque (cl); Django Reinhardt (gtr solo); Eugène Vées (gtr); Jean Storne (sb); Gaston Leonard (dms).
Engineer: Walter Ruhlmann

551 OSW 322-1 **Douce Ambiance** {2.17}
[***78*** Swi 183] [***LP*** Aff BOX107; Pat C054 16013] [***CD*** Arc CASTEL810562; Cls 905; Cly DIG12; Fmx FA312; Hab 111200; JSP 904; Mos MD 6-190]

552 OSW 323-1 **Manoir De Mes Rêves** {3.15}
[***78*** Swi 158] [***LP*** Pat C054 16013] [***CD*** Cls 905; Fmx FA312; JSP 904; Mos MD 6-190]

553 OSW 324-1 **Oui** {2.07}
[***78*** Swi 158] [***LP*** Aff BOX107; Pat C054 16013] [***CD*** Cls 905; Cly DIG12; Fmx FA312; JSP 904; Mos MD 6-190]

554 OSW 325-1 **Cavalerie** {2.33}
[***78*** Swi 183] [***LP*** Pat C054 16013] [***CD*** Cls 905; Fmx FA312; JSP 904; Mos MD 6-190]

Studio Pelouze, Paris Friday 26 February 1943

Personnel as last, without André Lluis.

555 OSW 326-1 **Vette** [**unissued**]

556 OSW 327-1 **Fleur D'Ennui** {2.31}
[***78*** Swi 176] [***LP*** Aff BOX107; Pat C054 16013] [***CD*** Cls 905; Cly DIG12; Fmx FA312; JSP 904; Mos MD 6-190]

Same session

Django Reinhardt, solo de guitare

Django Reinhardt (gtr solo) acc. by Eugène Vées (gtr); Jean Storne (sb); Gaston Leonard (dms).

557 OSW 328-1 **Blues Clair** {3.01}
[***78*** Swi 254] [***LP*** Aff BOX107; Pat C054 16013; Swa S1401] [***CD*** Cls 905; Fmx FA312; JSP 904; Mos MD 6-190; Recall SMDCD307]

Same session

Django Reinhardt, solo de guitare

Django Reinhardt (gtr solo).

558 OSW 329-1 **Improvisation No. 3 Pt. 1** {3.00}
[***78*** Swi 225] [***LP*** Aff BOX107; Pat C054 16013; Swa S1401] [***CD*** Cls 905; Fmx FA312; JSP 904; Mos MD 6-190]

559 OSW 329-2 **Improvisation No. 3 Pt. 2** {2.44}
[***78*** Swi 225] [***LP*** Pat C054 16013; Swa S1401] [***CD*** Cls 905; Cly DIG12; Fmx FA312; JSP 904; Mos MD 6-190]

Studio Albert, Paris Friday 12 March 1943

Django Reinhardt et son Orchestre (Fud Candrix and Son Orchestre)

Maurice Giegas, Janot Morales, Lucien Devroye (tpts); Nic Frerar, Lou Melon (tbns); Bobby Naret, Guy Plum (cl, as); Benny Pauwels (cl, fl, ts); Fud Candrix (ts); Django Reinhardt (gtr solo); Eugène Vées (gtr); Emmanuel Soudieux (sb); Pierre Fouad (dms).
Engineer: Eugène Ravenet

560 OSW 330-1 **Belleville** {2.41}
[***78*** Swi 162] [***LP*** Pat C054 16013] [***CD*** Cls 905; Fmx FA312]

561 OSW 331-1 **Oubli** {2.40}
[***78*** Swi 215] [***LP*** Pat C054 16014] [***CD*** Cls 905; Fmx FA312]

562 OSW 332-1 **Zuiderzee Blues** {2.36}
[***78*** Swi 180] [***LP*** Pat C054 16014] [***CD*** Cls 905; Fmx FA312]

563 OSW 333-1 **ABC** {2.17}
[***78*** Swi 180] [***LP*** Pat C054 16013] [***CD*** Cls 905; Fmx FA312]

Paris Tuesday 11 May 1943

'Harry Cooper et son Orchestre' record four titles for Swing records (matrix numbers OSW344–7). Musicians include 'H.P. Chadel' (Charles Delaunay), Robert Mavounzy and Lucien Simoens.
Two recorded titles, 'Caprice En Ut' and 'Lune Rousse' are written by Delaunay under the nom-de-plume 'H.P. Chadel'.

Paris Saturday 3 July 1943

The 'Académie du Jazz' stage a concert featuring Charles Henry (pno); Michel Warlop (vln) and Guy Paquinet (tb).

Studio Pelouze, Paris Wednesday 7 July 1943

Django Reinhardt et son Orchestre

Alex Renard, Alex Caturegli, Maurice Moufflard (tpts); Maurice Gladieu, Pierre Remy (tbns); Max Blanc (cl, as); Robert Merchez, Robert Mavounzy (as); André Lluis, Charles Hary (ts); Django Reinhardt (gtr solo); Eugène Vées (gtr); Jean Storne (sb); Pierre Fouad (dms) (1).
Michel Warlop, Paulette Izoird, Sylvio Schmidt, Raymond Goutard (vlns); Max Blanc, Robert Merchez (as); André Lluis, Charles Hary (ts); Django Reinhardt (gtr solo); Eugene Vées (gtr); Jean Storne (sb); Pierre Fouad (dms); Nelly Kay (vcl) (2).
Arr. by Django Reinhardt.
Engineer: Walter Ruhlmann

564 OSW 356-1 **Gaiement** (1) {2.38}
[**78 unissued** *Swing* test] [***LP*** Pat C054 16014; **KC107**] [***CD*** Cls 905; Fmx FA312]

565 OSW 357-1 **Mélodie Au Crépuscule** (2) {2.57}
[***78*** Swi 166] [***LP*** Pat C054 16014 (extract only)] [***CD*** Cls 905; Fmx FA312]

566 OSW 358-1 **Blues D'Autrefois** (Blues D'Outre Mer) (1) {2.34}
[***78*** Swi 215] [***LP*** Pat C054 16014] [***CD*** Cls 905; Fmx FA312]

567 OSW 359-1 **Place De Brouckère** (1) {2.54}
[***78*** Swi 166] [***LP*** Pat C054 16014] [***EP*** HMV 7EGF941] [***CD*** Cls 905; Fmx FA312]

London Wednesday 7 July 1943

Stéphane Grappelli records for Decca as 'Stephane Grappelly And His Quintet' (matrix numbers DR-7386–9). Musicians include Noel 'Chappie' d'Amato and vocalist Beryl Davis.

Paris Thursday 8 July 1943

'Gus Viseur et son Orchestre' record for Swing. Musicians include Robert Mavounzy.

Paris — **Friday 16 July 1943**

'Léo Chaullic et son Orchestre' record for Swing records. Musicians include Lucien Simoens.

Salbis, Loir-et-Cher, France — **c. late July 1943**

Django Reinhardt marries Sophie Zeigler, *aka* Naguine.

Switzerland — **mid–late 1943**

Django plays an engagement of undetermined length at an unnamed club in Zurich.

'Django played in a club there and was arrested when he attempted to leave Switzerland.' (Abrams)

See also Delaunay, page 116.

London — **Wednesday 6 October 1943**

Stéphane Grappelli, as 'Stephane Grappelly And His Quintet' record two titles for Decca (matrix numbers DR-7728–9). Musicians include Noel 'Chappie' d'Amato.

London — **Wednesday 8 December 1943**

Stéphane Grappelli, as 'Stephane Grappelly And His Quintet' records two titles for Decca (matrix numbers DR-7927–8). Musicians include Noel 'Chappie' d'Amato.

Paris — **Wednesday 15 December 1943**

'Jean Ferret et son Sixtette' record the Django Reinhardt composition 'Swing Guitars' (Pathé 2187, matrix CPT5783-1).

Buenos Aires — **late 1943**

'Oscar Alemán y su Quinteto de Swing' record for Odéon.

Santiago, Chile — **late 1943–early 1944**

'Quinteto Swing Hot de Chile' record for Victor. Musicians include Luis Silva. See Harlequin LP HQ2083 for two examples.

Chapelle de L'Institut de Jeunes Aveugles, Paris — **1944**

Léo Chaulliac performs Django Reinhardt's *Messe* (*Mass*) on the chapel organ. The recording of this 7' 33" performance is available on Iris Musique CD 3001 845.

Paris — **1944**

The probable time frame for the short, silent film of Django made at 'Bal Tabarin'.

England — **1944**

Noel 'Chappie' d'Amato features in the film *Round Rainbow Corner.*

London **January 1944**

The publication of Discography of the *Recorded Works of Django Reinhardt and the Quintette du Hot Club De France* by Billy Neil and E Gates, published by Clifford Essex Music Co. Ltd, 8 New Compton Street, Charing Cross Road, London WC2, a 24pp illustrated booklet, price 2/6d.
See Cherrett, pages 69–73 for a reproduction of the textual material from this booklet.

Paris **January 1944**

The Jazz Club Française is established, causing dissention in French jazz circles.

Paris **Sunday 9 January 1944**

'Ensemble Swing do Hot-Club Colonial' record for Polydor. Musicians include Robert Mavounzy.

Paris **Sunday 23 January 1944**

Django Reinhardt's 34th birthday.

Paris **March 1944**

Django appears with the Fud Candrix band and then joins them for a tour of France.

Normandy **Tuesday 6 June 1944**

The invasion of Europe begins with the landing of allied troops.

Paris [?] **Thursday 8 June 1944**

The birth of Django's son, Jean-Jacques (*aka* Babik).

Paris **Saturday 19 August 1944**

The 'Popular Uprising' begins when agents of De Gaulle seize the Préfecture of Police on the Ile de la Cité.
In the days following this event, numerous clashes occur throughout the city.

Paris **Thursday 24 August 1944**

The first allied tanks reach the city; General Von Choltiz surrenders to the allied forces at Hotel Meurice that afternoon, although sporadic fighting continues for two more days.

Paris **Friday 25 August 1944**

General de Gaulle arrives at L'Hôtel de Ville and appears at a balcony window, in front of enthusiastic crowds.

Beziers **Thursday 2 September 1944**

The Quintette appear in concert.
See Delaunay, page 259, for a photo of this event.

Salle Pleyell, Paris | Sunday 26 September 1944

The Quintette play a concert.

Studio Pelouze, Paris | Friday 3 November 1944

Noel Chiboust et son Orchestre

Christian Bellest, Alex Caturegli, Roger Hubert (tpts); Pierre Remy, Marcel Librecht (tbns); Hubert Rostaing (cl); Roger Jeanjean, Désire Duriez (as); André Lluis (ts, as); Gaston Rahier (ts), Noël Chiboust (ts, cl, ldr); Yves Raynal (bs); Léo Chauliac (pno); Django Reinhardt (gtr solo); Roger Chaput (gtr); Lucien Simoens (sb); Jerry Mengo (dms).

568 OSW 398-1 **Welcome Pt. 1** {2.37}
[*78* Swi 197] [*CD* Cls 945; Fmx FA312]

568a OSW 399-1 **Welcome Pt. II** {2.19}
[*78* Swi 197] [*CD* Cls 945; Fmx FA312]

Same location, date and engineer

Django's Music

Christian Bellest, Alex Caturegli, Roger Hubert (tpts); Pierre Remy, Marcel Librecht (tbns); Gérard Leveque (cl); Yves Raynal (bs); Léo Chauliac (pno); Django Reinhardt (gtr solo); Joseph Reinhardt (gtr); Lucien Simoens (sb); Jerry Mengo (dms).

569 OSW 400-1 **I Can't Give You Anything But Love** {2.19}
[*78* Swi 254] [*LP* Pat C054 16014] [*CD* Cls 945; Fmx FA312]

570 2SW 401-1 **Artillerie Lourde** {4.13}
[*78* **unissued**] [*LP* Pat C054 16014] [*CD* Cls 945; Fmx FA312]

30cm (12") master and release.

Paris | Autumn 1944

Django appears regularly at the newly opened 'Chez Django', formerly 'La Roulotte'.

La Chapelle de L'Institut des
Jeunes Aveugles, Paris | November or December 1944

Django Reinhardt (speech); unknown (comments); Léo Chaullic (organ).
Radio broadcast, acetate.

571 Interview with Django Reinhardt regarding his mass composition {2.12}
[**unissued**] [*CD* Fmx FA312]

Paris | 1945

Charles Delaunay publishes the second edition of *De la vie du jazz* (Editions Jazz Hot).

Paris | January 1945

The premier of Jean Cocteau's film *L'Aigle a deux têtes.*

Paris — Tuesday 23 January 1945

Django Reinhardt's 35th birthday.

Jazz Club Française auditorium, Paris — Thursday 25 January 1945

Jazz Club Mystery Hot Band

O. Saxo clarinette; V. Trompette; W. Piano; X. Guitarre; Y. Basse; Z. Drummer [*sic*]
Bernie Privin (tpt); Michael 'Peanuts' Hucko (cl, ts); Mel Powell (pno); Django Reinhardt (gtr); Josz Schulman (sb); Ray McKinley (dms).
Arr. by Mel Powell.

572 ST 1227-1 **How High The Moon** [**unissued**]

573 ST 1227-2 **How High The Moon** {2.21}
[***78*** ABC 120; Esq 10-043] [***CD*** Cas PIESD233; Cls 945; Fmx FA312]

574 ST 1228 **If Dreams Came True** {2.48}
[***78*** ABC 121; Esq 10-087] [***CD*** Cls 945; Fmx FA312]

575 ST 1229-2 **Hallelujah** {2.58}
[***78*** ABC 122; Esq 10-243; Victory 9032] [***LP*** Aff BOX107] [***CD*** Cls 945; Fmx FA312]

576 ST 1230 **Stompin' At The Savoy** {2.50}
[***78*** ABC 123; Esq 10-043] [***LP*** Aff BOX107] [***CD*** Cls 945; Fmx FA312]

ABC-JCF 122 carries the matrix number ST1229 but it is, nevertheless, the same as 1229-2 Victory 9032 issued as 'Beatin' The Hallelujah Drums'.
All four above also issued on Esquire ESQ-422, format unknown.

Paris — Fridays 9, 16 and 23 February 1945

A series of 'Trois Nuits de Jazz' featuring the orchestras of: Aime Barelli, Arthur Briggs, Léo Chaulliac, Noël Chiboust, Alix Combelle, André Ekyan, Charles Hary, Jerry Mengo, Alex Renard, Django Reinhardt, Hubert Rostaing, Michel Warlop 'and others'. (Unsigned, *Jazz Hot* Jan/Feb 1945)

Salle Pleyel, Paris — probably Sunday 25 February 1945

Django Reinhardt et son Orchestre

Alex Renard, Alphonse Marlier, Charles Suire (tpts); Pierre Remy, Maurice Gladieu (tbn); Gérard Leveque (cl); André Lamory (as, bs); Django Reinhardt (gtr solo); Joseph Reinhardt (gtr); Lucien Simoens (sb); Yvan Meyer (dms)
Concert 'Championat de France de Jazz'.

577 **Haevy Guns** (*sic*) (Artillerie Lourde) [**unissued**] [***CD*** Fmx FA312]

578 **Good Morning Blues** [**unissued**] [***CD*** Fmx FA312]

New York City — Thursday 1 March 1945

Article about Jean Ferret in *Down Beat* by 1st Lieut. Herb Caen.

See Cruickshank, page 87 for a reproduction.
Caen later became a columnist for the *San Francisco Chronicle.*

Star Sound Studios, London — Monday 12 March 1945

Stéphane Grappelli records two sides for radio broadcast with the Vic Lewis orchestra. Both were issued on Harlequin LP HQ3009.

Paris — March/April 1945

The results of the 1944 'Referendum do Hot Club' – the *Jazz Hot* readers' poll – are published:

Trompette	
Philippe Brun	393
Christian Bellest	162
Aime Barelli	157
Harry Cooper	86
Alex Renard	78
Trombone	
Albert Lirvat	321
Guy Paquinet	217
Eugène d'Hellemes	153
Gladieu	71
Clarinette	
Hubert Rostaing	407
André Ekyan	251
Christian Wagner	110
P Deloumaeu	47
Charles Hary	35
Alix Combelle	35
Alto sax	
André Ekyan	366
Robert Mavounzy	191
Hubert Rostaing	189
Chico Cristobal	118
Tenor sax	
Alix Combelle	427
Noël Chiboust	168
Hubert Rostaing	83
Charles Hary	64
Piano	
Léo Chauliac	417
Bernard Pfiefer	132
Emil Stern	74
Jacques Dieval	67
Jean Marion	59
Stéphane Grappelly	42

Guitare	
Django Reinhardt	452
Roger Chaput	137
Joseph Reinhardt	116
Serane Ferret	83
Pierre Ferret	42
Jan Maille	31
Basse	
Lucien Simoens	316
Louis Vola	287
Emmanuel Soudieux	185
Marcel Fabre	43
Fred Ermelin	40
Roger Grasset	37
Batterie	
Jerry Mengo	337
Pierre Fouad	231
Violon	
Stéphane Grappelly	366
Michel Warlop	173
Claude Lawrence	159
Divers	
Dany Kane	72
Willy Kett	36
Nelly Kat	34

The same issue of *Jazz Hot* reports that Django Reinhardt 'est dans le région du Marseille'.

Buenos Aires **Tuesday 17 and Thursday 19 April 1945**

'D'Hellemes Stompers' record 'The Jeep Is Jumpin' and 'The C-Jam Blues' on private acetates. Musicians include Eugène d'Hellemes.
Both recordings appear on Harlequin HDCD152.

New York City **Friday 11 May 1945**

'Dizzy Gillespie and His All Stars' record 'Salt Peanuts' for Guild records, the recording which will provide the catalyst for the split between Charles Delaunay and Hughes Panassié.

Buenos Aires **c. June 1945**

'Louis Vola del Quinteto del Hot Club de Francia' record at least 16 titles for Brazilian RCA. Musicians include Henri Salvador.
See Harlequin HQCD152 for an example.

Bal Tabarin, Salle Pleyel, Paris **Summer 1945**

The Quintette play an engagement which ends as a result of a ban on dancing in clubs.

Paris **Tuesday 10 July 1945**

As members of Jack Conner and his Orchestra, André Ekyan, Pierre Fouad, Hubert Rostaing and Emmanuel Soudieux record two titles for Swing records (matrix numbers OSW406, 407).
See Rust for details.

London **August 1945**

Article by Laurie Henshaw on Django in *BMG*.
See Cherrett, page 22, for a reproduction of this article.

Paris **October 1945**

The magazine *Jazz Hot* (No. 1) begins its post-war series with this issue, ignoring the pre-war numbering system; it features articles on Ray Ventura, Stéphane Grappelli and André Ekyan.
The same issue reports Django's return to Paris 'in a caravan' after six months of 'peregrinations sur la Riviera'. Abrams, however, reports that Django undertook a tour of US military camps at about this time.

AFN Studios, Paris **Friday 26 October 1945**

Django Reinhardt and The Air Transport Command Band

Herb Bass, Jerry Stephan, Robin Gould, Lonnie Wilfong (tpts); Bill Decker, Don Gardner, Shelton Heath, John Kirkpatrick (tbns); Jim Hayes (cl, as); Joe Moser (as); Bernie Cavaliere, Bill Zickenfoose (ts); Django Reinhardt (gtr solo); Ken Lowther (bs); Larry Mann (pno); Bob Decker (sb); Bill Bethel or Red Lackey (dms) (1).
Franco-American Quartet (Reinhardt, Mann, Decker, Bethel only) (2).
Arr. by Lonnie Wilfong.
AFN broadcast

Introduction {1.08}

579 **Djangology** (1) {3.33}
[***LP*** Vog 406505] [***CD*** Fmx FA312; Jass JCD 628]

580 **Honeysuckle Rose** (2) {2.40}
[***LP*** Vog 406505] [***CD*** Fmx FA312; Jass JCD 628; Vog 668003]

581 **Belleville** (1) {2.06}
[***LP*** Vog 406505] [***CD*** Fmx FA312; Jass JCD 628; Vog 668003]

582 **Uptown Blues** (1) {4.05}
[***LP*** Vog 406505] [***CD*** Fmx FA312; Jass JCD 628; Vog 668003]

583 **Moten Swing** (1) {4.00}
[***LP*** Vog 406505] [***CD*** Fmx FA312; Jass JCD 628; Vog 668003]

Paris **November 1945**

The magazine *Jazz Hot* (No. 2) features an article on and front cover photo of Django Reinhardt. It also reports on the first contact in six years, by telephone, of Django Reinhardt and Stéphane Grappelli.

See Delaunay, pages 130–1.

Paris — Thursday 1 November 1945

Django appears in concert with the ATC band.
See Delaunay, page 263, for a photo of the event.

Studio Albert, Paris — Tuesday 6 November 1945

Django Reinhardt and his American Swing Band – sous la direction de Jack Platt

Personnel as per (1) last session.

584 OSW 408-1 **Djangology** {2.35}
[***78*** Swi 221] [***LP*** Pat C054 16014] [***CD*** Cls 945; Fmx FA312]

585 OSW 408-2 **Djangology** [**unissued**]

586 OSW 409-1 **Swing Guitars** {2.22}
[***78*** Swi 208] [***LP*** Pat C054 16014] [***CD*** Cls 945; Fmx FA312]

587 OSW 409-2 **Swing Guitars** [**unissued**]

588 OSW 410-1 **Manoir De Mes Rêves** {3.12}
[***78*** Swi 221] [***LP*** Aff BOX107; Pat C054 16014] [***CD*** Cas PIESD233; Cls 945; DRG8493; Fmx FA312]

589 OSW 410-2 **Manoir De Mes Rêves** [**unissued**]

590 OSW 411-1 **Are You In The Mood?** {2.53}
[***78*** Swi 208] [***LP*** Pat C054 16014] [***CD*** Cls 945; Fmx FA312]

591 OSW 411-2 **Are You In The Mood** [**unissued**]

Paris — December 1945

The magazine *Jazz Hot* (No. 3) features articles on Arthur Briggs, André Ekyan and Garnet Clark. It also notes the return to Paris of Pierre Allier, following his extended stay in South America.

AFN Studios, Paris — Saturday 1 December 1945

Franco-American Quartette [Django Djams: The A.T.C. Small Group]

Django Reinhardt (gtr); Larry Mann (pno); Bob Decker (sb); Red Lacky (dms) (1).
As above, plus Les Leiber (as, penny-whistle) (2).
Radio broadcast, AFN 'Beaucoups de Musique'.

592 **Don't Be That Way** (1) {4.18}
[***LP*** Vog 406505] [***CD*** Fmx FA312; Jass JCD 628]

593 **Honeysuckle Rose** (2) {4.12}
[***LP*** KC107] [***CD*** Fmx FA312; Jass JCD 628]

594 **Sweet Sue, Just You** (2) {3.47}
[***CD*** Fmx FA312; Jass JCD 628]

Same location and date

Django Reinhardt, guitar solo

595 **Improvisation No. 6** [*sic*] {2.20}
[***LP*** Vog 406505] [***CD*** Fmx FA312; Jass JCD 628]

AFN Studios, Paris — Saturday 8 December 1945

Django Reinhardt and the ATC Band

Personnel as 26 October 1945 (1).
Radio broadcast 'NBC Bond Day'.

596 **Belleville** {2.06}
[***LP*** Vog 406505] [***CD*** Fmx FA312; Jass JCD 628; Vog 228E 6005]

597 **Moten Swing** {2.09}
[***LP*** Vog 406505] [***CD*** Fmx FA312; Jass JCD 628; Vog 228E 6005]

Salle Pleyel, Paris — Sunday 16 December 1945

Django Reinhardt and the ATC Band

Personnel as 26 October 1945 (1).
Radio broadcast: AFN/RDF.

598 **Introduction and Djangology** {0.47/3.31}
[***LP*** Vog 406505] [***CD*** Fmx FA312; Jass JCD 628; Vog 228E 6005]

599 **Moten Swing** {2.50}
[***LP*** Vog 406505] [***CD*** Fmx FA312]

600 **Are You In The Mood?** {2.41}
[***LP*** Vog 406505] [***CD*** Fmx FA312; Jass JCD 628; Vog 228E 6005]

601 **Uptown Blues** {3.16}
[***LP*** Vog 406505] [***CD*** Fmx FA312; Jass JCD 628; Vog 228E 6005]

602 **Apple Honey** {5.10}
[***LP*** Vog 406505] [***CD*** Fmx FA312; Jass JCD 628; Vog 228E 6005]

Paris — 1946

Django Reinhardt collaborates with André Hodier as music arranger for the film *Le village de la colère* directed by Raoul André.

Brussels — January 1946

The Belgian *Hot Club Magazine* features an article on Gus DeLoof.

London — Friday 4 January 1946

Django Reinhardt appears on BBC radio, broadcasting from Paris.

London — Saturday 12 January 1946

Reinhardt on the Air

The second in the 'Kings of Jazz' radio series on January 4 brought the music of the Hot Club de France guitarist Django Reinhardt to British listeners for the first time since the occupation of France, and displayed the gypsy maestro not only as still unchallengeable in his own particular field but also as composer of colourful and musically most interesting pieces.

Introduced by Pierre Lefevre, the programme was also notable for the excellent compering and a script by Charles Delaunay and Al Alvarez that interspersed these numbers with a wealth of information regarding the past and present of Django as well as giving listeners an insight of how the Nazi's ban on 'decadent' music was overcome. Django's '*Dinette*', for instance would need more than the vaunted perspicacity of the Gestapo to be recognized as '*Dinah*'!

Of Django's compositions, the exiting '*Rhythme Futur'*, a blues, '*Manoir de mes Reves*' and the hauntingly beautiful '*Melodie au Crepuscle*', written during a caravan ride from Cannes to Paris after losing all his money at baccarat early in the war, remain most vivid in the mind.

Backing came from an excellent group comprising tenor, clarinet, guitar, piano and drums. (Unsigned, *Melody Maker*)

Paris — Wednesday 23 January 1946

Django Reinhardt's 36th birthday.

London — Saturday 26 January 1946

Django arrives in London with his wife, son and Charles Delaunay.
See Cherrett, page 14 for a reproduction of the *Melody Maker* news report.
See Delaunay, pages 131–2.

EMI Studios, 3 Abbey Road, London NW8 — Thursday 31 January 1946

Django Reinhardt and le Quintette du Hot-Club de France

Stéphane Grappelli (vln); Django Reinhardt (gtr solo); Jack Llewellyn, Allan Hodgkiss (gtrs); Coleridge Goode (sb), (bowed sb) (1).
Engineer: Douglas Larter

603 OEF 25-1 **Coquette** (1) {2.44}
[*78* Swi 242] [*LP* Aff BOX107; HMV FELP247; Pat C054 16014; Swa S1389] [*CD* Cls 945; Fmx FA313; JSP 904; Mos MD 6-190]

604 OEF 26-1 **Django's Tiger** {2.36}
[*78* Swi 242] [*LP* Aff BOX107; HMV FELP208; Pat C054 16014; Swa S1389] [*CD* Cls 945; Fmx FA313; Gal GALE435; JSP 904; Mos MD 6-190; Recall SMDCD307]

605 OEF 27-1 **Embraceable You** {3.06}
[*78* Swi 229] [*LP* Aff BOX107; HMV FELP247; Pat C054 16014; Swa S1389] [*CD* Cls 945; Fmx FA313; JSP 904; Mos MD 6-190]

606 OEF 28-1 **Echoes Of France** (La Marseillaise) (1) {2.44}
[*78* Swi 229] [*LP* Aff BOX107; HMV FELP 208; Pat C054 16014; Swa S1389] [*CD* Cls 945; Fmx FA313; JSP 904; Mos MD 6-190; Recall SMDCD307]

Paris January–February 1946

The magazine *Jazz Hot* (No. 4) features articles on Django Reinhardt in Britain, Philippe Brun and Coleman Hawkins, and a front cover photo of Stéphane Grappelli.

Decca Studios, Broadhurst Gardens,
London NW6 Friday 1 February 1946

Django Reinhardt and Stephane Grappelli

Personnel as above.
Engineer: Arthur Lilley or Arthur Haddy

607 DR 10026-1 **Love's Melody** (Mélodie Au Crépuscule) [**unissued**]

608 DR 10026-2 **Love's Melody** (Mélodie Au Crépuscule) {3.10}
[***78*** **De F8604**, RD-40006, 625, 20299] [***LP*** AoC ACL1158]
[***CD*** Cls 945; Fmx FA313]

609 DR 10027-1 **Belleville** [**unissued**]

610 DR 10027-2 **Belleville** {2.56}
[***78*** **De F-8876**, F-41010, M32436; Har F-41010] [***LP*** AoC ACL1158]
[***CD*** Arc SOL517; Cls 945; Fmx FA313]

611 DR 10028-1 **Nuages** {3.16}
[***78*** **De F-8604**, RD-40006, 625, 20299] [***LP*** AofC ACL1158]
[***CD*** Arc SOL517; Cas MACCD132; Cls 945; Fmx FA313;
Gal GALE435]

612 DR 10028-2 **Nuages** {3.18}
[***78*** De F-8604] [***CD*** Fmx FA313]

613 DR 10029-1 **Liza** {2.51}
[***78*** **De F-8876**, F-41010, M322436; Har F-41010; Tel SH 104]
[***LP*** AoC ACL1158; Ast LP20102; Met MTM12] [***CD*** Arc SOL517;
Cls 945; Fmx FA313]

London Monday 11 February 1946

Django Reinhardt is taken ill and enters the French Hospital in London.
See Cherrett, page 13.

Paris March 1946

The magazine *Jazz Hot* (No. 4) features a front cover photo of Philippe Brun.

Brussels March 1946

The Belgian *Hot Club Magazine* features an article on Stan Brenders.

London March 1946

Article on Django by Sam Adams in *BMG*.
See Cherrett, page 19, for a reproduction of this article.

London — **Friday 8 March, Tuesday 12 March, Friday 22 March, Tuesday 26 March, Tuesday 2 April, Tuesday 9 April, Tuesday 16 April 1946**

BBC Radio appearances by the QHCF, scheduled prior to Django's illness, that did not take place.

Brussels — **April 1946**

The Belgian *Hot Club Magazine* features an article on Fud Candrix.

Brussels — **May 1946**

The Belgian *Hot Club Magazine* features articles on Stan Brenders and Josse Breyre.

Salle Pleyel, Paris — **Tuesday 7 May 1946**

Django Reinhardt plays a concert with André Ekyan's orchestra.

Studio Pelouze, Paris — **Thursday 16 May 1946**

Django Reinhardt and le Quintette du Hot-Club de France

Hubert Rostaing (cl, as) (1); Django Reinhardt (gtr solo); Jacques Dieval (pno); Lucien Simoens (sb); Arthur Motta (dms).
Engineer: Walter Ruhlmann

614 OSW 416-1 **Swing Time In Springtime** {2.49}
[***78*** Swi 218] [***LP*** HMV FELP247; Pat C054 16014] [***CD*** Cls 945; Fmx FA313; JSP 904; Mos MD 6-190]

615 OSW 417-1 **Yours And Mine** (1) {2.53}
[***78*** Swi 266] [***LP*** Pat C054 16015; Swa S1389] [***CD*** Cls 945; Fmx FA313; JSP 904; Mos MD 6-190]

616 OSW 418-1 **On The Sunny Side Of The Street** {2.46}
[***78*** Swi 249] [***LP*** Pat C054 16015; Swa S1389] [***CD*** Cls 945; Fmx FA313; JSP 904; Mos MD 6-190]

617 OSW 419-1 **I Won't Dance** {2.49}
[***78*** Swi 249] [***LP*** Pat C054 16015; Swa S1389] [***CD*** Cls 945; Fmx FA313; JSP 904; Mos MD 6-190]

Paris — **May–June 1946**

The magazine *Jazz Hot* (No. 7) features an article on Hubert Rostaing.

Zurich — **c. early summer 1946**

Django reportedly plays a month-long engagement in a Zurich nightclub.

Brussels — **June 1946**

The Belgian *Hot Club Magazine* features articles on Gus DeLoof and Arthur Briggs.

London — **June 1946**

Article in *Bandwagon* magazine on Stéphane Grappelli.
See Cherrett, page 14, for a reproduction of this article.

London **July 1946**

Short news item on Django Reinhardt in *BMG*.
See Cherrett, page 19, for a reproduction.

Paris **July/August 1946**

The magazine *Jazz Hot* (No. 8) features articles on Alix Combelle and Roger Chaput, and a front cover photo of André Ekyan.

Switzerland **September 1946**

Django tours with his new group. See Delaunay, page 135.

London **Thursday 24 October 1946**

Django Reinhardt arrives in London and appears at the 'Caribbean Club', London, the same evening.

London **Sunday 27 October 1946**

Django plays the 'Caribbean Club' accompanied by George Shearing (pno) and Coleridge Goode (sb).

London **Monday 28 October 1946**

Django leaves for New York aboard the 'Yankee Clipper'.

London **Thursday 31 October 1946**

Django's activities in London reported in *Melody Maker*.
See Cherrett, page 15, for a reproduction of this news report.

Brussels **November 1946**

The Belgian *Hot Club Magazine* features an article on Gus DeLoof.

New York City **Sunday 3 November 1946**

Django arrives in the USA.

The Music Hall, East 46 St and St Clair, Cleveland, OH **Monday 4 November 1946**

Django appears with the Duke Ellington Orchestra for the first time, at the Cleveland Public Music Hall. *Cleveland Plain Dealer* reporter Glenn Pullen said he played 'Tiger Rag', 'Blues In E Flat' and an unidentified tune; Max Abrams reports that he played 'Tiger Rag' and 'Honeysuckle Rose'.

Cleveland, OH **Tuesday 5 November 1946**

The *Cleveland Plain Dealer* newspaper reports on the previous night's concert with an article entitled 'French Guitar Artist Steals Duke's Concert', adding that 1,800 people attended the concert, which began at 9.15, delayed due to a lost baggage car containing the orchestra's instruments.

> The faithful followers of the popular composer-bandmaster did not seem to mind the long wait. They were offered extra compensation in the form

of Django Reinhardt, the noted French guitarist ... In the hands of this virtuoso, who resembles the screen's Adolph Menjou, an electric guitar acquires richer, magical qualities. His digital dexterity was remarkable, in intricate chords that were executed with such technical brilliance that the band musicians kept shouting *Go to it, master!*' (Glenn Pullen, *Cleveland Plain Dealer*)

Toronto, Ontario — Wednesday 6 November 1946

Django and the Ellington orchestra appear in concert.

Civic Opera House, Chicago, IL — Saturday 9 November 1946

Django and the Ellington orchestra appear in concert.

Civic Opera House, Chicago, IL — Sunday 10 November 1946

Django Reinhardt with Duke Ellington and his Orchestra

Shelton Hemphill, Harold Baker, Ray Nance, Cat Anderson (tpts); Lawrence Brown, Wilbur de Paris, Claude Jones (tbns); Russell Procope (cl, as); Johnny Hodges (as); Jimmy Hamilton, Al Sears (ts); Harry Carney (bs); Duke Ellington (pno); Django Reinhardt (elgtr solo); Oscar Pettiford (sb); William 'Sonny' Greer (dms) (1).
Django Reinhardt (elgtr solo) (2).
Acetates

618 Improvisation On Tiger Rag (Ride Red Ride) (1) {2.48}
[***LP*** Vog 500100] [***EP*** **Rar RA30**] [***CD*** Fmx FA313; Vog 228E 6005, 668003-1]

619 Blues Riff (1) {3.46}
[***LP*** Vog 500100] [***EP*** **Rar RA30**] [***CD*** Fmx FA313; Vog 228E 6005, 668003-1]

620 Honeysuckle Rose (1) {3.36}
[***LP*** Vog 500100] [***EP*** **Rar RA30**] [***CD*** Fmx FA313; Vog 228E 6005]

621 Improvisation No. 2 (2) {2.48}
[***LP*** Vog 500100] [***EP*** **Rar RA30**] [***CD*** Fmx FA313; Vog 228E 6005]

The Fremeaux issue of 618 fades early and lasts 2.14. Other issues may also vary.
This concert was specifically sponsored by *Down Beat* magazine.
Original recordings made by John Steiner

Rochester, MN — Monday 11 or Tuesday 12 November 1946

Django and the Ellington orchestra appear in concert.

Minneapolis, MN — Wednesday 13 November 1946

Django and the Ellington orchestra appear in concert. Django also writes to Gérard Leveque from the Hotel Nicollet.

Omaha, NB **Saturday 16 November 1946**

Django and the Ellington orchestra appear in concert.

The US tour continues with appearances in Buffalo NY, Kansas City MO (Play-Mor ballroom), Cincinnati OH, Boston MA, Detroit MI, Philadelphia PA, Pittsburgh PA, Norfolk VA, San Francisco CA and Lincoln NB. The specific dates for these appearances are currently unknown and some probably interpolate the above, logged, appearances.

Carnegie Hall, NYC **Saturday 23 and Sunday 24 November 1946**

Django and the Ellington orchestra appear in concert for the final time.
See Delaunay, pages 137–41.

New York **Monday 18 November 1946**

Article about Django Reinhardt published in *Time* magazine.

Article about Django Reinhardt published in *Down Beat* magazine. He also appears on the front cover of this issue.

See Cherrett, pages 14 and 117, for reproductions of these articles.

New York City **November–December 1946**

The time frame for the bulk of the amateur film made of Django Reinhardt by Harry Volpe.

Paris **Tuesday 3 December 1946**

'Jam Session No. 6' records for Swing. Musicians include Frank 'Big Boy' Goudie and Robert Mavouzny.

New York City **Thursday 5 December 1946**

Django writes to Stéphane Grappelli using notepaper from the Henry Hudson Hotel.

Cafe Society Club, New York City **December 1946–January 1947**

Django plays a month-long engagement in the company of Edmond Hall and Pete Johnson. See the film *Boogie Woogie Dream* (1941) for footage of Johnson, Albert Ammons, Lena Horne and Teddy Wilson, filmed in Cafe Society.

Paris **1947**

Charles Delaunay and Robert Goffin publish *Jazz 47* (Editions America, P Seghers).

London **1947**

Stéphane Grappelli appears in the film *Flamingo Affair*, also featuring the Eugene Pini Tango Orchestra. An extract appears on ***DVD*** MOE 001.

New York City **Thursday 24 January 1947**

Django Reinhardt's 37th birthday.

Paris January–February 1947

'Sarane Ferret et le Quintette de Paris' record five titles for Pacific records (matrix numbers ST1952–7). Musicians include Roger Grasset.

New York City Thursday 6 February 1947

Django Reinhardt leaves the USA and returns to Paris.
Harry Volpe makes amateur film of Django's departure.

Paris Thursday 13 February 1947

Django Reinhardt arrives back in Paris.

Brussels March 1947

The Belgian *Hot Club Magazine* features articles on Ivan DeBie and Gus deLoof.

Studio RDF, Paris March 1947

Django Reinhardt

Django Reinhardt (gtr); Eddie Barnard (pno).
Radio broadcast, 'Rendez-vous In Paris' (Program No. 7, North American Service of the French Broadcasting System); acetates made by the International Recording Company (allocated number B119-7).

[announcements and introduction]

622 **No Name Blues** (Minor Swing) {0.50}
[***CD*** Fmx FA313] [interview]

623 **Love's Melody** (Mélodie Au Crépuscule) {1.48}
[***CD*** Fmx FA313] [interview]

624 **Castle Of My Dreams** (Manoir De Mes Rêves) {0.45}
[***CD*** Fmx FA313]

[closing announcements]

The interviews, in English, by unnamed American radio presenters, are conducted as if they were with Django, but in fact they are with Charles Delaunay posing as Django.

Paris Thursday 6 March to c. early May 1947

Django appears in residence at Le Bœuf sur le Toit.

Paris Wednesday 19 March 1947

Stéphane Grappelli arrives in Paris and visits the headquarters of the Hot-Club de France at rue Chaptal.

Paris Thursday 20 March 1947

The death of Michel Warlop at age 36.

Studio Pelouze, Paris Wednesday 26 March 1947

Django Reinhardt and le Quintette du Hot-Club de France

Stéphane Grappelli (vln); Django Reinhardt (gtr solo); Joseph Reinhardt, Jean 'Matelot' Ferret (gtrs); Emmanuel Soudieux (sb).
Engineer: Walter Ruhlmann

625 OSW 449-1 **R-Vingt-Six** {2.27}
[**78** Swi 259] [***LP*** HMV FELP247; Pat C054 16015; Swa S1389] [***CD*** Cls 1001; Fmx FA313; JSP 904; Mos MD 6-190]

626 OSW 450-1 **How High The Moon** {2.35}
[**78** Swi 253] [***LP*** HMV FELP208; Pat C 054 16015; Swa S1389] [***CD*** Cls 1001; Fmx FA313; JSP 904; Mos MD 6-190]

627 OSW 451-1 **Lover Man** {3.17}
[**78** Swi 253] [***LP*** HMV FELP208; Pat C054 16015; Swa S1389] [***CD*** Cls 1001; Fmx FA313; Gal GALE435; Hab 111200; JSP 904; Mos MD 6-190]

628 OSW 452-1 **Blue Lou** {2.20}
[**78** Swi 259] [***LP*** Aff BOX107; HMV FELP 208; Pat C054 16015; Swa S1389] [***CD*** Avid AMSC648; Cls 1001; Fmx FA313; JSP 904; Mos MD 6-190]

629 OSW 453-1 **Blues** {2.35}
[**78** Swi 266] [***LP*** Aff BOX107; HMV FELP247; Pat C054 16015; Swa S1389; Swi 8420267] [***CD*** Cls 1001; Fmx FA313; JSP 904; Mos MD 6-190]

(probably) Technisor Studios, Paris Wednesday 16 April 1947

Django's Music (Django Reinhardt et son Orchestre du 'Boeuf Sur le Toit')

Vincent Casino, Louis Menardie, Jo Boyer (tpts); André Lafosse, Guy Paquinet (tbns); Michel de Villers (cl and as); Jean-Claude Fohrenbach (ts); Eddie Barnard (pno); Django Reinhardt (gtr solo); Joseph Reinhardt (gtr); Willy Lockwood (sb); Al Craig (dms).
Engineer: Robert Sergent

630 ST 1984-2 **Minor Blues** {2.45} (part 4006)
[**78** BS 59] [***LP*** Bar 80929/30] [***CD*** Cls 1001; Fmx FA313; Vog 228E 6005]

Same location, date and engineer

Django Reinhardt and le Quintette du Hot-Club de France

Django Reinhardt (gtr solo); Michel de Villers (cl) (1), (as) (2); Eddie Bernard (pno); Joseph Reinhardt (gtr); Willy Lockwood (sb); Al Craig (dms).

631 ST 1985 **Clair de Lune** (1) {2.47} (part 4007)
[**78 unissued**] [***LP*** Vog 403 500842, COF03] [***CD*** Cls 1001; Fmx FA313; Vog 228E 6005]

632 ST 1986 **Lancer Léger** (Pêche A La Mouche) (2) {2.32} (part 4008)
[***78*** BS 59] [***LP*** Bar 80929/30] [***CD*** Cls 1001; Fmx FA313]

633 ST 1987 **Lentement, Mademoiselle** {3.36} (part 4009)
[***78* unissued**] [***LP*** Vog 403 500842, **COF03**; KC109] [***CD*** Cls 1001; Fmx FA313; Vog 228E 6005]

634 ST 1988 **Love's Melody** (Mélodie Au Crépuscule) {2.35} (part 4010)
[***78* unissued**] [***LP*** Vog 403 500842, **COF03**] [***CD*** Cls 1001; Fmx FA313; Vog 228E 6005]

The above four titles were recorded for the soundtrack of an unfinished film *La Fleur de l'age* (dir. Marcel Carne).

Brussels mid-May 1947

The Quintette begin a tour of Belgium.

Studio Fonior, 218 Chaussée de Jette,
Koekelberg, Brussels Wednesday 21 May 1947

Django Reinhardt et son Quintette du Hot-Club de France

Django Reinhardt (elgtr solo); Hubert Rostaing (cl); Eugène Vées (gtr); Emmanuel Soudieux (sb); Pierre Fouad (dms).
Engineer: (possibly) Achille Palmans

635 Fo 1782-R **Porto Cabello** (Il Mexicano) [**unissued**]

636 Fo 1782-RB **Porto Cabello** (Il Mexicano) {3.18}
[***78* De F-9242**, MB-9242; Tel SH 107] [***LP*** Muse MU22] [***CD*** Cls 1001; DRG 8473; Fmx FA313; Mus 403222]

637 Fo 1783-R **Duke And Dukie** {3.16}
[***78*** De C16092, **F-9244**, MB-9244; 711] [***LP*** Muse MU22] [***CD*** Cls 1001; DRG 8473; Fmx FA313; Mus 403222]

638 Fo 1783-RB **Duke And Dukie** {3.21}
[***78* De SB-9244**; Har SB9244; Tel SH 104] [***LP*** Muse MU22] [***CD*** DRG 8473; Fmx FA313; Mus 403222]

639 Fo 1784-R **Song D'Automne** [**unissued**]

640 Fo 1784-RB **Song D'Automne** [**unissued**]

641 Fo 1784-RC **Song D'Automne** {2.58}
[***78*** De C-16092, **De F-9244**, M32332, MB-9244, 711; Har SB9244; Tel SH 109] [***LP*** Muse MU22] [***CD*** Cls 1001; DRG 8473; Fmx FA313; Mus 403222]

642 Fo 1785-R **Babik – Bi-Bop** {2.44}
[***78* De F-9242**; Tel SH 107] [***LP*** Muse MU22] [***CD*** Cls 1001; DRG 8473; Fmx FA313]

643 Fo 1785-RB **Babik – Bi-Bop** [**unissued**]

644 Fo 1785-RC **Babik – Bi-Bop** {2.48}
[***78*** **De F-9242**, MB 9242] [***LP*** Muse MU22] [***CD*** DRG 8473; Fmx FA313]

645 Fo 1786-R **Del Salle** {2.46}
[***78*** De MB-9243] [***LP*** Muse MU22; Vo DP05] [***CD*** Cls 1001; DRG 8473; Fmx FA313]

646 Fo 1786-RB **Del Salle** {3.09}
[***78*** De C-16177, **F-9243**; Tel SH 109] [***LP*** Muse MU22] [***CD*** DRG 8473; Fmx FA313]

647 Fo 1787-R **Just One Of Those Things** [**unissued**]

648 Fo 1787-RB **Just One Of Those Things** [**unissued**]

649 Fo 1787-RC **Just One Of Those Things** {2.49}
[***78*** De C-16177, **F-9243**, MB-9243] [***LP*** Ast LP20102; Met MTM12; Muse MU22] [***CD*** Cls 1001; DRG 8473; Fmx FA313; Mus 403222]

646 is not the same tune as 681.

Brussels — June 1947

The Belgian *Hot Club Magazine* features articles on Hubert Rostaing, Garland Wilson, Eddie Barclay and Blue Star Records.

Studio Technisor, Paris — Sunday 6 July 1947

Django Reinhardt and le Quintette du Hot-Club de France

Django Reinhardt (elgtr solo); Hubert Rostaing (cl); Joseph Reinhardt (gtr); Ladislas Czabanyck (sb); André Jourdan (dms).
Engineer: Robert Sergent

650 ST 2086-1 **For Sentimental Reasons** (part 4827) [**unissued**]

651 ST 2086-2 **For Sentimental Reasons** {2.53} (part 4827)
[***78*** BS 30] [***CD*** Cls 1001; Fmx FA313; Verve 835418-1]

652 ST 2087-1 **Danse Norvégienne** {2.58} (parts 5024, 5763)
[***78*** BS 38] [***25cm LP*** Dial(A) 218] [***LP*** Bar 80929/30; Ev FS230; Per(A) SPL304; 1201] [***CD*** Cls 1001; Fmx FA313; Verve 835418-1]

653 ST 2088-1 **Blues For Barclay** {2.58} (part 4828)
[***78*** unissued] [***25cm LP*** **Dial**(A) **218**] [***LP*** Bar 80929/30; Per(A) SPL1201] [***CD*** Cls 1001; Fmx FA314]

654 ST 2088-2 **Blues For Barclay** {2.50} (part 4828)
[***78*** BS 30] [***CD*** Cls 1001; Fmx FA313; Verve 836418-1]

655 ST 2089-1 **Folie A Amphion** (part 4830) [**unissued**]

656 ST 2089-2 **Folie A Amphion** (part 4830) [**unissued**]

657 ST 2089-3 **Folie A Amphion** {2.49} (part 4830)
[***78*** BS 33] [***LP*** Bar 80929/30, 84090] [***CD*** Cls 1001; Fmx FA314; Verve 835418-1]

658 ST 2090-1 **Vette** {3.11} (part 5766)
[***78*** BS 37] [***LP*** Bar 80929/30] [***CD*** Cls 1001; Fmx FA314; Verve 835418-1]

659 ST 2091-1 **Anniversary Song** {3.29} (part 4829)
[***78*** BS 33] [***25cm LP*** Dial 218] [***LP*** Bar 80929/30; 84090; Per SPL1201] [***CD*** Cls 1001; Fmx FA314; Verve 835418-1]

660 ST 2092-1 **Swing '48** {2.44} (part 5768)
[***78*** **BS 37**; Di 754] [***25cm LP*** Dial 214] [***LP*** Bar 80929/30; Per SPL1201, 1204] [***CD*** Cls 1001; Fmx FA314; Verve 835418-1]

Note that 2088-1 appears on FMX 314, while 2088-2 appears on FMX FA313. 657 'Folie A Amphion' is a different tune from 718.

Studio Technisor, Paris — Friday 18 July 1947

Django Reinhardt et le Quintette du Hot-Club de France

Django Reinhardt (elgtr); Hubert Rostaing (cl); Joseph Reinhardt (gtr); Emmanuel Soudieux (sb); André Jourdan (dms).
Engineer: Robert Sergeant

661 ST 2104-1 **September Song** {3.14}
[***78*** BS 46] [***LP*** Bar 80929/30] [***CD*** Cls 1046; Fmx FA314; Hab 111200; Verve 835418-1]

662 ST 2104-2 **September Song** {no timing available}
[***78*** Cel TZ 3013] [***25cm LP*** Dial 218] [***LP*** Per SPL1201]

663 ST 2105-1 **Brazil** {2.42}
[***78*** **BS 50**; Cel TZ 3011] [***25cm LP*** Dial 218] [***LP*** Bar 80929/30; Ev FS230; Per SPL1201] [***CD*** Cls 1046; Fmx FA314; Verve 835418-1]

664 ST 2106-1 **I'll Never Smile Again** {2.36}
[***78*** BS 42] [***LP*** Bar 80929/30, 84090] [***CD*** Fmx FA314; Verve 835418-1]

665 ST 2106-2 **I'll Never Smile Again** {2.42}
[***25cm LP*** Dial 218] [***LP*** Ev FS230; Per SPL1201] [***CD*** Cls 1046; Fmx FA314]

666 ST 2107-1 **New York City [unissued]**

667 ST 2107-2 **New York City [unissued]**

668 ST 2107-3 **New York City** {2.32}
[***78*** BS 46; Cel TZ 3013] [***LP*** Bar 80929/30, 84090] [***CD*** Cls 1046; Fmx FA314; Verve 835418-1]

669 ST 2108-1 **Django's Blues** {3.03}
[***78*** BS 38, Di 754] [***25cm LP*** Dial 214] [***LP*** Bar 80929/30; Per SPL1201, 1204] [***CD*** Cls 1046; Fmx FA314; Verve 835418-1]

670 ST 2109-1 **Love's Mood** {3.03}
[***78*** BS 98] [***LP*** Bar 80929/30] [***CD*** Cls 1046; Fmx FA314; Verve 835418-1]

671 ST 2112-1 **I Love You** {2.48}
[*78* BS 42] [***LP*** Bar 80929/30, 84090] [***CD*** Cls 1046; Fmx FA314; Verve 8354118-1]

Delaunay lists the second take of 'September Song', but it is ignored by Fremeaux and may not exist. If that is the case, then the release details for entry 662 properly belong in entry 661. Matrix numbers 2110 and 2111 remain untraced.

Germany — *c.* late July–August 1947

The Quintette tour US military bases.

Radio Diffusion Française Studios,
Montparnasse, Paris — Monday 25 August 1947

Django Reinhardt dans 'Surprise Partie'

Django Reinhardt (gtr solo); Maurice Meunier (cl); Eddie Bernard (pno); Eugène Vées (gtr); Emmanuel Soudieux (sb); Jacques Martinon (dms).
As above, without Meunier (1).
Engineer: Colette Barre

672 **Swing Guitars** {2.59}
[***25cm LP*** Per SPL1010; **Swi M33314**; Vog 049] [***EP*** Vo VRE5010] [***LP*** Per SPL1203; Swi LDM 30069; Vog 500100, CLVLX412, COF03] [***CD*** Fmx FA314; Vog 228E 6006, 668003-2]

673 **Babik** {2.02}
[***25cm LP*** Per SPL1101; **Swi M33315**; Vog LDE084] [***LP*** Ev FS230; Pe SPL1202; Vog 500100] [***CD*** Fmx FA314; Vog 228E 6006, 668003-2]

674 **What Kind Of Friend** {2.27}
[***LP*** KC107; MA MAL12234; Mo MDINT9148; Vo 500100; LD713] [***CD*** Fmx FA314; Vog 228E 6006, 668003-2]

675 **Nuages**
[***78*** Swi 438] [***25cm LP*** Jay 3008; Per 1102; Swi 33316; Vog LDE106] [***LP*** Des DLP113; Mo MDINT9103, 9315; Per SPL1203; SPL302; Vog 500100, COF03, DP05] [***EP*** Vog EPL7066, EPV1025, VRE5010] [***CD*** Cls 1046; Fmx FA314; Vog 228E 6006]

676 **Viper's Dream** {2.55}
[***LP*** **Swi LDM30069**; Vog 500100, CLVLX412, COF03] [***CD*** Fmx FA314; Mo MDINT9315, Vog 228E 6006, 668003-2]

677 **Blues Clair** (1) {2.39}
[***LP*** **Swi LDM30069**; Vog 500100, CLVLX412, COF03] [***45*** Vog {Pop} 17069] [***CD*** Vog 228E 6006, 668003-2]

Radio Diffusion Française Studios,
Montparnasse, Paris Friday 29 August 1947

Django Reinhardt dans 'Surprise Partie'

Django Reinhardt (elgtr); Maurice Meunier (cl); Eugène Vées (gtr); Emmanuel Soudieux (sb); Andre Jourdan (dms).
Engineer: Colette Barre

678 Minor Swing {2.47}
[***78*** Swi 439] [***25cm LP*** Per SPL1010; Swi 33314] [***LP*** Mo MDINT9315; Per SPL1202, 1204; Swi LDM30069; Vog 500100, CLVLX412, COF03] [***EP*** Vog EPL7068, EPV1025, VRE5010] [***CD*** Cls 1046; Fmx FA314; Vog 228E 6006, 668003-2]

679 Swing '39 {2.30}
[***25cm LP*** Per SPL3008; **Swi 33315**; Vog LDE084, 106] [***LP*** MA MAL1234; Per SPL1202, 1204; Vog 500100, COF03, DP05, LD713] [***EP*** Vog EPL7066] [***CD*** Fmx FA314; Vog 228E 6006, 668003-2]

680 Swing '41 {3.07}
[***25cm LP*** Per SPL1010; **Swi 33314**; Vog 049] [***LP*** Per SPL1202; Vog 500100] [***CD*** Fmx FA314; Vog 228E 6006, 668003-2, LD713]

681 Del Salle {3.17}
[***25cm LP*** Jay 3008; Per SPL3008; **Swi 33316**; Vog LDE106; [***LP*** MA MAL1234; Mo MDINT9148; Per SPL1102, 1203, 1204; Vog 500100, COF03, DP05] [***EP*** Vog EPL7066] [***CD*** Fmx FA314; Vog 228E 6006, 668003-2]

682 Les Yeux Noirs {3.08}
[***LP*** **Swi LDM30069**; Vog 500100, CLVLX412, COF03] [***CD*** Fmx FA314; Vog 228E 6006, 668003-2]

Period LPs are mistitled as 'Swing '40'. 681 is not the same tune as 645.

Paris Sunday 7 September 1947

Django Reinhardt dans 'Surprise Partie'

Django Reinhardt (elgtr); Hubert Rostaing (cl); Eugène Vées (gtr); Emmanuel Soudieux (sb); André Jourdan (dms).

683 Louise {2.27}
[***LP*** Vo 500813, COF03, DP05, LD491] [***CD*** Fmx FA314; Vog 228E 6006, 668003-2]

684 Django's Dream (Rêverie) {3.47}
[***LP*** Vog 500813, COF03, LD491] [***CD*** Fmx FA314; Vog 228E 6006]

685 Swingtime In Springtime {3.06}
[***25cm LP*** Per SPL1101*; **Swi 33316**; Vog LDE084*] [***LP*** Per SPL1202*; Vog 500813*, COF03, LD491] [***EP*** Vog EPV1208*] [***CD*** Fmx FA314; Gal GALE421; Recall SMDCD307; Vog 228E 6006, 668003-2]

686 Stockholm {3.17}
[***78*** Swi 438] [***25cm LP*** Jay 3008; Per SPL1102; Swi 33316]
[***LP*** Per SPL 1203, 1204; Vo 500813, COF03, LD491, LDE106]
[***EP*** Vog EPL1025, 7066, EPV1025] [***CD*** Cls 1046; Fmx FA314;
Vog 228E 6006]

687 Féerie {2.17}
[***25cm LP*** Per SPL1101; **Swi 33315**; Vog 084] [**25cm *LP*** Per SPL1102;
Vo COF03, LDE084] [***LP*** EV FS230; Vog LD491, 500813]
[***CD*** Fmx FA314; Vog 228E 6006, 668003-2]

688 Vendredi 13 {1.57}
[***25cm LP*** Jay 3008; Per SPL1101; **Swi 33316**; Vog LDE106]
[***LP*** Per SPL1202, 1204; Su 274; Vo 5001098, CLVLX313, COF03,
LDE106] [***EP*** Vog EPL7068] [***45*** Vog 45-68] [***CD*** Fmx FA314;
Vog 228E 6006, 668003-2]

689 Sweet Chorus {2.59}
[***25cm*** Jay 3008; Per SPL1102; **Swi 33316**; Vog LDE106] [***LP*** Per 1203;
Su 274; Vog 500813, COF03, DP05, LDE491] [***EP*** Vog EPL7068]
[***CD*** Fmx FA314; Mo MDINT9315; Vog 228E 6007]

690 Crépuscule {3.53}
[***LP*** Jay 3008; Per SPL1102; **Swi 33316**] [***LP*** Per SPL1203;
Vog LD491, LD106, 500813] [***EP*** Vog EPL7068] [***CD*** EV FS230;
Fmx FA314; Mo MDINT9315; Vog 228E 6007, 668003-2]

691 Songe D'Automne {3.19}
[***25cm LP*** Jay 3008; Per SPL1102; **Swi 33316**; Vog LDE106]
[***LP*** Per SPL1203, 1204; Su 274; Vog 500813, COF03, LD491]
[***CD*** Fmx FA314; Vog 228E 6007, 668003-2]

692 I Love You For Sentimental Reasons {3.06}
[***25cm LP*** **Swi 33330**] [***LP*** Vog 500813, COF03, LD491]
[***CD*** Fmx FA314; Vog 228E 6007]

693 Just One Of Those Things {3.14}
[***25cm LP*** **Swi 33330**] [***LP*** Vog 500813, COF03, DP05, LD491]
[***CD*** Vog 228E 6007, 668003-2]

'Swingtime In Springtime' is mistitled 'Manoir De Mes Rêves' on asterisked items.

Radio Diffusion Française Studios,
Montparnasse, Paris — Monday 15 September 1947

Django Reinhardt dans 'Surprise Partie'

Personnel as above.

694 Billet Doux {2.41}
[***25cm LP*** **Swi 33330**] [***LP*** MA MAL1234; Vog LD491, 500108]
[***CD*** Fmx FA314; Vog 228E 6007, 668003-2, COF03, DP05, LD713]

695 Porto Cabello {3.42}
[***25cm LP*** **Swi LDM30069**] [***LP*** Mo MDINT9315; 509031]
[***CD*** Fmx FA314; Vog 228E 6007, 668003-3, CLVLX412, DP05]

696 Swing Dynamique (Micro) {2.31}
[***25cm LP*** **Swi LDM30069**] [***LP*** Vog 500108] [***CD*** Vog 228E 6007, 668003-3, CLVLX412, COF03]

697 Lover Man {4.08}
[***25cm LP*** **Swi LDM30069**] [***LP*** Mo MDINT9148; Vog 500108, CLVLX412, DP05] [***CD*** Fmx FA314; Vog 228E 6007, 655611]

698 Rythme Futur {2.01}
[***LP*** Vog 500108] [***CD*** Fmx FA314; Vog 228E 6007]

Studio Lutetia, Paris — Saturday 4 October 1947

Django Reinhardt et le Quintette du Hot-Club de France

Django Reinhardt (elgtr); Hubert Rostaing (cl); Joseph Reinhardt (gtr); Emmanuel Soudieux (sb); André Jourdan (dms).
Engineer: probably Pierre Hamard

699 Part 4763-1 **Topsy** {3.01}
[***78*** **BS 53**; Esq 10-015; Wax 108] [***25cm LP*** Dial 214] [***LP*** Bar 80929/30, 84090; Col KC31478; Per SPL1201, 1204] [***EP*** Atl EP523]
[***CD*** Cls 1046; Fmx FA315; Verve 835418-2]

700 Part 4764-1 **Moppin' The Bride** (Micro) {2.19}
[***78*** BS 54] [***25cm LP*** Dial 214] [***LP*** Aff BOX107; Bar 80929/30, 84090; Col KC31478; EV FS230; Per SPL1201] [***EP*** Atl EP523] [***CD*** Cls 1046; Fmx FA315; Verve 835418-2]

701 Part 4765-1 **Insensiblement** {3.10}
[***78*** **BS 50**; Cel TZ3011] [***LP*** Bar 80929/30; Col KC31478]
[***CD*** Cls 1046; Fmx FA315; Verve 835418-2]

702 Part 4766-1 **Mano** {2.50}
[***78*** BS54] [***25cm LP*** Dial 214] [***LP*** Bar 80929/30, 84090; Col KC31478]
[***CD*** Cls 1046; Fmx FA315; Verve 835418-2]

703 Part 4767-1 **Blues Primitif** {2.40}
[***78*** **BS 55**; Esq 0-015; Wax 108] [***25cm LP*** Dial 218] [***LP*** Bar 80929/30; Col KC31478; Per SPL1201, 1204] [***EP*** Atl EP523] [***CD*** Cls 1046; Fmx FA315; Verve 835418-2]

704 Part 4768-1 **Gipsy With A Song** (Version 2) {2.55}
[***78*** BS 55] [***25cm LP*** Dial 218] [***LP*** Barc 80929/30, 84090; Col KC31478]
[***CD*** Cls 1046; Fmx FA315; Verve 835418-2]

705 Part 4769-1 **Gipsy With A Song** (Version 1 (*sic*)) {3.00}
[***78*** BS 55] [***LP*** Bar 80369] [***CD*** Cls 1046; Fmx FA315; Verve 835418-2]

Aff BOX107 mistitled as 'Mike'; Dial 214 mistitled as 'The Wedding March'. Dial 218 mistitled as 'Gypsy Without a Song'. Session supervised by Hughes Panassié.

Prague, Czechoslovakia — Tuesday 7 October 1947

The Fud Candrix orchestra play a concert at the 'Divadlo Voskovece and Werich'.

Radio Diffusion Française Studios,
Montparnasse, Paris — Wednesday 8 and Monday 13 October 1947

Django Reinhardt dans 'Surprise Partie'

Django Reinhardt (elgtr); Gérard Leveque (cl); Eugène Vées (gtr); Emmanuel Soudieux (sb); André Jourdan (dms).
Engineer: Colette Barre

706 **Artillerie Lourde** {4.13}
[***25cm LP*** Per 1010; **Swi 33314**; Vog 049] [***LP*** EV FS230; MA MAL1234; Per SPL102; Su 274; Vog 500108, LD713] [***CD*** Fmx FA315; Vog 228E 6007, 668003-3]

707 **Pêche A La Mouche** (Fly Fishing) {2.13}
[***25cm LP*** Per 1010; **Swi 33314**; Vog 049] [***LP*** EV FS230; Per SPL1202; Vog 500108, CLVLX313, COF03, LD713] [***EP*** Vog EPV1208] [***CD*** Fmx FA315; Vog 228E 6007]

708 **Belleville** {2.31}
[***25cm LP*** Per SPL1010; **Swi 33314**; Vog 049] [***LP*** Mo 509031, MDINT9315; Per SPL1203, 1204; Swi LD30069; Vog CLVLX412, COF03] [***EP*** Vog EPV1208] [***CD*** Fmx FA315; Vog 228E 6007, 670205]

709 **Douce Ambiance** {2.19}
[***78*** Swi 439] [***25cm LP*** Per SPL1010; Swi 33314; Vog 049] [***LP*** MA MAL1234; Per SPL1203, 1204; Vog 500108, COF03, LD713] [***EP*** Vog EPL7066, EPV 1025] [***45*** Vog 45-68] [***CD*** Cls 1046; Fmx FA315; Vog 228E 6007, 668003-3]

710 **Swing De Paris** {3.47}
[***25cm LP*** Per SPL1010; **Swi 33314**; Vog 049] [***LP*** Mode 509031, MDINT9103, 9315, 9841; Per SPL1203, Vog COF03] [***EP*** Vog EPL7068] [***45*** Vog 45-69] [***CD*** Fmx FA315; Vog 228E 6007]

711 **September Song** {3.22}
[***LP*** MA MAL1234; Mo MDINT9103; Vog COF05, DP05, LD713] [CD Fmx FA315]

712 **I Can't Give You Anything But Love** {2.45}
[***25cm LP*** Swi 33330] [***LP*** MA MAL1234; Mo MDINT9148; Vog 500108] [***CD*** Fmx FA315; Vog 228E 6007]

713 **Blues En Mineur** {3.26}
[***LP*** Vog 500100] [***CD*** Fmx FA315; Vog 228E 6007, 668003-3]

714 **It Had To Be You** {3.04}
[***25cm LP*** **Swi 33330**] [***LP*** MA MAL1234; Vog 500108, LD713] [***CD*** Fmx FA315; Vog 228E 6007, 668003-3]

715 **Manoir De Mes Rêves** {3.45}
[***25cm LP*** Per SPL110; **Swi 33315**; Vog LDE084] [***LP*** MA MAL1234; Per SPL1202; Vog 500108, CLVLX313] [***EP*** Vog EPV 1208] [***45*** Vog 45-67] [***CD*** Fmx FA315; Vog 228E 6008]

716 **Dinette** {2.50}
[***25cm LP*** Per 1101; **Swi 33316**; Vog LDE084] [***LP*** Mode 509031, MDINT9103, 9315; Per SPL1202, 1204; Vog COF03, LD713] [***45*** Vog 45-69] [***CD*** Fmx FA315; Vog 228E 6008, 668003-3]

717 **Mélodie Au Crépuscule** {3.14}
[***25cm LP*** Per(A) SPL1101; **Swing 33315**, LDM 30069; Vog LDE084] [***LP*** Des DLP113; Mo MDINT9148; Per SPL1202, SPL304; Vog 500108, COF03, DP05] [***EP*** Coll JEN8; Vog EPL 7996] [***CD*** Fmx FA315; Vog 228E 6008, 668003-3]

718 **Folie A Amphion** {2.56}
[***25cm LP*** Jay 3008; **Swi 33316**; Vog LDE 160] [***LP*** MA MAL1234; Mo MDINT9103, 9315; Per SPL1102, SPL120; Su 274; Vog COF03, LD713] [***EP*** Vog EPL7068] [***CD*** Fmx FA315; Vog 228E 6008, 668003-3]

719 **Place De Brouckère** {2.47}
[***25cm LP*** **Swi 30069**] [***LP*** Mode 50903, MDINT9315; Vog CLVLX412, COF03, DP05] [***EP*** Coll JEN8; Vo EPL7996] [***CD*** Fmx FA315; Vog 228E 6008]

720 **Symphonie** {2.36}
[***25cm LP*** **Swi 30069**] [***LP*** Vog 500108, CLVLX41, COF03] [***EP*** Coll JEN8; Vog EPL7996] [***CD*** Fmx FA315; Vog 228E 6008, 668003-3]

721 **Improvisation Sur La Danse Norvégienne** {2.47}
[***25cm LP*** **Swi 30069**] [***LP*** Vog 500108, CLVLX412, COF03] [***EP*** Coll JEN8; Vog EPL7996] [***CD*** Fmx FA315; Vog 228E 6008, 655611]

722 **Saint-Louis Blues** {4.05}
[***25cm LP*** **Swi 30069**] [***LP*** Mo MDINT9117, 9148, 9461, Per SPL304; Vog 500108, CLVLX412, COF03, DP05] [***EP*** Vog VRE5010] [***CD*** Fmx FA315; Vog 228E 6008, 668003-3]

Some discographers believe that 711 belongs in the August 1947 sessions rather than here.
718 Folie A Amphion is not the same tune as 657.

Paris — Thursday 16 October 1947

Django Reinhardt, Stéphane Grappelli, Joseph Reinhardt, Eugène Vées and bassist Fred Ermelin play a QHCF reunion concert at Salle Pleyel. Titles performed include 'Blue Drag', 'Swing Guitars', 'Swing '39', 'How High The Moon' and 'Old Man River'.

Paris Friday 17 October 1947

Stéphane Grappelli, accompanied by Joseph Reinhardt, Roger Chaput and Emmanuel Soudieux, records two titles for Swing records (matrix numbers OSW478 and OSW479), and two piano solos (matrix numbers OSW480 and OSW481). Lacquers of OSW479 and OSW480 were damaged in the manufacturing process and therefore only OSW478 and OSW481 were issued, coupled on Swing 271. Matrix OSW478 appears on Fmx FA315.

Studio Luteita, Paris Friday 14 November 1947

Django Reinhardt et le Quintette du Hot-Club de France

Stéphane Grappelli (vln); Django Reinhardt (gtr solo); Joseph Reinhardt, Eugène Vées (gtrs); Fred Ermelin (sb).
Engineer: Eugène Ravenet

723 OSW 482-1 **What Is This Thing Called Love?** {2.06}
[**78** Swi 285] [***LP*** HMV FELP208; Pat AT1002, C054 16015; Swa S1389] [***CD*** Cls 1046; Fmx FA315; JSP 904; Mos MD 6-190]

724 OSW 483-1 **Ol' Man River** {2.06}
[***78*** Swi 270] [***25cm LP*** An 60003] [***LP*** HMV FELP208; Pat C054 16015; Swa S1389] [***EP*** An 73007] [***CD*** Cls 1046; Fmx FA315; JSP 904; Mos MD 6-190]

725 OSW 484-1 **Si Tu Savais** {2.42}
[***78*** Swi 270] [***LP*** HMV FELP208; Pat C054 16016; Swa S1371] [***CD*** Fmx FA315; JSP 904; Mos MD 6-190]

726 OSW 485-1 **Eveline** {2.11}
[***78*** Swi 274] [***LP*** HMV FELP247; Pat C054 16016; Swa 1371] [***CD*** Fmx FA315; Gal GALE435; JSP 904; Mos MD 6-190]

727 OSW 486-1 **Diminushing** (*sic*) {3.13}
[***78*** Swi 274] [***25cm LP*** An 60003] [***LP*** HMV FELP247; Pat C054 16016; Swa 1371] [***EP*** An 73007] [***CD*** Fmx FA315; JSP 904; Mos MD 6-190]

Salle Pleyel, Paris Sunday 16 November 1947

The Quintet (Reinhardt, Grappelli, Joseph Reinhardt, Eugène Vées and Fred Ermelin) play a reunion concert. Among the titles performed are 'Blue Drag', 'Swing Guitars', 'Swing '39', 'How High The Moon' and 'Old Man River'.

Paris Monday 17 November 1947

The Quintet, with the same personnel as the previous evening, guest on the radio show *Actualities de Paris*, performing 'Viper's Dream'.
No recording is known to have survived.

Radio Diffusion Français Studios,
Montparnasse, Paris — Friday 21 and Friday 28 November 1947

Personnel as per last session, except: Django Reinhardt (gtr solo) (1).
Engineer: Colette Barre
Radio broadcast, RTF

728 **Ol' Man River** {3.31}
[***LP*** Mo MDINT9116; Vog 500813, COF03, DP05, LD 491]
[***EP*** **Vog EPL7728**] [***CD*** Fmx FA315; Vog 228E 6008]

729 **R-Vingt-Six** {2.52}
[***LP*** Vog 500813, COF03, LD491] [***EP*** **Vog EPL7728**]
[***CD*** Fmx FA315; Vog 228E 6008]

730 **How High The Moon** (Version 1) {2.58}
[***LP*** **Vog 406505**] [***CD*** Fmx FA315; Vog 228E 6008]

731 **Swing Guitars** {2.54}
[***LP*** Vog LD491, 500813] [***EP*** **Vog EPL7728**] [***CD*** Fmx FA315;
Vog 228E 6008, COF034, DP05]

732 **I Love You** {3.13}
[***LP*** Vog LD491; 500813, COF03, DP05] [***EP*** **Vog LDE7728**]
[***CD*** Fmx FA315; Vog 228E 6008]

733 **Tiger Rag** {2.50}
[***LP*** Vog 500842] [***CD*** Fmx FA315; Vog 228E 6008]

734 **Tears** {3.33}
[***LP*** Vog 500842] [***CD*** Fmx FA315; Vog 228E 6008, COF03, DP05]

735 **Dinah** {3.32}
[***LP*** Vog 500842, COF03] [***CD*** Fmx FA315; Vog 228E 6008]

736 **Them There Eyes** {2.11}
[***LP*** Vog 500842] [***CD*** Fmx FA315; Vog 228E 6008]

737 **How High The Moon** {2.50}
[***LP*** Vog 500842] [***CD*** Fmx FA315; Vog 228E 6009]

738 **Improvisation '47** (Improvisation No. 5) (1) {2.00}
[***LP*** Vog 500842] [***CD*** Fmx FA315; Vog 228E 6009]

739 **Daphné** {4.27}
[***LP*** Vog 500842, COF03, DP05] [***CD*** Fmx FA316; Vog 228E 6009]

740 **Manoir De Mes Rêves** {4.27}
[***LP*** Vog 500842] [***CD*** Fmx FA316; Vog 228E 6009, DP05]

741 **Danse Nuptiale** {2.36}
[***LP*** Vog 406505] [***CD*** Fmx FA316; Vog 228E 6009]

742 **Crazy Rhythm** {3.04}
[***LP*** Vog 406505] [***CD*** Fmx FA316; Vog 228E 6009]

742a **Tiger Rag** (incomplete) {2.37}
[***CD*** Fmx FA316]

Brussels December 1947

The Belgian *Hot Club Magazine* features an article on Frank 'Big Boy' Goudie.

The reunited QHCF tour Belgium.

Technisor Studios, Paris Wednesday 10 December 1947

Rex Stewart Quintette

Rex Stewart (ct); Hubert Rostaing (as); Django Reinhardt (gtr); Ladislas Czabanyck (sb); Ted Curry (dms).

743 ST2220-1 **Night And Day** [P5241] [**unissued**]

744 ST2220-2 **Night And Day** [P5241] {2.52}
[***78*** Fon BS 25086] [***CD*** Fmx FA316; Verve 835418-2]

745 ST 2220-3 **Night And Day** {2.50}
[78 **BS 73**; Cel TZ 3018; Fon 35] [***25cm LP*** Dial 218] [***LP*** Barc 80929/30, 84090; Ev FS230; Per SPL1201] [***CD*** Fmx FA316; Verve 835418-2]

746 ST 2221-1 **Confessin'** [P5242] [**unissued**]

747 ST 2221-2 **Confessin'** [P5242] [**unissued**]

748 ST 2221-3 **Confessin'** {2.55}
[***78*** **BS 73**; Cel TZ 3018; Fon BS 25086] [***25cm LP*** Dial 218] [***LP*** Bar 80929/30, 84090; Per SPL1201] [***EP*** Atl EP523] [***CD*** Fmx FA316]

Session supervised by Hughes Panassié.

probably Paris 1947–48

Django Reinhardt (gtr), probably Hubert Rostaing (clnt), uknown (gtr, sb).
Radio broadcast

Announcement {0.08}

748a **Pour Que Ma Vie Demure** {3.53} [**unissued**]

London 1948

Stéphane Grappelli appears in the short film *Stephane Grappelly and his Quartette.* The entire film appears on ***DVD*** MOE 001. See Filmography for details.

Paris Friday 23 January 1948

Django Reinhardt's 38th birthday.
The Quintette opens at the ABC Theatre in Paris.
See Cherrett, page 11, for a reproduction of this news item.

Paris February 1948

The magazine *Jazz Hot* (No. 20) features articles on Coleman Hawkins, Rex Stewart and the history of the Hot-Club de France (Part 1).

Dizzy Gillespie arrives in Paris. Louis Vola returns from South America.

Nice — Saturday 28 February 1948

Festival de Jazz de Nice

Stéphane Grappelli (vln); Django Reinhardt (gtr solo); Joseph Reinhardt, Challin Ferret (gtrs); Emmanuel Soudieux (sb).
Radio broadcast, RTF; acetates

749 **Nuages** {1.52}
[***CD*** Fmx FA316]

(Announcement by Gilbert Cazeneuve)

750 **Swing '42** {2.34}
[***CD*** Fmx FA316]

Paris — March 1948

The magazine *Jazz Hot* (No. 21) features the History of the Hot-Club de France (Part 2).

Studio Pelouze, Paris — Wednesday 10 March 1948

Django Reinhardt et le Quintette du Hot-Club de France

Stéphane Grappelli (vln); (pno) (1); Django Reinhardt (gtr solo); Joseph Reinhardt, Challin Ferret (gtrs); Emmanuel Soudieux (sb).

751 OSW 500-1 **Mike** {2.47}
[***78*** Swi 287] [***LP*** HMV FELP247; Pat C054 16016; Swa 1371]
[***CD*** Fmx FA316; JSP 904; Mos MD 6-190]

752 OSW 501-1 **Lady Be Good** {2.54}
[***78*** Swi 287] [***LP*** HMV FELP247; Pat C054 16016; Swa 1371]
[***CD*** Fmx FA316; JSP 904; Mos MD 6-190]

753 OSW 502-1 **Festival '48** {2.36}
[***78*** Swi 280] [***25cm LP*** An 60003] [***LP*** Aff BOX107; HMV FELP208; Pat C054 16016; Swa 1371] [***45*** An 73006] [***CD*** Fmx FA316; JSP 904; Mos MD 6-190]

754 SW 503-1 **Fantaisie** {2.52}
[***78*** Swi 280] [***LP*** HMV FELP247; Pat C054 16016; Swa S1371]
[***CD*** Fmx FA316; JSP 904; Mos MD 6-190]

755 OSW 504-1 **Brick Top** {3.05}
[***78*** Swi 283] [***LP*** HMV FELP247; Pat C054 16016; Swa S1371]
[***CD*** Fmx FA316; JSP 904; Mos Md 6-190]

756 OSW 505-1 **Just For Fun** {3.05}
[***LP*** **HMV FELP 208**; 247; Pat C054 16016; Swa S1371]
[***CD*** Fmx FA316; JSP 904; Mos Md 6-190]

757 OSW 506-1 **To Each His Own** – Symphony (1) {3.01}
[***LP*** **Pat C054 16016**; Swa S1371] [***CD*** Fmx FA316; JSP 904; Mos MD 6-190]

Grappelli plays pizzicato on 755.

Empire Theatre, Hackney, London E8 — Monday 15 March – probably Saturday 20 March 1948

The Quintette appear in a variety programme.

London — mid-March 1948.

Django Reinhardt and Stéphane Grappelli arrive to play a series of variety programmes organized by Lew Grade Entertainment.

BBC TV Studios, White City, Wood Lane, London W12 — Monday 22 March 1948

Django Reinhardt, Stephane Grappelly and Le Quintet Du Hot Club de France (*sic*)

Stéphane Grappelli (vln); Django Reinhardt (gtr solo); probably Alan Mindell and Malcolm Mitchell (gtrs); Teddy Wadmore (sb).
BBC Television, 'Stars In Your Eyes', broadcast at 3.00pm

Swing '42 {2.13}
The Bluest Kind Of Blues {3.30}
Belle Ville (*sic*) {2.00}

Programme presented by Michael Mills. Orchestra directed by Eric Robertson. Other artists appearing: Ronald Chesney, Cliff Gordon, Gail Kendall and Alicia Halama, Paul Konaski.
45 minutes' duration.

BBC TV Studios, White City, Wood Lane, London W12 — Saturday 27 March 1948

Django Reinhardt, Stephane Grappelly and le Quintet du Hot Club de France (1)

Stéphane Grappelli (vln); Django Reinhardt (gtr solo); probably Alan Mindell, Malcolm Mitchell (gtrs); Teddy Wadmore (sb).

Django Reinhardt and Stephane Grappelly at the piano (2)

BBC Television, 'Stars In Your Eyes', broadcast at 8.30pm

Swing '42 (1) {2.28}
To Each His Own (2) {1.39}
Diana (*sic*, probably Dinah) (2) [1.17]
The Bluest Kind Of Blues (1) {3.21}
Belle Ville (*sic*) (1) {2.05}

Programme credits as per 15 March, but also including Cyril Fletcher and Vera Lynn as guests, and duration 60 minutes.
Current research indicates that recordings of neither of these broadcasts, if indeed they ever existed, appear to have survived. However, the possibility of their retrieval cannot be discounted.

Paris **March–April 1948**

The magazine *Jazz Hot* (No. 22) features and article on Christian Bellest and the history of the Hot-Club de France (Part 3).

Empire Theatre, Wood Green, London N22 **Monday 29 March–probably Saturday 4 April 1948**

The QHCF appear in a variety programme.
See Cherrett, page 13, for a news item relating to this event.

Empire Theatre, Chiswick, London W4 **Monday 5–probably Saturday 10 April 1948**

The QHCF appear in a variety programme.
See Cherrett, page 13, for a news item relating to this event and page 21 for a reproduction of the programme.
See Delaunay, pages 149–50.

Brussels **April 1948**

The Belgian *Hot Club Magazine* features a front cover photo of Django Reinhardt and an article on Rex Stewart.

Paris **May 1948**

The magazine *Jazz Hot* (No. 23) features the History of the Hot-Club de France (Part 4).

London **May 1948**

Article about Django Reinhardt published in *BMG*.
See Cherrett, page 18, for a reproduction of this article.

Stockholm **Saturday 1 May–probably Saturday 8 or 15 May 1948**

The QHCF play an engagement, initially reported as one month long, at the China Theatre, Stockholm.
See Cherrett, page 13, for a news item relating to this event and page 15 for a report in *Melody Maker*.

London **between Saturday 16 and Sunday 23 May 1948**

Django Reinhardt and Stéphane Grappelli return to England to continue touring for Lew Grade Entertainment.

Hippodrome Theatre, Manchester **Monday 24 May–probably Saturday 29 May 1948**

The QHCF appear in a variety programme.
See Cherrett, page 18, for an advertisement pertaining to this.

Empire Theatre, Shepherd's Bush, London W12 **Monday 31 May–probably Saturday 5 June 1948**

The QHCF appear in a variety programme.
See Cherrett, page 18, for an advertisement pertaining to this.

Paris June–July 1948

The magazine *Jazz Hot* (No. 24) features the history of the Hot-Club de France (Part 5).

Probably Paris *c.* June–July 1948

Le Quintette du Hot-Club de France

Stéphane Grappelli (vln); Joseph Reinhardt (elgtr); Challin Ferret (gtr); probably Emmanuel Soudieux (sb).

757a Odette {2.01}
[***CD*** Fmx FA316]

Some doubt exists as to whether Django appears on this recording or not. See the notes to Fmx FA316 for further discussion.

Paris August–September 1948

The magazine *Jazz Hot* (No. 25) features the history of the Hot-Club de France (Part 6).

Paris October 1948

The magazine *Jazz Hot* (No. 26) features the history of the Hot-Club de France (Part 7).

Théâtre Edouard VII, Paris 10 October 1948

Hubert Rostaing et son Sextette, avec Django Reinhardt

Hubert Rostaing (cl, as); Roby Poutevin (vib); Armand Motta (pno); Django Reinhardt (elgtr); Lucien Galopian or Jean-Pierre Sasson (gtr); Ladislas Czabanyk (sb); Arthur Motta (dms).

(Announcements by Georges Baume and Charles Delauney {3.00})
[***CD*** Fmx FA316]

757b Diminution {3.45}
[***CD*** Fmx FA316]

757c Festival '48 {2.37}
[***CD*** Fmx FA316]

Paris November 1948

The premiere of Jean Cocteau's film *Les Enfants terribles.*

Paris November 1948

The magazine *Jazz Hot* (No. 27) features the history of the Hot-Club de France (Part 8).

Brussels November 1948

The Quintette appear in Brussels. See Delaunay, page 150.

Hubert Rostaing reportedly buys Django a tape-recorder.

Théâtre des Galeries, Brussels — late November–early December 1948

Quintette du Hot-Club de France December 1948

Hubert Rostaing (cl); Django Reinhardt (gtr solo); Henri 'Louson' Baumgartner (gtr); Louis Vola (sb); Arthur Motta (dms).
As above, without Rostaing (1).

758 MS277 **Artillerie Lourde** [see note]
[*25cm LP* Per SPL1103; **Swi 33317**] [*CD* Vog 228E 6009]

759 **Moppin' The Bride** (Danse Nuptial) {2.19}
[*LP* Su 274] [*EP* Vo VRE5020] [*CD* Fmx FA316; Vog 228E 6009]

760 MS277 **Troublant Boléro** {4.07}
[*25cm LP* Per 1103; **Swi 33317**] [*LP* Vog 530217] [*CD* Fmx FA316; Vog 228E 6009]

761 MS277 **Cadillac Slim** {2.52}
[*25cm LP* Per 1103; **Swi 33317**] [*LP* Su 274; Vog 530217]
[*CD* Fmx FA316; Vog 228E 6009]

762 MS277 **Nuages** {4.04}
[*25cm LP* Per 1103; Su 274; **Swi 33317**] [*LP* Vog 530217]
[*EP* Vo VRE5020] [*CD* Fmx FA316; Vog 228E 6009]

763 MS278 **Place De Brouckère** [see note]
[*25cm LP* Per 1103; **Swi 33317**] [*LP* Vog 530217]
[*CD* Vog 228E 6009]

764 MS278 **Improvisation Sur Une Danse Norvégienne** {2.42}
[*25cm LP* Per 1103; **Swi 33317**] [*LP* Vog 530217] [*CD* Fmx FA316; Vog 228E 6009]

765 MS 278 **Festival '48** {2.09}
[*25cm LP* Per 1103; **Swi 33317**] [*LP* Vog 530217] [*EP* Vo VRE5020]
[*CD* Fmx FA316; Vog 228E 6009]

766 MS 278 **Minor Swing** {2.33}
[*25cm LP* Per 1103; **Swi 33317**] [*LP* Vog 530217] [*CD* Fmx FA316; Vog 228E 6009]

767 **Symphonie** (1) {1.34}
[*LP* Vog 406505] [*CD* Fmx FA316; Vog 228E 6009]

MS277/278 are long-playing masters.
On all extant versions of this concert, the original versions of 'Artillerie Lourde' and 'Place De Brouckère', if indeed they ever existed, have been replaced with the corresponding tracks from the sessions of 8–13 November 1947. However, the possibility of their existence has not been dismissed.
These recordings were reportedly made with Django's newly-acquired tape recorder.
See Cherrett, page 13, for a news item relating to this event.

Paris December 1948

The magazine *Jazz Hot* (No. 28) features an article on Bill Coleman, and the final chapter of the history of the Hot-Club de France (Part 9).

Rome January 1949

The Italian tour begins.

Italy [?] Sunday 23 January 1949

Django Reinhardt's 39th birthday.

RAI Studios, Rome January–February 1949

Django Reinhardt and Stéphane Grappelly

Stéphane Grappelli (vln); Django Reinhardt (gtr); Gianni Safred (pno); Carlo Pecori (sb); Aurelio de Carolis (dms).
Django Reinhardt (gtr) only (1).
Recorded by Christian W. Livorness.

768 CW 18 **Over The Rainbow** {2.41}
[***LP*** **Pat C054 16016**; Swa S1371] [***CD*** EMI JT 7891032; Fmx FA316]

769 CW 19 **Night And Day** {3.02}
[***LP*** Pat C054 16020] [***CD*** EMIJT 7891032; Fmx FA316]

770 CW 20 **Minor Blues** [2.42}
[***LP*** **Pat C054 16016**; Swa S1371] [***CD*** EMIJT 7891032; Fmx FA316]

771 CW 21 **Nature Boy Blues** {3.32}
[***LP*** **Pat C054 16020**; Swa S1391] [***CD*** EMI JT 7891032; Fmx FA316]

772 CW 22 **The World Is Waiting For The Sunrise** {2.48}
[***LP*** RCA 731069; NL70671; 70929; 90448] [***CD*** Fmx FA316; RCA ND70929-2]

773 CW 23 **Vous Qui Passez Sans Voir** {2.47}
[***LP*** **Pat 054 16016**; Swa S1371] [***CD*** EMI JT 7891032; Fmx FA316]

774 CW 24 **Hallelujah** {3.05}
[***LP*** RCA 731069, NL70929, 90448] [***CD*** Fmx FA316; RCA ND70929-2]

775 CW 25 **Nagasaki** {2.49}
[***LP*** **Pat C054 16016**; Swa S1371] [***CD*** EMI JT 8274472; Fmx FA316]

776 CW 26 **I'll Never Be The Same** {3.58}
[***LP*** **Pat C054 16016**; RCA NL70761, 70929, 90448] [***CD*** Fmx FA316; RCA ND70929-2]

777 CW 27 **Swing '39** {3.11}
[***LP*** **Pat C054 16017**; RCA 731.769; Swa S1390] [***CD*** EMI JT 8274472; Fmx FA316]

778 CW 28 **Clopin Clopant** {3.04}
[***LP*** **Pat C054 16017**; Swa S1390] [***CD*** EMI JT 8274472; Fmx FA]

779 CW 29 **Honeysuckle Rose** {3.57}
[***LP*** RCA 731042, NL70761, 70929, 90448] [***CD*** BGO CD198; Fmx FA316; RCA ND70929-2]

780 CW 30 **All The Things You Are** {2.52}
[***LP*** RCA 731069, NL70671, 70929, 90448] [***CD*** Fmx FA316; RCA 70929-2]

781 CW 31 **Djangology** {2.43}
[***LP*** RCA 731042, NL70671, 70929, 90448] [***CD*** Fmx FA ; RCA ND70929-2]

782 CW 32 **Liza** {2.47}
[***LP*** **Pat C054 16017**; Swa S1390] [***CD*** EMI JT 8274472; Fmx FA]

783 CW 33 **For Sentimental Reasons** {3.23}
[***LP*** **Pat C054 16020**; Swa S1391] [***CD*** EMI JT 8274472; Fmx FA]

784 CW 34 **Daphne** {2.23}
[***LP*** RCA 731069, NL70671, 70929, 90448] [***CD*** Fmx FA ; RCA ND70929-2]

785 CW 35 **La Mer** (Beyond The Sea) {4.15}
[***LP*** RCA 731042, NN70671, 70929] [***CD*** Fmx FA ; RCA ND70929-2]

786 CW 36 **Sweet Georgia Brown** {3.13}
[***LP*** **Pat C054 16017**; Swa S1390] [***CD*** EMIJT 8274472; Fmx FA]

787 CW 37 **Lover Man** {3.06}
[***LP*** RCA 731042, NL70671, 70929, 90448] [***CD*** Fmx FA ; RCA ND70929-2]

788 CW 38 **Marie** {2.51}
[***LP*** RCA 731069, NL70671, 70929, 90448] [***CD*** Fmx FA ; RCA ND70929-2]

789 CW 39 **Stormy Weather** {3.27}
[***LP*** **Pat C054 16019**; Swa S1401] [***CD*** BGO CD366; EMI JT 8274472; Fmx FA]

790 CW 40 **Minor Swing** {2.34}
[***LP*** RCA 731042, NL70671, 70929, 90448] [***CD*** BGO CD198; Fmx FA ; RCA ND70929-2]

791 CW 41 **To Each His Own** {3.42}
[***LP*** **Pat C054 16020**; Swa S1391] [***CD*** EMI JT 8274472; Fmx FA]

792 CW 42 **What Is This Thing Called Love?** {3.48}
[***LP*** **Pat C054 16017**; Swa S1390] [***CD*** EMI JT 8274472; Fmx FA]

793 CW 43 **Ou Es-Tu, Mon Amour?** {3.17}
[***LP*** RCA 731042] [***CD*** Fmx FA ; RCA ND70929-2]

794 CW 44 **Undecided** {2.59}
[***LP*** Pat C054 16020] [***CD*** EMI JT 8274472; Fmx FA]

795 CW 45 **Improvisation No. 4** (1) {2.07}
[***LP*** **Pat C054 16020**; Swa S1391] [***CD*** EMI JT 8274472; Fmx FA]

796 CW 46 **I'm In The Mood For Love [unissued due to damage]**

797 CW 47 **Swing '42** {2.25}
[***LP*** RCA 731042, NL70671, 70929, 90448] [***CD*** Fmx FA ; RCA ND70929-2]

798 CW 48 **I Surrender Dear** {3.40}
[***LP*** RCA 731069, NL70671, 70929, 90448] [***CD*** Fmx FA ; RCA ND70929-2]

799 CW 49 **After You've Gone** {2.57}
[***LP*** RCA 731042, NL70671, 70929, 90448] [***CD*** Fmx FA ; RCA ND70929-2]

800 CW 50 **Mam'zelle [unissued due to damage]**

801 CW 51 **I Got Rhythm** {2.43}
[***LP*** RCA 731069; NL70671; 70929; 90448] [***CD*** Fmx FA , RCA ND70929-2]

802 CW 52 **I Saw Stars** {3.30}
[***LP*** RCA 731042] [***CD*** Fmx FA ; RCA ND70929-2]

803 CW 53 **Artillerie Lourde** {3.37}
[***LP*** RCA 731042, NL70761, 70929] [***CD*** Fmx FA ; RCA 70929-2]

804 CW 54 **It's Only A Paper Moon** {2.46}
[***LP*** RCA 731069, NL70671, 70929, 90448] [***CD*** Fmx FA ; RCA ND 70929-2]

RAI Studios, Rome — January–February 1949

Django Reinhardt and Stéphane Grappelly

Django Reinhardt (gtr); Stéphane Grappelli (vln); Gianni Safred (pno); Carlo Pecori (sb); Aurelio de Carolis (dms).
Reinhardt (gtr) and Grappelli (vln) only (1).
Recorded by Christian W Livorness.

805 CW 55 **Time On My Hands** {2.44}
[***LP*** **Pat C054 16020**; Swa S1391] [***CD*** EMI JT 8274472; Fmx FA]

806 CW 56 **Brick Top** {3.41}
[***LP*** RCA 731042, NL70761, 70929] [***CD*** Fmx FA ; RCA ND870929-2]

807 CW 57 **Improvisation On Tchaikowsky's Starry Night** (*aka* Pathétique) {3.40}
[***LP*** RCA 731069, NL70761, 70929] [***CD*** Fmx FA ; RCA ND70929-2]

808 CW 58 **My Blue Heaven** {3.27}
[***LP*** **Pat C054 16017**; RCA 731042; Swa S1390] [***CD*** EMI JT 8274472; Fmx FA]

809 CW 59 **Menilmontant** {3.00}
[***LP*** Pat C054 16017] [***CD*** Fmx FA ; RCA ND 70929-2]

810 CW 60 **Swing Guitars** {2.50}
[***LP*** RCA 731069, NL70671, 70929] [***CD*** Fmx FA ; RCA ND70929-2]

811 CW 61 **My Melancholy Baby** {3.29}
[***LP*** **Pat C054 16017**; Swa S1390] [***CD*** EMI JT 8274472; Fmx FA]

812 CW 62 **Truckin'** [**unissued due to damage**]

813 CW 63 **Webster** {1.57}
[***LP*** **Pat C054 16020**; Swa S1391] [***CD*** EMI JT 7891032; Fmx FA]

814 CW 64 **Micro** {2.15}
[***LP*** **Pat C054 16019**; Swa S1401] [***CD*** EMI JT 7891032; Fmx FA]

815 CW 65 **Micro** {2.25}
[***LP*** **Pat C054 161020**; Swa S1391] [***CD*** EMI JT 8274472; Fmx FA]

816 BL 108 **Dream Of You** {3.52}
[***LP*** **HMV CLP1389**, FELP 231; Pat C054 16017; RCA NL70671, 70929; Swa S1390] [***CD*** BGO CD198; Fmx FA ; RCA ND70929-2]

817 BL 109 **Begin The Beguine** {3.32}
[***LP*** **HMV CLP1389**, FELP 231; Pat C054 16017; Swa S1390]
[***CD*** BGO 198; Fmx FA]

818 BL 110 **How High The Moon** {3.25}
[***LP*** **HMV CLP1389**, FELP 231; Pat C054 16017; Swa S1390]
[***CD*** BGO 198; Fmx FA]

819 BL 111 **Nuages** {3.45}
[***LP*** Aff BOX107; **HMV CLP 1389**, FELP231; Pat C054 16017; RCA NL70671; 70929; Swa S1390] [***CD*** BGO 198; EMI JT 8274472; Fmx FA ; RCA ND70929]

820 BL 112 **I Can't Get Started** {3.35}
[***LP*** **HMV CLP1389**, FELP 231; Pat C054 16018; Swa S1401]
[***CD*** BGO 198; EMI JT 8274472; Fmx FA]

821 BL 113 **I Can't Give You Anything But Love** {3.26}
[***LP*** **HMV CLP 1389**, FELP231; Pat C054 16018; Swa S1401]
[***CD*** BGO 198; Fmx FA]

822 BL 114 **Manoir De Mes Rêves** (1) {3.13}
[***LP*** Aff BOX107; **HMV CLP 1389**; Pat C054 16018; RCA NL70671, 70929; Swa S1401] [***CD*** BGO 198; Fmx FA ; RCA ND70929]

823 BL 115 **Nuages** (No. 2) [**unissued due to damage**]

824 WL 208 **The Man I Love** {3.17}
[***LP*** **Pat C054 16019**; Swa S1401] [***CD*** BGO CD366; Fmx FA]

825 WL 209 **The Peanut Vendor** {3.56}
[***LP*** **Pat C054 16019**; Swa S1401] [***CD*** BGO CD366; Fmx FA]

826 WL 210 **Just A Gigolo** {3.28}
[***LP*** **Pat C054 16019**; Swa S1390] [***CD*** EMI JT 8274472; Fmx FA]

827 WL 211 **Troublant Boléro** {3.40}
[***LP*** **Pat C054 16019**; Swa S1390] [***CD*** Fmx FA]

828 WL 212b **Rosetta** {3.01}
[***LP*** **Pat C054 16017**; Swa S1390] [***CD*** Fmx FA]

829 WL 213 **Blue Skies** {4.11}
[***LP*** **Pat C054 16019**; Swa S1401] [***CD*** BGO CD366; Fmx FA]

830 WL 214 **It Might As Well Be Spring** {4.03}
[***LP*** **Pat C054 16019**; Swa S1401] [***CD*** BGO CD366; Fmx FA]

831 WL 215 **Blue Lou** {3.10}
[***LP*** **Pat C054 16020**; Swa S1391] [***CD*** Fmx FA]

832 WL 217 **Brazil** {2.50}
[***LP*** **Pat C054 16020**; Swa S1391] [***CD*** Fmx FA]

833 WL 218 **What A Difference A Day Made** {3.29}
[***LP*** **Pat C054 16020**; Swa S1391] [***CD*** Fmx FA]

834 WL 219 **Pigalle** {2.41}
[***LP*** **Pat C054 161020**; Swa S1391] [***CD*** Fmx FA]

835 WL 220 **Body And Soul** [**unissued due to damage**]

836 WL 221 **Que Reste-t-il Nos Amours?** [**unissued due to damage**]

WL 216 is untraced.
An unidentified culprit produces a random gaseous noise on the master of 820. See Delaunay, pages 150–1.

Paris **May 1949**

The magazine *Jazz Hot* (No. 33) features an article on Bill Coleman.

London **May 1949**

Review of Django Reinhardt and the Quintette of the Hot Club of France, 'Blues Primitiv'/'Topsy' (Esquire 10-105)

> Produced under the supervision of Hughes Panassié, this coupling presents the Quintette of the Hot Club of France, so famous of old, with a New Look, or rather a New Sound, and very pleasant it is too. The star of the record is, of course, Django Reinhardt, whose technique is absolutely staggering, but Hubert Rostaing runs him a close second. I haven't heard Reinhardt for a considerable time, and was surprised by the many changes that have taken place in his style, all (in my estimation) for the good. He is endowed with such extraordinary talent that his earlier work almost seemed too easy and 'off the cuff', without any thought behind it. Now this seeming casualness has been replaced by sincerity, bringing about an economy of conception and execution much preferable to the old flamboyance. (Unsigned, *Jazz Journal*)

Paris Sunday 8–Friday 13 May 1949

Folk and blues singer Huddie Leadbetter ('Leadbelly') appears at the Lyceum and other venues.

Paris October 1949

The magazine *Jazz Hot* (No.37) features an article on Dickie Wells.

Geneva Tuesday 25 October 1949

Django Reinhardt

Django Reinhardt (elgtr); André Ekyan (as, cl); François Vermeille (pno); Jean Bouchety (sb); Gaston Leonard (dms).
Radio broadcast, Radio Genève

837 Dream Of You {2.40}
[***LP*** Vog VG405] [***CD*** Fmx FA ; Vog 228E 6010, 668003]

838 Place De Brouckère {3.14}
[***LP*** Vog VG405] [***CD*** Fmx FA ; Vog 228E 6010, 668003]

839 Black Night {3.02}
[***LP*** Vog VG405] [***CD*** Fmx FA ; Vog 228E 6010, 668003]

840 Nuages {4.06}
[***LP*** Vog VG405] [***CD*** Fmx FA ; Vog 228E 6010, 668003]

841 Micro {2.30}
[***LP*** Vog VG405] [***CD*** Fmx FA ; Vog 228E 6010, 668003]

842 Danse Norvégienne No. 2 {2.48}
[***LP*** Vog VG405] [***CD*** Fmx FA ; Vog 228E 6010]

843 C Jam Blues {2.35}
[***LP*** Vog VG405] [***CD*** Fmx FA ; Vog 228E 6010]

844 Manoir De Mes Rêves {3.31}
[***LP*** Vog VG405] [***CD*** Fmx FA ; Vog 228E 6010]

Paris November 1949

The magazine *Jazz Hot* (No. 38) features articles on Dicky Wells and Coleman Hawkins.

Paris December 1949

The magazine *Jazz Hot* (No. 39) features an article on Coleman Hawkins.

London Monday 12 December 1949

Coleman Hawkins, accompanied by Jean Mengeon (pno), Pierre Michelot (sb) and Kenny Clarke (dms) appears at the Princess Theatre, Cambridge Circus. This was in direct contravention to aspects of the then-current Aliens Act, 1920.

Promotors 'Bix' Curtis and Tony Hughes, and *Jazz Illustrated* publisher Bert Wilcox, charged with the illegal appearance of Hawkins, brought to court and fined.

Paris | late 1949

Paul Baron and his Orchestra

Unknown personnel and Django Reinhardt (gtr solo).
Radio broadcast, 'This Is Paris' (Maurice Chevalier programme); acetate

845 Night and Day {3.01}
[***LP*** Vog VG405] [***CD*** Fmx FA ; Vog 228E 6010]

Paris | c. 1950

Paul Baron and his Orchestra [or] Wal Berg and his Orchestra

Radio broadcast

845a Nuages {0.29}
[**CD** Fmx FA ; Iris Musique 3001 845]

France | 1950

Jean Cocteau writes, directs and produces the film *Orphée.*

Rome | Sunday 15 January 1950

Django writes and dates a letter from the Café Greco.

Italy or France | Monday 23 January 1950

Django Reinhardt's 40th birthday.

Paris | March 1950

The magazine *Jazz Hot* (No. 42), celebrating its 15th year, features photos of Pierre Fouad, Jerry Mengo, Alix Combelle, André Ekyan, Louis Vola and Noël Chiboust.

Cannes | Wednesday 1 March 1950

The premiere of Jean Cocteau's film *Orphée.*

RAI Studios, Rome | April–May 1950

Django Reinhardt et le Quintette du Hot-Club de France

Django Reinhardt (elgtr); André Ekyan (as); (cl) (1); Ralph Schecroun (pno); Alf Masselier (sb); Roger Paraboschi (dms).
Recorded by Christian W Livorness.

846 CW1 **Anniversary Song** {4.17}
[***LP*** **RCA LPM2077**, 430336, 730596] [***CD*** Fmx FA ; RCA ND70929-2]

847 CW2 **Stormy Weather** {4.06}
[***LP*** **RCA LPM2077**, NL70671, 70929] [***CD*** Fmx FA ; RCA ND70929-2]

848 CW3 **Russian Songs Medley** {3.27}
[***LP*** **RCA LPM 2077**, 430336, 730596] [***CD*** Fmx FA ; RCA ND70929-2]

849 CW4 **Jersey Bounce** {2.56}
[***LP*** **RCA LPM 2077**, 430336, 730596, NL70761, 70929] [***CD*** Fmx FA ; RCA ND70929-2]

850 CW5 **Dînette** (1) {2.56}
[***LP*** Pat C054 16019] [***CD*** BGO CD366; EMI JT 827447-2; Fmx FA]

851 CW6 **Sophisticated Lady** {3.57}
[***LP*** **RCA LPM 2077**, 430336, 730596] [***CD*** Fmx FA ; RCA ND70929-2]

852 CW7 **Micro** {2.19}
[***LP*** Pat C054 16019] [***CD*** BGO CD366; Fmx FA]

853 CW8 **Dream Of You** (1) {2.53}
[***LP*** **RCA LPM 2077**, 430336, 730596] [***CD*** Fmx FA ; RCA ND70929-2]

854 CW9 **Nuages** (1) {3.58}
[***LP*** **RCA LPM 2077**, 430336, 730596] [***CD*** Fmx FA ; RCA 70929-2]

855 CW10 **Darktown Strutters' Ball** {2.45}
[***LP*** **RCA LPM 2077**, 430336, 730596] [***CD*** Fmx FA ; RCA 70929-2]

856 CW11 **Danse Norvégienne** (*aka* Improvisation on Grieg's Norwegian Dance) (1) {3.09}
[***LP*** Pat C054 16019] [***CD*** BGO CD366; Fmx FA]

857 CW12 **A Tisket A Tasket** {3.03}
[***LP*** **RCA LPM 2077**, 430336, 730596] [***CD*** Fmx FA ; RCA ND70929-2]

858 CW13 **Manoir De Mes Rêves** (1) {3.17}
[***LP*** RCA 731069] [***CD*** Fmx FA ; RCA ND70929-2]

859 CW14 **Place De Brouckère** (1) {2.51}
[***LP*** Pat C054 16019] [***CD*** BGO CD366; EMI JT 8274472; Fmx FA]

860 CW15 **September Song** {2.50}
[***LP*** **RCA LPM 2077**, NL70671, 70929, 430336, 730596] [***CD*** Fmx FA ; RCA ND70929-2]

861 CW16 **Royal Garden Blues** {2.34}
[***LP*** **RCA LPM 2077**, 430336, 730596] [***CD*** Fmx FA ; RCA ND70929-2]

862 CW17 **St Louis Blues** {2.34}
[***LP*** **RCA LPM 2077**, NL70671, 70929, 430336, 730596] [***CD*** Fmx FA ; RCA ND70929-2]

RAI Studios, Rome — April–May 1950

Django Reinhardt et le Quintette du Hot-Club de France

Django Reinhardt (elgtr); André Ekyan (as), (cl) (1); Ralph Schecroun (pno); Alf Masselier (sb); Roger Paraboschi (dms).
Recorded by Christian W Livorness.

863 BL101 **Sweet Georgia Brown** {3.32}
[***LP*** **HMV CLP1389**, FELP231; Pat C054 16018] [***CD*** BGO CD 198; Fmx FA]

864 BL102 **Minor Swing** (1) {2.17}
[***LP*** **HMV CLP1389**, FELP231; Pat C054 16018] [***CD*** BGO CD 198; Fmx FA]

865 BL103 **Double Whiskey** {2.38}
[***LP*** **HMV CLP1389**, FELP231; Pat C054 16018] [***CD*** BGO CD 198; Fmx FA]

866 BL104 **Artillerie Lourde** {3.30}
[***LP*** **HMV CLP 1389**, FELP231; KC 109; Pat C054 16018] [***CD*** BGO CD 198; Fmx FA]

867 BL105 **St James' Infirmary** (1) {2.23}
[***LP*** **HMV CLP1389**, FELP231; Pat C054 16018] [***CD*** BGO CD 198; Fmx FA]

868 BL106 **C Jam Blues** {3.18}
[***LP*** **HMV CLP1389**, FELP231; Pat C054 16018] [***CD*** BGO CD 198; Fmx FA]

869 BL107 **Honeysuckle Rose** {3.23}
[***LP*** **HMV CLP1389**, FELP231; Pat C054 16018]
[***CD*** BGO CD 198; Fmx FA]

870 WL201 **Stompin' At The Savoy** [**unissued due to damage**]

871 WL202 **Improvisation On Debussy's Rêverie** (1) {3.05}
[***LP*** Pat C054 16019] [***CD*** Fmx FA]

872 WL203 **Impromptu** [**unissued due to damage**]

873 WL204 **Black Night** {3.34}
[***LP*** Pat C054 16019] [***CD*** BGO CD366; Fmx FA]

874 WL205 **Boogie Woogie** {3.24}
[***LP*** Pat C054 16019] [***CD*** BGO CD366; Fmx FA]

875 WL206 **Boléro** [**unissued due to damage**]

'Double Whiskey' is titled 'Double Scotch' on CLP1389.
See Delaunay, page 152.

Paris July 1950

Django Reinhardt avec Jacques Helian et son Orchestre

Ernie Royal, Fred Gérard, Fernand Verstraete, André Cornille, Almond (tpts); Gaston Moat, Henry Taillourd, Gabriel Villain (tbns); Georges Cloud, Andre Rolland (as); Jacques Nasslet, Gaston Estienne (ts); Gerard Leveque (bs); Paul Guyot (pno); Django Reinhardt (gtr); Ladislas Czabanyck (sb); Christian Garros (dms) (1).
Royal, Guyot, Reinhardt, Czananyck, Garros only (2).
Radio broadcast, Radio Luxembourg

876 **Double Whiskey** (1) {timing not yet available}
[**unissued**] [***CD*** Fmx FA]

877 **I Got Rhythm** (2) {timing not yet available}
[**unissued**] [***CD*** Fmx FA]

Paris **December 1950**

The magazine *Jazz Hot* (No. 50) features a front cover photo of Django Reinhardt.

Paris **c. 1951**

Django Reinhardt (elgtr), acc. by Art Simmons (pno).
RTF radio broadcast

877a Yesterdays {2.26}
[**CD** Fmx FA ; Iris Musique 3001 845]

(interview with Django Reinhardt)
[**CD** Fmx FA ; Iris Musique 3001 845]

Paris **1951**

Charles Delaunay publishes *Hot discographie encyclopédique* Vol. 1 [A–B] (Editions Vogue).

Paris **January 1951**

The magazine *Jazz Hot* (No. 51) features an article on Bill Coleman.

Paris **January 1951**

Django Reinhardt et l'Orchestre Symphonique National

Django Reinhardt (gtr solo); acc. by Orchestre Symphonique National (unknown number of musicians and instruments) under the direction of Wal Berg.
Radio broadcast, Radio Luxembourg

878 Troublant Boléro {4.34}
[***LP*** Vog 406505] [***CD*** Fmx FA]

Paris **January 1951**

The magazine *Jazz Hot* (No.52) features articles on Benny Carter and Bill Coleman.

Paris **Tuesday 23 January 1951**

Django Reinhardt's 41st birthday.

Paris **February 1951**

Django begins a five-month engagement at Club Saint-Germain-des-Prés.
See Delaunay, page 155.

Club Saint-Germain-des-Prés, Paris **Saturday 10 February 1951**

Django Reinhardt au club Saint-Germain

Django Reinhardt (gtr); Bernard Hullin (tpt); Hubert Fol (as); Raymond Fol (pno); Pierre Michelot (sb); Pierre Lemarchand (dms).
Radio broadcast; acetates

879 **Lover** {3.03}
[***LP*** Vog LP NEC Plus Ultra 502008] [***CD*** Fmx FA ; Vog 228E 6010]

880 **Nuages** {3.37}
[***LP*** Vog COF03, LP NEC Plus Ultra 502008] [***CD*** Fmx FA ; Vog 228E 6010]

881 **Impromptu** {5.10}
[***LP*** Vog NEC Plus Ultra 502008] [***CD*** Fmx FA ; Vog 228E 6010]

882 **Margie** {3.07}
[***LP*** Vog NEC Plus Ultra 502008] [***CD*** Fmx FA ; Vog 228E 6010]

883 **Diminushing Blackness** (*sic*) {2.29}
[***LP*** Vog NEC Plus Ultra 502008] [***CD*** Fmx FA ; Vog 228E 6010]

Club Saint-Germain-des-Prés, Paris — Tuesday 20 February 1951

As above, except Maurice Vander (pno) replaces Raymond Fol.

884 **Dream Of You** {5.20}
[***LP*** Vog NEC Plus Ultra 502008] [***CD*** Fmx FA ; Vog 228E 6010]

885 **Manoir De Mes Rêves** {3.55}
[***LP*** Vog NEC Plus Ultra 502008] [***CD*** Fmx FA ; Vog 228E 6010]

886 **I Can't Give You Anything But Love** {4.40}
[***LP*** Vog NEC Plus Ultra 502008] [***CD*** Fmx FA ; Vog 228E 6010]

887 **Jumping With Symphony Sid** {4.11}
[***LP*** Vog NEC Plus Ultra 502008] [***CD*** Fmx FA ; Vog 228E 6010]

London — Thursday 15 March 1951

Article about Django Reinhardt published in *Melody Maker* issue dated 17 March. See Cherrett, page 33, for a reproduction of this article.

Paris — April/May (?) 1951

Django Reinhardt

Reinhardt (gtr solo) acc. by unknown studio musicians.
La Route du bonheur film soundtrack

888 7 TLA 1586 **Belleville** {5.19}
[***LP*** Pat C054 16018] [***EP*** **HMV 7EMF130**] [***CD*** Fmx FA ; RCA74321 237692]

889 7 TLA 1587 **Nuages** {6.17}
[***LP*** HMV FELP247; Pat C054 16018] [***EP*** **HMV 7EMF130**] [***CD*** Fmx FA ; RCA74321 237692]

The short section of the film featuring Django, miming to 'Nuits de St Germain des Prés', appears on ***DVD*** MOE 001.
HMV 7EMF130 is a two-track extended-play record, not a 45rpm single.

Paris Friday 11 May 1951

Django Reinhardt et son Quintette

Django Reinhardt (elgtr solo); Bernard Hullin (tpt); Hubert Fol (as); Raymond Fol (pno); Pierre Michelot (sb); Pierre Lemarchand (dms) (1).
As above, without Hullin (2).

890 P 851 **Double Whiskey** (1) {2.53}
[***78*** **De MF-21413**; 28145; Om 21413] [***45*** Decca (A) 9-28145] [***LP*** Mus MU222] [***CD*** DRG 8473; Fmx FA ; Mus 403222]

891 P 852 **Dream Of You** (1) {3.14}
[***78*** De MF-21413; Om 21413] [***LP*** Mus MU222] [***CD*** DRG 8473; Fmx FA ; Mus 403222]

892 P853 **Impromptu** (1) {2.42}
[***78*** **De MF-21414**, 28145; Om 21414] [***45*** Decca (A) 9-28145] [***LP*** Mus MU222] [***CD*** DRG 8473; Fmx FA ; Mus 403222]

893 P 854 **Vamp** (2) {2.32}
[***78*** **De (F) MF-21414**, 214141; Om 21414] [***LP*** Mus MU222] [***CD*** DRG 8473; Fmx FA ; Mus 403222]

Knokke, Belgium Summer 1951

Django Reinhardt plays the summer season at the Knokke Casino Theatre, and in August jams with American trumpeter Oran 'Hot Lips' Page.
See Cherrett, pages 45 and 111, for articles pertaining to this event.
See Delaunay, page 156.

Paris September 1951

Blues singer Big Bill Broonzy appears in Paris and records for Vogue.

London November 1951

Review of Stephane Grappelly, 'Someday Sweetheart'/'Henderson Stomp' (Decca F9745)

> A rather belated and unexpected coupling of two old Decca recordings under the direction of former Hot Club violinist, Stephane Grappelly, which fail to live up to the promise of the titles.
>
> The fine old standard tune on the first side receives a very stereotyped performance from the Grappelly Sextet, with a plodding rhythm section, and a vocal by Beryl Davis, not at her best. The Fletcher Henderson stomp on the reverse is at least livelier, and is cheered by the presence of George Shearing who takes an excellent solo. This side recommended for Shearing fans. (Peter Tanner, *Jazz Journal*)

Paris 1952

Charles Delaunay publishes *Hot discographie encyclopédique* Vol. 2 (C–E) (Editions Vogue).

Paris 1952

Django Reinhardt

Reinhardt (elgtr); Hubert Fol (as); Sadi Lallemand (vib); Maurice Vander (pno); Pierre Michelot (sb); Pierre Lemarchand (dms).

899 **Nuit De St Germaine Des Près** {1.44}
[***CD*** Fmx FA ; Vog 228E 6010]

Belgium Wednesday 23 January 1952

Django Reinhardt's 42nd birthday.

Théâtre de Galeries, Brussels Sunday 20 January 1952

Django performs at a Hot Club of Belgium concert.
See Delaunay, page 159.

Brussels Friday 25 January 1952

Django performs in concert at the Hot Club of Belgium.

Paris Wednesday 30 January 1952

Django Reinhardt et son Quintette

Django Reinhardt (elgtr); Roger Guerin (tpt); Hubert Fol (as); Raymond Fol (pno); Barney Spieler (sb); Pierre Lemarchand (dms).

894 P 1179 **Keep Cool** {3.05}
[***78*** De MF-21718] [***LP*** De ACL831; Mus MU222] [***45*** De 45-5581] [***CD*** DRG 8473; Fmx FA ; Mus 403222]

895 P1179-3 **Keep Cool** {no timing available}
[***78*** De MF-21718] [***CD*** Fmx FA]

896 P 1180 **Flèche D'Or** {3.00}
[***78*** De MF-21718] [***LP*** De ACL891; Mus MU222] [***45*** De 45-5581] [***CD*** DRG 8473; Fmx FA ; Mus 403222]

897 P 1181 **Troublant Boléro** {3.30}
[***78*** De MF-21719] [***LP*** De ACL831; Mus MU222] [***CD*** DRG 8473; Fmx FA ; Mus 403222]

898 P 1182 **Nuits De St Germaine Des Prés** {3.05}
[***78*** **De MF-21719**, 21719] [***LP*** Astan LP20102; De ACL 831; Met MTM12; Mus MU222] [***CD*** DRG 8473; Fmx FA ; Mus 403222]

Paris June 1952

The magazine *Jazz Hot* (No. 67) features an article on Benny Carter.

Paris October 1952

The magazine *Jazz Hot* (No. 70) features an article on Dickie Wells.

Paris November 1952

Django Reinhardt acc. by Aime Barelli et son Orchestre

Aime Barelli, Alex Caturegli, Jean Mauclaire, Georges Gay, Marcel Simino (tpts); Benny Vasseur, Nat Peck (tbns); Jean Aldegon, Paul Jean-Jean (as); Jean Fourmanoir, Léon Soen (ts); Armand Miggiani (bs); Pierre Foucault (pno); Leo Petit (gtr) Django Reinhardt (elgtr solo); Antoine Giaccardo (sb); André Jourdan (dms) (1).
Jam session: Barelli, Vasseur, Attenoux, Reinhardt, Fol only (2).
ORTF radio broadcast, 'Jazz Variétés'.

900 **Yesterdays** (1) {2.59}
[***LP*** DJM 22049] [***CD*** Fmx FA]

901 **Lover** (1) {3.02}
[***LP*** DJM 22049] [***CD*** Fmx FA]

902 **Blues** (2) {4.08}
[***LP*** La Roulotte MA-3] [***CD*** Fmx FA]

London Thursday 13 November 1952

Article published in *Melody Maker* week ending 15 November on the QHCF. See Cherrett, page 34, for a reproduction of this article.

Paris 1953

Charles Delaunay publishes *Hot discographie encyclopédique* Vol. 3 (E–He) (Editions Vogue).

Paris January 1953

Norman Granz, promoter of 'Jazz At the Philharmonic', meets Django with a view to planning an album. See 10 March 1953, *qv.*

Django plays a one-month engagement at 'Club Riverside' in Paris.

Paris Friday 23 January 1953

Django Reinhardt's 43rd birthday.

Paris Friday 30 January 1953

Django Reinhardt et son Quintette

Django Reinhardt (elgtr); Roger Guerin (tpt); Hubert Fol (as); Maurice Vander (pno); Pierre Michelot (sb); Pierre Lemarchand (dms) (1).
As above, without Guerin (2).
Reinhardt, Vander, Michelot and Lemarchand only (3).

903 P 1616 **Crazy Rhythm** (1) {3.10}
[***78*** De MF-36124] [***25cm LP*** De FM133088] [***LP*** De ACL831; Met MTM12; Mus MU222] [***45*** De 45-5510] [***CD*** DRG 8473; Fmx FA ; Mus 403222]

904 P 1617 **Anouman** (2) {2.42}
[***78*** De MF-36124] [***25cm LP*** De 133088] [***LP*** De ACL831; Mus 222]
[***45*** De 45-5581] [***CD*** DRG 8473; Fmx FA]

905 P 1618-2 **D R Blues** (3) {3.18}
[***78*** De MF-36125] [***25cm LP*** De 133088] [***LP*** De ACL831;
Mus MU222] [***CD*** DRG 8473; Fmx FA ; Mus 403222]

906 P 1619-1 **Fine And Dandy** (2) {3.10}
[***78*** De MF-36125] [***LP*** De ACL831; Mus 222] [***45*** De 45-5510]
[***CD*** DRG 8473; Fmx FA ; Mus 403222]

Paris — Sunday 1 February 1953

Django Reinhardt acc. par Tony Proteau et son Orchestre

Bernard Hullin, Jean Lissée, Roger Guérin, Fernan Verstraete (tpts); Nat Peck, Guy Paquinet, André Paquinet (tbns); Jack Ary, Robert Cuinet (as); Daniel Dallolmo, Andre Ross (ts); Henri Aspar (bs); Andre Persiany (pno); Django Reinhardt (gtr solo); Charlie Blareau (sb); Gerard Pochonnet (dms).
ORTF broadcast, 'Jazz Variétés'.

907 **Time After Time** {2.43}
[***LP*** La Roulotte (A) MA-3] [***CD*** Fmx FA]

908 **Blues** {2.56}
[***LP*** La Roulotte (A) MA-3] [***CD*** Fmx FA]

Same date

Jam Session

Jean Lissée, Roger Guérin, Bernard Hullin, Fernand Verstraete (tpts); Nat Peck (tbn); Andre Ross (ts); Claude Bolling (pno); Django Reinhardt (gtr solo).

909 **Fine And Dandy** {5.57}
[***LP*** DJM 22049] [***CD*** Fmx FA]

Brussels — Saturday 28 February 1953

Django appears in concert.
See Delaunay, page 159.

Paris — Tuesday 10 March 1953

Django Reinhardt et ses Rythmes

Reinhardt (elgtr); Maurice Vander (pno); Pierre Michelot (sb); Jean-Louis Viale (dms).

910 **Brazil** {2.25}
[***25cm LP*** **BS 6830**; Clef MGC516; Fel EDL87005; Pampa LRM 25308]
[***LP*** Bar 80369, 80929/30; Col KK31478; Ri RLP6575; Verve MGV8015]
[***EP*** Clef EP509; BS EP12002] [***CD*** Fmx FA ; Verve 835418-2]

911 September Song {2.33}
[***25cm LP*** **BS 6830**; Clef MGC516; Fel EDL87005; Pampa LRM25308]
[***LP*** Bar 80369, 80929/30; Col KC31478; Ri RLP6575; Verve MGV8015]
[***45*** Clef EP509] [***CD*** Fmx FA ; Verve 835418-2]

912 Confessin' {3.37}
[***78*** Pa BN3007] [***25cm LP*** **BS 6830**; Clef MGC516; Fel EDL 87005; Pampa LRM25308] [***LP*** Barclay 80929; Col KC 31478; Ri RLP6575; Verve MGV8015] [***EP*** BS12002; Clef EP509, Verve EP26122]
[***CD*** Fmx FA ; Verve 835418-2]

913 Manoir De Mes Rêves {2.35}
[***25cm LP*** **BS 6830**; Clef MGC516; Fel EDL87005; Pampa RM25308]
[***LP*** Bar 80929/30; Col KC31478; Ri RLP6575; Verve MG8015]
[***EP*** BS12008; Clef EP509] [***CD*** Fmx FA ; Verve 835418-2]

914 Night And Day {2.50}
[***25cm LP*** **BS 6830**; Clef MGC516; Fel EDL87005; Pampa LRM25308]
[***LP*** Bar 80929/30; Col KC 31478; Ri RLP6575; Verve MGV8015]
[***EP*** BS EP12002; Clef EP516; Verve EP26122] [***CD*** Fmx FA ; Verve 835418-2]

915 Blues For Ike {3.21}
[***25cm LP*** **BS 6830**; Clef MGC516; Fel EDL 87005; Pampa LRM25308]
[***LP*** Bar 80929/30; Col KC31478; Ri RLP6575; Verve MGV8015]
[***EP*** BS12008; Clef EP516; Verve EP26122] [***CD*** Fmx FA ; Verve 835418-2]

916 Nuages {3.15}
[***25cm LP*** **BS 6830**; Clef MGC516; Fel EDL 87005; Pampa LRM 25308]
[***LP*** Bar 80829/30; Col KC 31478; Ri RLP6575; Verve MGV8015]
[***EP*** BS EP12002; Clef EP509; Verve EP26122] [***CD*** Fmx FA ; Verve 835418-2]

917 Insensiblement {3.06}
[***78*** Pa BN3007] [***25cm LP*** **BS 6830**; Clef MGC516; Fel EDL87005; Pampa LRM 23805] [***LP*** Bar 80929/30; Col KC31478; Ri RLP6575; Verve MG8015] [***EP*** **BS 12008**; Clef EP516] [***CD*** Fmx FA ; Verve 835418-2]

All titles on Columbia KC 31478 feature rhythm, overdubbed in 1968, by the French group Guitars Unlimited.
The exact recording order of items 910–17 cannot be confirmed.

Paris **April 1953**

The magazine *Jazz Hot* (No. 76) features an article on Alix Combelle.

Paris | Wednesday 8 April 1953

Django Reinhardt

Django Reinhardt (elgtr); 'Fats' Sadi Lallemand (vib); Martial Solal (pno); Pierre Michelot (sb); Pierre Lemarchand (dms).

918 P 1723-1 **Le Soir** {2.54}
[***78*** De F-10219, **De MF-36165]** [***25cm LP*** De FM133088]
[***LP*** De ACL831; Mus MU222] [***EP*** De 45-5581] [***CD*** DRG 8473; Fmx FA]

919 P 1724-1 **Chez Moi** {3.00}
[***78*** De MF-36166] [***25cm LP*** De FM133088; Lon WB91056]
[***LP*** De ACL831; Mus MU222] [***EP*** De 45-5581] [***CD*** DRG 8473; Fmx FA ; Mus 403222]

920 P 1725-1 **I Cover The Waterfront** {3.24}
[***78*** De MF-36166] [***25cm LP*** De FM 133088] [***LP*** Astan LP 20102; De ACL831; Met MTM12; Mus MU222] [***EP*** De 45-5581]
[***CD*** DRG 8473; Fmx FA ; Mus 403222]

921 P 1726-1 **Deccaphonie** {3.15}
[***78*** De F-10219, **MF-36165**] [***25cm LP*** De 133088; Lon WB91074]
[***LP*** De ACL831; Mus MU222] [***EP*** De 45-5581] [***CD*** DRG 8473; Fmx FA ; Mus 403222]

922 P1726-2 **Deccaphonie** [**unissued**]

Switzerland | early May 1953

Django tours for two weeks.

Samois-Sur-Seine | Friday 15 May 1953

Django Reinhardt returns home from his last overseas tour, in Switzerland.

Samois-Sur-Seine | Saturday 16 May 1953

Django Reinhardt dies.
See Cherrett pages 27, 36, 37, 39, 46, and 112; Cruickshank, pages 112 and 114, Delaunay pages 160–1 and 292 and *Jazz Hot* No. 78, June 1953, for reports and obituaries.

Samois-Sur-Seine | Tuesday 19 May 1953

Django Reinhardt is buried in the Samois cemetery.
See Cherrett, page 11.

78rpm releases

References to record reviews are indicated by a month(s)/year code preceded by the code for the journal in which the review may be found. The transcript of that review may be found in the main body of this work in chronological order, eg *JH* 4–5/36 indicates *Jazz Hot* for April/May of 1936; the following are the codes employed:

EMV = *L'Edition Musicale Vivante*
GP = *The Gramophone*
HCM = *Hot Club Magazine*
JH = *Jazz Hot*
JI = *Jazz Information*
JJ = *Jazz Journal*
JT = *Jazz-Tango*
RM = *Rhythm*
SM = *Swing Music*

Release number	*Allocated recording numbers*	*Review found in*
ABC-JCF		
120	573/rev. not Django	
121	574/rev. not Django	
122	575/rev. not Django	
123	576/rev. not Django	
Blue Star		
BS30	651/654	*D* 2/48; *JH* 4/48
BS33	657/659	*D* 2/38: *JH* 4/48
BS37	658/660	
BS38	652/669	*D* 9–10/48; *JH* 4/48
BS42	664/671	
BS46	661/668	
BS50	663/701	*D* 9–10/48
BS53	699/703	
BS54	700/702	*D* 2/38
BS55	704/705	
BS59	630/632	
BS73	745/748	
BS98	670/rev. not Django	

Brunswick

A9884	176/177	
A9909	188/189	
A9943	174/187	
A9945	174/187	'possibly non-existent' (Abrams)
A9987	185/186	
A81047	141/157	
A81187	143/144	
A81206	154/155	
A81304	108/142	
A81436	337/343	
A81503	335/340	
A81603	336/342	
A81685	339/341	
A81692	384/385	
A81901	377/379	
A82082	395/398	
A82135	395/398	
A82504	176/177	
A82559	337/343	
500.016	176/187	
500.604	146/187	
500.613	185/186	
505.267	384/441	
505.268	440/442	
505.269	335/340	
505.270	336/339	
505.271	337/440	
505.272	409/426	
505.273	408/425	
505.274	423/424	
505.275	395/398	
505.276	373/375	
505.277	377/379	
505.278	185/186	
505.279	176/424	
505.280	174/187	

Celson

TZ3011	663/701
TZ3013	662/668
TZ3018	745/748

Columbia

BF404	057/058

CQ2225	519/rev. by Charles Trenet	
DB5037	367/371	*GP* 9/38
DB5047	364/368	
DCF62	519/rev. by Charles Trenet	
[DF878/DF941/DF942]	These Don Baretto releases appear in Delaunay's 1960 discography, but have subsequently been proved to be without Django's presence.	
DF1191	036/037	
DF1406	038/042	
DF1487	182/183	
DF1506	057/058	
DF1672	085/rev. by Jean Sablon acc. by Garland Wilson	
DF1690	093/094	
DF1714	088/089	
DF1847	194/195	
DF2344	331/333	
DF2427	364/370	
DF2444	366/368	
DF2886	519/rev. by Charles Trenet	
GN5035	270/273	
GN5036	325/328	
GN5038	268/269	
GN5039	255/256	
GN5041	351/rev. by Fletcher Allen	
GN5044	314/330	
GN5059	294/rev. by Bill Coleman	
MC5037	371/338	
MC5047	364/367	
MZ239	364/371	
R14124	395/398	
R14231	422/441	
4178-M	088/089	
4191 M	057/058	
4222-M	183/195	
100.001	088/089	

Decca

C16092	637/641	
C16177	646/649	
F5780	176/177	*D* 11/38 (*sic*); *GP* 12/35; *SM* 11–12/35
F5824	174/187	*D* 11/38 (*sic*); *GP* 3/36; *SM* 3/36
F5831	188/189	
F5943	185/186	*D* 11/38; *GP* 6/36

F6002	154/156	
F6077	141/157	
F6150	128/155	*GP* 12/36
F6406	143/144	
F6531	108/142	
F6616	337/343	*D* 11/38; *GP* 3/38 (*sic*)
F6639	335/340	*D* 4/38; *GP* 4/38
F6675	336/342	*GP* 6/38
F6721	344/345	*GP* 9/38
F6769	339/341	
F6776	384/385	*GP* 10/38
F6828	389/390	
F6875	377/379	*JH* 7–8/39
F6899	373/375	*JH* 7–8/39; *RM* 1/39
F6935	387/391	*RM* 2/39
F7009	346/347	
F7027	395/396/398 (395 and 396 are alternate takes released under the same issue number)	
F7100	401/402/408 (401 and 402 are alternate takes released under the same issue number)	
F7133	399/409/410 (409 and 410 are alternate takes released under the same issue number)	
F7140	440/442	
F7198	393/394/422 (393 and 394 are alternate takes released under the same issue number)	*GP* 10/39
F7390	441/443	*GP* 3/40
F7568	372/424 'non-existent' (Abrams)	
F8068 or 8086	337/343 (it is not known which is the correct release number)	
F8604	608/611/612 (611 and 612 are alternate takes released under the same issue number)	
F8876	610/613	
F8917	'Though reading as by the QHCF, this is a Grappelly–Shearing group' (Abrams)	
F9045	336/339	
F9242	636/642/644 (642 and 644 are alternate takes released under the same issue number)	*HCM* 10/47
F9243	646/649	*JH* 1/48; *HCM* 9/48
F9244	637/641	*HCM* 9/48
F9428	336/339	*JH* 5–6/38
F9433	384/385	*JH* 7–8/39
F10219	920/923	
F41010	610/613	

F42144	154/rev. by Nat Gonella	
F42166	340/342	
F49019	174/187	
MB9242	636/642	
MB9243	646/649	
MB9244	637/641 (MB9200 series are photo-labels, featuring a head-and-shoulders portrait of Django)	
MF21413	890/891	
MF21414	892/893	
MF21718	894/895/896 (894 and 895 are alternate takes released under the same issue number)	
MF21719	897/898	
MF36124	903/904	
MF36125	905/906	
MF36165	918/921	
MF36166	919/920	
RD40006	608/611	
SB9244	637/638/641 (637 and 638 are alternate takes released under the same issue number)	
SB41010	610/613	
Y5062	174/187	
Y5105	185/186	
Y5120	154/156	
Y5178	143/144	issued June 1938
Y5204	141/157	
Y5205	128/155	
Y5212	337/343	
Y5227	336/342	
Y5262	344/345	
Y5266	389/390	
Y5270	377/379	
Y5348	373/375	
Y5408	402/408	
Y5450	399/409	
Y5580	393/422	issued July 1941
538	335/340	
542	336/342	
572	377/379	
573	339/341/375 (339 and 341 found coupled with 375 under the same issue number)	
587	395/398	
597	402/408	
606	399/409	
615	393/422	

616	440/441	
625	607/611	
711	637/641	
20299	608/611	
23002	141/143	
23003	128/157	
23004	108/156	
23021	176/185	
23031	185/188	
23032	174/189	
23065	336/340	
23066	335/343	
23067	337/342	
23077	385/386	
23079	344/346	
23098	345/347	issued September 1939
23152	341/402	
23261	379/405	
23262	375/398	
23263	372/399	
23264	377/409	
	(23002/23003/23004/23021 also issued as Decca album 207, with graphics; 23261/23262/23263/23264 also issued as Decca album 334, with graphics and notes by Les Leiber, Hal Davis and Milton Gabler)	
28145	892	
32332	641/–(?)	
32436	610/613	
333016	377/379/408 (some copies couple 337 with either 379 or 408)	
59006	423/424	
59018	440/442	
59019	408/425	
59023	409/426	
59045	441/443	
89045	339/rev. not Django	
115213	403/404	

Dial

754	660/669

Electrola

EG3537	098/100
EG3695	103/rev. not Django
EG3717	214/220

EG3776	216/217	
EG3882	221/228	
EG3918	226/227	
EG6088	235/248	
EG6178	233/249	
EG6560	238/239	
EG6561	243/246	

Esquire

10-015	698/703
10-043	572/576
(10-053)	(credited in error to Django Reinhardt on the label; it does not contain any Django performances)
10-087	574/rev. not Django
10-243	575/rev. not Django

Fonit

BS25086	744/748
35	745
606	399/409
615	422/393/394 (393/394 are alternate takes, both found coupled with 422)

Gramophone Co Ltd (*aka* HMV)

(see abbreviation appendix for country identification and linguistic variations)

AL2366	226/227	
AL2404	235/248	
AL2436	233/249	
AL2492	245/250	
AM4737	193/194	
B8388	098/100	
B8420	103/rev. by Freddie Jenkins' Harlem Seven	*GP*4/36
B8463	214/220	*GP*8/36
B8479	216/217	
B8494	102/rev. by Paul Whiteman and his orchestra	
B8518	221/228	
B8532	223/224	
B8534	226/227	
B8574	255/256	
B8587	252/253	
B8598	241/245	*GP*9/37
B8606	235/248	*GP*9/37
B8614	243/246	
B8629	233/249	

B8669	237/242	
B8690	238/239	*GP*2/38
B8718	236/240	*GP*3/38
B8737	245/250	*GP*5/38
B8754	255/256	*GP*7/38
B8763	271/272	*GP*8/38
B8778	281/282	*GP*9/38
B8799	268/269	*GP*10/38
B8812	257/258	
B8826	270/273	*RM* 1/39
B9154	416/rev. by Frank Newton and his orchestra	
EA2540	255/256	
GW1509	233/249	
GY297	238/242	
GY333	233/249	
GY432	235/248	
HN2495	243/246	
HN4476	103/rev. not Django	
JK2048	235/248	
JK2049	238/239	
JK2332	233/249	
JK2639	257/258	
JK2823	191/rev. not Django	
JO15	235/248	
JO16	235/rev. not Django	
JO148	255/256	
K5454	002/003	
K5469	001/004	
K6339	019/rev. not Django	
K6542	018/020	
K6861	023/025	
K6862	021/rev. by Eliane deCreus	
K6863	027/029	
K7193	045/049	
K7238	050/053	
K7256	047/055	
K7305	059/rev. by Germaine Sablon	
K7314	051/061	*EMV* 11/34; *JT* 11/34
K7373	070/073	
K7374	069/072	
K7437	054/rev. by Le Petit Mirsha	
K7455	098/102	
K7464	092/097	
K7479	060/rev. by Le Petit Mirsha	
K7517	129/130	

K7527	100/103	
K7618	190/192	
K7645	191/rev. not Django	
K7704	212/216	
K7706	214/220	
K7707	217/219	*D* 2/37
K7790	224/226	
K7843	221/228	*D* 3/37
K7898	223/227	*D* 7/37
K8112	362/363	
K8366	412/rev. not Django	
K8396	235/248	
K8511	257/258	
K9185	259/rev. not Django	
L1046 (30cm/12")	307/310	*JH* 4–5/38
N4450	279/280	
N4469	216/217	
N4472	103/rev. by Freddy Jenkins' Harlem Seven	
SG364	255/256	
SG365	279/280	
SG367	301/302	
SG20001	270/273	
SG20002	271/272	
X4496	100/103	
X4497	098/102	
X4593	191/rev. not Django	

Harmonic

(Decca pressings with stickers pasted over the logo; they may be illegitimate issues)

F41010	610/613
SB9244	638/641

Henry

848	011
962	016/017
966	012
968	014/015

Hot Record Society

HRS1003	413/414
HRS1004A	416/418
HRS1004B	416/420
HRS1026	418/rev. by Buck Clayton

Ideal

(vertical cut, 30cm (12"), 80rpm)

8543/8544	005/006
8545/8546	007/008
8547/8548	009/010

Jazz Club Français – *see* ABC-JCF *qv*

Joe Davis

DA-17, 1–8 (box set)	080/081/110/125/126/128/153/155
8003	081/082
8004	080/152
8005	110/142

Odéon

(F)250.418	030/032
(F)250.419	034/035
(F)250.420	031/033
(0)264997	441/rev. not Django
(0)283286	402/408
(0)284357	337/341
(0)284393	335/336
(0)284563	402/408
(0)284773	377/424
(0)284778	377/rev. not Django
(0)284865	176/177
(0)284997	440/441
(0)286044	080/379
(0)286192	372/373
(0)286347	402/408
(0)291032	364/368

Olympia

5017	537/538

Omega

(Decca pressings)

21413	890/891
21414	892/893

Oriole

LB1000	080/082
LB1001	081/083
LB1002	110/111
LB1003	125/126
LB1004	109/127

LV100	080/082	*GP* 6/35; *SM* 6/35
LV101	081/083	*GP* 6/35; *SM* 6/35
LV102	110/111	*GP* 10/35; *SM* 10/35
LV103	125/126	*GP* 10/35; *SM* 10/35
LV104	109/127	*GP* 1/36; *SM* 11–12/35

Pampa

BN3007	912/917

Pathé

AT1002	723	
N44126	493/rev. not Django	
PA466	077/078	
PA467	076/079	
PA468	074/075	*JT* 5/35
PA530	104/105	
PG532	493/500	
PA537	106/112	*JT* 5/35
PG538	107/113	*JT* 5/35
PA667	135/139	*JT* 9/35
PA668	137/140	
PA669	136/138	*JT* 9/35
PA805	196/rev. by Jean Trenchant	
P1041	493/500	
P1042	229/230	
P1059	231/232	
P1476	348/349	
PI1062	416/418	
PN44126	493/rev. not Django	
20172	440/442 (pressed in Shanghai)	

Polydor

A-142	141/143
A-197	108/128
A-230	156/157
A-315	335/340
F512.467	173/rev. not Django
F512.468	181/rev. not Django
F512.469/F512.470	André Pasdoc
F512.471	(now confirmed as being without Django)
F512.648	205/rev. not Django
F512.736	206/207
F512.737	208/209
F512.738	210/211
F524.108	163/167

F524.111	168/rev. not Django	
F524.185	(by Edith Piaf; at the time thought to have been a Django item, in fact it features Matelot Ferret)	
F580.016	176/187	
F580.017	423/424	
624024	176/177	
624076	336/337	
624110	336/342	
624112	174/187	
624113	100/346	

Regal-Zonophone

G23542	367/371
G23613	364/368

Royal

1753	080/081	*JI* 10/39
1754	082/rev. by 52nd St Boys	(issued October 1939)
1778	152/rev. by Freddy Taylor	*JI* 11/39
1780	109/141	*JI* 11/39
1785	126/128	*JI* 12/39
1788	125/142	(issued December 1939)
1798	154/155	*JI* 12/39
1807	127/153	*JI* 12/39

Rythme

D5016	535/536
D5017	537/538
D5018	541/542
D5024	546/549
D5025	547/548
D5026	543/550
D5030	539/540
D5500	544/545

Sofradi

05017	537/538

Supraphon

B22638	123/146
B22639	110/128
B22640	111/127
B22641	081/083
B22642	080/082

Swing

1	255/256	
2	234/244	
4	274/275	
6	268/269	
7	279/280	
8	281/282	
12	284/285	
13	316/317	*JH* 2–3/38
14	289/290	*JH* 2–3/38
15	325/328	*JH* 2–3/38
16	271/272	*JH* 4–5/38
18	297/304	*JH* 4–5/38
20	350/352	*JH* 6–7/38
21	254/287	*JH* 6–7/38
23	301/302	*JH* 6–7/38
26	323/356	*JH* 8–9/38
27	270/273	*JH* 10–11/38
28	312/313	*JH* 10–11/38
31	295/296	*JH* 10–11/38
32	292/293	*JH* 10–11/38
34	354/355	
35	315/320	
36	351/rev. by Fletcher Allen	
40	305/306	*JH* 7–8/39
42	294/rev. by Bill Coleman	*JH* 7–8/39
43	314/330	*JH* 7–8/39
44	329/357	
45	283/303	*JH* 7–8/39
54	322/353	*JH* 7–8/39
56	413/420	
65	436/439	
67	428/429	
69	318/319	
70	416/418	
72	446/450	
73	452/456	
74	286/rev. by Michel Warlop and Garland Wilson	
77	311/434	
79	465/468	
80	457/458	
81	454/455	
82	466/467	
83	472/474	

84	480/481	
85	478/479	
86	482/484	
87	490/491	
88	493/500	
89	512/513	
91	516/rev. by Jazz de Paris; dir. Alix Combelle	
93	451/477	
95	517/492	
96	507/508	
97	486/487	
98	461/462	
102	509/510	
103	499/503	
108	511/515	
117	505/506	
118	494/501	
119	489/rev. by Noël Chiboust	
123	496/523	
126	514/rev. by Pierre Allier	
127	520/521	
128	433/504	
X129	525/rev. without Django	
137	498/524	
146	522/434	
151	527/rev. not Django	
158	552/663	
162	533/560	
166	565/567	
176	502/556	
180	562/563	
183	551/554	*JH* 11/45
X186	529/531	
190	459/460	
194	463/464	
197	568/rev. by Noël Chiboust	*JH* 12/45
199	437/438	
200	271/rev. by Dickie Wells	
201	350/351	
202	462/464	
203	414/rev. by Léo Chauliac	*JH* 1–2/46
205	447/448	
208	586/590	*JH* 7–8/46
211	321/435	*JH* 7–8/46
215	561/566	*JH* 9–10/46

218	504/614	
221	584/588	
225	558/559	
229	605/606	*JH* 1/47
242	603/604	
249	616/617	
253	626/627	
254	557/569	
259	625/628	*JH* 11/47
266	615/629	*D* 1/46; *JH* 12/47
270	706/707	
274	708/709	*D* 5/48; *JH* 6–7/48
280	753/754	
283	705/755	
287	751/752	
438	675/686	
439	678/709 (label states 'fin de series')	

Swing Society

1045	258/259

Telefunken

A1958	125/126
A1958-522	125/126
A1959	080/081
A1960	143/144
A1961	145/146
A-1961-523	145/146
SH104	613/638
SH109	641/646
TK104	513/638
TK107	636/644

Ultraphone

AP1314	131/132	
(AP1408/AP1409)	(these are Nane Cholet items, now proven not to be Django recordings)	
AP1422	080/082	*JH* 3/35; *JT* 2/35
AP1423	081/083	*JH* 3/35; *JT* 2/35
AP1443	110/111	*JH* 4/35
AP1444	108/109	*JH* 4/35
AP1478	123/124	
AP1479	125/126	*JH* 7–8/35
AP1484	127/128	*JH* 7–8/35; *JT* 6/35
AP1485	122/rev. not Django	

AP1511	143/144	*JH* 9–10/35
AP1512	141/142	*JH* 9–10/35
AP1527	145/146	
AP1544	152/153	
AP1547	154/155	
AP1548	156/157	
AP1552	158/159	
AP1567	113/rev. by Boyce and Grappelli, without Django	
B14286	080/082	
B14287	081/083	
B14288	111/127	
B14289	110/128	
B14290	125/126	
B14291	123/146	

Varsity

8376	082/128
8377	080/155
8378	126/152
8379	141/142
8380	081/127

Victor

A-1182	252/rev. not known
A-1204	21.4/220
A-1277	227/245
A-1286	350/352
A-1294	255/256
A-1419	098/103
DC-15	103/rev. not known
JA-856	214/220
JA-860	098/102
JA-874	212/216
JA-910	218/217
JA-1012	221/226
JA-1078	221/226
JA-1119	223/224
JA-1363	227/245
JB-215 (30cm/12")	307/310
25511	217/220
25558	221/226
25601	223/rev. by Lionel Hampton
26218	301/302
26219	255/256
26220	268/269

26221	350/352
26222	281/282
26223	292/293
26506	216/219
26578	224/227
26617	272/rev. by Dickie Wells
26733	233/235
27272	305/306
27313	294/rev. by Dickie Wells
20-2760	226/rev. by Duke Ellington
40-122	214/228
40-123	239/242
40-124	237/243
40-125	246/248 (40-122–5 issued as a 78rpm box set with graphics and notes)
68–0684	214/220
(68–0737	
68–0790	
90–0073	
92–2173)	(all these discs issued as 'Louis Vola del Quinteto del Hot Club de France', but recorded by Vola in Argentina and not Django items)

Victory

9032	575/rev. not Django

Wax

108	698/703

Vinyl releases

Items in italics are known to exist but have not been available for checking.

Label	*Catalogue no.*	*Title*	*Date of issue*
17.5cm (7") 45rpm vinyl			
Decca [F] 903; 906	45-5510		
Decca [F] 894; 896	45-5581	(labels of both sides of this release read 'Recorded In Belgium' [*sic*])	
Decca [A] 890; 892	28145		
HMV [F] 279; 493	MF1040		
HMV [F] 516	MF20021		
HMV [F] 525	MF20022		
Pop [F] 677	73007		
Vogue [F]	1205		
Vogue [F] 675; 725	45-67		
Vogue [F] 688; 709	45-68		
Vogue [F] 710; 716	45-69		
17.5cm (7") 45rpm EP			
Angel [A] 472; 493; 724; 727 (drawn from Angel 60003 LP)	73006	Le Jazz Hot par Django Reinhardt et QHCF Part 1	
Angel [A] 311; 503; 522; 724	73007	Le Jazz Hot par Django Reinhardt et QHCF Part 2	
Atlantic [A] 413; 414; 699; 700	EP523		

Ausland [G] 7EGW8505
234; 244; 255; 277

Ausland [G] 7EGW8588
(same as Electrola E41098)

Barclay [F] 74041

Barclay [F] 74042

Blue Star BEP12002
910; 912; 914; 916

Blue Star BEP12008
911; 913; 915; 917

Clef [A] EP509
910; 911; 912; 913; 916

Clef [A] EP510
910; 911; 912; 913
(also issued in Australia under the same catalogue number)

Clef [A] EP516
814; 915

Collector [E] JEN6 Swing Guitars
(same as Vogue EPL7728)

Collector [E] JEN8 Improvisation
717; 719; 720; 721

Columbia SEG7619 Boum! – Song Successes of Charles Trenet (*anthology*)
519

Columbia [E] SEG7775 Larry Adler with the Quintet of the Hot Club of France
364; 366; 368; 370

Columbia [Au] SEGO7775
(same as SEG 7775, *qv*)

Decca [E] 45-5581
918; 919; 920; 921

Decca [E] DFE6366 Stephane and Django
128; 155; 176; 177
(also issued in Australia on DFEA6366)

Electrola [G] E40920 Django Reinhardt
234; 244; 255; 256

Electrola [G] E41098
228; 301; 436; 493

Esquire [E] ESQ302 Glenn Miller's Uptown Hall Gang, 1945

HMV [H] DJE4005

HMV [It] EGF650
(same as HMV [F] 7EMF165)

HMV [It] *EGF941*

HMV [E] 7EG8132 Django's Guitar
(same as HMV [F] 7EMF40)

HMV [E] 7EG8324 Eddie South and Stephane Grappelly
284; 297; 303; 304
(also issued in Australia as HMV 7EGO8324)

HMV [E] 7EG8361 Eddie South and his Jazz Violin
281; 282; 295; 296

HMV [E] 7EG8393 Coleman Hawkins All Stars with Django Reinhardt
255; 256; 257; 258
(also issued in Australia as HMV 7EGO8393)

HMV [E] 7EG8447 Rex Stewart and His Footwarmers
(same as Pathé EA26)

HMV [F] 7EGF650 Django Reinhardt et Le Quintette du Hot-Club de France
228; 301; 436; 493

HMV [F] 7EGF941
500; 524; 567; 584

HMV [E] 7EGH1001
216; 220; 223; 226

HMV [E] 7EGH1002
228; 301; 436; 493

HMV [E] 7EGH1003
233; 238; 240; 250

HMV [E] 7EGH1004
244; 279; 283; 287

HMV [E] 7EGH1005
284; 285; 286; 296

HMV [E] 7EGH1006
302; 305; 311; 314

HMV [F] 7EMF26 Benny Carter – Coleman Hawkins
255; 256
(the Carter recordings are without Django)

HMV [F] 7EMF34
268; 269

HMV [F] 7EMF40 Django Reinhardt – Solos de Guitare
252; 253; 279; 321

HMV [F] 7EMF130
888/889 (*sic*)

HMV [F] 7EMF165
228; 301; 436; 493

HMV [F] 888; 889	7EMF310	Django Reinhardt
HMV [H]	*7EGW8505*	
HMV [It] (same as HMV [F] 7EMF40)	7EMQ5	
HMV [It] 228; 301; 436; 493	7EMQ12	Django Reinhardt e il Quintetto dell Hot Club de France
HMV [Au] (same as HMV 7EG8324)	7TLA23	
HMV [Au] (same as HMV 7EG8393)	7TLA29	
Oriole [E] 080; 082; 083; 126	EP7045	Django
Pathé [F] 413; 416; 418; 419	EA26	Rex Stewart and his Feetwarmers
Pathé [F] 229	EGC3002	(*anthology*)
Rarities [E] 618; 619; 620; 621	30	Django with the Duke
RCA [G] 103; 224; 238; 240 (same as RCA [N] EPC1100-1)	EPC-1100-1	Django
RCA [G] 100; 226; 253; 416 (same as RCA [N] EPC 1100-2)	EPC-1100-2	Django
RCA [G] 216; 217; 236; 252 (same as RCA [N] EPC1100-3)	EPC-1100-3	Django
Supraphon [Cz] 080; 081; 082; 083	SUK35615	Le Quintette du Hot-Club de France
Verve [G] 912; 914; 915; 916	26122	Django Reinhardt
Vogue [F] 675; 681; 686; 709	EPL 7066	Django Reinhardt et son Quintette du Hot-Club de France Vol. 1
Vogue [F] 688; 689; 690	EPL 7067	Django Reinhardt et son Quintette du Hot-Club de France Vol. 2
Vogue [F] 673; 678; 679; 718	EPL 7068	Django Reinhardt et son Quintette du Hot-Club de France Vol. 3
Vogue [F] 728; 729; 731; 732	EPL 7728	

Vogue [F] *EPL 7996*
717; 719; 720; 721

Vogue [F] EPL 1025
675; 678; 686; 709
(also issued as Vogue EPV 1025 in UK)

Vogue [E] EPV1208 Django Reinhardt and his Quintette of the Hot Club of France
[*also issued in Australia as Vogue EPVA1208*]

Vogue [E] VRE5010 Le Disque d'Or du Jazz
672; 675; 678; 722

Vogue *VRE5020* *Django Reinhardt-Festival 48*
759; 762; 765 and 1 track without Django

25cm (10") 33rpm Vinyl

Angel [J] PW1001
(same as HMV DLP1045)

Angel [A] 60003 Le Jazz Hot par Django Reinhardt et QHCF
311; 472; 493; 503; 522; 753

Angel [A] 60011 Django's Guitar
280; 315; 320; 321; 435; 436; 439; 557; 558; 559

Ausland [G] WDLP1045
(same as HMV DLP 1045)

Blue Star [F] 6830
(same as CLEF MGC516)

Brunswick [G] LPB86018 In Memoriam – Django Reinhardt (und das Quintete des Hot Club de France)
174; 176; 177; 187; 337; 338; 341; 343

Clef [A] MGC516 The Great Artistry Of Django Reinhardt
910; 911; 912; 913; 914; 915; 916; 917
(also issued in Australia, with the same catalogue number)

Club National Du Disque [F] CND580
252; 253; 301; 304; 307; 420; 439; 493

Columbia [F] FP1164 (*anthology*)
057; 194; 195

Columbia [E] *33CS580* (*anthology*)

Decca [E] LF1139 Swing From Paris
336; 339; 341; 347; 373; 377; 391; 441
(same as London LL1344; also issued in Australia as Decca LFA1139)

Decca [F] 123998 Django Reinhardt et Stéphane Grappelli avec le Quintette du Hot-Club de France
185; 186; 375; 385; 396; 398; 401

Decca [F] 124015 Django Reinhardt et Stéphane Grappelli avec le Quintette du Hot-Club de France
335; 340; 384; 388; 390; 408; 409; 424

Decca [F] FM133088 Django Reinhardt
903; 904; 905; 918; 919; 920; 921

Dial [A] 214 Django Reinhardt – Quintette of the Hot Club of France
660; 699; 700; 702; 703; 704

(Dial 215 Ellingtonia)
(despite being credited on the sleeve, Django does not appear on this album)

Dial [A] 218 Django Reinhardt
652; 653; 659; 662; 663; 665; 669; 745; 748

Electrola E60068
(same as HMV DLP1045)

Felstead [E] BDL87005 Django Reinhardt and His Rhythm
(same as Clef MGC516)

HMV [Au] ODLP7512

HMV [E] DLP1045 Django Reinhardt 1954
466; 467; 492; 493; 498; 500; 501; 524; 567; 584

HMV [E] DLP1055 Coleman Hawkins All Stars 1954 (*anthology*)
103; 255; 256; 257; 258
(remainder of album comprises recordings by Hawkins from 1939 to 1945)

HMV [F] FFLP 1027 Django Reinhardt
244; 279; 280; 287; 301; 302; 315; 320; 321

HMV [F] FFLP 1118 Eddie South
281; 282; 283; 284; 285; 295; 296; 297; 303; 304

HMV [F] FFLP 1120
(same as Trianon [F] 5354)

HMV [F] FFLP1138
220; 330; 467; 492; 493; 498; 500; 524; 567; 584

HMV [F] FOLP8004 Bill Coleman (*anthology*)
289; 292; 293; 294
(also contains six titles by Coleman recorded between 1936 and 1937.

HMV [Br] MQDB12
(same as HMV ODLP7512)

HMV [Au] ODLP1045
(same as HMV [E] DLP1045)

HMV [It] QCLP12019

HMV [It] QFLP4026

Jay [A] 3008 The Best of Django Reinhardt
(same as Swing M33316, but reprogrammed)

Jay [A] *3012* *Concert Recital For Django Reinhardt*

London [A] LL1344 Swing From Paris
(same as Decca LF1139)

London [RE] WB90156 (*anthology*)
919

London [E] WB91074 (*anthology*)
921

Omega [F] 123998
(same as Decca 123998)

Omega [F] 124015
(same as Decca 124015)

Oriole [E] MG10019 Django 1957
080; 081; 082; 083; 099; 100; 101; 102

Pacific [F] LDPA1317 Les Premiers Enregistrements du Quintette du HCF
143; 144; 145; 146; 152; 153; 154; 155; 156; 157

Pampa [Ar] LRM25308
(same as CLEF MGC516)

Pathé [F] 33AT1002 Surprise Partie (*anthology*)
500 (also features titles by Arthur Briggs, Alix Combelle and others)

Pathé [F] ST1012 Django Reinhardt
(same as HMV DLP1045)

Pathé Vox VX610 Three Fingered Lightening
(same as HMV DLP1045)

Period [A] 1010 Django Reinhardt Memorial Vol. 1
(same as Swing 33314)

Period [A] 1101 Django Reinhardt Memorial Vol. 2
673; 679; 685; 687; 688

Period [A] 1102 Django Reinhardt Memorial Vol. 3
(same as Swing M33316)

Period [A] 1103
758; 760; 761; 762; 763; 764; 765; 766

RCA [Ar] AVLT6
216; 217; 223; 224; 233; 235; 248; 249

RCA [A] LEJ-10 The RCA Victor Encyclopaedia of Recorded Jazz Vol. 10 (*anthology*)
239

RCA [A] LPT27 Great Tenor Sax Artists (*anthology*)
256

Riviera [F] RLP6575
(same as CLEF MGC516)

Swing [F] LDM30069
695; 696; 697; 719; 720; 721; 722

Swing [F] M33314 Souvenirs de Django Reinhardt Vol. 1
672; 678; 680; 706; 707; 708; 709; 710

Swing [F] M33315 Souvenirs de Django Reinhardt Vol. 2
673; 679; 687; 715; 717

Swing [F] M33316 Souvenirs de Django Reinhardt Vol. 3
681; 685; 686; 688; 689; 690; 691; 716; 718

Swing [F] M33317 Concert Django Reinhardt à Bruxelles
(same as Period 1103)

Swing [F] M33330 Django Reinhardt Vol. 4
692; 693; 694; 712; 714

Trianon [F] 5354 Django Reinhardt Joue avec André Ekyan et son Orchestre
297; 299; 300; 301; 326; 327; 329; 376

Vogue LDE049 Souvenirs of Django Reinhardt Vol. 1
(same as Swing 33314)

Vogue [E] LDE084 Souvenirs of Django Reinhardt Vol. 2
673; 679; 685; 687; 716; 717

Vogue [E] LDE106 Souvenirs of Django Reinhardt Vol. 3
(same as Swing M33316)

Vox – see Pathé, *qv*

30cm (12") 33rpm vinyl

Ace of Clubs [E] ACL1158 Django Reinhardt and Stéphane Grappelli with the Quintet of the Hot Club of France 1964
335; 336; 337; 339; 340; 341; 342; 343; 385; 440; 607; 610; 611; 613
(also issued in Australia as ACLA1158)

Ace of Clubs [E] ACL1189 Parisian Swing 1965
128; 154; 155; 157; 347; 387; 389; 390; 391; 440; 442; 443
(also issued in Australia as ACLA 1189)

Affinity [E] BOX107 Django 1987
185; 212; 214; 216; 217; 219; 220; 221; 223; 224; 226; 227; 228; 233; 234; 235; 236; 237; 238; 239; 240; 241; 242; 243; 244; 245; 246; 247; 248; 249; 250; 253; 254; 255; 256; 257; 258; 268; 272; 273; 279; 280; 281; 283; 284; 285; 286; 289; 290; 292; 296; 297; 303; 305; 306; 307; 311; 316; 318; 319; 322; 323; 325; 330; 350; 352; 413; 414; 416; 418; 420; 433; 434; 435; 436; 439; 459; 466; 473; 492; 493; 494; 495; 497; 499; 501; 502; 503; 504; 533; 551; 553; 556; 557; 558; 575; 576; 588; 603; 604; 605; 606; 700; 743; 822

Amiga 850018 Duke Ellington–Django Reinhardt
234; 255; 279; 283; 436
(remainder of LP by Duke Ellington)

Amiga 855241 Django Reinhardt and Stéphane Grappelli
(same as HMV CLP1491)

Archive of Folk Music – see Everest, *qv*

Ariston ARLP12031 Duke's Fabulous Recordings (*anthology*)
618; 619; 620
(remainder of LP by Duke Ellington)

Astan [E] LP20102 Nuages 1986
255; 256; 258; 270; 396; 493; 613; 649; 898; 920; 921

Astor [Au] Django Reinhardt Vol. 1

Astor [Au] GGS1065 Django Reinhardt Vol. 2
(same as Everest FS230)

Ausland [G] WCLP631

Ausland [G] WCLP684

Barclay [F] 920.366 Django Reinhardt et Le QHCF Vol. 1
(same as Harmony HFL8033 plus 664; 671; 702; 704)

Barclay [F] 920.417 Django Reinhardt et le Quintette du Hot-Club de France

Barclay [F] 80369 Django Reinhardt joue avec Guitars Unlimited
705; 910; 911; 912; 913; 914; 915; 916; 917

Barclay [F] 80929/30 Django's Story 1947–53
630; 632; 652; 653; 657; 658; 659; 660; 661; 663; 664; 668; 669; 670; 671; 699; 700; 701; 702; 703; 704; 745; 748; 910; 911; 912; 913; 914; 915; 916; 917

Barclay [F] 84076

Barclay [F] 84090 L'Incomparable Django Reinhardt
657; 659; 664; 668; 671; 699; 700; 702; 704; 745; 748

Barclay [F] 820050

BBC Records [E] REB680 Hot Violins (*anthology*) 1988
239; 303

BBC Records [E] REB698 Coleman Hawkins 1927–39 (*anthology*) 1990
255; 256; 257; 258

Black Tulip [E] LP28052 The Very Best of Stephane Grappelli 1995

Black Tulip [E] LP2636771 Swing That Music 1988

Bluebird [E] NL90448 Djangology '49 1990
(see RCA NL90448, *qv*)

Blue Star [F] *30*

Brunswick 87520 Swing From Europe (*anthology*)
174

Brunswick [G] 87921 Django Reinhardt (Europe's Greatest Contribution To Jazz)
535; 536; 537; 538; 539; 540; 541; 542; 543; 544; 545; 546; 547; 548; 549; 550

Capitol [A] T2045 Django Reinhardt and The QHCF
495; 497; 499; 501; 503; 504; 523; 551; 553; 554; 556

Capitol [A] T10457 Best of Django Reinhardt Vol. 1
233; 236; 237; 238; 239; 240; 241; 242; 243; 245; 246; 248

Capitol [A] T10458 Best of Django Reinhardt Vol. 2
273; 292; 301; 305; 306; 307; 413; 414; 416; 418; 420; 586

Capitol [A] TBO10226 The Best Of Django Reinhardt – 24 Classic Performances
(T10457/8 are the same as TBO10226)

Capitol [A] W2140 The Jazz Story Vol. 4 (*anthology*)
493

CBS [E] 52213 Django
(same as Oriole MG10019 and Realm RM213, of which this is a direct reissue)

CBS [F] 63052 Paris 1945 (*anthology*)
573; 574; 575; 576
(the remainder of this album is by members of the Glenn Miller army band)
(issued in Australia on Columbia BP233919)

Columbia [F] 2C054-15382 Jean Sablon Chante (*anthology*)
195

Columbia [G] C2033/34 Django Reinhardt
(same as IC188-10395/96]

Columbia [F] CCTX 240853 Eddie South
281; 282; 283; 284; 285; 295; 296; 297; 303; 304
(also contains 'Doin' The Raccoon'/'Two Guitars' from South's 1928 Paris session)

Columbia [F] CTX40295 Charles Trenet – Je Rechante (*anthology*)
519

Columbia [G] HZE813
See Hör Zu HZE813BL

Columbia [G] IC188-10395/96 Django Reinhardt
(same as Pathé 2C054-10395/96)

Columbia	KC31479	Django Reinhardt – Swing It Lightly	1968
699; 700; 701; 702; 703; 704 (same as Barclay 80369)			
Decca [F]	*ACL831*	*Django Reinhardt et son Quintette*	
894; 896; 897; 898; 903; 904; 905; 906; 918; 919; 920; 921			
Decca [E] (Eclipse)	ECM 2051	Swing '35–'39	1970
174; 176; 177; 185; 186; 187; 188; 189; 372; 373; 377; 379; 398			
Decca [E]	MOR530	Swinging Affair 1939	
344; 346; 424; 425; 426			
Decca [F]	115.120–124	Django Reinhardt et le Quintette du Hot-Club de France avec Stéphane Grappelli [5LP box]	
174; 176; 178; 185; 186; 187; 188; 189; 335; 336; 337; 339; 340; 341; 342; 343; 344; 345; 346; 347; 372; 373; 375; 377; 379; 384; 394; 395; 396; 396; 398; 399; 400; 401; 402; 403; 404; 405; 408; 409; 410; 411; 422; 423; 424; 425; 426; 440; 441; 442; 443; 607; 611; 612; 613			
Decca [F]	115.213A		
403; 404			
Decca [F]	168003	Django Reinhardt–Stéphane Grappelli avec le Quintette du Hot-Club de France	
(same as Ace of Clubs 1158)			
Decca [F]	168004	Swing de Paris	
(same as Ace of Clubs ACL1189)			
Decca [F]	99017	Django Reinhardt et son Quintette	
(same as Decca ACL831)			
Design [A]	DLP113	Jazz Hall of Fame Vol. 2 (*anthology*)	
675; 717			
Disques Swing	SW8420267	Djangologie/USA	
DJM [E]	22049		1976
900; 901; 909			
Electrola [G]	E83035		
051; 223; 234; 244; 249; 254; 279; 280; 283; 287; 302; 305; 306			
Electrola [G]	E83216	(*anthology*)	
228 (excerpt only)			
Electrola [G]	*E83270*	*Das Program Geht Weiter (anthology)*	
Electrola [G]	*E83315*		
Electrola [G]	O83347	Jatz von Jestern (*anthology*)	
098; 228 (incomplete); 416			
Emarcy [A]	*MGE26004*	*Django Reinhardt – Le Jazz Hot!*	
(also issued in electronic stereo as SRE66004)			

Ember [E] *CJS810* *Requiem For a Jazzman*
(same as CLEF MGC516 plus four tracks by a Stéphane Grappelli group without Django)

Ember [E] CJS831 Gypsy of Jazz – Django Reinhardt 1971
(same as Everest FS212)

EMI *EMS1363* *Paris by Night (anthology)* *1990*

EMIDisc [F] C048-50660 Jean Sablon avec Django Reinhardt et Garland Wilson
036; 038; 042; 057; 058; 085; 088; 089; 194; 195
(and two titles by Sablon with Garland Wilson)

Everest [A] FS212 Django Reinhardt Vol. 1

Everest [A] FS230 Django Reinhardt Vol. 2
652; 663; 665; 673; 687; 690; 700; 706; 707; 745

Everest [A] FS255 Django Reinhardt Vol. 3
(same as Period 1204)

Everest [A] *FS306* *Django Reinhardt Vol. 4*

Family [A] 717 (*anthology*)
098; 100
(and ten additional titles by Coleman Hawkins 1933–35)

For Discriminating Collectors FDC 1021
(never released; material planned for this album first appeared on Ariston 12031)

Gala [GB] GLP357 (*anthology*)
675

GNP-Crescendo GNP9001 Django Reinhardt – Stéphane Grappelli with the Quintette of the Hot Club of France
(same as Ace of Clubs ACL1158)

GNP-Crescendo [A] GNP9002 Parisian Swing
(same as Ace of Clubs ACL1189)

Happy Days CHD134 Jean Sablon
027; 029; 038; 057; 085

Happy Days CHD165
100; 154; 157; 217; 228; 237; 243; 246; 247; 337; 343; 344; 345; 377; 379; 502

Harmonie [C] *HFL8033* *Django Reinhardt*

Harmony [Ar] 7139 Django Reinhardt y el Quinteto del Hot Club de Francia
(same as Realm 213)

HMV [F] CHTX 240550 Django – Selection
220; 227; 234; 236; 252; 253; 279; 280; 284; 285; 301; 302; 557

HMV [F]	CHTX 240551	Django et ses Amis Americains	

255; 256; 257; 258; 268; 269; 281; 294; 351; 413; 414; 416; 418; 420

HMV [F]	CHTX 240646	Les Classiques de Django	

103; 228; 237; 241; 244; 250; 278; 283; 304; 319; 321; 436; 606

HMV [E]	CLP1054	Dickie Wells In Paris	

(same as HMV [It] QCLP12019)

HMV [E]	CLP1249	Django	1959

223; 234; 235; 244; 249; 251; 254; 279; 280; 283; 301; 302; 305; 306

HMV [E]	*CLP1340*	*The Art Of Django*	
HMV [E]	CLP1389	Django The Unforgettable	1960

816; 817; 819; 820; 821; 822; 863; 864; 865; 866; 867; 868; 869

HMV [E]	*CLP1491*	*Django And Stephane Originals*	
HMV [E]	CLP1817	The Legendary Django	

285; 286; 311; 315; 315; 318; 320; 433; 434; 435; 439; 472; 496

HMV [E]	CLP1890	Django And His American Friends 1	

100; 102; 103; 190; 191; 193; 255; 256; 257; 258; 268; 269; 270; 271; 272; 273

HMV [E]	CLP1907	Django And His American Friends 2	1965

281; 282; 289; 290; 292; 294; 295; 296; 350; 351; 352; 413; 414; 416; 418; 420

HMV [F]	FELP153		

(same as HMV [It] QCLP12019)

HMV [F]	FELP154	Django Reinhardt Vol. 1	1957

051; 103; 212; 214; 216; 217; 219; 220; 221; 223; 224; 226; 227; 228; 306

HMV [F]	FELP171	Django Reinhardt Vol. 2	1957

233; 236; 237; 238; 239; 240; 241; 242; 243; 245; 246; 248; 250

HMV [F]	FELP174	Django Reinhardt Vol. 3	

234; 235; 244; 249; 254; 255; 256; 257; 258; 275; 279; 280; 283; 287

HMV [F]	FELP181	Django Reinhardt Vol. 4	

252; 253; 282; 283; 284; 285; 286; 292; 293; 294; 295; 296; 297; 304

HMV [F]	FELP184	Django Reinhardt Vol. 5	

272; 273; 301; 302; 303; 305; 306; 307; 309; 311; 312; 313; 314

HMV [F]	FELP197	Django Reinhardt Vol. 6	

315; 317; 318; 319; 321; 351; 413; 414; 416; 418; 42; 436; 439;

HMV [F]	FELP203	Django Reinhardt Vol. 7	

321; 330; 433; 434; 435; 468; 472; 492; 493; 496; 498; 502; 517

HMV [F]	FELP208	Django Reinhardt Vol. 8	

522; 552; 557; 559; 604; 606; 626; 627; 628; 753; 758

HMV [F]	FELP231	Django Reinhardt Vol. 9
(same as HMV [E] CLP1389)		
HMV [F]	FELP236	Django Reinhardt Vol. 10
494; 495; 497; 499; 501; 503; 504; 523; 533; 534; 551; 553; 554; 556;		
HMV [F]	FELP239	Django et Stephane (Vol. 11)
(same as HMV [E] CLP1491)		
HMV [F]	FELP247	Django Reinhardt Vol. 12
603; 605; 614; 625; 629; 726; 727; 751; 752; 754; 755; 756; 757; 889		
HMV [H]	*HCLP103*	
HMV [H]	HCLP120	
(same as HMV [F] FELP154)		
HMV [H]	HCLP122	
(same as HMV [F] FELP171)		
HMV [H]	HCLP124	
(same as HMV [F] FELP174)		
HMV [F]	HTX40124	Django Anthologie Vol. 1
(also issued as CHTX40124)		
HMV [F]	HTX40125	Django Reinhardt et Stephane Grappelly
(also issued as CHTX40125: same as HMV [E] CLP1491)		
HMV [F]	HTX40158	Django Anthologie Vol. 2
(same as HMV [F] FELP171)		
HMV [F]	HTX40159	Django Anthologie Vol. 3
(same as HMV [F] FELP174)		
HMV [F]	HTX40160	Django Anthologie Vol. 4
(same as HMV [F] FELP181)		
HMV [F]	HTX40233	Jean Tranchant – Belles Années du Music
229		Hall (*anthology*)
HMV [F]	HTX40271	Django Anthologie Vol. 5
(same as HMV [F] FELP154)		
HMV [F]	HTX40272	Django Anthologie Vol. 6
(same as HMV [F] FELP184)		
HMV [F]	HTX40273	Django Anthologie Vol. 7
(same as HMV [F] FELP197)		
HMV [F]	HTX40274	Django Anthologie Vol. 8
(same as HMV [F] FELP208)		
HMV [F]	HTX30275	Django Anthologie Vol. 9
(same as HMV [F] FELP236)		
HMV [F]	HTX40276	Django Anthologie Vol. 10
(same as HMV [F] FELP247)		

HMV [F] HTX40238 Bill Coleman in Paris Vol. 1 (*anthology*)
190; 191; 289; 290

HMV [F] HTX40239 Dickie Wells In Paris
(same as HMV [It] QCLP12019)

HMV [F] HTX40268 Bill Coleman In Paris Vol. 2
(same as Odéon [Ar] LDF4374

HMV [F] HTX40239 Dickie Wells In Paris
(same as HMV QCLP12019)

HMV [F] HTX40628 Bill Coleman In Paris Vol. 2
(same as Odéon LDF4374)

HMV [Au] OCLP1491
(same as HMV CLP1491)

HMV [Au] OCLP1817
(same as HMV CLP1817)

HMV [Au] OCLP1890
(same as HMV CLP1890)

HMV [Au] OCLP1907
(same as HMV CLP1907)

HMV [Au] OCLP7529
(same as HMV [F] FELP154

HMV [Au] OCLP7542
(same as HMV [F] FELP171)

HMV [Au] ODLP7512
244; 279; 280; 287; 301; 302; 311; 315; 320; 321

HMV [Au] OXLP7554
(same as either Emidisc C048-50660 or Parlophone PMC7134

HMV [It] QCLP4026
(same as HMV [Au] ODLP7512)

HMV [It] QCLP12019 Dickie Wells a Parigi (*anthology*)
268; 269; 270; 271; 272; 273

Hör Zu [G] HZE813BL Django Reinhardt – Die Andere Seite
100; 245; 287; 297; 301; 304; 320; 370; 436; 466; 493; 495; 497; 606

Jazz Legend 5 Rex Stewart 1947 (anthology)

KC [E] 109 Unissued Titles 37–41
278; 308; 403; 444; 445; 471; 564; 593; 633; 674; 866

La Roulotte MA2

La Roulotte MA3 Later Years
902; 907; 908

Living Era [E] AJA5054 The Hawk In Europe 1988
100; 255; 256; 257; 258

Living Era [E] AJA5070 Swing From Paris
177; 185; 186; 187; 188; 189; 335; 337; 339; 342; 373; 375; 377; 379; 385; 398; 441

Living Era [E] AJA5267 (*anthology*)
155; 171

London LL1344
128; 154; 155; 157; 336; 337; 339; 341; 347; 390; 391; 441

Marble Arch *MAL1234* *Django*
674; 679; 681; 694; 706; 709; 712; 714; 711; 716; 718

Meteor MTM12 I Got Rhythm 1986
177; 335; 336; 396; 493; 613; 649; 898

Mode [F] MDINT9103 Deux Géants du Jazz – Sidney Bechet–Django Reinhardt Vol. 1 (*anthology*)
675; 710; 711; 716; 718

Mode [F] MDINT9116 Les Grands du Jazz (*anthology*)
728

Mode [F] MDINT9117 Just Blues (*anthology*)
722

Mode [F] MDINT9148 Deux Géants du Jazz Vol. 2 – Sidney Bechet et Django Reinhardt
674; 681; 697; 712; 717; 721

Mode [F] MDINT9315 Le Disque d'Or de Django Reinhardt
675; 676; 678; 689; 690; 695; 708; 710; 716; 717; 719

Mode [F] MDINT9461 Les Classiques du Jazz (*anthology*)
722

Mode [F] MDINT9841 Jazz Greats – Paris (*anthology*)
663

Mode [F] 509031
695; 708; 719

Musidisc [F] MU222 Django Reinhardt 1947–53
636; 637; 638; 641; 642; 644; 645; 646; 649; 890; 891; 892; 893; 894; 896; 897; 904; 905; 906; 918; 919; 920; 921

Music For Pleasure [E] MFP1054 Djangology
(same as HMV [E] DLP1045)

Music For Pleasure [E] MFP1408 Larry Adler (*anthology*)
364; 366; 368; 370

Music For Pleasure *MFP5164* *Django Reinhardt*

NEC Plus Ultra *45040*

NEC Plus Ultra 502008
879; 880; 881; 882; 883; 884; 885; 886; 887

NPU 502000 At The Club St Germain 1951

NPU 502010 At The Club St Germain 1949

Odéon [Ar] LDF4374 Bill Coleman en Paris (*anthology*)
292; 293

Odéon [Ar] LDM7346
(same as HMV DLP1045)

Old Bean [E] OLD 12 In Paris 1987
128; 154; 155; 157; 185; 186; 187; 188; 189; 216; 217; 221; 226; 227; 228

Pacific [F] LDPD 6272 Les Premières Enrigistrements du Quintette du H C F
080; 081; 082; 083; 108; 109; 110; 111; 125; 126; 127; 128; 141; 142

Parlophone [E] PMC7105 Bill Coleman à Paris Vol. 2 1936–38 (*anthology*)
293

Parlophone [E] PMC7134 Jean Sablon/Django Reinhardt (*anthology*)
036; 037; 038; 042; 057; 058; 085; 088; 089; 129; 130; 194; 195
(also includes two tracks by Sablon accompanied by Garland Wilson)

Parlophone [E] PMC7146 Django In Rome 1949–50
(also issued as PCS7146; same as Pathé 2C05416019)

Pathé [F] 2C 054-10395/96 Toutes les Cordes de Django
001; 020; 025; 195; 368; 370; 437; 438; 451; 465; 473; 476; 481; 486; 514; 515; 519; 527; 531; 532; 558; 568; 569; 570; 588; 590; 615; 616; 617

Pathé [F] 2C 054-11841 Django Reinhardt
256; 257; 279; 304; 465; 467; 472; 480; 492; 493; 500; 584; 588; 606

Pathé [F] 2C 054-11842 Django Reinhardt et Stéphane Grappelli
(same as HMV [E] CLP1491)

Pathé [F] 2C 054-16001 Djangologie Vol. 1 1928–36
002; 020; 025; 051; 098; 100; 102; 103; 190; 191; 193; 212; 214; 216

Pathé [F] 2C 054-16002 Djangologie Vol. 2 1936–37
217; 219; 220; 221; 223; 224; 226; 227; 228; 233; 234; 235; 236; 237

Pathé [F] 2C 054-16003 Djangologie Vol. 3 1937
238; 239; 240; 241; 242; 243; 244; 245; 246; 247; 248; 249; 250; 252

Pathé [F] 2C 054-16004 Djangologie Vol. 4 1937

253; 254; 255; 256; 257; 258; 268; 269; 270; 271; 272; 273; 274; 275

Pathé [F] 2C 054-16005 Djangologie Vol. 5 1937

279; 280; 281; 282; 283; 284; 285; 286; 287; 289; 290; 292; 293; 294

Pathé [F] 2C 054-16006 Djangologie Vol. 6 1937

295; 296; 297; 301; 302; 303; 304; 305; 306; 307; 310; 311; 312; 313

Pathé [F] 2C 054-16007 Djangologie Vol. 7 1937–38

314; 315; 316; 317; 318; 319; 320; 321; 322; 324; 328; 330; 350; 351

Pathé [F] 2C 054-16008 Djangologie Vol. 8 1938–39

352; 364; 366; 368; 370; 413; 414; 416; 418; 420; 428; 429; 433; 434

Pathé [F] 2C 054-16009 Djangologie Vol. 9 1939–40

435; 436; 437; 438; 439; 450; 451; 457; 463

Pathé [F] 2C 054-16010 Djangologie Vol. 10 1940

464; 465; 466; 467; 468; 472; 473; 474; 475 (extract only); 476; 480; 481; 484; 486

Pathé [F] 2C 054-16011 Djangologie Vol. 11 1940

487; 490; 491; 492; 493; 494; 495; 496; 497; 498; 499; 500; 501; 502

Pathé [F] 2C 054-16012 Djangologie Vol. 12 1940–41

503; 504; 508; 509; 514; 515; 516; 517; 521; 522; 523; 524; 525 (extract only)

Pathé [F] 2C 054-16013 Djangologie Vol. 13 1942–43

527; 529; 531; 533; 534; 551; 552; 553; 554; 556; 557; 558; 559; 560

Pathé [F] 2C 054-16014 Djangologie Vol. 14 1943–46

561; 562; 563; 564; 565; 566; 567; 569; 570; 584; 586; 588; 590; 614

Pathé [F] 2C 054-16015 Djangologie Vol. 15 1946–47

603; 604; 605; 606; 615; 616; 617; 625; 626; 627; 628; 629; and 2 NYE

Pathé [F] 2C 054-16016 Djangologie Vol. 16 1947–49

751; 752; 753; 754; 755; 756; 757; 768; 770; 773; 775; 776; 777; 778; 782; 783; 786

Pathé [F] 2C 054-16017 Djangologie Vol. 17 1949
777; 778; 782; 792; 808; 811; 816; 817; 818; 819; 826; 827; 828

Pathé [F] 2C 054-16018 Djangologie Vol. 18 1949–50
820; 821; 822; 863; 864; 865; 866; 867; 868; 869; 888; 889

Pathé [F] 2C 054-16019 Djangologie Vol. 19 1949–50
789; 814; 824; 825; 826; 829; 830; 831; 850; 856; 859; 871; 873; 874

Pathé [F] 2C 054-16020 Djangologie Vol. 20 1949 (*sic*)
769; 771; 783; 791; 794; 795; 805; 813; 815; 831; 832; 833; 834

Pathé [F] 2C 054-16024 Swing Sessions Vol. 4 (*anthology*)
325; 329; 355; 446; 449; 452; 455; 456; 507
and tracks by Alix Combelle and Fletcher Allen without Django

Pathé [F] 2C 054-16025 Swing Sessions Vol. 5 (*anthology*)
482; 525
(and tracks by Barelli, Chiboust, Foaud, Rostaing, Warlop)

Pathé [F] FELP305 Bruno Coquatrix (*anthology*)
088

Pathé [F] FPX483 Charles Trenet [13 volumes] (*anthology*)
519

Period [A] SPL302 Jazz Digest Vol. 1 (*anthology*)
(same as Design DLP113)

Period [A] SPL304 Jazz Digest Vol. 2 (*anthology*)
652; 717; 722

Period [A] SPL1201 Django Reinhardt Memorial Vol. 1
652; 653; 659; 660; 662; 663; 775; 669; 699; 700

Period [A] SPL1202 Django Reinhardt Memorial Vol. 2
673; 678; 679; 680; 685; 686; 706; 707; 715; 716; 717

Period [A] SPL1203 Django Reinhardt Memorial Vol. 3
672; 675; 681; 686; 689; 690; 691; 708; 709; 710

Period [A] SPL1204 The Best of Django Reinhardt
660; 669; 678; 679; 681; 686; 688; 691; 699; 703; 708; 709; 716

Period [A] SPL1302

Polydor [F] 46451 Europe's Greatest Contribution To Jazz

Polydor [F] 512467
180; 181

Polydor [F] 512648
205

Polydor [F] *512736*

Polydor [F] *512737*

Polydor [F] *512738*

Polydor [F] *524108*

Polydor [F] 524111

Polydor [F] *530187*

Polydor [F] 2344 146
535; 536; 537; 538; 539; 540; 541; 542; 543; 544; 545; 546; 547; 548; 549; 550

Polydor [F] 2489188 Django Reinhardt et Compagnie 1934–37
163; 167; 168; 205; 206; 207; 208; 209; 210; 211
(also contains tracks by Micheline Day and Wal Berg et son Jazz, believed at the time to include Django but now believed not to)

Polydor [G] 236510 Django
(same as Brunswick 87921)

Polydor [G] 423232 Django Reinhardt And Dickie Wells In Paris
(same as HMV [It] QCLP12019)

Polydor [G] *LPHM46451* *Django Reinhardt – Europe's Greatest Contribution To Jazz*

Prestige [A] 7593 Dickie Wells In Paris 1937
(same as HMV [It] QCLP12019)

Prestige [A] 7614 First Recordings!
080; 081; 082; 110; 125; 126; 127; 128; 141; 142; 153; 155

Prestige [A] 7633 Django Reinhardt and the American Jazz Giants
098; 100; 102; 103; 190; 191; 193; 255; 256; 257; 258; 350; 351; 352

Pye [Au] ILP1007
(same as Reprise [Ar] 12475)

Pye [Au] ILP1032 One More Time (*anthology*)
677

Pye – Golden Guinea [E] *GGL0306* *Two Giants Of Jazz*
(one side only – reverse by Sidney Bechet)

RCA [Au] L 101245 Djangology
(same as RCA 430.392)

RCA [A] LEJ-10 The RCA-Victor Encyclopaedia of Recorded Jazz Vol. 10 (*anthology*)
239

RCA [A] LPM1100 Django Reinhardt – In Memoriam 1908–1954 (*sic*)
(same as RCA [N] EPC1100-1, 2, 3)

RCA [A] LPM2077
(same as RCA [F] 430336]

RCA [A] LPM2319 Djangology 1961
(same as RCA 430.392); (also issued in France as LPM2319)

RCA [It] LPM10043 La Storia del Jazz-Swing (*anthology*)
255

RCA [E] NL70671 The Indispensable Django Reinhardt 1986
772; 776; 780; 781; 784; 785; 787;788; 790; 797; 798; 799; 801; 803; 804; 806; 807; 810; 816; 819; 822; 847; 849; 860; 862;

RCA (Jazz Tribune) NL70929 The Indispensable Django Reinhardt 1987
(same as NL70671)

RCA [E] NL90448 Djangology '49 1990
(same as NL70671)

RCA [E] RD27236 Djangology
(same as RCA [F]430392)

RCA [F] 430.336 Newly Discovered Masters by Django Reinhardt
846; 847; 848; 849; 851; 853; 854; 855; 857; 860; 861; 862

RCA [F] 430.392 Djangology
779; 781; 785; 787; 790; 793; 797; 799; 802; 803; 806; 808

RCA [F] 730.596 Django Reinhardt and le Quintette du Hot Club de France Vol. 1 1950
(Black and White series Vol. 11)
(same as RCA 430.336)

RCA [F] 731.042 Django Reinhardt and le Quintette du Hot Club de France Vol. 2 1949
(Black and White series Vol. 32)
(same as RCA 430.392)

RCA [F] 731.069 Django Reinhardt and le Quintette du Hot Club de France Vol. 3 1949–50
772; 784; 788; 798; 801; 804; 807; 810; 858

RCA [F] 731.769

RCA 7055 [3-LP BOX]

Realm [E] RM184 The Incomparable Django Reinhardt
(same as Barclay 84090)

Realm [E] RM213 Django 1964
(same as CBS 52213 and Oriole MG10019)

Regal [E] REG2022 En Avril à Paris – Charles Trenet (*anthology*)
519

Reprise [A] R6075 The Immortal Django Reinhardt
(also issued in electronic stereo as R96075 and in mono in Argentina as Reprise 12.475)

Riviera [F] RLP6575
(same as Clef MGC516 (*sic*))

Saga [E] ERO8034 The Blues (*anthology*)
675

Sutton [A] SU274 Django Reinhardt and his Jazz Guitar
681; 688; 689; 690; 691; 706; 718; 759; 761; 762
(also issued in electronic stereo as SSU 274; all tracks grossly mistitled)

Swaggie [Au] S1251 Django Rhythm 1935–37
(same as HMV CLP1890)

Swaggie [Au] S1252 Django Swing 1937–39 undated
(same as HMV CLP1907)
(also issued on Swaggie as 'Django Swing – Jazz From The Swinging Years' bearing the same catalogue number)

Swaggie [Au] S1305 QHCF VOL. 1 undated
217; 219; 220; 221; 223; 224; 226; 227; 228; 233; 234; 235; 236; 237

Swaggie [Au] S1306 QHCF VOL. 2 undated
238; 239; 240; 241; 242; 243; 244; 245; 246; 247; 248; 249; 250; 252

Swaggie [Au] S1307 Bill Coleman in Paris Vol. 1 1935–38 1981
190; 193

Swaggie [Au] S1308 Bill Coleman in Paris Vol. 2 1936–38 1981
292; 293; 294

Swaggie [Au] S1370 Swingin' With Django 1976
295; 296; 297; 301; 302; 303; 304; 305; 306; 307; 310; 311; 312; 313

Swaggie [Au] S1371 Reinhardt and Grappelli '47–'49 1976
725; 726; 727; 751; 752; 753; 754; 755; 756; 757; 768; 770; 771; 773; 775

Swaggie [Au] S1389 QHCF 1946–47 1980
603; 604; 605; 606; 615; 616; 617; 625; 626; 627; 628; 629; 723; 724

Swaggie [Au] S1390 In Rome Vol. 1 1980
777; 778; 782; 786; 792; 808; 811; 816; 817; 818; 819; 826; 827; 828

Swaggie [Au] S1391 In Rome Vol. 2 1980
783; 791; 795; 805; 813; 816; 831; 832; 833; 834

Swaggie [Au] S1399 1936–37 1981
212; 214; 216; 253; 254; 279; 280; 283; 284; 285; 286; 287; 315; 316; 317; 318

Swaggie [Au] S1400 1937–39 1983
319; 320; 321; 322; 330; 364; 366; 368; 370; 433; 434; 435; 436; 437; 438; 439

Swaggie [Au] S1401 1943–50 1983
557; 558; 559; 789; 814; 820; 821; 822; 824; 825; 829; 830

Swing [F] LDM30069 Memorial Django Reinhardt
(same as Vogue CLVLX 412)

Swing [F] 8045 Eddie South In Paris (anthology)

Swing [F] 8420267
020; 075; 106; 183; 212; 214; 216; 217; 219; 220; 221; 223; 224; 226; 227; 228; 229; 230; 233; 234; 235; 236; 237; 238; 239; 240; 241; 242; 243; 244; 246; 247; 248; 249; 250; 252; 253; 254; 255; 256; 257; 258; 268; 270; 272; 273; 279; 280; 281; 285; 286; 287; 289; 290; 292; 294; 296; 297; 301; 302; 303; 305; 306; 307; 311; 315; 316; 318; 319; 322; 323; 325; 330; 331; 333; 350; 352; 413; 414; 416; 418; 420; 433; 434; 435; 436; 438; 439; 471; 475; 492; 493; 629

Topline [E] Crazy Rhythm

Verve [A] MGV8015 Jazz from Paris – Dizzy and Django
(same as Clef MGC516 for the Django performances)
(also issued in Australia under the same catalogue number)

Verve [E] 8451504 Jazz Club Mainstream – Guitar and Bass 1991

Victor – see RCA Victor, *qv*

Vogue VG405 NEC Plus Ultra Vol. 2
837; 838; 839; 840; 841; 842; 843; 844; 845

Vogue CDF03 [4-LP BOX]

Vogue [F] CLD745 Django 1934
(same as Oriole MG10019 plus 108; 109; 110; 111; 114)

Vogue [F] CLVLX313 Django, Mon Frère
(same as Marble Arch 1234 plus 688; 707; 715)

Vogue [F] CLVLX342 (*anthology*)
676

Vogue [F] CLVLX412 Django Reinhardt
672; 676; 677; 678; 682; 695; 696; 697; 708; 719; 720; 721; 722

Vogue [F] COF 03 Coffret Souvenir [5-LP box]
080; 081; 082; 083; 125; 127; 143; 144; 154; 155; 156; 157; 631; 633; 634; 672; 675; 676; 677; 678; 679; 680; 681; 682; 683; 684; 685; 686; 687; 688; 689; 690; 691; 692; 693; 694; 696; 707; 708; 709; 710; 711; 717; 718; 719; 720; 721; 722; 728; 729; 731; 732; 733; 734; 735; 739; 880

Vogue [F] DP05 Le Grande Parade du Django Reinhardt
080; 125; 143; 156; 157; 645; 675; 679; 683; 689; 693; 694; 695; 697; 711; 717; 719; 722; 728; 731; 732; 734; 739; 740

Vogue [E] LAE12251 Django Reinhardt Memorial
(same as CLVLX 412]

Vogue [E] LD419

Vogue [F] LD 491
683; 684; 687; 689; 691; 692; 693; 694; 728; 729; 631; 732
(same as Reprise R6075)

Vogue [F] LD 610-30 Concert à Bruxelles 1948
(same as Period 1103)

Vogue [F] LD 668-30 Django Reinhardt Memorial
674; 680; 769; 681; 694; 706; 707; 709; 711; 712; 714; 716; 718

Vogue [F] LD 713

Vogue [E] LDE048 Django Reinhardt Quintet

Vogue [E] LDE106 Souvenirs of Django Reinhardt
(same as Swing M33316)

Vogue [It] SLBVG 83007 Il Disco d'Oro di Django Reinhardt
(same as Vogue CLD 745)

Vogue [It] SLBVG 83016 Django Reinhardt – Il Secondo Disco d'Oro
141; 142; 143; 144; 145; 146; 152; 153; 154; 155; 156; 157

Vogue [E] VJD502 Djangology 1935–47 [2-LP set]

Vogue [E] VJD526 Django Reinhardt 1947 [2-LP set]

Vogue [F] 0000315

Vogue [It] 30-034

Vogue [F] 406505 Django and The ATC Band
065; 066; 444; 445; 579; 580; 581; 582; 583; 592; 595; 596; 597; 598; 599; 600; 601; 602; 730; 741; 742; 767

Vogue [F] 500064 The Versatile Giant
064

Vogue [F] 500100
618; 619; 620; 621; 672; 674; 657; 676; 677; 678;

Vogue [F] 500108 1947
685; 694; 696; 697; 698; 706; 707; 709; 712; 714; 715; 717; 720; 721; 722

Vogue [F] 500740
067; 068; 080; 081; 082; 083; 108; 109; 110; 111; 125; 126; 127; 128; 679; 680; 681; 682

Vogue [F] 500740
080; 081; 082; 083; 108; 109; 110; 111; 125; 126; 127; 128

Vogue [F] 500745 Django 1934 – Les Premiers Enregistrements 1972

Vogue [F] 500813 For Collectors Only
683; 684; 685; 686; 687; 689; 690; 691; 692; 693; 728; 729; 731; 732

Vogue [F] 500842 L'Inoubliable, 1947
631; 633; 634; 733; 734; 735; 736; 737; 738

Vogue (Mode) [F] 509031 Le Disque D'or

Vogue [F]	530187	Django 1935
141; 142; 143; 144; 145; 146; 152; 153; 154; 155; 156; 157		
Vogue [F]	530217	Concert de Bruxelles
760; 761; 762; 763; 764; 765; 766		
Vogue [F]	*610-30*	*Concert à Bruxelles 1948*
Vogue [F]	*668-30*	*Django Reinhardt Memorial*
Vogue [F]	*403500842*	
World Record Club [E]	T821	The Legendary Django
World Record Club [E]	SH368	Jean Sablon and Django Reinhardt 1933–35
036; 038; 057; 058; 085; 089; 194; 195		
World Record Club [E] (same as HMV CLP1491)	ST1004	Django Reinhardt and Stephane Grappelly – Together Again
World Record Club [E]	T821	The Legendary Django
Xtra [E] (same as Everest FS–230)	1092	Django Reinhardt

16" 33rpm transcription

Office of War Information	OWI-133	
350		

Compact disc releases

Label — *Catalogue no.* — *Title* — *Date of issue*

AA — **24**

068; 075; 080; 081; 082; 083; 100; 108; 109; 110; 111; 125; 126; 127; 142; 152; 154; 155; 156; 157; 185

ABM — **CD1194** — **Continental** — **1999**

080; 081; 082; 083; 109; 110; 111; 125; 126; 177; 221; 223; 226; 268; 301; 352

Affinity — **AFS10035** — **Swing in Paris 1936–40**

212; 214; 216; 217; 219; 220; 221; 223; 224; 226; 227; 228; 233; 234; 235; 236; 237; 238; 239; 240; 241; 242; 243; 244; 245; 246; 247; 248; 249; 250; 252; 253; 254; 255; 256; 257; 258; 268; 269; 270; 271; 272; 273; 279; 280; 281; 282; 283; 284; 285; 286; 287; 289; 290; 292; 293; 294; 295; 296; 297; 303; 304; 305; 306; 307; 310; 311; 315; 318; 319; 320; 321; 322; 323; 325; 328; 329; 350; 351; 352; 371; 413; 414; 416; 418; 419; 433; 434; 435; 436; 439; 465; 466; 467; 468; 472; 476; 492; 493; 494; 495; 496; 497; 499; 500; 501; 502; 503; 504

ARC — **CASTEL810562** — **Django Reinhardt: Genius of Jazz** — **1998**

143; 157; 217; 224; 244; 257; 258; 273; 301; 413; 459; 492; 493; 502; 510; 516; 531; 551

SOL 507 — **Nuages**

217; 220; 223; 224; 226; 233; 235; 239; 240; 244; 258; 273; 301; 352; 493

SOL 517 — **Hot-Club de France**

125; 126; 128; 143; 154; 155; 156; 157; 221; 234; 393; 404; 441; 442; 443; 610; 611; 613

AVID — **AMSC648** — **The Quintette of the Hot Club of France** — **1999**

125; 126; 188; 189; 214; 216; 217; 220; 224; 226; 233; 236; 237; 238; 240; 243; 246; 247; 248; 249; 250; 337; 340; 343; 344; 345; 346; 373; 375; 377; 384; 387; 390; 393; 395; 399; 404; 405; 409; 441; 442; 628

Beat Goes On — **BGOCD198** — **The Art Of; Unforgettable** — **1993**

233; 236; 237; 238; 239; 240; 241; 242; 243; 246; 247; 250; 779; 789; 790; 816; 817; 818; 819; 820; 821; 822; 824; 825; 829; 830; 850; 852; 856; 859; 863; 864; 865; 866; 867; 868; 869; 873; 874

	BGOCD249	**Django and His American Friends 1–2**	

100; 102; 103; 190; 191; 192; 255; 256; 256; 257; 258; 268; 270; 272; 273; 281; 282; 289; 290; 292; 293; 296; 330; 350; 352; 413; 414; 416; 418; 419

	BGOCD366	**Django; Live In Rome 49–50**	**1998**

244; 249; 254; 279; 280; 283; 284; 286; 301; 302; 305; 306; 459; 824; 825; 829; 830; 859

Best Music	**BSTCD9101**	**King of the Gypsies**	**1992**

223; 224; 226; 227; 233; 234; 235; 238; 239; 240; 244

Castle	**PIESD233**	**Guitar Genius**	**2000**

100; 109; 174; 252; 253; 254; 256; 270; 279; 280; 294; 315; 352; 391; 413; 435; 466; 473; 492; 493; 573; 588

Castle Collector	**MACCD132**	**Django Reinhardt and Stéphane Grappelli**	**1995**

080; 082; 128; 157; 174; 185; 189; 233; 234; 236; 244; 248; 372; 375; 409; 611

Charly	**CDDIG 12**	**Swing de Paris**	

080; 081; 083; 100; 111; 142; 145; 152; 155; 157; 212; 216; 217; 220; 221; 223; 224; 226; 228; 240; 241; 248; 249; 252; 253; 254; 255; 256; 257; 258; 268; 270; 272; 273; 279; 280; 281; 283; 285; 289; 290; 292; 293; 294; 296; 297; 301; 302; 307; 311; 315; 316; 317; 322; 330; 352; 413; 414; 416; 418; 419; 435; 439; 460; 467; 468; 473; 492; 493; 494; 499; 501; 502; 503; 504; 533; 534; 551; 553; 556; 559

Classics	**602**	**Coleman Hawkins Vol. 2**	**1991**

098; 100; 102; 103

	703	**Chronological 1934–35**	**1993**

051; 061; 064; 065; 066; 067; 068; 074; 075; 076; 077; 078; 079; 080; 081; 082; 083; 106; 107; 112; 113

	707	**Eddie South Vol. 1 1927–37**	**1993**

281; 282; 283; 284; 295; 296; 297

	708	**Stéphane Grappelly 1935–40**	**1993**

174; 176; 177; 185; 186; 187; 188; 189; 286; 318; 319; 344; 345; 346; 347; 437; 438

	714	**Alix Combelle Vol. 1**	**1993**

152; 153; 451; 452; 453; 454; 455; 456; 477; 478; 479; 480; 481

	727	**Chronological 1935**	**1993**

108; 109; 110; 111; 125; 126; 127; 128; 135; 136; 137; 138; 139; 140; 141; 142; 143; 144; 145; 146; 154; 155

737 **Eddie South Vol. 2** **1993**

303; 304

739 **Chronological 1935–36** **1993**

156; 157; 190; 191; 193; 206; 207; 208; 209; 210; 211; 212; 214; 216; 217; 219; 220; 221; 223; 224; 226; 227; 228

748 **Chronological 1937** **1994**

233; 234; 235; 236; 237; 238; 239; 240; 241; 242; 243; 244; 245; 246; 247; 248; 249; 250; 252; 253; 274; 275

751 **Alix Combelle Vol. 2 1940–41** **1994**

505; 506; 507; 508

762 **Chronological 1937 Vol. 2** **1994**

277; 278; 279; 280; 301; 302; 305; 306; 307; 310; 311; 312; 313; 314; 315; 316; 317; 320; 321; 322; 323; 325; 328

777 **Chronological 1937–38** **1994**

329; 330; 335; 336; 337; 339; 340; 341; 342; 343; 348; 349; 353; 354; 355; 356; 357; 364; 366; 368; 370; 372; 373

793 **Chronological 1938–39** **1994**

377; 379; 384; 385; 386; 387; 389; 390; 391; 393; 396; 398; 399; 401; 404; 405; 408; 409; 413; 414; 416; 418; 419

813 **Chronological 1939–40** **1995**

422; 423; 424; 425; 426; 427; 428; 429; 430; 431; 433; 434; 435; 436; 439; 440; 441; 442; 443; 457; 458; 460

831 **Chronological 1940** **1995**

461; 462; 463; 464; 465; 466; 467; 468; 471; 472; 473; 474; 475; 476; 482; 483; 484; 485; 486; 487; 489; 490; 491

852 **Chronological 1940–41** **1995**

492; 493; 494; 495; 496; 497; 498; 499; 500; 501; 502; 503; 504; 509; 510; 511; 512; 513; 514; 517; 519

877 **Chronological 1941–42** **1996**

520; 521; 522; 523; 524; 525; 527; 529; 530; 535; 536; 537; 538; 539; 540; 541; 542; 543; 544; 545

905 **Chronological 1942–43** **1996**

546; 547; 548; 549; 550; 551; 552; 553; 554; 556; 557; 558; 559; 560; 561; 562; 563; 564; 565; 566; 567

945 — Chronological 1944–46 — 1997

568; 568A; 569; 570; 572; 573; 574; 575; 576; 584; 586; 588; 590; 603; 604; 605; 606; 608; 610; 611; 613; 614; 615; 616; 617

1001 — Chronological 1947 — 1998

625; 626; 627; 628; 629; 630; 631; 632; 633; 634; 635; 636; 641; 642; 645; 649; 651; 652; 653; 654; 657; 658; 659; 660

1046 — Chronological

661; 663; 664; 665; 668; 669; 670; 671; 678; 686; 699; 700; 601; 702; 703; 704; 705; 723; 724

Crown Collection — CWNCD2010 — The Quintette of the Hot Club of France — 1995

174; 217; 221; 233; 235; 237; 239; 240; 244; 301; 305; 385; 398; 399; 493

Digimode — CO3506 — Best Recordings No. 1 — 1997

080; 156; 176; 189; 190; 217; 223; 224; 236; 239; 337; 339; 385; 390; 399; 441; 501

CO3507 — Best Recordings No. 2 — 1997

157; 185; 212; 214; 216; 228; 233; 235; 237; 240; 244; 246; 247; 249; 301; 335; 336; 341; 344

DRG — Brussels 1947

636; 637; 638; 641; 642; 644; 645; 646; 649; 890; 891; 892; 893; 894; 895; 896; 897; 898; 903; 904; 905; 906; 918; 919; 920; 921

8493 — Django with his American Friends — 1998

098; 100; 102; 103; 190; 191; 193; 212; 217; 224; 250; 251; 252; 253; 254; 255; 256; 258; 268; 269; 270; 272; 273; 281; 283; 284; 285; 289; 290; 292; 293; 294; 296; 303; 304; 350; 352; 364; 366; 368; 413; 414; 416; 418; 419; 446; 588

Eagle — EABCD71 — The Masters: Django Reinhardt — 1997

080; 081; 156; 224; 241; 254; 255; 256; 257; 270; 279; 283; 290; 302; 311; 330; 345; 404

Empress — RAJCD808 — Plays The Great Standards — 1993

082; 214; 217; 220; 221; 224; 226; 233; 235; 237; 239; 241; 242; 243; 255; 256; 257; 258; 279; 501; 504

Flapper — PASTCD9738 — Django Reinhardt and Stéphane Grappelly — 1991

212; 214; 216; 217; 220; 221; 223; 226; 227; 228; 233; 235; 236; 237; 238; 239; 240; 246; 247; 248; 249

	PASTCD9792	**Django Reinhardt and Friends**	**1992**

098; 102; 103; 190; 315; 316; 494; 499; 501; 502

Fremeaux (2-CD sets)	**FA301**	**Presentation Stomp 1928–34**	**1996**

001; 002; 003; 004; 005; 006; 007; 008; 009; 010; 011; 012; 013; 104; 015; 018; 019; 020; 021; 023; 025; 027; 029; 030; 031; 032; 033; 036; 037; 038; 042; 044; 045; 046; 047; 049; 050; 051; 053; 055

	FA302	**I Saw Stars 1934–35**	**1996**

057; 058; 059; 060; 061; 064; 065; 066; 067; 068; 069; 070; 072; 073; 074; 075; 076; 077; 078; 079; 080; 081; 082; 083; 085; 088; 089; 092; 093; 094; 096; 097; 098; 100; 102; 103; 104; 105; 106; 107

	FA303	**Djangology 1935**	**1996**

108; 109; 110; 111; 112; 113; 118; 122; 123; 124; 125; 126; 127; 128; 129; 130; 131; 132; 133; 134; 135; 136; 137; 138; 139; 140; 141; 142; 143; 144; 145; 146; 152; 153; 154; 155; 156; 157; 158; 159; 173

	FA304	**Magic Strings 1935**	**1996**

163; 167; 168; 174; 176; 177; 179; 180; 181; 183; 185; 186; 187; 188; 189; 190; 191; 192; 193; 194; 195; 196; 197; 198; 199; 200; 201; 202; 203; 204; 205; 206; 207; 208; 209; 210; 211; 212

	FA305	**Mystery Pacific 1936–37**	**1997**

214; 216; 217; 219; 220; 221; 223; 224; 226; 227; 228; 229; 230; 231; 232; 233; 234; 235; 236; 237; 238; 239; 240; 241; 242; 243; 244; 245; 246; 247; 248; 249; 250; 251; 252; 253; 254; 255; 256; 257; 258; 259; 260; 261; 262; 283; 264; 265; 266; 267

	FA306	**Swinging With Django 1937**	**1997**

268; 269; 270; 271; 272; 273; 274; 275; 277; 278; 279; 280; 281; 282; 283; 284; 285; 286; 287; 288; 289; 290; 291; 292; 293; 294; 295; 296; 297; 298; 299; 300; 301; 302; 303; 304; 305; 306; 307; 308; 309; 310; 311; 312; 313; 314

	FA307	**Orchestral Swing 1937–38**	**1997**

315; 316; 317; 318; 319; 320; 321; 322; 323; 325; 328; 329; 330; 331; 335; 336; 337; 338; 339; 340; 341; 342; 343; 344; 345; 346; 347; 348; 349; 350; 351; 352; 353; 354; 355; 356; 357; 358; 359

	FA308	**Swing From Paris 1938–39**	**1998**

360; 361; 362; 363; 364; 366; 367; 368; 370; 371; 372; 373; 375; 377; 379; 381; 382; 383; 384; 385; 386; 387; 388; 389; 390; 391; 392; 393; 394; 395; 396; 398; 399; 401; 402; 403; 404; 405; 408; 409; 410; 412

FA309	**H C Q Strut 1939–40**	**1998**

413; 414; 416; 418; 419; 422; 423; 424; 425; 426; 427; 428; 429; 430; 431; 432; 433; 434; 435; 436; 437; 438; 439; 440; 441; 442; 443; 444; 445; 446; 447; 448; 449; 450; 451; 452; 453; 454; 455; 456; 457; 458; 459; 460

FA310	**Nuages 1940**	**1999**

461; 462; 463; 464; 465; 466; 467; 468; 469; 470; 471; 472; 473; 474; 475; 476; 477; 478; 479; 480; 481; 482; 483; 484; 485; 486; 487; 489; 490; 491; 492; 493; 494; 495; 496; 497; 498; 499; 500; 501; 502; 503; 504; 509; 510 (*sic*)

FA311	**Swing '42 1940–42**	**1999**

505; 506; 507; 508 (*sic*); 511; 512; 513; 514; 515; 516; 517; 518; 519; 520; 521; 522; 523; 524; 525; 526; 527; 529; 531; 533; 534; 535; 536; 537; 538; 539; 540; 541; 542; 543; 544; 545; 546; 547; 548; 549; 550

FA312	**Manoir De Mes Rêves 1943–45**	**1999**

551; 552; 553; 554; 556; 557; 558; 559; 560; 561; 562; 563; 564; 565; 566; 567; 568; 568A; 569; 570; 571; 572; 573; 574; 575; 576; 577; 578; 579; 580; 581; 582; 583; 584; 585; 586; 588; 590; 592; 593; 594; 595; 596; 597; 598; 599; 600; 601; 602

FA313	**Echoes of France 1946–47**	**2000**

603; 604; 605; 606; 608; 610; 611; 612; 613; 614; 615; 616; 617; 618; 619; 620; 621; 622; 623; 624; 625; 636; 627; 628; 629; 630; 631; 632; 633; 634; 636; 637; 638; 7641; 642; 644; 645; 646; 649; 651; 652; 654 (*sic*)

FA314	**Django's Dream 1947**	**2001**

653 (*sic*); 657; 658; 659; 660; 661; 663; 664; 665; 668; 669; 670; 671; 672; 673; 674; 675; 676; 677; 678; 679; 680; 681; 682; 683; 684; 685; 686; 687; 688; 689; 690; 691; 692; 693; 694; 695; 696; 697; 698

FA315	**Gypsy With A Song 1947**	**2001**

699; 700; 701; 702; 703; 704; 705; 706; 707; 708; 709; 710; 711; 712; 713; 714; 715; 716; 717; 718; 719; 720; 721; 722; 723; 724; 725; 726; 727; 728; 729; 730; 731; 732; 733; 734; 737; 783 (*sic*)

FA316	**Festival '48**	**2002**

739; 740; 741; 742; 742a; 748; 749; 750; 751; 752; 753; 754; 755; 756; 757; 757a; 757b; 757c; 760; 761; 762; 764; 765; 766; 767; 768; 769; 770; 771; 772; 773; 774; 775; 776; 777; 778; 779; 780

FA317

FA318

FA319

	FA320		
Frog	**DGF50**	**The Swing Sessions Vol. 1**	**2001**

234; 244; 254; 255; 256; 257; 258; 268; 269; 270; 271; 272; 263; 274; 275; 277; 278; 279; 280; 281; 282; 283; 284; 285; 286; 287

Frog	**DGF52**	**The Swing Sessions Vol. 2**	**2002**

289; 290; 291; 292; 293; 294; 295; 296; 297; 298; 299; 300; 301; 302; 303; 304; 305; 306; 307; 308; 309; 310; 311

Gallerie	**GALE419**	**A Portrait of Jean Sablon**	**1997**

027; 029; 037; 038; 042; 057; 085; 089; 129; 182; 183; 195

	GALE435	**A Portrait of Stéphane Grappelli**	

143; 144; 154; 156; 174; 176; 177; 186; 187; 188; 189; 226; 233; 237; 239; 243; 247; 254; 287; 304; 318; 319; 343; 346; 347; 373; 375; 438; 604; 611; 627; 726

Habana	**111200**	**The Triumphs of Jazz**	**2000**

080; 125; 236; 245; 256; 257; 279; 294; 301; 302; 316; 339; 391; 433; 441; 443; 493; 501; 551; 627; 661

Happy Days	**CDHD165**	**Swing from Paris**	

100; 154; 156; 157; 217; 221; 226; 228; 237; 243; 246; 247; 337; 343; 344; 345; 375; 377; 379; 409; 502

	CDHD206	**Swinging with Django**	**1993**

128; 174; 187; 216; 220; 235; 248; 249; 301; 305; 306; 355; 336; 339; 340; 372; 385; 393; 396; 398; 399; 401; 408; 426

	CDHD230	**The Hawk Takes Flight**	**1993**

098; 100; 102; 103; 255; 256; 257; 258

	CDHD234	**Django!**	**1994**

082; 125; 142; 143; 156; 176; 185; 186; 188; 233; 234; 236; 235; 240; 243; 244; 252; 317; 364; 368; 435

Iris Musique	**3001 845**	**Gypsy Jazz School – Django's Legacy**	**2002**

845a; 877a

Jass	**JA628**		

579; 580; 581; 582; 583; 592; 593; 596; 597; 598; 600; 601; 602

Jazz Collection	**CTPCD05**	**That's Jazz**	

176; 233; 234; 236; 237; 238; 239; 240; 242; 244; 246; 247; 248; 249; 250

	Oro 74	**Django Reinhardt**	

233; 234; 235; 236; 237; 239; 240; 242; 244; 246; 247; 249; 250

Jazz Hour	**JHR73509**	**I Got Rhythm**	**1999**

220; 221; 223; 224; 226; 233; 234; 235; 239; 240; 244; 256; 258; 268; 270; 352; 399

Jazzterdays	**JTD102415**	**Are You In The Mood?**	

212; 214; 216; 217; 219; 220; 221; 223; 224; 226; 227; 228; 235; 236; 237; 238; 239; 240; 241; 243; 244

Jazztime	**7891032**		

768; 769; 770; 771; 773; 813; 814

	8274472		

775; 777; 778; 782; 783; 786; 789; 791; 792; 794; 795; 797; 798; 799; 801; 802; 803; 804; 805; 808; 811; 815; 819; 820; 826; 850; 859

JSP	**341**	**The Chronological Django Reinhardt Vol. 1**	**1992**

067; 068; 080; 081; 082; 083; 108; 109; 110; 111; 125; 126; 127; 128; 141; 142; 143; 144; 145; 146; 152; 153; 154; 155; 156; 157

	342	**The Chronological Django Reinhardt Vol. 2**	**1993**

335; 336; 337; 338; 339; 340; 341; 342; 343; 344; 345; 346; 347; 384; 385; 386; 387; 388; 389; 390; 391; 392; 440; 441; 442; 443

	343	**The Chronological Django Reinhardt Vol. 3**	

372; 373; 375; 377; 379; 393; 394; 395; 396; 398; 399; 401; 402; 403; 404; 405; 408; 409; 410; 422; 423; 424; 425; 426

	344	**The Chronological Django Reinhardt Vol. 4**	

098; 100; 102; 103; 174; 176; 177; 185; 186; 187; 188; 189; 212; 214; 216; 217; 219; 220; 221; 223; 224; 226; 227; 228

	349	**The Chronological Django Reinhardt Vol. 5**	

190; 191; 193; 233; 234; 235; 236; 237; 238; 239; 240; 241; 242; 243; 244; 245; 246; 247; 248; 2459; 250; 252; 253; 254

	904	**Paris and London 1937–1948**	

251; 279; 280; 298; 299; 301; 302; 305; 306; 307; 308; 309; 310; 311; 315; 318; 319; 320; 321; 433; 434; 435; 436; 437; 438; 439; 471; 472; 473; 474; 475; 476;

492; 493; 494; 495; 496; 497; 498; 499; 500; 501; 502; 503; 504; 516; 522; 523; 524; 526; 533; 534; 551; 552; 553; 554; 556; 557; 558; 559; 603; 604; 605; 606; 614; 615; 616; 617; 625; 626; 627; 628; 629; 723; 724; 725; 726; 727; 751; 752; 753; 754; 755; 756; 757

Kaz	**EUKCD913**	**Django Reinhardt and Stéphane Grappelly**	**1994**

080; 082; 100; 128; 154; 157; 174; 185; 187; 189; 233; 234; 235; 244; 248; 372; 375; 379; 398; 399; 409; 435; 493

Living Era	**CDAJA5138**	**Django Reinhardt and Stéphane Grappelli**	

080; 081; 082; 083; 100; 110; 111; 125; 126; 128; 142; 155; 157; 221; 228; 240; 242; 391

	CDAJA5267	**Quintessential Django Reinhardt and Stéphane Grappelly**	**1998**

080; 082; 083; 110; 155; 157; 174; 176; 177; 217; 221; 234; 235; 243; 252; 301; 335; 336; 337; 341; 375; 435; 493

Magic Music	**TMM22**	**Stéphane Grappelli; Django Reinhardt**	**1994**

068; 075; 080; 081; 082; 100; 108; 109; 111; 125; 126; 127; 128; 142; 143; 144; 152; 154; 157; 250; 279

Milan	**74321308652**	**Jazz au Masculin**	

080; 125; 186; 212; 214; 233; 235; 243; 244; 245; 246; 247; 248; 249; 250; 251; 252; 253; 254; 283; 284; 285; 286; 287; 301; 303; 305; 306; 318; 319; 335; 337; 342; 373; 377; 393; 438

Mosiac	**MD6–190**	**The Complete QHCF HMV; Swing Recordings, 1936–48**	**1998**

212; 214; 216; 217; 219; 220; 221; 223; 224; 226; 227; 228; 233; 234; 235; 236; 237; 238; 239; 240; 241; 242; 243; 244; 245; 246; 247; 248; 249; 250; 251; 252; 253; 254; 279; 280; 298; 299; 301; 302; 305; 306; 307; 308; 309; 310; 311; 315; 318; 319; 320; 321; 433; 434; 435; 436; 437; 438; 439; 471; 472; 473; 474; 475; 476; 492; 493; 495; 496; 498; 499; 500; 501; 502; 503; 504; 516; 522; 523; 524; 533; 534; 551; 552; 553; 554; 556; 557; 558; 559; 603; 604; 606; 606; 614; 615; 616; 617; 625; 626; 627; 628; 629; 723; 724; 725; 726; 727; 751; 752; 753; 754; 755; 756; 757

Music	**CD6048**	**Crazy Rhythm**	**1996**

080; 081; 142; 152; 156; 157; 220; 221; 224; 256; 257; 258; 268; 270; 273; 279; 283; 301; 335

Musidisc **MU403222**

636; 637; 638; 641; 649; 890; 891; 892; 893; 894; 895; 896; 897; 903; 905; 906; 918; 919; 920; 921

Old Bean **DOLD12** **In Paris 1935–36**

154; 155; 156; 157; 174; 176; 177; 185; 186; 187; 188; 189; 216; 217; 221; 223; 226; 227; 228

QED **QED71** **Djangology** **1996**

080; 081; 082; 083; 100; 108; 109; 110; 111; 125; 126; 127; 128; 142; 143; 144; 152; 154; 155; 156; 157; 174; 185

RCA **ND709292**

772; 774; 776; 779; 780; 781; 784; 785; 786; 787; 788; 790; 793; 797; 798; 799; 801; 802; 803; 804; 806; 807; 809; 810; 816; 819; 822; 846; 847; 848; 849; 851; 853; 854; 855; 857; 858; 860; 861; 862

Recall **SMDCD307** **Djangology**

080; 081; 082; 157; 214; 220; 223; 228; 233; 234; 235; 237; 239; 240; 244; 249; 250; 279; 301; 337; 339; 346; 398; 433; 439; 471; 492; 501; 503; 504; 533; 557; 604; 606; 685

Retro **RZCD7002** **The Gold Collection** **1997**

083; 110; 125; 126; 127; 128; 144; 155; 174; 176; 177; 185; 186; 187; 188; 189; 216; 219; 220; 227; 233; 234; 237; 238; 239; 240; 241; 242; 243

Swing **CDSW8403** **Coleman Hawkins and Benny Carter** **1985**

098; 100; 102; 103; 255; 256; 257; 258; 350; 352

CDSW8413 **Djangologie**

212; 214; 216; 217; 219; 220; 221; 223; 224; 226; 227; 228; 233; 234; 235; 236; 237; 238; 239; 240; 241; 242; 243; 244; 246; 247; 248; 249; 250; 252; 253; 254; 255; 256; 257; 258; 268; 270; 272; 283; 279; 280; 282; 283

CDSW8419 **Rare Django**

002; 003; 014; 020; 027; 029; 038; 055; 067; 068; 075; 092; 094; 106; 182; 183; 220; 229; 277; 278; 219; 323; 331; 353; 354; 355; 356; 357

CDSW8426

284; 285; 296; 297; 301; 302; 303; 305; 306; 307; 311; 315; 316; 318; 319; 322; 323; 325; 350; 352; 413; 414; 416; 418; 419; 433; 434; 435; 436; 438; 492; 493

Verve **835418–1**

651; 652; 654; 657; 658; 659; 660; 661; 663; 664; 665; 668; 669; 670; 671

835418–2

699; 700; 701; 702; 703; 704; 705; 744; 748; 910; 911; 912; 913; 914; 915; 916; 917

Vogue **668003**

081; 082; 083; 109; 125; 126; 141; 142; 143; 145; 146; 154; 156; 579; 580; 581; 582; 583; 618; 619; 672; 673; 647; 676; 677; 678; 679; 680; 681; 682; 683; 685; 687; 688; 690; 691; 693; 694; 695; 706; 709; 713; 614; 716; 717; 718; 720; 722; 837; 838; 839; 840; 841

22E6005

596; 597; 598; 600; 601; 602; 618; 619; 620; 621; 630; 631; 633; 634; 679; 680; 681; 682; 683; 684; 685; 686; 687; 688

228E6006

672; 673; 674; 675; 676; 677; 678; 679; 680; 681; 682; 683; 684; 685; 686; 687; 688

228E6007

689; 690; 691; 692; 693; 694; 695; 696; 697; 698; 706; 707; 708; 709; 710; 712; 713; 714

228E6008

715; 716; 717; 718; 719; 720; 721; 722; 728; 729; 730; 731; 732; 733; 734; 735; 736

228E6009

736; 737; 738; 739; 740; 741; 742; 758; 759; 760; 761; 762; 763; 764; 765; 766; 767; 737; 738; 739; 740; 741; 742

228E6010

837; 838; 839; 840; 841; 842; 843; 844; 845; 879; 880; 881; 882; 883; 884; 885; 886; 887

Cassette releases

Cat. No.	*Equivalent CD*	*Equivalent LP*	*Pub. date*
Ace of Clubs KACC1158	AH1158		
Avid AVM533	AVC533		
BBC ZCF680	BBCCD680		
BBC ZCF698	BBCCD698	ZBBC2167	1998
Decca KECC2051	ECM2051		1970
Galaxy MCGAL46	GAL46		
Happy Days MCHD165	CDHD165		1989
Happy Days MCHD206	CDHD206		
Happy Days MCHD230	CDHD230		
Happy Days MCHD234	CDHD234		
Jazz Café 74321214494	74321214492 (*sic*)		
Jazz Collection ORT82	ORO82		
Jazz Hour			1994
Jazz Time 64035-4			1994
Kaz EUKMC913	EUKCD913		
Living Era ZCAJA5054	CDAJA5054		
Living Era ZCAJA5117	CDAJA5117		
Living Era ZCAJA5267	CDAJA5267		
Old Bean COLD12	DOLD12	OLD12	
Swing 8405		8405	

Compact disc releases by associated and contextual artists

This file is not exhaustive, and is intended only as a general guide to the music of those artists who were, in one way or another, contemporaries of Django Reinhardt, or who worked either within the same time frames and geographical areas or within the same fields as Django.

Alemán, Oscar

Acoustic Disc ACD29	1938–57 [2-CD]
Fremeaux FA020	1928–43

Baker, Josephine

Fremeaux FA156	1927–39 [2-CD]

Briggs, Arthur

EPM 158.472	1927–33

Carter, Benny

Classics 530	1933–36
541	1936
552	1937–39
579	1939–40
631	1940–41
923	1943–46

Coleman, Bill

Classics 764	1936–38

Combelle, Alix

Classics 714	1935–40
751	1940–41
782	1942–43

Grappelli, Stéphane

Classics 708	1935–40
779	1941–43
EPM 159222	1933–47 (includes titles with Gregor et ses Gregorians)

Hawkins, Coleman

Classics 587	1929–34
602	1934–37
613	1937–39
634	1939–40
807	1943–44
842	1944

863	1944–45
926	1945
984	1946–47
Fremeaux FA213	1926–44 [2-CD]

Johnson, Freddy

Classics 829	1933–39

Lewis, Willie

Classics 822	1932–36
847	1936–38
880	1941

Normann, Robert

Hot Club Vol. 1 CD40	1938–41
Hot Club Vol. 2 CD41	1941–52

Rico's Creole Band

Harlequin CD41	1931–34

Sablon, Jean

Fremeaux FA062	1933–46 [2-CD]

Salvador, Henri

Fremeaux FA186

South, Eddie

Classics 707	1923–37
Classics 737	1937–41
Frog DGF36	1927–37

Stellio

Fremeaux FA023	1929–31 [2-CD]

Stewart, Rex

Classics 931	1934–46
1016	1946–47

Valvert, Félix

Fremeaux FA188	1944–48

Ventura, Ray

Fremeaux FA5005	1929–38

Viseur, Gus

Fremeaux FA010	1934–42

Warlop, Michel

EPM 158192	1934–38

Wells, Dickie

Classics 937	1929–46

Wilson, Garland

Classics 808	1931–33

Various artists

Accordéon, 1913–1941 1913–41
Disques des Halles DH002

Accordéon Vol. 1
Fremeaux DH002 1913–41 [2-CD]

Accordéon Vol. 2
Fremeaux FA005 1925–42 [2-CD]

Biguine Vol. 1
Fremeaux FA007 1927–40 [2-CD]

Biguine Vol. 2
Fremeaux FA027 1930–43 [2-CD]

Biguines from Martinique
Arhoolie CD7013 1929–51

Buenos Aires to Paris – Argentine Tango Performers in France
Harlequin HQCD99 1924–38
(includes four recordings by Manuel Pizarro)

Cubans in Europe Vol. 1
Harlequin CD37 1929–32

Cubans in Europe Vol. 2
Harlequin CD56 1932–34

Jazz Gitane
EPM 159472 1940s
(includes performances by the Ferret brothers)

Jazz in Argentina 1929–46
Harlequin HQCD152
(includes performances by d'Hellemes Stompers and Louis Vola)

Jazz In Norway 1920–40
Harlequin HJCD9001
(includes performances by Robert Normann)

Jazz Violin
EPM 158002 1926–42

Les Cingles du music-hall
Fremeaux CMH29-43 1929–43
(10 volumes of Parisian music-hall artists)

Music of Martinique
Flyright CD947 1929–50

Swing Caraïbe
Fremeaux FA069 1929–46 [2-CD]

Tango à Paris
Fremeaux FA012 1907–41 [2-CD]

Tziganes
Fremeaux FA006 1910–35

Violon Jazz
Fremeaux FA052

Bibliography

Anonymous, *Discographie du Django Reinhardt*, Disques Vogue, 1951

Antonietto, Alain, *see* Billard, François

Ayeroff, Stan, *Django Reinhardt*, New York, Consolidated Music Publishers, 1978

Billard, François, and Antonietto, Alain, *Django Reinhardt: un géant sur son nuage*, Paris, Editions Lieu Commun, 1993

Balmer, Paul, *Stéphane Grappelli With and Without Django Reinhardt*, London, Sanctuary Publishing, 2003

Brierre, Jean-Dominique, *Le Jazz français*, Paris, Editions Hors Collection, 2000

Charle, François, *The Story of Selmer Maccaferri Guitars*, self-published, 1999 (see 'Useful addresses' for details)

Cherrett, Ted, *The Genius that was Django*, self-published, 1997 (see 'Useful addresses' for details)

Cruickshank, Ian, *Django's Gypsies: The Mystique of Django Reinhardt and his People*, London, Ashley Mark/Hal Leonard Publishing Corporation, 1994

Dadi, Marcel, *Django Reinhardt: 'Swing Guitare'* (scores and tablatures), Paris, Editions Francis-Day

Delaunay, Charles, *Django Reinhardt: Souvenirs*, Paris, Editions Jazz Hot, 1954

—, *Django, mon frère*, Paris, Editions Jazz Hot, 1960 [Also published as: *Django Reinhardt* (trans. Michael James), London, Cassells, 1961; republished as: *Django Reinhardt*, New York, Da Capo Press, 1982; republished in 1988 with a revised discography and expanded photo section as: *Django Reinhardt*, Newcastle-upon-Tyne, Ashley Mark Publishing Company]

—, *Delaunay's Dilemma – de la peinture au jazz*, Mâcon, Editions W, 1985

Dregni, Michael, forthcoming biography of Django Reinhardt, in press

Horricks, Raymond, *Stéphane Grappelly*, Midas Books, 1983

Nabe, Marc-Edouard, *Nuage*, Paris, Edition Le Dilettante, 1993

Neill, Billy, and Gates, E, *Discography Of The Recorded Works Of Django Reinhardt And The Quintette Of The Hot Club of France*, London, Clifford Essex Music, 1944

Panassié, Hughes, *Douze années de jazz*, Paris, Editions Corea, 1946

Peters, Mike, *Django Reinhardt Anthology* (transcriptions and tablature), [place?], Goodman Music Group, 1984

du Peuty, Philippe and Ody, Joëlle, *Django Reinhardt* (Book and CD), Paris, Editions Vade retro, 1997

Ruppli, Michel, with Charles Delaunay, *Swing (discographies vol.1)*, Paris, AFAS, 1989

Schmitz, Alexander, and Maier, Peter, *Django Reinhardt: sein Leben, seine Musik, seine Schallplattern*

von Schultes [Schulteis?], Jochen, *Chronik von Djangos Musik*

Smith, Geoffrey, Stéphane Grappelli – a biography, London, Pavillion Books, 1987

Spautz, Roger, *Django Reinhardt, Mythe et Réalitié*, Luxemburg, Editions RTL, 1983
Tournes, Ludovic, *New Orleans sur Seine*, Paris, Editions Fayard, 1999
Volpe, Harry, *Souvenir Jazz Album*, Miami Beach, FL, n.d.
Williams, Patrick, *Django Reinhardt*, Paris, Editions du Limon, Collection 'Mood Indigo', 1998
Zwerin, Mike, *La Tristesse de St Louis*, London, Quartet Books, 1985

Filmography

1 ***Gregor et ses Gregorians***
Paris, *c.* January 1930
Directed by Roger Lion; production company uncredited
Duration: 3m 30s
Short sound feature including Stéphane Grappelli.

2 ***Clair de Lune***
Cannes, 1932
Starring Claude Dauphin and Blanche Montel
Music by Django Reinhardt, Sylvio Schmidt, Louis Vola
Almost certainly lost.

3 Unknown title (or possibly untitled)
Probably The Hague, Holland, *c.* spring 1937
Produced by Poligon
Duration: 2m
Promotional short featuring Coleman Hawkins (introductory comments and tenor saxophone solo, 'I Wish I Were Twins', accompanied by an unidentified pianist).

4 Unknown title (possibly 'Swing Night')
On stage, The Hague, Holland, Sunday 10 October 1937
Probably produced by Poligon
Duration: 27s (part of a longer film)
Quintette du Hot-Club de France on stage (see entry 288 in main discography).

5 Naples Kissed by Fire (*Naples au baiser du feu*)
France, 1937
Directed by Augusto Genini, produced by Paris Film Productions
Starring Tino Rossi. Django Reinhardt is purported to be involved in this production, but this is currently unconfirmed.

6 ***Feaux de joie***
probably Paris, *c.* 1938, produced by Pathé Baby
Duration: 44m
Musical short featuring Ray Ventura et ses Collégiens; musicians featured include Philippe Brun, Gus DeLoof, Louis Gaste and Guy Paquinet.

7 Jazz Hot
probably Paris, *c.* April/May 1938
Possibly produced by British Gaumont
Duration: 6m 20s

A short promotional film featuring the Quintette du Hot-Club de France (see entries 360 and 361 in main discography). Charles Delaunay remembers there being two further tunes filmed for this session.

8 *Carrefour*
Paris, 1938
Directed by Kurt Bernhardt
Una Mae Carlisle appears, singing 'Darling Je Vous Aime Beaucoup', accompanied by Garland Wilson. Further details unknown.

9 Quintette du Hot-Club de Paris
London, Wednesday 16 August 1939
Produced by BBC Television
See main text for details. Almost certainly lost.

10 Unknown title (probably *Le Bal tabarin*)
Paris, *c.* 1944
Duration: *c.* 15s
'Very short sequence with dancers and dubbed, inconsistent sound. Initially, the band is playing "Night and Day", but when it cuts to Django, the sound jumps and he briefly plays something that is too short to identify for certain. The caption that appears on the screen indicates that it was probably part of a documentary of some sort.' (François Rousseau's website)

11 Time Flies
England, 1944
Directed by Walter Ford; produced by Gainsborough/Gaumont British
Duration: 85m
Guest appearance by Stéphane Grappelli as 'A Troubador' (*sic*) accompanying Evelyn Dall singing 'Ring Along Bells'.

12 Untitled
New York City, late 1946
8mm home movies filmed by American guitarist Harry Volpe. Reportedly shows Harry Volpe walking down a street with Django Reinhardt near the Henry Hudson hotel, Reinhardt and Volpe playing together and eating spaghetti with friends, and Reinhardt leaving for Paris by boat.

13 *Le Village de la colère*
France, 1946
Directed by Raoul André
Soundtrack music arranged by Django Reinhardt and André Hodier.

14 Flamingo Affair
London, *c.* 1947
Stéphane Grappelli is featured playing violin in a brief night-club scene.

15 Untitled
Paris, *c.* 1948

Duration: 15s
Said to have been given to Alain Antionetto by a gypsy. Visual evidence suggests that the second guitar player is Eugène Vées, and that the clarinettist may possibly be Hubert Rostaing. No positive visual identification can be made for the drummer, but it may be Pierre Fouad.

16 Stephane Grappelli and his Quartet
London (Viking Film Studios), 1948
Directed by Horace Shepherd; produced by Inspiration-Ariston Productions
Duration: 12m 50s
Short film featuring Grappelli accompanied by George Shearing (pno), Dave Goldberg (gtr), Coleride Goode (sb), Ray Ellington (dms), performing 'Stephane's Blues', 'Piccadilly Stomp', 'Wendy', 'Sweet Georgia Brown', 'Evelyne' and 'Stephen's Blues' (reprise).

17/18 Stars in Their Eyes
July 1948; produced by BBC Television
See main text for details. Almost certainly lost.

19 *La Fleur de l'âge*
France, 1950/51
Directed by Marcel Carn
Unfinished project.

20 *La Route du bonheur*
France, 1952
Directed by Maurice Labro and Giorgio Simonelli
Distributed by René Chateau Video (*c.* 1992)
Duration of appearance: 1m 40s
Django appears miming to a soundtrack in a scene set in a railway carriage.

21 Django Reinhardt
Paris, 1957
Directed by Paul Paviot; produced by Pavox Films
Duration: 22m
The musicians participating in this recreation of the Quintette Du Hot-Club de France are Stéphane Grappelli, Henri Crolla, Alix Combelle, Hubert Rostaing, André Ekyan, Jarko Jugdino and Joseph Reinhardt. See the website www.silcom.com/~dlp/Passagen/cm.research.html for further details in French. 'An evocation of the life and career of the guitarist Django Reinhardt. Made after his death, the film describes the world of the founder of the Hot Club de France (*sic*) and investigates his Manouches origins.' (from the website description)

22 *Mon pote le gitan*
Probably Paris, 1958
Featuring Joseph Reinhardt and singer Jacques Verieres.

23 Unknown title
Probably Paris, late 1950s–early 1960s
Joseph Reinhardt (gtr) acc. Pierre Romanet (gtr) (1), (vln) (2); (uk, pno, sb, dms) (2), performing (1) Bric-à-brac {2.30}; (2) Sonny Boy {1.48}
The scene takes place in a nightclub; probably part of a longer feature film.

24 Paris Blues
Paris, 1961
Directed by Martin Ritt; produced by Pennebaker Productions
Duration: 99m
A fictional account of two ex-patriot jazz musicians in Paris. Joseph Reinhardt appears, in a non-musical, non-speaking role as a guest at a roof-top party. His appearance is uncredited in the film.

25 Django Reinhardt – Die Legende ein Jazz Gitaristen
c. 1970s
Produced by Balance Film Productions
Duration: 40m
Documentary on the life of Django Reinhardt, featuring interviews with Eddie Barclay, Charles Delaunay, Stéphane Grappelli, Jean Sablon, Dietrich Schulz-Köhn and Louis Vola, and footage of Joseph Reinhardt.

26 Le Jazz Hot – The Story of Jazz in France
Paris and London, 1986
Directed by Philip Speight; produced by Jazzology Productions for BBC-TV
Duration: 90m
Documentary tracing the development of jazz in France. Includes interviews with Stéphane Grappelli, Jacques Bureau, Arthur Briggs, Charles Delaunay, Bill Dillard, Philippe Brun, Tommy Benford, Matelot Ferret. Film of Joseph Reinhardt, including film clips 4, 15 and 20.

27 Django Legacy
Samois-sur-Seine, France, 1990
Directed by John Jeremy; produced by Jazzology Productions for UK Channel 4
Duration: 52m
A documentary focusing on the annual guitar festival at Samois-sur-Seine, and including an interview with Babik Reinhardt.

28 Stephane Grappelli – A Life in the Jazz Century
Paris and London, 2002
Directed by Paul Balmer; produced by Music on Earth Productions
Duration: 120m including extra footage
Biography of Stéphane Grappelli, including extensive interview footage with Grappelli, Coleridge Goode, Diz Dizley, and others. Also includes, complete and unedited, films 1, 4, 7, 9, 15, 16, relevant scenes from films 14 and 20, and the Hot Club reunion section of film 21. See 'Useful addresses' for details of how to obtain this DVD.

Catalogue of photographs

Subject	*Found in*	*Page*
Adler, Larry		
on stage with QHCF at the Alhambra	Delaunay	249
Alemán, Oscar		
various	Acoustic Disc CD ACD-29	
Allier, Pierre		
on stage at L'Amiral	Delaunay	253
Ambrose, Bert		
with Django and Duke Ellington	Delaunay	269
ATC Band		
with Django, 1945, two poses	Delaunay	263
Barclay, Eddie		
with Django at Pierre Gerardot's home	Delaunay	281
Barrelli, Aime		
studio portrait with instrument	FMX FA310	
Belest, Christian		
on stage at L'Amiral	Delaunay	253
Benford, Tommy		
with Eddie South, 1937	FMX FA306	
Bernard, Eddie		
with Django in Germany, post-1945	Delaunay	274
Brenders, Stan		
with Fud Candrix and Jean Omer	FMX FA311	
Breyere, Josse		
studio portrait with instrument, 1930s	FMX FA307	
Briggs, Arthur		
studio portrait with instrument	FMX FA309	
middle trumpet in booklet photo-montage	Classics CD 829	
at Django's funeral, 1953	Cherrett	37
Brun, Philippe		
studio portrait, 1930s	FMX FA307	
studio portrait with instrument	FMX FA309	
with instrument, 1930s	FMX FA310	
Candrix, Fud		
with Stan Brenders and Jean Omer	FMX FA311	

Delaunay, Charles		
on the HCF balcony, Marseilles, 1935	FMX FA308	
with Django and Naguine Reinhardt	FMX FA310	
	Delaunay	232
with Django and AFN band members	FMX FA312	
with Django and record collection	FMX FA313	
	Delaunay	256
at Antwerp Railroad station *c.* 1936	Delaunay	236
with Django and Naguine at Antwerp	Delaunay	249
with Django, playing chess	Delaunay	256
with Django and Warren Bryan, AFN studios, 1945	Delaunay	265
with Django and AFN Orchestra, 1945	Delaunay	266
with Django, Pinkart and others, New York, 1946	Delaunay	271
Ekyan, André		
at Paris Airport, 1934	FMX FA302	
	Delaunay	223
with Django and Stéphane, 1934	FMX FA302	
	Delaunay	220
studio portrait with instrument (1)	FMX FA306	
studio portrait with instrument (2)	FMX FA309	
studio portrait with cigarette	FMX FA310	
at Moulin Rouge, 1941	FMX FA311	
	Delaunay	253
with Django in Rome	Delaunay	281
Ellington, Duke		
at the Hot-Club offices, 1939	FMX FA309	
	Delaunay	250
with Django in USA, 1946 (1)	FMX FA313	
with Django in USA, 1946 (2)	FMX FA313	
Fernandez, Juan		
holding double bass (in booklet photo-montage)	CLASSICS CD829	
Ferreri, Albert		
with Django and AFN band members	FMX FA312	
	Delaunay	266
Ferret, Jean 'Matelot'		
at Samois-sur-Seine, 1987	Cruickshank	40 and 42
Ferret, Pierre		
with Django at La Boîte à Matelots, 1931	Delaunay	218
Fol, Hubert and Raymond		
at Club St-Germain	Delaunay	285

with QHCF, Cambridge Theatre programme 1938	Delaunay	248
at Decca recording studios, London, 1938	FMX FA307	
	Delaunay	243
with Django Reinhardt, Stockholm, 1939	FMX FA308	
	Delaunay	244
on stage with the QHCF, 1939	FMX FA309	
with Reinhardt, both smoking, 1939	FMX FA309	
with Reinhardt, London, 1946	Cruickshank	19
with Reinhardt, 1946	Delaunay	277
with Django in London, 1946	Cherrett	51
with his daughter, Evelyne, 1947	FMX FA315	
at Nice, 1948	FMX FA316	
with Django, Louis Vola at Nice, 1948	Delaunay	280
with Django, 1948	Delaunay	280
in London, 1970	Cherrett	85
Grassett, Roger		
with the Quintette, 1936, two poses	Delaunay	236 and 237
on stage with the QHCF, 1939	FMX FA309	
Guérino		
in 'La Boîte à Matelots', 1932–33	FMX FA301	
Hawkins, Coleman		
Paris, 1935	FMX FA302	
with Freddy Taylor, 1935	FMX FA303	
portrait by Charles Delaunay	FMX FA305	
studio portrait with instrument	FMX FA305	
at Nice, 1948	Delaunay	273
Hodgkiss, Allan		
with Django and Stéphane in London, 1946	Cherrett	51
Hullin, Bernard		
at Club St Germain	Delaunay	285
Johnson, Freddy		
montage of vintage photos	CLASSICS CD829	
Johnson, George		
studio portrait, with instrument, 1935	FMX FA304	
Jourdan, André		
with Django and Leveque	Delaunay	258
sketch by Chaput	FMX FA315	
Lemarchand, Pierre		
at Club St Germain	Delaunay	285
Leveque, Gérard		
with Django and Eugène Vées	FMX FA312	

Nourry, Pierre		
with QHCF, 1935	FMX FA304	
	Delaunay	225
Page, Oran 'Hot Lips'		
with Django in Belgium	Cherrett	111
Pasdoc, André		
studio portrait	FMX FA304	
Pinkart		
with Django and Delaunay in New York, 1946	Delaunay	271
Platt, Jack		
with Django and AFN orchestra members, 1945	FMX FA312	
with Django, 1945, three poses	Delaunay	264 and 266
Quintette du Hot-Club de France		
first publicity photo (cropped)	FMX FA302	
as above, in full	Delaunay	222
Place Pigalle, summer 1934	FMX FA302	
	Delaunay	220
autographed Ultraphone publicity sheet, 1934	FMX FA303	
	Delaunay	224
	Cruickshank	78
on stage, *c.* 1935	FMX FA303	
studio portrait, with Pierre Nourry, *c.* 1935	FMX FA304	
	Delaunay	225
at 'Nuites Bleues', 1935	Delaunay	231
three poses, including 'All Strings', 1936	Delaunay	236 and 237
with the QHCF at The Hague, October 1937	Delaunay	232
at 'Casanova', 1937	Delaunay	231
at the 'Big Apple', 1937	FMX FA305	
at Bricktop's club, 1937	FMX FA306	
on stage with Larry Adler, *c.* 1937	Delaunay	249
at Decca recording studios, London, 31 January or 1 February, 1938	FMX FA307	
studio portrait, London, 1938	FMX FA308	
	Delaunay	243
in unnamed club, Paris, 1938	FMX FA308	
on a balcony in Paris, 1938	FMX FA308	
from the Cambridge Theatre programme, 1938	Delaunay	248
on stage, 1939	FMX FA309	
on stage, October 1940	Delaunay	250 and 252
at Moulin Rouge, 1941	FMX FA311	
post-war, two poses	Delaunay	276
wartime portrait, autographed by Django	Cruickshank	12

Reinhardt, Babik

with Django, 1947	Cruickshank	9
with Django, 1949	Cruickshank	27 and 115
with Naguine and Les Paul, early 1950s	Cherrett	10
with Naguine, 1958	Cruickshank	21
as above plus two more poses	Delaunay	278–9

Reinhardt, Django

birth certificate	FMX FA301	
	Delaunay	213
with his family at age 10	Delaunay	213
with banjo, 1923	FMX FA301	
	Delaunay	214
head and shoulders, 1927	Delaunay	214
Toulon, 1931	Delaunay	217
Cannes, 1931	Delaunay	217
with Louis Vola, 1932	FMX FA301	
in 'La Boîte à Matelots' 1932–33	FMX FA301	
	Delaunay	218
leaning against motor car, Cannes, 1932	Delaunay	219
with Louis Vola, Cannes, 1932	Delaunay	219
still from *Clair de Lune*, 1932	FMX FA301	
	Delaunay	218
studio portrait, *c.* 1933	FMX FA301	
	Delaunay	227
Paris Airport, 1934	FMX FA302	
	Delaunay	223
with QHCF, Place Pigalle, summer 1934	Delaunay	220
with Grappelli and Ekyan, 1934	Delaunay	220
first official QHCF photo, 1934	Delaunay	222
autographed Ultraphone publicity sheet, 1934	Delaunay	224
studio portrait, *c.* 1935	FMX FA302	
studio portrait by Jacques Hellian, *c.* 1935	Cruickshank	2
head and shoulders studio portrait, *c.* 1935	Cruickshank	117
on the HCF balcony, 1935	Delaunay	227
at the Hotel Emile Goudeau, *c.* 1935, 2 poses	Delaunay	230
at 'Stage B' with Combelle and Grappelli 1935	FMX FA303	
	Delaunay	228
with QHCF at 'Nuites Bleues', 1935	Delaunay	231
with QHCF and Pierre Nourry, *c.* 1935	FMX FA304	
	Delaunay	225
with Grappelli, in evening dress,	FMX FA305	
with instruments, *c.* 1935	Delaunay	234
with QHCF at 'Nuites Bleues', 1935	Delaunay	231

with Grappelli, in evening dress, *c.* 1935	FMX FA304	
	Delaunay	223
at Antwerp Railroad station, *c.* 1936	Delaunay	236
with the Quintette, three poses, 1936	Delaunay	236 and 237
with the QHCF, The Hague, October 1937	Delaunay	232
with the QHCF at the 'Big Apple', 1937	FMX FA305	
	Delaunay	238
with the QHCF, studio portrait, 1937	Delaunay	238
with QHCF at 'Casanova', 1937	Delaunay	231
drawing by Jean Cocteau, 1937	FMX FA306	
	Delaunay	frontispiece
with Delaunay and Naguine at Antwerp	Delaunay	249
Django and Joseph's hands by Juliette Lasserre	FMX FA306	
at Decca recordings studios, London, 1938	FMX FA307	
with Naguine and Leslie McDonald, 1938	Cherrett	108
with the QHCF, London, 1938	Delaunay	243
Cambridge Theatre programme, 1938	Delaunay	246 and 248
Paris club, in front of microphone, 1938	FMX FA308	
	Delaunay	230
in front of microphone with guitar	FMX FA308	
with Grappelli in Stockholm, 1939	FMX FA308	
	Delaunay	244
on stage with the QHCF, 1939	FMX FA309	
with Grappelli, both smoking, 1939	FMX FA309	
at the Hot-Club offices, with Ellington, 1939	FMX FA309	
	Delaunay	250
with Naguine and Charles Delaunay	FMX FA310	
	Delaunay	232
with QHCF, October 1940	FMX FA310	
	Delaunay	252
on stage, October 1940	Delaunay	250 and 252
with Joseph and G Leveque, 1940	Delaunay	251
cartoon by Roger Chaput, from 'Jazz Hot'	FMX FA310	
with orchestra at Le Bal Tabarin, 1941	FMX FA312	
playing violin in recording studio, 26 September 1941	FMX FA311	
studio portrait with Macafferri guitar	FMX FA311	
	Delaunay	116
with Naguine and Joseph, *c.* 1940s	Cruickshank	102
on stage at L'Amiral	Delaunay	253
with Pierre Fouad at Moulin de la Galette, 1942	Delaunay	257
with 'MacKac' at Moulin de la Galette, 1942	Delaunay	257
playing chess with Delaunay	Delaunay	256
inspecting records with Delaunay	Delaunay	256

with friends at Ave Frochot	Delaunay	256
with Edith Piaf, 1942	FMX FA312	
studio portrait, 1943	Delaunay	258
studio portrait, undated, *c.* 1943	Delaunay	259
on stage at Béziers, 1943	Delaunay	259
with Marcel Rouffle, wartime	Delaunay	258
at Rue de Acacias, wartime, with Leveque	Delaunay	258
with Lonnie Wilfong at Nice, *c.* 1944	FMX FA312	
	Delaunay	261
with Eugène Vées and Gérard Leveque	FMX FA312	
with guitar, Paris, 1944	Cruickshank	34
with AFN band	FMX FA312	
with Leveque and Léo Chauliac, 1945	Delaunay	260
with Leveque, 2 poses	Delaunay	260
with his orchestra at 'La Tabarin'	Delaunay	261
at 'Bœuf sur le Toit'	Delaunay	261
with the ATC Band, 1945, 3 poses	Delaunay	263 and 266
studio portrait, *c.* 1945	Delaunay	262
with Jack Platt, 1945, 2 poses	Delaunay	264
with Warren Bryan and Delaunay at AFN studios	Delaunay	265
at the microphone of the AFN studio, 1945	Delaunay	267
at the AFN studios, 2 poses, 1945	Delaunay	268
with unknown woman, 1945	Delaunay	266
studio portrait, *c.* 1945	FMX FA313	
with Eddie Bernard in Germany, post-1945	Delaunay	274
pen sketch by Roger Chaput, *c.* 1946	Delaunay	274
with Stéphane in London, 1946	Cherrett	10
with Lionel Hampton, 1946	FMX FA313	
in Hospital, London, 1946	Cherrett	13
with Grappelli in London, 1946	Cherrett	12
with Duke Ellington in USA, 1946 (1)	FMX FA313	
with Duke Ellington in USA, 1946 (2)	FMX FA313	
with Duke Ellington in USA, 1946 (3–4)	Delaunay	269
with Ellington band members, 1946	Delaunay	269
studio portrait, USAS, 1946	Delaunay	269
with the post-war quintet, two poses	Delaunay	276
with members of McPartland orchestra, USA	Delaunay	270
with Jimmy and Marion McPartland, USA	Delaunay	271
with unknown woman, *c.* 1946	Delaunay	270
with Harry Volpe, USA, 1946	Delaunay	272
with Grappelli, London, 1946	Cruickshank	19
with his paintings, three poses, 1947	Delaunay	274–5
rehearsing at 'Bœuf sur le Toit'	Delaunay	272
with Charles Delaunay and record collection	FMX FA313	

on stage with guitar	FMX FA314	
at a Manouche campsite with Joseph	FMX FA314	
	Cruickshank	cover and 7
with M Meunier, 1947	FMX FA314	
working on a painting, 1947	Cruickshank	75
with Babik, 1947	Cruickshank	9
at Nice, 1948, two poses	Delaunay	273
with Stéphane and Vola at Nice, 1948	Delaunay	280
with guitar at Nice, 1948	Cherrett	41
with Stéphane, 1948	Delaunay	280
with the 'Bœuf sur le Toit' orchestra	Delaunay	280
on tour with British musicians Alan Mindel Teddy Wadmore and Malcolm Mitchell in Sweden	FMX FA316	
at Nice in 1948	FMX FA316	
at Nice with Louis Armstrong, 1948	FMX FA316	
with Grappelli, Jack Teagarden and Earl Hines, Paris, 1948	FMX FA316	
with guitar, showing left hand, 1949	Cruickshank	81
relaxing, 1949	Cruickshank	85
with Babik, five poses, 1940s	Delaunay	278–9
with Babik, 1949	Cruickshank	27, 28 and 115
head and shoulders, in hat, with tie and jacket	FMX FA314	
eating, with Joseph playing guitar	FMX FA314	
'Harcourt' studio portrait, Paris	Cruickshank	51
close-up of Django's left hand, undated	Cruickshank	66
	Delaunay	215
at an exhibition of his paintings	Cruickshank	70
studio portrait, early 1950s	Delaunay	283
with classic guitar, two poses	Delaunay	284
at Club St-Germain, 1951	Delaunay	285
with Benny Goodman	Delaunay	286
with Dizzy Gillespie, Brussels 1952	Delaunay	287
with orchestra at Club St-Germain, 1951	Delaunay	285
with Les Paul in Paris	Delaunay	285
with Tony Proteau orchestra, four poses	Delaunay	288–9
with guitar, *c.* 1952	Cruickshank	56
fishing at Samois, 1952	Delaunay	290
playing billiards at Samois, 1952	Delaunay	290
with guitar, Samois, 1953	Delaunay	291
Reinhardt, Joseph		
Toulon, 1931	Delaunay	217
Cannes, 1931	Delaunay	217
with QHCF, Place Pigalle, summer 1934	Delaunay	220

with Django and Babik, 1940s	Delaunay	278
with Babik and Les Paul, early 1950s	Cherrett	10
with Babik, 1958	Cruickshank	21
Rostaing, Hubert		
studio portrait with instrument (1)	FMX FA310	
studio portrait with instrument (2)	FMX FA315	
cartoon by Roger Chaput	FMX FA311	
with QHCF, wartime	Cruickshank	12
on stage with QHCF, 1940	Delaunay	252
Sablon, Germaine		
1933	FMC FA301	
Sablon, Jean		
Paris Airport, 1934	FMX FA302	
	Delaunay	223
portrait by Paul Colin, *c.* 1935	FMX FA304	
Sablon, Germain and Jean		
dueting, *c.* 1935	FMX FA303	
Savitry, Emile		
Toulon, 1931	Delaunay	217
Schmidt, Sylvio		
on the set of *Claire de lune*, Cannes, 1932	Delaunay	218
Siniavine, Alec		
Paris Airport, 1934	FMX FA302	
	Delaunay	223
Snow, Valaida		
with trumpet, 1930s	FMX FA308	
Soudieux, Emmanuel		
at Nice, 1948	Delaunay	273
South, Eddie		
studio portrait with instrument	Frog DGF–36	
and his Alabamians, 1937	FMX FA306	
with violin, undated	Cherrett	32
Stewart, Rex		
at the Hot-Club offices, with Ellington, 1939	FMX FA309	
	Delaunay	250
Taylor, Freddy		
and Swing Men from Harlem, *c.* 1935	AD ACD–29	
with Coleman Hawkins, 1935	FMX FA303	
portrait by Charles Delaunay	FMX FA305	
Teagarden, Jack		
with Django, Grappelli and Vola at Nice, 1948	Delaunay	280

at Nice, 1948, two poses	Delaunay	273
at Nice, 1948	FMX FA316	
with Django and Stéphane at Nice 1948	Delaunay	280
Volpe, Harry		
with Django in New York, 1946	Delaunay	272
Wadmore, Teddy		
with Django on tour in Sweden, 1948	FMX FA316	
Wagner, Christian		
studio portrait with instrument	FMX FA310	
Warlop, Michel		
studio portrait with instrument (1), *c.* 1935	FMX FA304	
studio portrait with instrument (2)	FMX FA306	
studio portrait with instrument (3), 1938	FMX FA307	
Wells, Dickie		
at Boudon, *c.* 1937	FMX FA306	
Wilfong, Lonnie		
with Django	FMX FA312	
78rpm record labels		
ABC Jazz Club 123	FMX FA312	
Blue Star 33	FMX FA314	
Blue Star 53	FMX FA315	
Blue Star 55	Cherrett	9
Blue Star 73	FMX FA316	
Championnat unnumbered	FMX FA312	
Decca F6616 (French)	FMX FA307	
Decca F6675 (English)	Cherrett	26
Decca F7390 (French)	FMX FA309	
Decca F9242 (French) picture label	FMX FA313	
Decca 23261	FMX FA308	
Henry 966	FMX FA301	
Ideal 8545	FMX FA301	
Oriole LV100	Cherrett	9
Pathé PA537	FMX FA303	
Polydor 512.737	FMX FA304	
Polydor 524.108	FMX FA304	
Rythme 5025	FMX FA311	
Swing 1	FMX FA305	
Swing 16	FMX FA306	
Swing 65	FMX FA309	
Swing 83	Cherrett	9
Swing 88	FMX FA310	
Swing 91	FMX FA311	
Swing 229	FMX FA314	

Index of artists

Index of songs

Code	Publisher
AHC	Ascherberg, Hopwood & Crew
BH	Boosey & Hawkes (Editions Hawkes in France)
BM	Bellwin Music
CC	Campbell-Connelly
CD	Choudens
CH	Chappell
CM	Cinephonic Music
DI	Darewski
FDH	Francis, Day and Hunter
FM	Feldman
FS	Francis Salabert
GM	Good Music
IB	Irving Berlin
KP	Keith Prowse
LEDP	Les Editions de Paris
LF	La Fleur
LW	Lawrence Wright
MM	Mills Music
PM	Peter Maurice
SF	Sam Fox

Parisian music business addresses 1929–1950

Gramophone record shops

Art Radiophonique	31 rue Marbroeuf 8e
Assimil	4 rue Lefebvre 15e
(specialists in foreign-language recordings)	
Baron	3 rue Dancourt 18e
Boîte à Musique	133, blvd Raspail, 6e
('Grande Spécialité de Disques Hot'; established 1929)	
Broadway	79 ave des Champs-Elysées 8e
Chant du Monde	32 rue Beaujon, 8e
Conn	3 rue Duperré 9e
Discobole	27 Galerie des Marchands 8e
Disques-Exchange	11 rue de Vintimille 9e
Disques-Office	9 rue de L'Odéon 6e
Durand	3 place de la Madeleine 8e
Francis-Salabert	35 blvd des Capucines 2e
Gramophone (La Voix de son maître)	18 blvd Haussmann 9e
Hamm	135–9 rue de Rennes 6e
Maison de la Musique	40 rue Ballu 9e
Maison du Jazz	24 rue Victor-Massen 9e
Maud	4 ave de Villiers 17e
Music-Shop	67 rue Pierre-Charron 8e
Ondes Sonores	85 rue de la boette 8e
Paramount Radio	43 rue de Mauberge 9e
Phono-Graf	57 avenue Victor-Hugo 16e
Radio-Havre	107 rue Saint-Lazare 9e
The Record	55 rue d'Amsterdam 9e
Remond	124 ave de Neuilly
Robert Guy	145 place de Vaugirard 15e
Sinfonia	68 ave de Champs-Elysées 8e
SML	144 blvd de la Villette 19e
Sofradi	29 rue Vernet 8e
The Music Shop	70 rue de Ponthieu 8e *(until at least 1935)* 67 rue Pierre-Charron 8e *(by 1938)*
Vittoz	6 rue Grange-Batelière 9e

Instrument and music shops

Centre d'Etudes de Jazz	42 rue de l'Echiquier 10e
Connétable	28 blvd Poissonnière 9e
Couesnon	94 rue d'Angoulême 11e
Hohner	24 rue des Petites-Ecuries 10e
(also distributors for Brunswick-Polydor records until 1931)	
Lyra	9 rue Notre Dame de Lorette 9e
La Maison du Jazz	25 rue Victor-Masse 9e
Major	3 rue Duperré 9e
Paul Beuscher	27 blvd Beaumarchais 3e
Pierret	84 rue de la Folie-Mericourt 11e 207 blvd Voltaire 11e
Rar Robinson	74 rue Blanche 9e
Selmer	4 place Dancourt, 18e
Stand du Jazz	33 rue de Navarin 9e
Strasser–Marigaux–Lemaire	144–6 blvd de la Villette 19e

Jazz societies

Hot-Club de France	5 rue de l'Isy 8e *(from inception)* 15 rue de Conservatoire 9e *(until summer 1938)* 14 rue Chaptal 9e *(from September 1938)*
Jazz Club Française	22 rue Bergère 9e *(offices)* 32 rue de Ranelagh, 16e *(auditorium)*

Journals

Disques	12 rue du Helder 9e
L'Edition Musicale Vivant	5 rue de Cardinal-Mercier 9e
Jazz Hot	15 rue de Conservatoire 9e *(until summer 1938)* 14 rue Chaptal, 9e *(from September 1938)*
Jazz-Tango	117 rue Réaumur 3e
Radio-Magazine	61 rue Beaubourg 4e

Music publishers

Benjamin	27 & 41 rue de l'Echiquier 10e
Breton & Co	148 rue Montmartre 2e
Campbell-Connelly	10 rue Grange-Batelière *(to end 1935)* 83 rue de Provence 9e *(by 1937)*
Chappell SA	86 blvd Haussmann 8e
Charles Brul	18 rue de Provence 8e
Charles Gras	12 rue la Chaussée-d'Antin 9e

Choudens	30 blvd des Capucines 1e
	95 Faubourg Saint-Honoré 8e
	38 rue Montaigne 8e
Coda	12 rue Lafayette
Editions de Paris	14 Faubourg Poissonnière 10e
Eimef	31 rue Bergère 9e
Europa	27 rue de l'Echiquier 10e
Européennes	40 rue du Faubourg Poissonnière 10e
Feldmann	32 & 41 rue de l'Echiquier 10e
Fortin	93 rue de Richelieu 2e
France-Melodie	2 square Trudaine *(to end 1935)*
	39 rue Condorcet 9e *(by 1937)*
Francis-Day	30 rue de l'Echiquier 10e
Francis Salabert (see Salabert, *qv*)	
Hawkes	16 rue du Faubourg Saint-Denis 10e
International de Musique	31 rue Bergère 9e
International Music Co	33 rue de Navarin 9e
Jacques Rosenberg	3 rue Rossini 9e
	11 rue Junot
Joubert	25 rue d'Hauteville 10e
Lawrence Wright	17 rue de l'Echiquier 10e
Maurice Decruck	28 blvd Poissonnière 9e
Max Eschig	48 rue du Rome 8e
Musicales Universelles	42 rue le Peletier 9e
Pan	12 rue de l'Echiquier 10e
Paris-Monde	28 blvd Poissonnière 9e
Paul Beuscher	27 blvd Beaumarchais 3e
Peter Maurice	29 blvd Poissonnière 9e
Philippe Pares	46 rue Laffitte 9e
Raoul Breton et Co.	148 rue Montmartre 2e
Ray Ventura & Cie	28 blvd Poissonnière 2e
Rex	33 rue de Navarin 9e
Roudanez	9 rue de Medecis
Salabert	22 rue Chauchat 9e
Sam Fox	40 bis rue du Poissonnière 10e
Selmer	33 rue le Peletier 9e
SEMI (Société d'Editions Musicales Internationales)	12 rue du Ct Leandri 15e
Smyth	17 Faubourg Montmartre 9e
	40 Faubourg Poissonnière 10e
Sterny	42 Faubourg Saint-Martin 10e
Stubbs du Peron	7 rue Manuel, 9e
Sylvia	86 blvd Haussmann 8e
Vedette	4 rue de Trévise 9e

Radio stations

Radio Citie	1 blvd Haussmann 9e
Radio Diffusion Française	Montparnasse 14e
Poste Parisien (RDF)	116 blvd des Champs-Elysées, 8e

Record companies

Edison–Bell–Cristal *(Brunswick, Decca, Polydor)*	38 rue d'Hauteville 10e
Gramophone	7–9 blvd Haussmann 9e
Odéon	11 Faubourg Poissonnière 9e
Pathé	30 blvd des Italiens 9e
Swing	251–253 Faubourg Saint-Martin 10e
Telefunken	46 rue de la Bienfaisance 8e
Ultraphone (Société Ultraphone)	46 rue de la Bienfaisance 8e
	36 blvd Haussmann 9e

Recording studios

AFN	26 rue Françoise 1er 8e
Brunswick	(see Polydor, *qv*)
Columbia	61 rue Albert 13e
Decca	(see Polydor, *qv*)
Kennedy	10 villa Victor Hugo 16e *(1937)*
Lutetia	31 ave de Wagram 17e
Odéon	rue Albert 13e
Pathé	69 ave de la Grande Armée 17e
Pelouze	5 rue de Pelouze, 8e
Polydor	72–74 blvd de la Gare 13e
Publicis	1 blvd Haussmann, 4e
Studio Albert	(see Columbia, *qv*)
Technisor	26 rue Françoise 1er 8e
Ultraphone	13 ave du Maine 14e

Venues

ABC Music Hall	blvd Poissonnière, Montmartre 2e
Les Ambassadeurs	1 ave Gabriel 8e
Apollo	rue de Clichy 9e
La Bagatelle	rue de Clichy 9e
Barclay Club *(Eddie Barclay's private club from at least late 1945; every Tuesday, Saturday and Sunday 4.30–7.00pm)*	83–85 ave de la Grand Armée 16e
Big Apple	rue Pigalle 9e

Bœuf sur le Toit	28 rue Boissy D'anglas *(21 December 1921–28)*
	43 bis ave Pierre 1e-de-Serbie *(by July 1937)*
	34 rue du Colisée *(by 1951)*
Bricktop's	rue Pigalle 9e *(1928–39)*
Casanova Club	rue Fromention 9e
Casino de Paris	16 rue de Clichy 9e
Chez Boudon	rue Fontaine and rue Mansart 9e
Chez Django Reinhardt (La Roulotte)	rue Pigalle 9e *(1944)*
Chez Florence	rue Blanche 9e
Chez Jane Stick	rue de Ponthieu 8e
La Cigale	124 blvd Rochechouart 9e
Club Saint-Germain	13 rue Saint-Benoît 6e
Coliseum	65 rue Rochechouart 9e
Le Croix de Sud	Montparnasse
Le Doyen	Jardin des Champs-Elysées 8e
L'Ecole Normale de Musique	78 rue Cardinet at blvd Malesherbes 17e
Embassy Club	ave des Champs-Elysées 8e
Harlem Club	*(opened by Freddy Taylor 1937–38)*
Hotel Claridge	74 Ave de Champs-Élysées 8e
Hot Feet	rue Notre Dame de Lorette 9e *(1939–)*
Jimmy's Bar	rue Huyghens, 14e
Moulin de la Galette	77 rue Lepic 17e (Montmartre)
(Aux) Nuits Bleues	7 rue Fromentin 9e *(Summer 1935–)*
Olympia	28 blvd des Capucines 9e
Le Perroquet	16 rue de Clichy 9e
Plantation Club	58 rue Notre Dame de Lorette 9e
Royal Box	16 rue Fontaine 9e
Salle Chopin	rue Daru 8e
Salle Gaveau	45 rue de la Boette 8e
Salle Lafayette	27 rue de Petits-Hotels 10e
Salle Pleyel	252 rue du Faubourg Saint Honore 8e
Salle Rameau	252 Faubourg St-Honoré 8e
Swing Time	rue Fromentin 9e
Villa d'Este	4 rue Arsene-Houssaye 8e

Comparative table of allocated recording numbers

This table allows users to easily and quickly cross-reference allocated recording numbers between this work and the earlier works by Abrams and Delaunay. Titles without matrix numbers are indicated by the first letters of each word in the title.

Vernon	*Delaunay*	*Abrams*	*Matrix or title*
001	9	1	BT4115-1
002	7	2	BT4116-1
003	8	3	BT4118-1
004	10	4	BT4119-1
005	1	5	ID999
006	2	6	ID1000
007	3	7	ID1001
008	4	8	ID1002
009	5	9	ID1003
010	6	10	ID1004
011			H848-B
012			H966-A
013			H966-B
014			H968 (A)
015			H968 (B)
016			H962-A
017			H962-B
018	11	11	OG762-1
019		13	OG764-1
020	12	12	OG765-1
(Abrams allocated 14 to OG763, which does not feature Django.)			
021	13	15	OPG639-1
022		16	OPG640-1
023		17	OPG640-2
024		18	OPG641-1
025		19	OPG641-2
026	14	20	OPG642-1
027		21	OPG642-2
028	15	22	OPG643-1
029		23	OPG643-2
030			KI 5902-1

031			KI 5906-1
032			KI 5905-1
033			KI 5907-1
034			(Odéon 250.419)
035			(Odéon 250.419)
036	16	24	CL4257-1
037	17	25	CL4258-1

(Abrams allocated 26 to a second take of CL4258, which does not appear to exist.)

038	18	27	CL4661-1
039		28	CL4661-2
040		29	CL4662-1
041		30	CL4662-2
042	19	31	CL4663-1
043		32	CL4663-2
044		33	CL4664-1
045	20	34	OPG 1296-1
046	21	35	OPG 1297-1
047		36	OPG 1297-2
048		37	OPG 1298-1
049	22	38	OPG 1298-2

(Delaunay's original discography assigned this number to OPG1292. He then correctly identified the matrix/title relationship in his updated version.)

050	23	38a	OPG 1362-1
051	24	39	OPG 1415-1
052		40	OPG 1415-2
053	25		OPG 1416-1
054			OPG 1416-2
055	26	41	OPG 1417-1
056		42	OPG 1417-2
057	27	43	CL4807-1
058	28	44	CL4808-1
059	29	45	OPG 1572-1
060	30	46	OPG 1573-2
061	31	47	OPG 1574-1
062		48	OPG 1574-2
063		49	TR
064		52	TR

(Delaunay assigned 32 to 'Tiger Rag', listing it without bassist Fernandez. This take, if indeed it ever existed, remains unfound.)

065		50	AYG
066		51	C
067	33	53	1071

068	34	54	1072

(Abrams allocates 55–58 to OLA8-11 by Eliane DeCreus, which do not feature Django.)

069	35	59	OLA 148-1
070	36	60	OLA 149-1
071		61	OLA 149-2
072	37	62	OLA 150-1
073	38	63	OLA 151-1
074	44	64	CPT 1700-1
075	39	65	CPT 1701-1
076	40	66	CPT 1702-1
077	41	67	CPT 1703-1
078	42	68	CPT 1704-1
079	43	69	CPT 1705-1
080	45	70	P 77161
081	46	71	P 77162
082	47	72	P 77163
083	48	73	P 77164
084		74	CI 5176-1
085	49	75	CI 5176-2
086		76	CI 5178-1
087		77	CI 5178-2
088	50	78	CI 5178-3
089	51	79	CI 5179-1
090		80	OLA 300-1
091		81	OLA 301-1
092	52	82	OLA 302-1
093		83	CL 5220-1
094		84	CL 5221-1
095		85	OLA 330-1
096	53	86	OLA 330-2
097	54	87	OLA-331-1
098	55	88	OLA 346-1
099			OLA 346-2
100	56	89	OLA 347-1
101			OLA 347-2
102	57	90	OLA 348-1
103	58	91	OLA 349-1
104	59	92	CPT 1841
105	60	93	CPT 1842
106	61	94	CPT 1843
107	62	95	CPT 1844
108	65	98	P 77240
109	66	99	P 77241
110	67	100	P 77242

111	68	101	P 77243
112	63	96	CPT 1857
113	64	97	CPT 1858
114		102	VD
115		103	BD
116		104	SW
117		105	HCYDMLYD
118			K-169
119			MDA
120			BD
121			HCYDMLYD
122	69	P 77333	
123	70	P 77334	
124		(108)	P 77335
125	74	109	P 77351
126	75	110	P 77352
127	76	111	P 77353
128	77	112	P 77354
129	72	113	OLA 520-1
130	73	114	OLA 521-1
131	78	117	P 77373
132	79	118	P 77374
133		115	WADADM
134		116	TSOA
135	80	119	CPT 2142
136	81	120	CPT 2143-1
137	82	121	CPT 2144-1
138	83	122	CPT 2145-1
139	84	123	CPT 2146
140	85	124	CPT 2147-1
141	86	125	P 77434
142	87	126	P 77435
143	88	127	P 77440
144	89	128	P 77441
145	90	129	P 77468
146	91	130	P 77469
146a			BE
147		131	CL 5487-1
148		132	CL 5487-2
149		133	CL 5488-1
150		134	CL 5488-2
151		135	CL 5489-1
152	92	136	P 77522
153	93	137	P 77523
154	97	141	P 77537

155	98	142	P 77538
156	99	143	P 77539
157	100	144	P 77540
158	101	145	P 77541
159	102	146	P 77542
160			1968-3/1HPP
161			1968-3/2HPP
162			1968-3/3HPP
163	94	138	1968-3/4HPP
164			1969-4/1HPP
165			1969-4/2HPP
166			1969-4/3HPP
167	95	139	1969-4/4HPP
168	96	140	1970-HPP
169		147	TR
170		148	SGB
171		149	W
172		150	TBSCM
173	113	169/170	P 77574-1
174	105	151	2009-HPP
175		152	2010-HPP
176	106	153	2035-HPP
177	107	154	2036-1/2HPP
178		155	2037-HPP
179			2038-HPP
180		156	2039-HPP
181		157	2040-HPP

(Abrams allocates 158–163 to an André Pasdoc session, about which he had doubts, and which now is generally agreed not to feature Django.)

182			CL 5487-1
183			CL 5488-1
184			CL 5489-1
185	108	164	2079-HPP
186	109	165	2080-1/2HPP
187	110	166	2081-HPP
188	111	167	2082-HPP
189	112	168	2083-HPP
190	114	171	OLA 730-1
191	115	172	OLA 731-1
192		173	OLA 731-2
193	116	174	OLA 732-1
194	103	175	CL 5487-3
195	104	176	CL 5518-1

196		177	CPT 2428-1

(Abrams allocates 178 to a non-musical item, the presentation of the programme.)

197		179	2117
198			2118
199		180	2119
200		181	2120
201		182	2121
202			LJEB
203			MOR/BD
204			BD
205			2354-HPP
206	117	183	2422-HPP
207	118	184	2423-HPP
208	119	185	2424-HPP
209	120	186	2425-HPP
210	121	187	2426-HPP
211		188	2427-HPP
212	123	189	OLA 1057-1
213		190	OLA 1057-2
214	124	191	OLA 1058-1
215		192	OLA 1508-2
216	125	193	OLA 1059-1
217	126	194	OLA 1060-1
218		195	OLA 1060-2
219	127	196	OLA 1061-1
220	128	197	OLA 1062-1
221	129	198	OLA 1290-1
222		199	OLA 1290-2
223	130	200	OLA 1291-1
224	131	201	OLA 1292-1
225		202	OLA 1292-2
226	132	203	OLA 1293-1
227	133	204	OLA 1294-1
228	134	205	OLA 1295-1
229	135	206	CPT 2931-1
230	136	207	CPT 2932-1
231	137	208	CPT 2969-1
232	138	209	CPT 2970-1
233	139	210	OLA 1702-1
234	140	211	OLA 1703-1
235	141	212	OLA 1704-1
236	142	213	OLA 1705-1
237	143	214	OLA 1706-1
238	144	215	OLA 1707-1

239	145	216	OLA 1708-1
240	146	217	OLA 1709-1
241	147	218	OLA 1710-1
242	148	219	OLA 1711-1
243	149	220	OLA 1712-1
244	150	221	OLA 1713-1
245	151	222	OLA 1714-1
246	152	223	OLA 1715-1
247	153	224	OLA 1716-1
248	154	225	OLA 1717-1
249	155	226	OLA 1718-1
250	(156)	(227)	OLA 1719-1

(Delaunay allocated matrix OLA1737-1 to 250/156, which was in error. Abrams allocated 227 to the same title.)

251		228	OLA 1738-1
252	157	229	OLA 1739-1
253	158	230	OLA 1740-1
254	159	231	OLA 1741-1
255	160	232	OLA 1742-1
256	161	233	OLA 1743-1
257	162	234	OLA 1744-1
258	163	235	OLA 1745-1
259		236	PFH
260		238	ELY
261		239	ITSOTN
262		240	F
263		237	IGS No. 1
264		241	IGS No. 2
265			D
266		242	LB
267		243	B

(Abrams allocated 237a to the unissued 'Sweet Chorus'.)

268	164	244	OLA 1884-1
269	165	245	OLA 1885-1
270	166	246	OLA 1886-1
271	167	247	OLA 1887-1
272	168	248	OLA 1888-1
273	169	249	OLA 1889-1
274	170	250	OLA 1890-1
275	171	251	OLA 1891-1
276		252	OLA 1950-1
277		253	OLA 1950-2
278		254	OLA 1951-1
279	172	255	OLA 1952-1
280	173	256	OLA 1953-1

281	174	257	OLA 2145-1
282	175	258	OLA 2146-1
283	176	259	OLA 2147-1
284	177	260	OLA 2148-1
285	178	261	OLA 2149-1
286	179	262	OLA 2150-1
287	180	263	OLA 1738-2(R)
288			ISS
289	181	264	OLA 1979-1
290	182	265	OLA 1980-1
291		266	OLA 1980-2
292	183	267	OLA 1981-1
293	184	268	OLA 1982-1
294	185	269	OLA 1983-1
295	186	270	OLA 1984-1
296	187	271	OLA 1985-1
297	188	272	OLA 1986-1
298		273	OLA 1987
299		274	OLA 1988
300		275	OLA 1989
301	189	276	OLA 1990-1
302	190	277	OLA 1991-1
303	191	278	OLA 1992-1
304	192	279	OLA 1993-1
305	193	280	OLA 1994-1
306	194	281	OLA 1995-1
307	195	282	X2LA 1996-1
308		283	X2LA 1996-2
309		284	X2LA 1997-1
310	196	285	X2LA 1997-2
311	197	286	OLA 1998-1
312	198	287	OLA 1999-1
313	199	288	OLA 2000-1
314	200	289	OLA 2214-1
315	201	290	OLA 2215-1
316	202	291	OLA 2216-1
317	203	292	OLA 2217-1
318	204	293	OLA 2218-1
319	205	294	OLA 2219-1
320	206	295	OLA 2220-1
321	207	296	OLA 2221-1
322	208	297	OLA 2222-1
323		298	OLA 2223-1
324	209	299	OLA 2223-2
325	210	300	OLA 2308-1

326		301	OLA 2308-2
327		302	OLA 2309-1
328	211	303	OLA 2310-1
329	212	304	OLA 2311-1
330	213	305	OLA 2312-1
331	214	306	CL 6502-1
332		307	CL 6502-2
333	215	308	CL 6503-1
334		309	CL 6503-2
335	216	310	DTB 3523-1
336	217	311	DTB 3524-1
337	218	312	DTB 3525-1
338		313	DTB 3526-1
339	219	314	DTB 3526-2
340	220	315	DTB 3527-1
341	221	316	DTB 3528-1
342	222	317	DTB 3529-1
343	223	318	DTB 3530-1
344	224	319	DTB 3531-1
345	225	320	DTB 3532-1
346	226	321	DTB 3533-1
347	227	322	DTB 3534-1
348	228	323	CPT 3836-1
349	229	324	CPT 3837-1
350	230	325	OSW 4-1
351	231	326	OSW 5-1
352	232	327	OSW 6-1
353	233	328	OSW 7-1
354	234	329	OSW 8-1
355	235	330	OSW 9-1
356	236	331	OSW 10-1
357	237	332	OSW 11-1
358		333	D
359		334	Da
360			J-1
361			J-2
362			OLA 2513-1
363			OLA 2514-1
364	238	335	CL 6716-1
365		336	CL 6716-2
366	239	337	CL 6717-1
367	239a	338	CL 6717-2
368		339	CL 6718-1
369		340	CL 6718-2
370	241	341	CL 6719-1

371	241a	342	CL 6719-2
372	242	343/344	4209-1/2HPP
373	243	345	4210-HPP
374		346	4210-1/2HPP
375	244	347	4211-HPP
376		348	CBD4211-1/2HPP(*sic*)
377	245	349	4212-HPP
378		350	4212-1/2HPP
379	246	351	4213-HPP
380		352	4213-1/2HPP
381			Medley-1
382			Medley-2
383			SS
384	247	353	DR 2878-1
385	248	354	DR 2879-1
386	249	355	DR 2880-1
387	250	356	DR 2903-1
388	250a	357	DR 2903-2
389	251	358	DR 2904-1
390	252	359	DR 2907-1
391	253	360	DR 2908-1
392		360a	DR 2908-2
(Abrams erroneously gives the matrix numbers as DR 2980-1 and 2.)			
393	254	361	4967-HPP
394	254a	362	4967-1/2HPP
395	255	363	4968 HPP
396	255a	364	4968-1/2HPP
397		365	4969-HPP
398	256	366	4969-1/2HPP
399	257	367	CAX4970-HPP
400		368	4970-1/2HPP
401	258	369	4971-HPP
402	258a	370	4971-1/2HPP
403		371	4972-HPP
404		372	4972-1/2HPP
405	259	373	4973-HPP
406		374	4973-1/2HPP
407	260	375	4974-HPP
408	260a	376	4974-1/2HPP
409	261	377	CA4975
410	261a	378	4975-1/2HPP
411		379	4976-HPP
412			OLA 3017-1
413	262	380	OSW 63-1
414	263	381	OSW 64-1

415		382	OSW 64-2
416	264	383	OSW 65-1
417		384	OSW 65-2
418	265	385	OSW 66-1
419		386	OSW 66-2
420	266	387	OSW 67-1
421		388	OSW 67-2
422	267	389	5080-HPP
423	268	390	5081-HPP
424	269	391	5082-HPP
425	270	392	5083-HPP
426	271	393	5084-HPP
427	272	394	OSW 72
428	273	395	OSW 73-1
429	274	396	OSW 74-1
430	275	397	OSW 75
431	276	398	OSW 76
432			TR
433	277	399	OPG 1719-1
434	278	400	OPG 1720-1
435	279	401	OPG 1721-1
436	280	402	OPG 1722-1
437	281	403	OPG 1723-1
438	282	404	OPG 1724-1
439	283	405	OPG 1725-1
440	284	406	DR 3861-1
441	285	407	DR 3862-1
442	286	408	DR 3863-1
443	287	409	DR 3864-1
444		410	D
445		411	IHTBY
446	288	412	OSW 95-1
447	289	413	OSW 96-1
448	290	414	OSW 97-1
449		415	OSW 98-1
450	291	416	OSW 99-1
451	292	417	OSW 104-1
452	293	418	OSW 105-1
453		419	OSW 106-1
454	294	420	OSW 107-1
455	295	421	OSW 108-1
456	296	422	OSW 109-1
457	297	423	OSW 110-1
458	298	424	OSW 111-1
459	299	425	OSW 112-1

460	300	426	OSW 113-1
461	301	427	OSW 114-1
462	302	428	OSW 115-1
463	303	429	OSW 116-1
464	304	430	OSW 117-1
465	305	431	OSW 118-1
466	306	432	OSW 119-1
467	307	433	OSW 120-1
468	308	434	OSW 121-1
469			SS
470			AI
471		435	OSW 127-1
472	309	436	OSW 128-1
473		437	OSW 129-1
474	310	438	OSW 130-1
475		439	OSW 131-1
476		440	OSW 132-1
477	311	441	OSW 133-1
478	312	442	OSW 134-1
479	313	443	OSW 135-1
480	314	444	OSW 136-1
481	315	445	OSW 137-1
482	316	446	OSW 138-1
483		447	OSW 138-2
484	317	448	OSW 139-1
485		449	OSW 139-2
486	318	450	OSW 140-1
487	319	451	OSW 141-1
488		452	OSW 141-2
489	320	453	OSW 142-1
490	321	454	OSW 143-1
491	322	455	OSW 144-1
492	323	456	OSW 145-1
493	324	457	OSW 146-1
494	325	458	OSW 147-1
495	325a	459	OSW 148-1
496	326	460	OSW 149-1
497	326a	461	OSW 150-1
498	327	462	OSW 151-1
499	328	463	OSW 152-1
500	329	464	OSW 153-1
501	330	465	OSW 154-1
502	331	466	OSW 155-1
503	332	468	OSW 156-1

504	333	469	OSW 157-1

(Abrams allocates 467 to OSW145-2R which appears to be only a remastering of OSW145-1.)

505	334	470	OSW 162-1
506	335	471	OSW 163-1
507	336	472	OSW 164-1
508	337	473	OSW 165-1
509	338	474	OSW 166-1
510	339	475	OSW 167-1
511	340	476	OSW 168-1
512	341	477	OSW 169-1
513	342	478	OSW 170-1
514	343	479	OSW 171-1
515	344	480	OSW 172-1
516	345	481	2SW 173-1
517	346	481a	OSW 174-1
518		482	CL7419
519	347	483	CL7420-1
520	348	485	OSW 225-1
521	349	484	OSW 226-1
522	350	486	OSW 227-1
523	351	487	OSW 228-1
524	352	488	OSW 229-1
525	353	489	2SW 235-1
526		490	2SW 235-2
527	354	491	OSW 261-1
528		492	OSW 261-2
529	355	493	2SW 262-1
530		494	2SW 262-2
531	356	495	2SW 263-1
532		496	2SW 263-2
533	357		OSW 265-1
534	358		OSW 266-1
535	359	499	16189
536	360	500	16190
537	361	501	16191
538	362	502	16192
539	363	503	16194
540	364	504	16195
541	365	505	16196
542	366	506	16197
543	367	507	16218
544	368	508	16219
545	369	509	16220
546	370	510	16221

547	371	511	16222
548	372	512	16223
549	373	513	16224
550	374	514	16225
551	375	515	OSW 322-1
552	376	516	OSW 323-1
553	377	517	OSW 324-1
554	378	518	OSW 325-1
555		519	OSW 326-1
556	379	520	OSW 327-1
557	380	521	OSW 328-1
558	381	522	OSW 329-1
559	382	523	OSW 329-2
560	383	524	OSW 330-1
561	384	525	OSW 331-1
562	385	526	OSW 332-1
563	386	527	OSW 333-1
564		528	OSW 356-1
565	387	529	OSW 357-1
566	388	530	OSW 358-1
567	389	531	OSW 359-1
568	390	532	OSW 398-1
568a	390	532	OSW 399-1
569	391	533	OSW 400-1
570		534	2SW 401-1
571			interview
572	392	535	ST 1227-1
573		536	ST 1227-2
574	393	537	ST 1228
575	394/394a	538/539	ST 1229-2
576	395	540	ST 1230
577			HG
578		541	GMB
579			D
580			HR
581			B
582			UB
583			MS
584	396	542	OSW 408-1
585		543	OSW 408-2
586	397	544	OSW 409-1
587		545	OSW 409-2
588	398	546	OSW 410-1
589		547	OSW 410-2
590	399	548	OSW 411-1

591		549	OSW 411-2
592		554	DBTW
593		551	HR
594			SSJY
595			I. No. 6
596		553	B
597		552	MS
598		550	D
599		557	MS
600			AYITM
601		555	UB
602		559	AH
603	400	560	OEF 25-1
604	401	561	OEF 26-1
605	402	562	OEF 27-1
606	403	563	OEF 28-1
607	404	564	DR 10026-1
608	405		DR 10026-2
609		565	DR 10027-1
610	406	566	DR 10027-2
611	407	567	DR 10028-1
612		568	DR 10028-2
613	408	569	DR 10029-1
614	409	570	OSW 416-1
615	410	571	OSW 417-1
616	411	572	OSW 418-1
617	412	573	OSW 419-1
618		574	TR
619		575	BR
620		577	HR
621		576	Imp No. 2
622			NNB
623			LM
624			COMD
625	413	581	OSW 449-1
626	414	582	OSW 450-1
627	415	583	OSW 451-1
628	416	584	OSW 452-1
629	417	585	OSW 453-1
630	418	586	ST 1984-2
631		587	ST 1985
632	419	588	ST 1986
633		589	ST 1987
634		590	ST 1988
635		591	Fo 1782-R

636	420	592	Fo 1782-RB
637	421	593	Fo 1783-R
638	421a	594	Fo 1783-RB
639			Fo 1784-R
640			Fo 1784-RB
641	422	595	Fo 1784-RC
642	423	596	Fo 1785-R
643			Fo 1785-RB
644	423a	597	Fo 1785-RC
645	424	589 (*sic*)	Fo 1786-R
646	424a	590 (*sic*)	Fo 1786-RB
647			Fo 1787-R
648			Fo 1787-RB
649	425	591 (*sic*)	Fo 1787-RC
(Abrams repeats three numbers in error and omits 598–600 inc.)			
650		601	ST 2086-1
651	426	602	ST 2086-2
652	427	603	ST 2087-1
653	428	604	ST 2088-1
654	428a	605	ST 2088-2
655		606	ST 2089-1
656		607	ST 2089-2
657	429	608	ST 2089-3
658	430	609	ST 2090-1
659	431	610	ST 2091-1
660	432	611	ST 2092-1
661	433	612	ST 2104-1
662	433a	613	ST 2104-2
663	434	614	ST 2105-1
664	435	615	ST 2106-1
665	435a	616	ST 2106-2
666		617	ST 2107-1
667		618	ST 2107-2
668	436	619	ST 2107-3
669	437	620	ST 2108-1
670	438	621	ST 2109-1
671	439	624	ST 2112-1
(Abrams does not use 622 or 623.)			
672	440	625	SG
673	441	626	B
(Delaunay allocates 442 to 'Blues En Mineur', explaining that it is a mistitling of 441. Abrams allocates 627 to the same title.)			
674		628	WKOF
675	443	629	N
676	444	630	VD

677	445	631	BC
678	446	632	MS
679	448	634	S39
680	447	633	S41
681	449	635	DS
682	450	636	LYN
683	451	637	L
684	452	638	DD
685	453	639	SIS
686	454	640	S
687	455	641	F
688	456	642	V13
689	457	643	SC
690	458	644	C
691	459	645	SA
692	460	646	ILYFSR
693	461	647	JOOTT
694	462	648	BD
695	463	649	PC
696	464	650	SD
697	465	651	LM
698	466		T
699	466	652	4763
700	467	653	4764
701	468	654	4765
702	469	655	4766
703	470	656	4767
704	471	657	4768
705	472	658	4769
706	473	659	AL
707	474	660	PALM
708	475	661	B
709	476	662	DA
710	477	663	SDP
711	480	666	SS
712	479	664	ICGYABL
713	–	–	BEM
714	478	665	IHTBY
715	481	667	MDMR
716	483	669	D
717	482	668	MAC
718	484	670	FAA
719	486	671	PDB
720	485	672	S
721	487	673	ISUDN

722	488	674	SLB
723	489	675	WITTCL
724	490	676	OMR
725	491	677	STS
726	492	678	E
727	493	679	D
728	494	681	OMR
729	495	682	RVS
730	(495)	683	HHTM
731	496	684	SG
732	497	685	ILY
733	(497)	686	TR
734	(497)	687	T
735	(497)	688	D
736	(497)	689	TTE
737	(497)	691	HHTM
738		694a	I.47
739		690	D
740		692	MDMR
741		693	DN
742		694	CR
742a			TR
743		695	N&D
744	498	696	ST2220-2
745	498A	697	ST2220-5
746		698	ST2221-1
747		699	ST2221-2
748		700	ST2221-3
748a			PQMVD
749		701	N
750		702	S.42
751	500	703	OSW500
752	501	704	OSW501
753	502	705	OSW502
754	503	706	OSW503
755	504	707	OSW504
756	505	708	OSW505
757		708A/B	OSW506
757a			O
757b			F.48
757c			D
758	506	709	AL
759		710	NTB
760		711	TB
761	506	712	CS

762	(506)	713	N
763	(506)	714	PDB
764	(506)	715	ISUDN
765	(506)	716	F.48
766	(506)	716A	MS
767		717	S
768		719	CW18
769		720	CW19
770		721	CW20
771		722	CW21
772		723	CW22
773		724	CW23
774		725	CW24
775		726	CW25
776		727	CW26
777		728	CW27
778		729	CW28
779		730	CW29
780		731	CW30
781		732	CW31
782		733	CW32
783		734	CW33
784		735	CW34
785		736	CW35
786		737	CW36
787		738	CW37
788		739	CW38
789		740	CW39
790		741	CW40
791		742	CW41
792		743	CW42
793		744	CW43
794		745	CW44
795		778 (*sic*)	CW45
796		746	CW46
797		747	CW47
798		748	CW48
799		749	CW49
800		750	CW50
801		751	CW51
802		752	CW52
803		753	CW53
804		754	CW54
805		755	CW55
806		756	CW56

807		757	CW57
808		758	CW58
809		759	CW59
810		760	CW60
811		761	CW61
812		762	CW62
813		762A	CW63
814		763	CW63
815		763A	CW64
816	508	764	BL108
817	509	765	BL109
818	510	766	BL110
819	511	767	BL111
820	512	768	BL112
821	513	769	BL113
822	514	777 (*sic*)	BL114
823		770	BL115
824		771	WL208
825		772	WL209
826		773	WL210
827		774	WL211
828		774A	WL212B
829		775	WL213
830		776	WL214
831		776A	WL215
832		776C	WL217
833		776D	WL218
834		776E	WL219
835		776F	WL220
836		776G	WL221
837			DOY
838			PDB
839			BN
840			N
841			M
842			DN
843			CJB
844			MDMR
845			N&D
845a			N
846	515	779	CW1
847	516	780	CW2
848	517	781	CW3
849	518	782	CW4
850		783	CW5

851	519	784	CW6
852		785	CW7
853	520	786	CW8
854	521	787	CW9
855	522	788	CW10
856		789	CW11
857	523	790	CW12
858		791	CW13
859		792	CW14
860	524	793	CW15
861	525	794	CW16
862	526	795	CW17
863	527	796	BL101
864	528	797	BL102
865	529	798	BL103
866	530	799	BL104
867	531	800	BL105
868	532	801	BL106
869	533	802	BL107
870		803	WL201
871		804	WL202
872		805	WL203
873		806	WL204
874		807	WL205
875		807A	WL206
876		808	DW
877		809	IGR
877a			Y
878		813	TB
879		814	L
880		815	N
881		816	I
882		817	M
883		818	DB
884		819	DOY
885		820	MDMR
886		822	ICGYABL
887		821	JWSS
888		810	7TLA1586
889		811	7TLA1587
890	534	823	P851
891	535	824	P852
892	536	825	P853
893	537	826	P854
894	538	827	P1179

895	538A	828	P1179-3
896	539	829	P1180
897	540	830	P1181
898	541	831	P1182
899			NDSGDP
900		832	Y
901		833	L
902		834	B
903	542	835	P1616
904	543	836	P1617
905	544	837	P1618-2
906	545	838	P1619
907		839	TAT
908		840	B
909		841	FAD
910	546	848	B
911	547	843	SS
912	548	849	C
913	549	846	MDMR
914	550	844	NAD
915	551	842	BFI
916	552	847	N
917	553	845	I
918	554	850	P1723
919	555	851	P1724
920	556	852	P1725
921	557	853	P1726-1
922			P1726-2

Total number of recordings catalogued – 931

922 catalogued + 146a, 568a, 742a, 748a, 757a, 757b, 757c, 845a, 877a

Unissued

022, 026, 024, 028, 039, 040, 041, 043, 048, 052, 054, 056, 062, 071, 084, 086, 087, 090, 091, 095, 099, 107, 114, 115, 116, 117, [119, 120, 121], 146a, 147, 148, 149, 150, 151, 161, 162, 164, 165, 166, 169, 170, 171, 172, 175, 178, 184, 192, 213, 215, 218, 222, 225, 276, 300, 324, 326, 327, 332, 334, 365, 369, 374, 376, 378, 380, 397, 400, 406, 407, 411, 415, 417, 419, 421, 483, 485, 488, 518, 530, 532, 555, 572, 585, 587, 589, 591, 607, 609, 635, 639, 640, 643, 647, 648, 650, 655, 656, 666, 667, 743, 746, 747, 749, 750, 796, 800, 812, 823, 835, 836, 870, 872, 875, 876, 877, 922 (117)

Unfound

034, 035, 063, 662, 758, 763 (6), and also possibly both sides of Polydor 512612, 512618 and 512619

Unreissued in any form

016, 017 (2)

Disputed

030, 031, 032, 033, 034, 035, 118 (119, 120, 121 included in [**unissued**]), 133, 134, 432, 757a (11)

Not Django

525

If these 137 recordings are not included, this gives us a total of 794 undisputed available Django Reinhardt recordings. 016, 017, 146a, 175, 178 are known to exist but remain unissued, which would make 799. If Polydor 512612, 512618, 512619 were found and do feature Django this would add a further six. There are, finally, three recordings that may or may not feature Django: Columbia BF938 by the Alexandre Orchestra (Apres l'Amour/Le Capitaine Craddock), *c.* 1928, which are reported to feature Django playing rhythm banjo, and 'A Sur La Place De L'Opéra' (016), which is reported also to exist on Ideal 8780, coupled with 'La Parisienne'. If these three recordings do include Django, we have a grand total of 808 recordings.

Useful addresses

About Django
www.aboutdjango.com
An excellent French website dedicated to Django. All the known film of Django is on this website and is downloadable to be viewed with a suitable software application.

Ashley Mark Publishing
Oslover House, 43 Sackville Road, Newcastle upon Tyne NE6 5TA, UK
Importers of Hal Leonard titles.

François Charle
17 galerie Vero-Dodat, 75001 Paris, France
Author/publisher of *The Story of The Maccaferri Guitars*; write for details of price and availability.

Ted Cherrett
73 Woodham Park Road, Woodham, Addlestone, Surrey KT15 3TJ, UK
Author/publisher of *The Genius that was Django*; write for details of price and availability.

Classics Records
50 Rue Stendhal, 75020 Paris, France
Richly detailed catalogue available on request.

Django Reinhardt Welcome Centre
An excellent website with a great deal of information relating to Django.

Django Swing Page
Another excellent Django-dedicated website that includes a well-organized on-line mail-order facility.

Fred Sharp
Fsharp8@comcast.net
A series of lectures by Fred Sharp on the life and works of Django, available as a CD; email for details.

Fremeaux & Associates
20 rue Robert Giraudineau, 94300 Vincennes, France
T 01.43.74.90.24
F 01.43.65.24.22
Richly detailed catalogue available on request.

Dave Gould
An excellent source for discographical and other information.

Hal Leonard Publishing

7777 West Bluemond Road, PO Box 13819, Milwaukee, WI 53213, USA
Specialist books including the reprint of Cruickshank's *Django's Gypsies* and Delaunay's *Django Reinhardt.*

Maporama

A website that enables you to pinpoint any address in any major city of the world simply by typing in the address. The site will show you both a map and instructions on how to get to the chosen address.

Music On Earth Productions

42 Barnfield Road, Ealing, London W5 1QT, UK
Contact: Judy Caine
T 020 8998 5675
F 020 8248 7404
The source for the code-free, all-zones 2-DVD Stéphane Grappelli film documentary that also contains all the important Django footage, digitalized, complete and unedited.

***Quintette* Magazine**

Zwaluw 33, 8103 AS Raalte, The Netherlands
T/F +31 (0) 572 35 86 33
A quarterly publication dedicated to Django and the followers of Django's music.

Red Lick Records

Porthmadog, Gwynedd LL49 9DJ, UK
T 01766 512151
F 01766 512851
www.redlickrecords.com
email sales@redlickrecords.com
Excellent discount mail-order service for most specialist record labels, music books, videos and DVDs. Catalogue available on request.

Vestapol Videos

PO Box 802, Sparta, NJ 07871, USA
The Django Legacy video available along with many other guitar-oriented videos and DVDs.

Advice for the beginner

There is no doubt that if you want the complete recorded works of Django Reinhardt, there is only one choice: the Fremeaux Intégral series, a set of currently 17 – and ultimately 20 – 2-CD issues that will present the entire canon in chronological order. They are well mastered, superbly illustrated and accompanied by intelligent and insightful notes in French and English. Note that, because this series is still in progress and is likely to be so for some time, physical space has been allocated in this work for the reader to infill future issues.

Django was involved in a wide variety of musical styles in Paris, and even deep into his jazz career was to be found accompanying popular commercial artists whose connections to jazz were, at best, tenuous. Perhaps the most startling example of these juxtapositions can be heard by comparing his recordings with Jacotte Perrier on 5 January 1938 to the very next session on 31 January with the Quintette. In short, the Fremeaux collection presents every facet of the Django experience from Musette to Bop. They are not cheap, but they represent the ultimate collection, including much that is unavailable elsewhere.

If you find that a little overwhelming, and you want the best of the classic QHCF output, then the two JSP boxed sets will furnish you with most of your needs. They are at once beautifully mastered and very affordable. While they are not as lavishly illustrated as the Fremeaux set, they have the advantage of delivering most of the great Quintet recordings. The only serious gaps are the 1934 test recordings (numbers 064–6) and the 1937 Grappelli–South–Reinhardt sessions (numbers 281–7 and 295–7), omissions remedied by obtaining Classics 703 by Django Reinhardt and the chronological Eddie South recordings on Classics 707 and 737.

The French Classics series takes the middle ground, including more than JSP but less than Fremeaux. If you are going to collect Django on Classics, you will also need to look at compilations by associated artists in the same series to achieve any measure of completeness. Mastering is generally good, presentation uniform and notes informative.

Beyond these, the reader will encounter many collections on many labels, in a variety of levels of quality. All of them will contain excellent music, but the mastering, programming and presentation can and will vary widely from superb to unacceptable. Details of some further CD releases not listed in this volume can be obtained on Dave Gould's excellent website.

The starting point for literature has to be Charles Delaunay's classic book *Django*, but try to obtain the Hal Leonard edition for the extraordinary gallery of photos and illustrated memorabilia. Ted Cherrett's *The Genius that was Django* is a labour of love by a fan. In rescuing some 35 years' worth of cuttings from a wide variety of journals and newspapers, he has provided the aficionado with a unique and fascinating scrapbook. Ian Cruickshank's *Django's Gypsies* is a useful and fascinating collection of Django-related memorabilia that also contains a sensitively written and well-argued reappraisal of his work. An upcoming biography by Michael Dregni promises to be well written and informative. The publication date for this work is currently unconfirmed.

The opportunity to savour what little film there is of Django can be thoroughly satisfied by obtaining the zone-free DVD *Stéphane Grappelli: A Life in the Jazz Century*, which contains all the known Django footage in the best possible condition.

If you wish to continue keeping abreast of Django-related developments, then you are advised to subscribe to the excellent and knowledgeable Dutch magazine *Quintette*, and also visit the recommended websites. Contact information for all the organizations listed above can be found in the 'Useful addresses' section.

Index